Wildlife management and habitat creation on landfill sites

A manual of best practice

Wildlife management and habitat creation on landfill sites
A manual of best practice

Ecoscope Applied Ecologists

Written by Duncan Watson & Valerie Hack
with additional contributions from Matthew Fasham

Edited by Matthew Fasham

Published by Ecoscope Applied Ecologists

Citation

Ecoscope (2000). Wildlife Management and Habitat Creation on Landfill Sites: A Manual of Best Practice. Ecoscope Applied Ecologists, Muker.

The techniques described in this book do not necessarily reflect the policies of the partner organisations or individuals involved in its production.
No responsibility can be accepted for any loss, damage or unsatisfactory results arising from the implementation of any of the recommendations within this book.

Published by

Ecoscope Applied Ecologists, Crake Holme, Muker, Richmond, North Yorkshire, DL11 6QH

Design by
Phil Cottier and Tim Sidaway

Figures by
Matthew Fasham

Printed by
Grillford Limited on Mondial Silk (ECF)

ISBN No: 0-9539189-0-4

Cover photographs:
Front cover: Grassland and wetland: David Hill
Cowslips: David Hill
Gulls: Duncan Watson
Hay meadow: Melvyn Foxton
Back cover: Hay meadow: Melvyn Foxton

Contents

Case studies

Boxes

Figures

Tables

ACKNOWLEDGEMENTS

The authors would like to thank the following people:

- Mark Fishpool (Programmes Manager for Tees Valley Wildlife Trust), who managed this project on behalf of the Tees Valley Wildlife Trust.
- John Garner for immense support, enthusiasm and common sense as well as being a wealth of knowledge on aquatic ecology
- Angela Darwell for expert advice on aquatic macrophytes
- Nigel and Sue Harris for providing valuable assistance and giving constructive criticism on many aspects of ecology and habitat management
- Claire Cornish for expert advice on the NVC
- Richard Brown for expert advice on seed harvesting and marketing and grassland creation

We are grateful to the following people for their comments on drafts of this book:

- Penny Anderson (Penny Anderson Associates); John Dickson (NBC (Environmental Services) Ltd); Sue Everett (Floralocale); Mark Fishpool, Jane Ellis and Jeremy Garside (Tees Valley Wildlife Trust); Melvyn Foxton (former Senior Restoration Officer, West Yorkshire Waste Management); Steven Haymes (Biffa Waste Services); Elizabeth Simmons (Enviros Aspinwall); and Nathalie Stephenson, Deborah Brown, David Hill and Graham Tucker (Ecoscope Applied Ecologists).

We would also like to thank all those who provided information on potential case studies, particularly the following people, who took the time to show us around sites that they were involved with:

- Henry Austin (Shanks Ltd); William Brayford (Merseyside Waste Disposal Authority); Sarah Carver (Waste Recycling Group plc); Catherine Elwin and Steven Bacon (Groundwork Wirral); Trevor Fletcher and Mike Swiss (Viridor Waste Management Ltd); Melvyn Foxton; Pete Gotham (RSPB); Derek Richardson (Knowsley Metropolitan Borough); Steve Simmonds (Powys County Council); Eric Smith (Dorset County Council); and Mike Sutcliffe and Julian Morley (Cheshire County Council).

We are also grateful to Biffa Waste Services for the use of their sites in the bird control trials. In particular, we would like to thank Stuart Tunnicliffe, Andrew Ives and Tim Darby for helping to organise the operation of the trials.

The following people and organisations provided photographs for inclusion in this book:
Melvyn Foxton, Chris Gomersall, Valerie Hack, David Hill, Khyber Associates, NBC (Environmental Services) Ltd, Duncan Watson and Windrush.

The funding for this project was provided by Biffaward, a multi-million pound scheme set up by Biffa Waste Services using the Landfill Tax Credits.

SECTION A

Introduction and essential background

1 Introduction

This manual has been produced to provide best practice guidelines for a comprehensive range of wildlife and ecology related issues at landfill sites. Two major issues are specifically addressed:

- The management of pest species attracted to landfill sites during site operation
- The creation of habitats of ecological value through the site restoration process

The project has been undertaken independently of the waste management industry by Ecoscope Applied Ecologists with additional input and project management from the Tees Valley Wildlife Trust. Funding for the manual was provided solely through 'Biffaward – Investing in the Environment'.

1.1 Demand for best practice standards

1.1.1 Wildlife management at operational sites

The waste management industry has recently come under pressure to remove the increased risk of bird-strike resulting from the situating of landfill sites close to airfields. Large numbers of birds and other pest species can also have a number of other impacts, from potential effects on human health to a generally detrimental effect on local amenity. Control of pest species can be very successful if carried out to a sufficiently high standard, but is often less effective at some UK sites, mainly due to a lack of clear direction on the most effective techniques. As a result, the industry is in need of standard guidance on best practice, both on the assessment of wildlife-related problems and the best methods of tackling such problems when they arise. Best practice guidance on the management of wildlife pest species attracted to operational landfill sites is presented in this manual.

1.1.2 Habitat creation at landfill sites

The UK Biodiversity Action Plan (Anon, 1994) has identified a number of targets for the conservation of habitats and species over the coming years. There is a major opportunity for industry to contribute to this process, particularly in the case of the landfill industry in which a substantial quantity of land is released through the site restoration process. Habitat creation on landfill sites can also help to relieve increasing pressure on the waste management industry to demonstrate that after-uses at restored landfill sites may be beneficial, both to the local community and the environment.

A wide range of literature on habitat creation is currently available (e.g. Gilbert & Anderson, 1998; Baines & Smart, 1991; Parker, 1995). Unfortunately, restored landfill sites present a unique environment requiring the modification of standard techniques. The waste management industry is therefore in need of a set of best practice guidelines targeted specifically at the creation of habitats on landfill sites in order that opportunities to benefit biodiversity and demonstrate beneficial after-use are not missed. This manual provides best practice guidance on all aspects of habitat creation at landfill sites right through from the choice of an appropriate after-use scheme to practical information on the creation of a comprehensive range of habitat types.

1.2 Intended readership

Best practice guidance in this manual is aimed at all involved in wildlife-related issues within the landfill industry. Specifically this includes:

- Landfill site operators
- Planning authorities
- Industry regulators
- Conservation organisations
- Environmental consultants
- Pest control companies

1.3 Scope and content of the manual

Whilst the best practice guidance in this manual is applicable to all landfill developments to a certain extent, it has been particularly aimed at modern landfill sites which accept controlled wastes, especially those still at the planning stage. These are sites with pollution control infrastructure, and a cap and restoration soil depth as recommended in Table F.1.1.

The need for complex engineering and environmental control at these sites is principally responsible for the unique landfill environment for which specialist habitat creation advice is necessary. Habitat creation at sites which have only accepted inert waste follows similar principles, but with fewer constraints on what can be achieved.

Brief guidance on habitat creation at older, closed landfill sites is also provided – habitat creation at such sites largely follows the same principles as for modern sites, but there may be additional constraints (e.g. woodland cannot be planted on old landfills with insufficient soil depth covering the waste).

Section A.2 of the manual describes the processes taking place within a landfill and describes the methods used to control the outputs (leachate and gas) from a closed landfill site. **Section A.3** describes the planning process and other legislative considerations relating to landfill sites (e.g. international biodiversity initiatives). **Section A.4** outlines the stages in the development of a landfill site, and emphasises that all aspects of site development should be fully considered at the outset of site design.

Section B describes the process of Ecological Impact Assessment (EcIA), and its role in landfill site operation and habitat creation.

Section C deals with wildlife management on operational landfill sites, and details the potential impacts arising from populations of birds, rats and insects at landfill sites. Best practice control methods are proposed for all three groups, with particular emphasis on the control of scavenging birds. This section of the manual is relevant to the control of pests at all landfill sites at which an element of putrescible waste is accepted (i.e. controlled waste landfills – those accepting domestic, commercial and industrial wastes). Landfill sites accepting only relatively inert wastes are unlikely to attract wildlife pest species.

In addition, the results of independent trials of a range of bird control methods carried out by Ecoscope Applied Ecologists are presented in Appendix 1.

Section D outlines the process of landfill site restoration, including engineering systems to control landfill outputs and the basics of site design. The constraints on habitat creation imposed by the restored landfill environment are briefly considered.

Section E introduces the types of after-use appropriate for restored landfill sites, and discusses the key concepts involved in habitat creation. General guidelines for habitat creation for nature conservation after-uses are also given, including advice on selecting habitat type, community type and species.

Section F focuses on practical guidelines for habitat creation. **Section F.1** provides general guidance on soils and vegetation, including soil type and depth; the soil conditions necessary for successful habitat creation; site preparation (including the use of nurse species to stabilise soil and increase fertility); and weed control. **Sections F.2 – F.6** provide specific guidance for the creation of grassland, woodland, heathland, wetlands and agricultural habitats respectively.

In addition, nine case studies detailing examples of habitat creation methods carried out on a range of landfill sites are presented.

1.4 Key definitions
A full list of definitions is provided in the glossary. However, definitions of a few key terms are provided here to prevent misunderstanding.

1.5 Useful contacts
A list of organisations which may be able to provide useful information and services for the planning, design and creation of habitats on landfills is provided in Appendix 2.

2 The process of landfilling wastes

2.1 Introduction
A basic understanding of the processes involved in the landfilling of wastes is useful for all readers of this book and particularly invaluable with respect to those involved in planning or implementing habitat creation on landfill sites. Landfill sites present a unique environment for habitat creation, both directly from the outputs of processes acting within the landfill (i.e. landfill gas and leachate), and indirectly as a result of measures employed to control such outputs. A good understanding of this environment, and the limitations and constraints it imposes upon habitat creation, will therefore greatly enhance the likelihood of successful habitat creation on landfill sites.

This chapter provides a brief outline of the processes taking place within a landfill site and the most common means of controlling them in order to prevent pollution. The main implications for habitat creation are also outlined and the reader referred to sources of further information where necessary. Note that most of this manual is directed at landfill sites that accept or have accepted controlled wastes.

2.2 The importance of landfill
Up to 96% of controlled wastes (domestic, commercial and industrial wastes) are currently disposed of at landfill sites, of which over 50% are potentially biodegradable (Simmons & Baines, 1998). Whilst these wastes make up only 26% of the total waste arising in the UK, around 400 million tonnes per annum, much of the remainder is agricultural and mining wastes which are not disposed of at licensed landfill sites. A substantial proportion of wastes going to landfill is therefore made up of controlled wastes.

There are alternatives to waste disposal by landfill, including waste minimisation, re-use and recycling, and new technologies involving incineration and heat recovery. In response to the EC Landfill Directive (1999), the UK has set a target of recovering 45% of municipal waste and recycling 30% of domestic waste by the year 2010 (DETR, 1999b). However, despite this commitment it is still likely that a significant quantity of waste will be disposed of to landfill for at least the foreseeable future. With the future requirement for landfill seemingly assured there is therefore a clear need for the establishment of best practice guidelines for wildlife management and habitat creation at landfill sites.

2.3 Processes taking place within a landfill
The main processes taking place at controlled waste landfill sites are outlined in brief below, and shown in

Key definitions	
Aftercare	Work carried out following soil placement to establish and maintain the after-use. Aftercare includes soil treatment, cultivation, planting and other management within the initial five-year aftercare period.
After-use	The long-term use established on a landfill site following restoration, e.g. nature conservation, agriculture, amenity, etc.
Habitat creation	The creation of habitats of nature conservation interest on a site where they do not currently exist (regardless of whether or not they previously existed on the site).
Long-term management	Work carried out after the aftercare period to maintain / enhance the after-use. Also termed post-closure management.
Restoration	The process that returns a landfill site to a condition suitable for its after-use.

A synthetic liner being installed into a new cell on an operational landfill site.

Figure A.2.1. For further information on any of the aspects covered, consult the range of government Waste Management Papers (e.g. DoE, 1986; DoE, 1994a; DoE, 1995; Environment Agency, in prep.).

2.3.1 Inputs into the system

A relatively high proportion of controlled wastes going to landfill is comprised of putrescible waste. Added to this may be inert or low reactivity wastes, whilst the other main input to the landfill system is water, most of which enters the landfill as rainfall during the operational period (the construction of a low-permeability cap prevents infiltration by rainwater once filling has ceased). Additional water can also enter some sites with the waste, particularly where liquid wastes or sludges are accepted.

2.3.2 Processes acting within the landfill

Biodegradable wastes in landfills are broken down by bacterial action, and the availability of water is essential for such biodegradation to take place. A number of phases of degradation occur, starting with a short-lived aerobic phase, progressing through anoxic conditions to fully anaerobic conditions before finally the exhaustion of degradable materials results in ultimate stabilisation. Our understanding of the processes that take place within a landfill is limited and therefore it is very difficult to predict the length of time required to achieve this ultimate stabilisation. What is clear is that stabilisation time is very site-specific and dependent on a variety of factors, from moisture availability to the surface : volume ratio of particles within the fill. A number of chemical reactions are also known to take place during the degradation process, many of which can affect the composition of the leachate (see A.2.3.3).

2.3.3 Outputs from the landfill

The major outputs from a biodegrading landfill are:

- Landfill gas
- Leachate

Landfill gas is principally made up of methane and carbon dioxide, at an average ratio of 6:4. The exact composition varies from site to site and over time but other common elements present include nitrogen, carbon monoxide, hydrogen, hydrogen sulphide and oxygen. Trace elements of volatile organic compounds can also be present depending on waste composition.

Leachate is formed through the solubilisation of biological and chemical reaction products and the release of inorganic and organic compounds. As with landfill gas, its exact composition is variable, but it commonly contains high levels of ammonia and has a high Biological Oxygen Demand (BOD) and Chemical Oxygen Demand (COD). A high BOD results from the presence of decomposing organic matter whilst a high COD results from the oxidisation of reduced compounds.

Landfill gas and leachate production are nearly always greatest during the first few years after landfilling, when biological activity is at its peak. If not controlled, landfill gas can cause serious problems. Within the filled waste itself, there should be no voids and insufficient oxygen for an explosive amount of landfill gas to accumulate. However, explosive conditions can potentially occur in off-site enclosed spaces (e.g. service ducts or cellars) if the gas migrates. Landfill gas can migrate both laterally and vertically through porous rocks and soils and through cracks and fissures. In addition to the potential for explosions, this can also

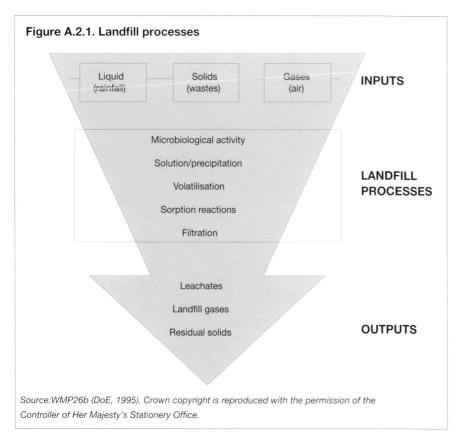

Figure A.2.1. Landfill processes

Source:WMP26b (DoE, 1995). Crown copyright is reproduced with the permission of the Controller of Her Majesty's Stationery Office.

lead to the replacement of soil oxygen with landfill gas within and beyond the site, which can result in vegetation die-back. The breakout of leachate into the local water catchment area can also cause great damage, especially through ammonia pollution and deoxygenation of the water caused by the high BOD and COD of the leachate.

A further consequence of the processes acting within a landfill is settlement of the waste. At older landfill sites, some settlement can occur as a result of the gradual consolidation of uncompacted waste. At modern sites, waste is substantially compacted during the operational phase, and most settlement occurs as a result of a reduction in waste mass through biodegradation of organic material and removal as landfill gas or leachate. At all sites settlement is generally greatest during the first two to five years after landfilling is completed, during which time landfill gas and leachate production are at their highest. Factors influencing the rate of degradation, such as waste type and water availability can therefore also have a profound effect on the rate and amount of settlement. In general, a minimum of 10% settlement (of original waste depth) can be expected, with up to 30% at some sites.

The phasing of operation at landfill sites, whereby discrete parts of the site are filled to a pre-determined sequence, can mean that adjacent phases are at different stages in the biodegradation process. Differences in waste composition between adjacent cells can also lead to differential settlement, whereby settlement takes place at different rates on adjacent sections of the landfill. This can have considerable implications for the restoration and aftercare of the site.

2.4 Control of pollution from landfill sites

2.4.1 Modern sites

Modern landfill sites incorporate a number of engineering features designed to contain leachate and control the migration of gas (see figure A.2.2 below). At most sites the main features comprise:

- An impermeable lining around the base and sides of the site formed either by densely compacted clay or a synthetic material – designed to prevent leachate from entering the surrounding water catchment whilst also preventing lateral migration of landfill gas into surrounding areas.
- A low-permeability cap formed either by densely compacted clay or a synthetic material – designed to minimise infiltration of rainwater into the landfill and hence reduce leachate production whilst also controlling the vertical migration of

landfill gas. The cap is further covered by a soil layer to protect it from weathering, dessication and erosion, and to enable the establishment of vegetative cover.

- A 'domed' landform – designed to maximise surface water runoff and thus reduce the potential for rainwater infiltrating the fill.
- Landfill gas and leachate control systems – landfill gas is usually actively extracted via a network of collection wells and pipes to a gas plant where it may be utilised to produce electricity or simply flared. Similarly, leachate is collected via a network of wells and pipes and either treated on site and discharged, or pumped away for treatment off-site.

Further information on each of these processes is given in Section D.

2.4.2 Accelerated stabilisation

The Government's strategy for sustainable development requires that wastes should be dealt with by the generation that produces them. Effectively this requires all landfilled wastes to be stabilised within 30-50 years. However, most modern landfills are characterised by a very low permeability cap and liner that prevents infiltration by rainwater, which may in turn reduce the

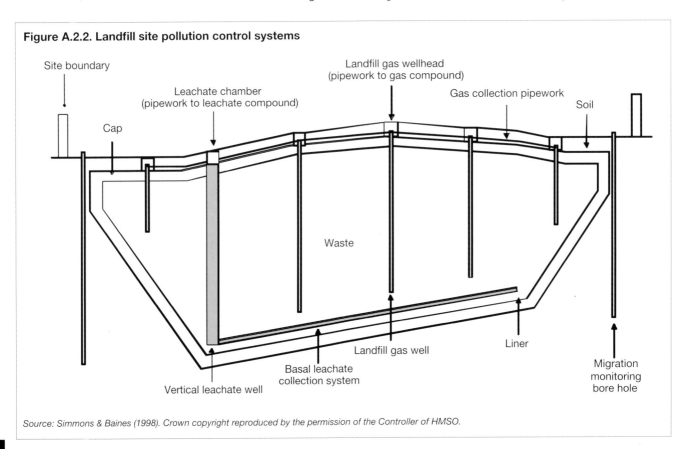

Figure A.2.2. Landfill site pollution control systems

Site boundary

Leachate chamber
(pipework to leachate compound)

Landfill gas wellhead
(pipework to gas compound)

Gas collection pipework

Soil

Cap

Waste

Vertical leachate well

Basal leachate
collection system

Landfill gas well

Liner

Migration
monitoring
bore hole

Source: Simmons & Baines (1998). Crown copyright reproduced by the permission of the Controller of HMSO.

rate of biodegradation so much that stabilisation may take many decades to achieve. Maintenance of pollution control systems will therefore be a long-term commitment, and thus in contradiction to the Government's sustainable development strategy. As a result, site designs that accelerate the stabilisation of waste through the introduction of water and repeated circulation are now being investigated. Implications for habitat creation from the adoption of such techniques are potentially large. For example, large-scale infrastructure works would be required including pipes, access points and underground chambers. In addition, rates of settlement could be increased so much that a temporary cap might be required which could delay final restoration for many years. However, research into these methods is still at a very early stage and the techniques are not currently common practice. Accelerated stabilisation is therefore not considered further in this manual, but see WMP26b (DoE, 1995) for further details.

2.4.3 Older sites

Older sites, which may have been poorly or incompletely restored, can be good candidates for habitat creation. Grants for the beneficial restoration of derelict land may be available for older sites in urban areas where restoration was not originally a planning requirement. There may be other grants which are available, or there may be the possibility of habitat creation in association with remedial works to control excessive pollution. Older sites are not generally characterised by the same standard of pollution control features as modern sites, frequently being based on non-containment or dilute-and-disperse techniques, which give little control over landfill gas migration or leachate breakout. Some sites may have a relatively thin cap or indeed no cap at all, little or no basal lining and no method of gas or leachate control. Consequently, the implications for habitat creation at such sites may be considerably different to those at modern sites, with landfill gas, heat and possibly leachate all potentially having a direct impact. Whilst the guidance in this book is aimed primarily at modern sites, further information on undertaking habitat creation work at older sites is provided in Section D.

2.4.4 Implications of the landfill process for wildlife management and habitat creation

The domed landform, heavily compacted clay cap and poorly structured soil characteristic of a large proportion of modern restored landfill sites can present a harsh environment for habitat creation and vegetation growth. These characteristics must therefore be carefully considered in the design of habitat creation schemes.

The biodegradation process at landfill sites results in a variety of outputs that can also seriously inhibit a habitat creation scheme. Direct damage to created habitats from gas and leachate is only likely at older sites where engineered pollution control measures do not exist. At modern sites with an engineered cap, basal liner and active gas and leachate extraction systems, direct impacts from gas or leachate are likely to be minimal. However, the large-scale infrastructure required to control and remove landfill gas and leachate and the potential need for re-engineering following settlement can all have a major influence on habitat creation. A full discussion of constraints presented by the restored landfill environment upon habitat creation is presented in Section D of this manual, whilst guidelines for the creation of various habitat types on landfill site are covered in depth in Sections E and F.

5

3 Planning and legal considerations at landfill sites

3.1 Introduction

The design, planning, operation and restoration of landfill sites is primarily regulated by two different types of legislation:

1. Planning system legislation
2. Pollution control legislation

The planning system controls the development and use of land in the public interest. With respect to landfill sites it principally exists to control the location and design of sites in order to minimise adverse effects on existing and surrounding land-use and the restoration and aftercare of land to ensure that land is suitably restored and returned to a beneficial after-use.

Operational activities at landfill sites are principally regulated through pollution control legislation in the form of site licensing, although some operational activities that affect local amenity are also subject to planning controls. Prior to and following site operation, licensing is almost exclusively concerned with the functioning of pollution control measures – all other aspects of site planning and design are covered by the planning process.

The role of the planning system in particular is so fundamental to wildlife management and habitat creation at landfill sites that it is essential that all readers of this book have at least a basic understanding of the processes involved. This chapter therefore provides an outline of the major functions of the planning process, particularly with regard to landfill sites. The role of the planning system in addressing nature conservation issues, including recent initiatives to promote biodiversity conservation is also covered. Pollution control and waste management licensing are of less overall importance to the subjects of this book, although they can impact substantially on wildlife management at operational sites and may also impact, through the operation of pollution control systems, on habitat creation. A brief outline of the legislation and licensing process is therefore also given in this chapter.

3.2 The planning system – background information

3.2.1 Planning legislation

The planning system is principally controlled by the following pieces of legislation:

- Town & Country Planning Act 1990 / Town & Country Planning (Scotland) Act 1972

- Planning & Compensation Act 1991
- Town & Country Planning (Environmental Impact Assessment) (England and Wales) Regulations 1999 / The Environmental Assessment (Scotland) Regulations 1988 (as amended)

Note that the above is not a comprehensive list of all planning legislation potentially relevant to landfill sites.

3.2.2 Development plans

Development plans must be produced at a range of levels, taking into account national (e.g. Planning Policy Guidance Notes) and regional guidance. Development plans can take the form of:

- Structure Plans – setting out general policies and proposals for the development and other use of land at a county scale.
- Local Plans – relating the policies of the structure plan to precise areas of land at a local district level.
- Unitary Development Plans (Parts I and II) – combining the functions of structure and local plans.

In areas controlled by unitary authorities or metropolitan authorities, Unitary Development Plans (Parts I and II) must be produced whilst Structure and Local Plans must be produced in areas controlled by county and district level authorities. In the national parks a slightly different system exists, and a slightly different system is also in place in Scotland.

3.2.3 The planning process at waste management facilities

For most developments, planning applications and permissions are dealt with at a district level. However, planning issues relating specifically to waste management facilities are considered at a larger scale by the Waste Planning Authority (WPA). In England the WPA is usually the county or unitary authority. Since 1996, in Wales and Scotland, waste planning has been the function of the unitary councils. Following the Town & Country Planning Act 1990, every WPA is required to produce a Waste Local Plan (WLP). The role of the WLP is to provide detailed proposals for waste management in relation to other land-use policies, as set out in the normal structure plan, local plan, etc. Examples of information that should be contained within a WLP include:

- the amount of spare capacity at existing waste management sites;
- proposed locations for potential new

waste management sites;
- areas in which waste management is inappropriate, for example designated sites of conservation importance, areas designated for landscape importance or sites of archaeological interest; and
- criteria by which future waste management proposals can be assessed.

The WLP therefore effectively takes the place of the Local Plan with respect to waste, although note that policies for older, closed landfills are still covered by standard Local Plans.

3.2.4 The planning control function of the Waste Planning Authority

All waste disposal developments (except for a limited exception for certain types permitted under the General Permitted Development Order 1995, for example the disposal of river dredgings by the relevant drainage authority or the disposal of colliery spoil on land designated for that purpose) require planning permission from the relevant WPA, which may only be given after the WPA has received a full planning application. Whilst in most cases there is a presumption in favour of development proposals which support WLP policies, in granting permission the WPA may impose a number of planning conditions designed to minimise impacts from site preparation and operation upon a number of interests, including nature conservation. Conditions are also made to secure effective restoration and aftercare of sites; for example, developers may be asked to restore sites to a specific after-use such as a particular habitat type. The choice of after-use is ultimately made by the site operator or landowner, although the WPA can (and should) comment, and influence, this decision. The WPA also has powers to impose an aftercare condition for a period of five years, following completion of restoration, by the end of which time the majority of habitat creation (where this is the agreed after-use) should be complete. Note that the aftercare period should not begin until the restoration conditions have been complied with (i.e. after interim restoration – see Section D).

3.2.5 Environmental and ecological assessment

Most planning applications require a range of supporting information to be provided before permission is granted. At certain types of waste management facility, including many landfills, a formal Environmental Impact Assessment (EIA) is a mandatory requirement (see Section B). This should contain information on a wide range of environmental issues, including ecology and nature conservation, but also including issues such as landscape, amenity and soils. Ecology and nature conservation impacts are best addressed through an Ecological Impact Assessment (EcIA) which will normally form part of the overall EIA. However, even at landfill sites where formal EIA is not required, the WPA should ask for an EcIA to accompany all planning applications for landfill. The findings, whether incorporated within a formal EIA or not, should then be used by the WPA to impose conditions upon the planning permission to ensure that any damage to certain habitats is prevented or, if unavoidable, sufficiently mitigated for. Such conditions should include where appropriate, the creation of habitats as part of site restoration and the long-term management of any such habitats. Further information on the processes involved in EcIA is provided in Section B, and includes guidance on the preparation of an EcIA at a proposed landfill site.

3.2.6 Consultations

Prior to the formal acceptance of a planning application for a landfill, the WPA is required to carry out a number of consultations with interested parties. Comments made can then be taken into consideration by the Planning Officer in deciding whether the application is acceptable and what conditions should be imposed to minimise impacts. Consultation with certain organisations is statutory on all applications, for example the utilities, the local highways department and MAFF. For landfill developments within 13 km of airfields, the Civil Aviation Authority or Ministry of Defence are also statutory consultees with respect to the increased bird-strike risk (see Section C), whilst from a nature conservation perspective the relevant government agencies (English Nature, Countryside Council for Wales, Scottish Natural Heritage and the Countryside Agency) are statutory consultees on all waste planning applications. The Environment Agency (or SEPA in Scotland), as the Waste Regulatory Authority, will also be consulted throughout the planning process. Consultation with certain other organisations (often including voluntary conservation organisations such as the RSPB and the local Wildlife Trust) takes place on a non-statutory basis. This means that although there may be

objections to a proposal on nature conservation grounds, the Planning Officer is not obliged to take such objections into account when deciding on the acceptability of the proposal or on the imposition of conditions. For a full list of statutory and non-statutory consultees please refer to the Town and Country Planning (General Permitted Development) Order 1995.

3.2.7 Rights of appeal and enforcement

Following the issue of a planning permission, a number of further procedures may take place, including the right of a developer to appeal to the Secretary of State if he or she considers the decision of the Planning Authority or the imposition of certain conditions to be unacceptable. The WPA has the power to take enforcement action at any time should the developer be in breach of any of the planning conditions agreed. A comprehensive list of WPA powers and the rights of developers is beyond the scope of this manual; for further information on this or any other subject covered in this chapter it is therefore recommended that the reader consults alternative sources such as the range of government Waste Management Papers and Planning Policy Guidance Notes.

3.3 The incorporation of nature conservation into the planning process

3.3.1 Nature conservation in development plans

Following the Town & Country Planning Act 1990 and the Planning & Compensation Act 1991, it is a legal requirement for nature conservation plans and policies to be incorporated into development plans at all levels of local government (i.e. in structure, local and unitary plans). Waste Local Plans must also promote policies with regard to waste management that are fully consistent with the nature conservation plans and policies outlined in the relevant structure plan and government guidelines.

3.3.2 Identification of important sites

In accordance with the government's Planning Policy Guidance Note (PPG) number 9 (DoE, 1994b), development plans should identify all designated sites of nature conservation importance within the development plan area. Sites containing UK BAP priority habitats or species should also be identified, as should species identified by Local Biodiversity Action Plans (see below).

Identification of key sites in

development plans enables their existence to be fully considered in the context of other plan policies. For example, there will usually be a presumption against development if Sites of Special Scientific Interest (SSSIs) will be adversely affected.

3.3.3 Additional policies with regard to nature conservation

The Town & Country Planning Act 1990 states that development plans should not only be concerned with designated areas with regard to nature conservation, but that additional policy areas should also be addressed. These include the following:

- The conservation and management of major landscape features such as rivers and hedgerows. These may act as wildlife corridors and therefore be crucial for the migration and dispersal of many species. The EU Habitats Directive (1992) requires that development plans, at all levels, contain policies to ensure their protection.
- The possible provision of new habitats. The Town & Country Planning Act 1990 and the Planning & Compensation Act 1991 require development plans to include policies for the improvement of the physical environment. This in effect requires local authorities to identify opportunities for habitat creation within development plans, in addition to developing policies to promote the conservation of existing habitats. Such habitat creation policies may of course be relevant to landfill sites.

Additional conditions relating to nature conservation can be added to planning permissions through a Section 106 agreement negotiated under the Town & Country Planning Act (1990). These agreements are essentially contracts or legal agreements between the planning authority and the applicant, and can be used to ensure that conservation losses caused by a development are adequately mitigated for, and that long-term management of conservation areas created / enhanced is secured.

3.3.4 The incorporation of biodiversity initiatives into development plans

Since the signing of the Biodiversity Convention at the Earth Summit in Rio, in 1992, a number of measures to facilitate the conservation of biodiversity have been initiated. Box A.3.1 provides some basic background to biodiversity conservation and its role in development planning.

Box A.3.1. Biodiversity conservation

Biodiversity (or Biological Diversity)
"The variability among living organisms from all sources including, inter alia, terrestrial, marine and other aquatic ecosystems and the ecological complexes of which they are part; this includes diversity within species, between species and of ecosystems." (Article 2 of the Convention on Biological Diversity, 1992)

Biodiversity conservation at a global scale – the Convention on Biological Diversity
In 1992 at the United Nations Conference on Environment and Development in Rio de Janeiro, over 150 countries signed up to the Convention on Biological Diversity, including the UK. It was signed in response to widespread concern about the continuing global loss of animal and plant species and genetic resources and committed signatories, including the UK, to the production of plans and the implementation of programmes of action to conserve biodiversity.

A number of other conventions were signed and declarations made at the Earth Summit including Agenda 21, which effectively requires a wide range of activities, including development such as landfill sites, to be environmentally sustainable. The conservation of biodiversity is of course an integral part of sustainable development.

Biodiversity conservation at a national scale – The UK BAP
The UK Biodiversity Action Plan (the UK BAP) was published in 1994 and broadly outlined the government strategy for biodiversity conservation until 2015. The UK BAP was followed by the UK Steering Group Report (1995), which identified a number of habitats and species as priorities for action on the basis of factors such as their conservation importance or threatened status. These priority habitats and species now form the central basis for actions to conserve biodiversity in the UK.

Individual action plans have now been produced for all 38 priority habitats and for a large proportion of the 400 priority species. Each action plan sets a number of conservation objectives and defines specific targets by which the success of conservation action, at a national scale, can be measured. Targets commonly relate to the conservation and enhancement of existing habitats and species but may also relate to the creation of new habitats. For example the action plan for the priority habitat of lowland heathland includes a target to encourage the "re-establishment" of 6000 ha of heathland by the year 2005.

Biodiversity conservation at a local scale - local BAPs
A key delivery mechanism for national objectives and targets is the preparation of Local Biodiversity Action Plans (Local BAPs). Local BAPs may be produced at any number of scales from regional to single site-specific, although they are most commonly produced at a local authority area level. Indeed, as part of their Local Agenda 21 initiatives, required as part of the government's commitment to sustainable development, all local authorities are expected to prepare a local BAP (or at least contribute to the preparation of one).

The key functions of a Local BAP include the following:
- establishment of a database and review of existing information on local biodiversity;
- identification of priority species and habitats within a national, regional and local context;
- definition of specific objectives and targets for the conservation of each priority species or habitat at a local level;
- identification of delivery mechanisms for the achievement of targets;
- implementation of agreed programmes of action; and
- monitoring of the effectiveness of the plan in achieving national and local targets.

(following UK Local Issues Advisory Group guidance for local BAPs)

Unfortunately Local BAPs have yet to be published for the majority of local authority areas (although for most an outline is available, which should at least list Priority habitats and species with relevant objectives and targets). In such cases alternative guidance does exist for planners. English Nature's Natural Area profiles for example, provide a list of prioritised objectives for conservation within 120 distinct Natural Areas, based on ecological and physical ecological characteristics rather than political boundaries[1].

Application of biodiversity initiatives to the planning system
Local BAPs are an excellent means by which key biodiversity issues relevant to a particular local area can be identified and incorporated fully into development plans. In this way development plans should include, for example, information on the existence and location of all priority species and habitats in an area, in order that such information is incorporated into planning policy and decisions.

Furthermore, through its planning control function, each local planning authority (or Waste Planning Authority) can actually help to meet both local and national biodiversity targets. This may be achieved both by the safeguarding of key habitats / species and by various mitigation and compensation conditions which could include a requirement for habitat restoration or creation on certain types of site, including landfill.

1 Comprehensive information on a range of sources of guidance for those involved in habitat creation planning at landfill sites, including Natural Areas and Local BAPs, is provided in Section E of this manual. Note that Natural Areas are only applicable in England. .

3.3.5 Consideration of nature conservation in the assessment of development proposals (including landfill sites)

The identification of key sites of nature conservation importance within development plans should ensure that nature conservation is fully considered in the assessment of development proposals. These key sites may incorporate not only statutorily designated sites such as SSSIs but also locally designated (e.g. SNCIs) or undesignated sites containing priority species or habitats and major landscape features with value as wildlife networks or corridors.

The identification of all key sites of conservation importance in the WLP should ensure that potential waste management developments have the minimum detrimental effect on listed sites of nature conservation value.

However, some conflict between development and nature conservation is often unavoidable. For example, there is a tendency for landfill sites to be situated in old quarries, many of which have considerable ecological interest. This conflict is especially likely on sites carrying a lower weight of designation at which it might be argued that the benefits of development outweigh the nature conservation importance of the site. Where such conflict is likely, PPG9 (DoE, 1994b) states that planning conditions should be used by the planning authority (or WPA) to secure measures from developers that avoid damaging impacts on wildlife or physical features and / or compensate for any features lost.

Planning conditions should be imposed that are consistent with nature conservation policies within development plans, which should in turn be consistent with local BAP and Natural Area objectives. Planning conditions must also be consistent with ecological information specific to individual sites. For these purposes an Ecological Impact Assessment (EcIA) should be carried out at the request of the local planning authority / WPA for all major development projects, including landfills. EcIA should identify all habitats and species of importance likely to be affected by a development, establish the extent to which each will be affected and include proposals to mitigate for adverse impacts and ensure that there is no long-term net loss of biodiversity. See Section B for further information on Ecological Impact Assessment with respect to landfill sites.

3.4 Waste management licensing – background information

3.4.1 Pollution control legislation

Waste management licensing is principally controlled by the following pieces of legislation:

- Environmental Protection Act 1990
- Controlled Waste Regulations 1992
- Waste Management Licensing Regulations 1994

Note that the above is not a comprehensive list of all pollution control legislation potentially relevant to landfill sites.

3.4.2 The purpose of waste management licensing

The Environmental Protection Act 1990 prohibits the deposit of controlled waste without a valid waste management licence. This is intended to control processes and substances which can have potentially harmful effects on the environment and human health or have a detrimental effect on amenity. Licensing therefore principally covers pollution control and a variety of operational activities. However, licensing is not simply restricted to the operational life of a site. Indeed, a site licence can only be surrendered and a certificate of completion issued once the site is unlikely to cause further pollution to the environment (i.e. once organic waste has completely stabilised). As described previously, this may not happen for many decades.

3.4.3 The role of EA/SEPA

Waste management licensing is the responsibility of the Environment Agency (EA) in England and Wales, and the Scottish Environmental Protection Agency (SEPA) in Scotland. Their principal functions are:

- the issue of Waste Management Licences; and
- the enforcement of Waste Management Licence conditions.

3.4.4 The issuing of waste management licences

An application for a waste management licence must be submitted to EA/SEPA prior to operation of a site. The application should include a working plan containing

---

Box A.3.2. Issues controlled by the planning system and waste management licensing with specific respect to wildlife management and habitat creation at landfill sites

	Issues covered
Planning System	- Assessment of the acceptability of planning applications, based on supporting information with planning application. Formal EIA may be required – ecological impacts on the site and surrounding area should be identified at all sites. - Imposition of planning conditions to reduce impacts. Conditions may utilise mitigation measures such as habitat creation to reduce long-term ecological impacts. - Certain operational considerations may be reflected in planning conditions including protection of local amenity and safeguarding at sites within 13 km of airfields. - Choice of after-use (made by site operator). - Design and implementation of restoration and aftercare including habitat creation schemes. - Implementation of after-use management agreements.
Waste Management Licensing	- Control of operational activities that may cause harm to human health or environmental pollution, including a possible requirement for bird control / pest control. - Installation, maintenance and monitoring of environmental protection and pollution control systems.

detailed design proposals and the results of a range of site investigations. EA/SEPA are then obliged to consult a variety of interested parties (both statutory and non-statutory) before issuing a license, usually with a number of conditions attached.

On all licences, conditions are imposed to ensure that human health and environmental quality, particularly water quality, are safeguarded throughout the operational life of the site and beyond, until a completion certificate is issued. In effect, licence conditions provide a set of site operating standards covering a number of aspects from the phasing of operation and use of daily cover material to the long-term integrity of pollution control systems. With respect to wildlife management on landfill sites, licence conditions are often primarily responsible for the control of pest species such as birds, rodents or insects during site operation (see Section C), although these issues can also be covered by planning conditions.

3.4.5 The enforcement of waste management licences

In addition to the issuing of licences it is also the duty of EA/SEPA to enforce compliance with license conditions. In effect, this requires regular site visits by EA/SEPA inspectors to ensure that license conditions are being adhered to. In the event of license conditions being breached, the EA/SEPA has powers to prosecute site operators. In extreme cases it has the power to revoke a license.

3.4.6 Interaction between licensing and the planning system

A waste management licence cannot be issued unless the site has obtained relevant planning permission. A site may have a planning consent without a licence, but cannot operate as such without a licence. Ideally, the two applications are made together and considered over the same (or similar) timescale; consultations between the WPA and EA/SEPA are important to ensure that conditions are not conflicting. Informal consultations between the site developer, the WPA and EA/SEPA are therefore essential throughout the pre-application process.

Issues controlled by the planning and licensing system, with specific examples relating to wildlife management and habitat creation on landfill sites are summarised in Box A.3.2 (note that there can be considerable overlap on several activities).

4 Stages in the development of a landfill site

4.1 Introduction

The development of a landfill site passes through a number of stages from initial site selection to the actual planning application and from Construction, through Operation to Restoration and Aftercare. A general understanding of the landfill site development process is essential for all involved in landfill site planning and operation, including those involved in wildlife management or habitat creation issues. With respect to the readership of this book, an understanding of these stages must be gained in order that planning for wildlife management and habitat creation should take place at the optimum time in the development process. This should ensure that negative impacts from wildlife during site operation are minimised and that maximum benefits to biodiversity through habitat creation are obtained.

Figure A.4.1 shows the main stages in the development of a landfill site in a simplified, diagrammatic form. The relevance of each stage to those involved in wildlife management and habitat creation at landfill sites is also outlined. Note that Figure A.4.1 represents a very simplified version of the landfill site development process – the operation of site-specific factors may result in variations to this diagram applying at a high proportion of sites. Note also that as described below, the process of landfill site development must be regarded as a holistic one, with each stage represented in Figure A.4.1 fully integrated with the rest of the process.

4.2 Landfill site development as a holistic process

The concept of landfill site development as a holistic process (i.e. considering all aspects of site development, including nature conservation, from the outset) is now central to the latest government guidance on waste management. Waste Management Paper 26e (Environment Agency, in prep.) suggests that restoration and environmental protection must be considered together throughout the life of the site in order to maximise the success of restoration, aftercare and habitat creation. This approach requires that the various stages from construction and operation to restoration and aftercare are considered together as one fully integrated process at the outset of site planning. Sufficiently detailed designs of each stage should be completed at the planning stage, before construction and operation of the site begins.

The benefits of such an approach are clear. For example, cases of expensive restoration being destroyed by uncoordinated pollution control works should be avoided, sites should be restored to a landform design that is suitable for the agreed after-use and complex aftercare schemes that require detailed planning or phasing should be successfully put into practice. Potential requirements for wildlife management during site operation and opportunities for habitat creation should therefore be identified at the EIA / EcIA stage and plans produced accordingly. Further information on EIA and EcIA is provided in Section B of this manual.

The production of integrated designs for all stages of the site development process is now usually a prerequisite of being granted planning permission, although designs may of course be altered over time in response to the existence of previously unidentified factors – it is usual to provide outline indicative designs at the planning stage, and develop these into detailed proposals during the licensing stage. Clearly this is of most relevance to sites currently still at the planning stage. However, even at older sites detailed restoration plans, if not already in existence, should still be designed at the earliest possible opportunity to enable the benefits of restoration to be maximised. There may also be scope for existing plans to be reviewed and old restoration plans that might now be outdated (many agricultural restoration schemes for example) to be improved.

4.2.1 Planning for wildlife management during site operation

A proactive rather than a reactive approach to wildlife management during site operation, achievable by planning at the outset of landfill site development, is likely to have a number of benefits. Firstly, detrimental impacts may be avoided from the outset. Also, wildlife management planned at the outset is likely to be far more cost-effective than programmes introduced at a later stage. For example, deterring gulls from sites which they have never gained access to should be much easier than deterring gulls from sites which they have become accustomed to feeding on. It is also far more cost-effective to prevent an infestation of rats or flies than to exterminate an infestation once established.

Potential impacts must therefore be identified at the EIA / EcIA stage. Where appropriate, programmes of bird control and pest control should be instigated at the outset of site operation. For detailed information on the assessment of likely wildlife management issues see Section C.

4.2.2 Planning for habitat creation

Detailed planning at the outset of site design can also have far-reaching benefits for successful habitat creation. For example, the retention of existing key habitat features within the site design, even if only in small areas or on the periphery of the site, may greatly benefit restoration by speeding up colonisation of the restored areas. Good quality soils can greatly benefit habitat creation, and early planning can improve restoration by ensuring that the most appropriate soils

(i.e. those originally in place at the site) are used in restoration. The use of restoration materials from local sources is also possible if carefully planned; planting with seeds or cuttings taken from nearby habitats not only conserves local genetic stock, but may also prove to be more successful than habitat creation using soils and plant propagules imported from outside the local area.

Early consideration of habitat creation should also enable constraints on potential restoration plans to be identified at an early stage. Also, site engineers can fully incorporate post-use habitat creation plans into engineering designs, and site operators can avoid activities that may compromise the success of restoration.

Opportunities for habitat creation should therefore be identified at the EIA / EcIA stage. The incorporation of existing ecological information for the site is perhaps the single most important factor in successful habitat creation, particularly at sites where important biodiversity may be lost during site construction. Habitat creation must therefore be considered at the outset of site development. Even where existing ecological interest is limited, designs for the creation of additional habitats that enhance the conservation value of the site, should still be produced at the outset of site development. Further information on habitat creation at sites where existing ecological interest is limited is given in Section E.

Figure A.4.1. Simplified diagram showing the main stages of landfill site development and outlining the importance of each stage to wildlife management and habitat creation

Initial site selection
The identification of a provisional site, following guidance in Structure Plans and Waste Local Plans.
Key sites of nature conservation importance should be avoided at this stage.

Design
- Conceptual design: identification of fundamental constraints and consideration of final after-use.
- Main design: incorporation of site investigation results into detailed designs for construction, operation, restoration and aftercare.
Potential requirements for wildlife management during operation and opportunities for habitat creation identified and detailed designs produced.

Planning and waste management licence applications
Applications must be supported by a range of information and designs agreed during informal consultation with EA / SEPA and the WPA.
Key sites of nature conservation importance should be avoided at this stage.

Preparation of site and construction
Preparation of the site to enable it to receive wastes. Includes the construction of site infrastructure and engineering systems designed to prevent pollution, such as the site lining.
Mitigation to minimize adverse ecological impacts, and possibly the retention of key ecological features as identified in the EcIA.

Operation
The actual landfilling of wastes - likely to be in discrete phases enabling phased restoration of the site.
**Wildlife management programme implemented where appropriate.
Preliminary works necessary for habitat creation carried out.**

Restoration[*]
The process that returns the site to a condition suitable for its after-use.
Restoration includes design, initial landscaping works, soil spreading and aftercare.
Close consultation between habitat creation designers and restoration engineers is required at this stage to ensure that restoration meets specifications necessary to support the proposed habitat creation.

Aftercare[*]
Work done after the replacement of the full soil profile to bring the land up to the required standard for the after-use, comprising cultivating, fertilising, planting, draining and other land treatments.
Implementation of habitat creation works and ongoing management.

Post-closure management[*]
Works done to maintain pollution control systems and monitor their effectiveness during the post-closure period.
Long-term habitat monitoring and maintenance.
Amendments to habitat management methods should be considered based on monitoring of habitat creation success.

[*] Definitions given are consistent with those given in Waste Management Paper 26e (Environment Agency, in prep.)

SECTION B
Ecological Impact Assessment and its role in wildlife management and habitat creation at landfill sites

1 Introduction

Ecological Impact Assessment (EcIA) is a relatively new discipline, usually performed as part of the formal Environmental Impact Assessment (EIA) process. It is designed to ensure that all potential impacts upon ecosystems from development projects, including landfill, are fully considered within the planning process and that all unavoidable impacts are adequately mitigated for before, during and after development.

A full discussion of EcIA methods is beyond the scope of this book. However, the EcIA process is an integral part of the identification of wildlife management issues and the design of habitat creation schemes at a considerable number of landfill sites. Indeed, even at sites where existing ecological interest is limited the EcIA should always be seen as the starting point for habitat creation design.

Given that EcIA is such an important part of the wildlife management and habitat creation process at landfill sites, it is essential that the reader has a basic understanding of the requirements and processes involved. This chapter therefore aims to make all those involved in landfill site planning, operation and restoration fully aware of the EcIA process, both within and outside the formal EIA process. More detailed guidance is also given on specific factors that should be considered within EcIA at landfill sites, several of which may affect wildlife management and habitat creation. Further information on the applications of EcIA to the choice of after-use and habitat creation design is given in Section E.

2 Environmental Impact Assessment at landfill sites

Environmental Impact Assessment (EIA) can be defined as the process of identifying, estimating and evaluating the environmental consequences of current or proposed actions (Vanclay & Bronstein, 1995).

This process can be applied to current or proposed actions at a strategic (i.e. planning authority or governmental) scale or, as is more usually the case, to individual development projects. The main objectives of EIA include the design, planning and implementation of development that meets environmental standards and the subsequent enforcement and testing of designs and plans through post-development monitoring and audit. To meet these objectives, legislation requiring EIA for a wide range of development projects now exists in the UK and a large number of other countries.

The scope of an EIA should be wide-ranging, addressing the potential effects of development on all relevant aspects of the environment including human beings, flora and fauna, soil, water, air, climate, material assets including architectural and archaeological heritage, landscape, and the inter-relationship between these factors (EU Directive 85/337/EEC). The findings of EIA are usually presented in an Environmental Statement which should contain a description of the project, the data necessary to assess the main effects on the environment and a description of the mitigation measures (measures to be taken to avoid, reduce or remedy significant adverse effects).

A detailed outline of Environmental Impact Assessment procedures is beyond the scope of this book. For further information on EIA it is therefore suggested the reader consult the references in Box B.2.1.

With respect to landfill sites in the UK, EIA is not a formal requirement at all sites, although following recent changes to the regulations it is now mandatory at most sites. The Town and Country Planning (Environmental Impact Assessment) (England and Wales) Regulations 1999 define two tiers of projects:
- Schedule 1 projects – EIA is mandatory in all cases; and
- Schedule 2 projects – the requirement for EIA is determined by member states on consideration of a project's size, nature and location.

With the exception of sites accepting hazardous wastes (as defined by Council Directive 91/689/EEC), waste disposal by landfill comes under Schedule 2 of the regulations. EIA is required where:
- The area of the development exceeds 0.5 hectares; or
- The installation is to be sited within 100 metres of any controlled waters.

With respect to wildlife management and habitat creation on landfill sites the assessment of impacts on habitats and species is perhaps of greater relevance than the process of EIA as a whole. At landfill sites where EIA is mandatory an *Ecological Impact Assessment* (EcIA) will usually be carried out as part of the EIA. However, as stated above an EIA is not required at all landfill developments. Ecological information for the site is however essential for the effective management of wildlife issues during site operation and successful habitat creation. An EcIA should therefore be carried out at all proposed landfill sites. Whilst there is currently no formal requirement for EcIA at sites not subject to formal EIA, the WPA has the power to insist upon it at all sites through exercise of its statutory powers under the following regulations:
- General Information for Full Applications – Article 4 of the Town & Country Planning (Applications) Regulations 1988

- Outline Applications – Article 3 of the Town & Country Planning (General Applications: Development Procedures) Orders 1995
- European sites – Regulation 48 of the Conservation (Natural Habitats etc.) Regulations 1994

Further background information on EcIA is provided in section B.3.

Box B.2.1. Sources of further information on Environmental Impact Assessment

Morris & Therivel (1995). *Methods of Environmental Impact Assessment.*

Petts & Eduljee (1994). *Environmental Impact Assessment for waste treatment and disposal facilities.*

Petts (1999). *Handbook of Environmental Impact Assessment.*

Treweek (1999). *Ecological Impact Assessment.*

Vanclay & Bronstein (1995). *Environmental and Social Impact Assessment.*

Wood (1995). *Environmental Impact Assessment – a comparative review.*

See the references section for full reference details.

---

3 The process of Ecological Impact Assessment

3.1 The concept of Ecological Impact Assessment

Ecological Impact Assessment (EcIA) can be defined as "the process of identifying, quantifying and evaluating the potential impacts of defined actions on ecosystems or their components" (Treweek, 1999).

Whilst it is usually carried out as part of the EIA process, EcIA relates solely to the impacts of development upon habitats and species, whereas EIA must consider all potential environmental impacts. Note that the impacts of species associated with the development (e.g. pest species attracted to landfill sites) should also be considered as well as the impacts of the development upon existing species. Although EcIA usually forms part of EIA it can also be conducted independently, for example at landfill sites which do not require formal EIA.

The results of the ecological impact assessment should provide the basis for ecologically informed decisions to be made during the planning process, which can be subsequently enforced through the imposition of conditions on planning permissions. EcIA also provides the basis for the production of a Conservation Management Plan, through which ecological issues are considered and mitigated for throughout the life of a development project and beyond.

It must be stressed that EcIA is still a relatively new concept and as a consequence not all EcIA is as effective as it might be. The lack of a formal review procedure frequently results in wide variations in the quality of assessments. A further common failing is the lack of adequate monitoring; without monitoring the effects of development upon habitats and species we cannot be sure that impacts have been predicted accurately, and without monitoring the results of mitigation measures we cannot know that they have been successful.

3.2 Temporal and spatial considerations

EcIA, whether part of a formal EIA or not, must be carried out as early as possible in the design phase of a project. In part this is because an effective assessment may require a considerable amount of time to carry out; site survey must take place at appropriate times of year for all potentially important ecological features to be identified. For example, breeding bird surveys can only be carried out during the bird breeding season (April – July). It is also essential that the results of an EcIA

are considered early enough in the design process to allow mitigation for potential impacts to be properly incorporated into site design. Mitigation is likely to be far less effective if instigated during the later stages of site development; best results will be obtained by fully predicting impacts from the outset and including appropriate mitigation in the initial site design. Due to the interdependence of ecosystem components the potential effects of development projects can be wide-ranging and must therefore be considered beyond simply the area to be developed. Ecological impacts are likely to extend beyond the site boundary for many types of development, including landfill. Noise, for example, can result in reduced densities of breeding birds in areas outside the site of development – densities were found to be reduced for up to 2.8 km from a busy motorway in the Netherlands (Reijnen, 1995). The concept of a minimum viable population size, whereby a population of a particular species must contain a certain number of individuals in order to retain genetic viability, must also be considered. Where discrete populations of particular species (e.g. isolated colonies of certain butterfly species) straddle the site boundary, loss of part of the population may reduce the population size to below the critical level necessary for long-term survival. A suitable scale for the study must therefore be designed which allows all potential impacts to be addressed.

It is also essential that the potential of an area to hold habitats and species of ecological importance is never underestimated and a full EcIA always carried out. Despite widely-held misconceptions, areas of ecological importance do exist outside designated sites; they can occur in existing industrial areas, areas previously subject to disturbance and very small areas, even though such sites may seem very unlikely to contain important wildlife. Species of conservation importance can occur in the most unlikely locations, including newly restored landfill sites (see Pennyhill case study number 8).

3.3 Processes involved in EcIA

The following section is intended simply as a brief overview of the various stages involved in an EcIA, from conception through to post-development monitoring. For more detailed information it is recommended the reader consult additional texts such as those listed in Box B.2.1.

3.3.1 Scoping studies

Scoping is in many ways the most critical stage of the EcIA process as it involves the definition of the scale and timing of all future aspects of the study. Ecologically important areas omitted at this stage are unlikely to be properly considered later in the process.

The main roles of the scoping process are as follows:

- To identify areas of potential ecological importance – for example by Phase I habitat survey (see NCC, 1990a). Areas requiring more detailed study, due for example to the potential presence of rare or protected species, should also be identified.
- To identify the major sources of potential impacts likely to result from the proposed development – including both direct and indirect impacts.

3.3.2 Additional surveys

The complexity and scale of ecosystems invariably means that data cannot be collected on all ecosystem components. Attention should therefore be focused on particular areas including potentially important habitats identified by the Phase I survey and areas considered likely to hold rare or protected species, in combination with areas where likely impacts are greatest. The primary objective of these specialised ecological surveys should be to establish a set of baseline ecological conditions from which ecological importance may be evaluated, the scale of impacts predicted and the extent of actual impacts measured through future monitoring.

3.3.3 Impact Prediction

The process of predicting impacts is an integral part of the EcIA process upon which the overall ecological impact of a development project is assessed and appropriate mitigation proposed. Whilst some impacts such as land take are relatively simple to predict, considerable uncertainty often exists in the prediction of the exact scale of less direct impacts on habitats and species (such as air pollution or minor alterations to drainage regimes) due to the inherent complexity of ecosystems. Considerable uncertainty also exists where there are complex interactions between species, many of which may not be fully understood (for example, the dependence of certain orchid species upon a single soil fungus for seed germination). In such cases a direct impact on one component of the ecosystem may indirectly affect a large

number of other organisms, impacts on which will be almost impossible to predict.

3.3.4 Evaluation

EcIA must provide an indication to developers and decision-makers of the most important ecological features and areas within a site, particularly in relation to areas where predicted impacts are greatest, in order for informed, ecologically sound decisions to be made. Evaluation usually involves the highlighting of species or habitats of importance according to various standard criteria, which in the UK include:

For habitats:

- Standard Nature Conservancy Council criteria such as size, rarity and naturalness (see the NCC (1989) guidelines for the selection of biological SSSIs).
- Site designation – both statutory (e.g. SSSI, SAC and SPA) and non-statutory (e.g. SNCI and County Wildlife Sites).
- Priority habitats identified by the UK BAP.

For species:

- Special protection under Schedules 1, 5 and 8 of the Wildlife & Countryside Act (1981). Note that in many cases protection is limited to the species itself, but the habitat of some species is also protected (e.g. bat roosts are protected all year round regardless of the length of time they are occupied for).
- Special protection under Regulation 39 of the Conservation (natural habitats etc.) Regulations (1994). This legislation protects species listed on Annex II of the EU Habitats and Species Directive (1992), and affords these species (and their habitat) a greater level of protection than they previously received under the Wildlife & Countryside Act.
- Rarity – e.g. inclusion in red data books.
- Threatened status – e.g. UK BAP species or bird species on the JNCC List of Birds of Conservation Importance (JNCC, 1996).

Ideally, attention should not simply be restricted to protected habitats or species. Consideration should also be given to keystone species (species whose presence is central to the functioning of a particular habitat type), key processes (such as water availability, grazing and nutrient cycling) and habitat attributes (such as soil type, soil conditions, aspect, shading). Considering these factors will assist in successful habitat design and creation.

3.3.5 Mitigation

The term mitigation refers to any action designed to avoid, reduce or compensate for impacts upon the nature conservation interest of a site. Five common forms of mitigation are recognized (adapted from Treweek, 1999) as follows:

- **Impact avoidance** – involves the retention of key ecological features within the site design, for example key habitats or habitats that contain key species conserved *in situ*. This is perhaps the best form of mitigation although care must be taken to ensure that additional impacts from the development do not impinge upon the integrity of the retained habitats. Retained habitats must also be large enough to be self-sustaining (e.g. 5 ha in the case of woodland). Alternatively, links (e.g. hedgerows, watercourses) to similar habitat should be provided.
- **Impact reduction** – involves the construction of features designed to reduce impacts upon ecologically important areas. Examples include noise screens to reduce impacts from noise-generating developments on breeding birds and wildlife-proof fences, which are designed to prevent certain species entering impact areas, where they may come to harm. Wildlife-proof fences have been used with some success on certain amphibian species and mammals such as water vole (Ecoscope Applied Ecologists, 1999).
- **Rescue or translocation** – entails the removal of individual plants or animals to an alternative site, or at a larger scale the movement of an entire habitat through the stripping and replacement of soil and turves. Note that monitoring translocated species and habitats has shown that translocations are rarely wholly successful and almost always result in a reduction in the nature conservation value of a habitat. Translocation can also be very expensive and requires very careful matching of conditions at the donor and receptor sites. It is therefore important that translocation is only viewed as a last resort – retention of habitats *in situ* almost always results in a greater probability of long-term survival.
- **Restoration** – includes the creation of habitats on a site once damaging impacts have ceased. It is especially relevant for development projects at which impacts from development are only temporary in nature, such as landfill, and forms one of the main

themes of this book. Note that habitat creation is not a substitute for the retention of habitats *in situ*, which will result in a greater probability of successful conservation in the long term.

- **Compensation –** this can include the enhancement of existing habitat (through sensitive management) or the creation of new habitat on land outside the impacted areas as compensation for the habitats damaged or lost as a result of the project. It may take place on an area of land within the site, set aside for such a purpose, or on land completely independent of the development area.

3.3.6 Monitoring

Monitoring of the actual impacts upon habitats and species and the effectiveness of mitigation measures, measured against baseline data, should form an integral part of every EcIA. In addition to evaluating whether planning conditions have been complied with, monitoring can also contribute greatly to the improvement of best practice standards by enabling more accurate impact prediction and the implementation of proven mitigation techniques. At present, detailed monitoring requiring a long-term commitment on the part of the developer (i.e. several years) is rarely carried out. This situation is improving, and the requirement for ecological monitoring is now frequently included as a planning condition on development projects.

Monitoring of habitats and species will usually involve the replication of surveys undertaken as part of the initial EcIA. Results should be comparable with baseline surveys and the impact of the development on particular habitats or species can then be assessed. Monitoring should take place for several years after the project has been completed, in order to measure long-term effects, although the actual frequency of monitoring required will vary from habitat to habitat and species group to species group. There must also be provision for action to be taken if impacts are greater than anticipated or if mitigation is unsuccessful. Such provision ideally needs to be included in planning conditions on the development.

4 Ecological Impact Assessment at landfill sites

4.1 Introduction

Many of the impacts arising from landfill developments are to a certain extent temporary in that site restoration is required once operation has ceased. Although it is impossible to create an exact replicate of habitats damaged or destroyed during site construction and operation, ecological mitigation in the form of habitat creation after the completion of landfilling activities offers a major opportunity to compensate for the habitats destroyed.

The processes involved in conducting EcIA at landfill sites are generally similar to those employed for other developments. However, a number of impacts on habitats and species may occur that are more or less specific to landfill sites, in addition to basic land-take. This chapter therefore provides guidance on a number of landfill-specific factors that must be addressed by those carrying out EcIA at landfill sites. This includes information on:

- potential impacts specifically resulting from the construction and operation of landfill sites;
- specific habitats and species in the surrounding area that are especially sensitive to impacts from landfill sites; and
- potential impacts specific to landfill site restoration.

Note that this section is particularly aimed at modern landfill sites where EcIA should be carried out as part of the planning process. Some form of ecological assessment should also be carried out at old sites prior to restoration works, but there are different requirements (see Section B.4.5).

This chapter also examines the opportunities for mitigation of impacts at landfill sites. Of most relevance is the potential for the creation of habitats at landfill sites. It is recommended that all landfill developments which impact on features of high ecological value should incorporate an adequate degree of habitat creation into site restoration (see Section E).

4.2 Potential impacts on ecosystems during landfill site construction and operation

Clearly, landfill site construction and operation will result in the loss of habitats present on the site. Landfill operation can also give rise to a number of impacts on ecosystems that are unlikely to occur at other types of development. The most

common of these are therefore outlined in this section as a guide for practitioners involved in EcIA at landfill sites. This information will also allow site operators and planners to check the quality and completeness of ecological information provided with planning applications. A summary is provided in Table B.4.1. Note that the extent of impacts at all landfill sites will vary widely depending on factors such as:

- waste type(s) accepted;
- site size;
- site topography; and
- characteristics of the surrounding area.

The EcIA must therefore take these into consideration accordingly.

4.2.1 Scavenging birds

Sites accepting putrescible wastes are all likely to attract large numbers of scavenging birds, particularly gulls and corvids (see Section C for detailed information on birds at operational landfill sites). Impacts from large flocks of birds include air-strike risk, damage to amenity and concerns over human health; the potential for such impacts should be addressed as part of the formal EIA. However, large numbers of scavenging birds can also have a number of damaging impacts upon local habitats, which should be addressed as part of an EcIA. Predation is the most common impact on other species resulting from large numbers of gulls and corvids (particularly the eggs and young of ground-nesting birds). Eutrophication, caused by the deposition of large quantities of gull guano, is the most common impact on habitats (particularly nutrient-poor terrestrial and aquatic habitats). Such impacts are of greatest concern where rare or endangered species or habitats are concerned, and rare habitats or species that may be impacted upon must therefore be identified by the EcIA.

Gulls frequently travel long distances (up to 50 km) between landfills and roosting or breeding sites, and they frequently stop at water bodies or alternative feeding sites en route. Impacts can therefore occur over a very wide area. EcIA must therefore identify all sites where important ground-nesting bird colonies exist (e.g. gravel pits and beaches) within a wide radius of the landfill site itself (up to 10 km) and along the entire length of likely flight-lines to and from roost / breeding sites.

Gull guano, if deposited in large enough quantities, will raise nutrient levels. The species composition of nutrient-sensitive habitats is likely to be altered, and rarer species may be out-competed by aggressive grasses and weedy species such as nettles. Important terrestrial habitats that are nutrient-sensitive, such as heathland and semi-natural grassland, are only likely to be affected relatively close to a landfill site (within 1 km) where they may be used as loafing sites by gulls. However, aquatic habitats could be affected over a much wider radius (up to 10 km) if waterbodies are used by large numbers of gulls. Although such impacts are sometimes considered trivial by site operators, they must not be overlooked and should always be fully considered during the EcIA process.

4.2.2 Other pest species
Although infestations of rats and insects at landfill sites are most commonly associated with impacts upon humans (see Sections C.3 & C.4), ecologically damaging impacts can also occur. For example, rats are known to predate a number of animals including legally protected species such as slow-worm. Rats may also predate eggs and young birds, and therefore may cause problems if rare ground-nesting species are present close to the site. Landfill site EcIAs should therefore pay particular attention to identifying the presence of species susceptible to rat predation.

4.2.3 Dust
The potential impact of dust created during site construction and operation upon local amenity is likely to be fully covered as part of the main EIA for the site. However, an EcIA must ensure that potential impacts on habitats are fully considered. Dust can affect habitats by reducing plant photosynthesis, reducing oxygen content of water and (if the dust is nutrient-rich) causing eutrophication. Impacts from dust contamination are possible for many habitat types, both terrestrial and aquatic. Important habitats or species close to a site (within 1 km), particularly downwind of the prevailing wind direction, must therefore be identified by the EcIA. Where appropriate, mitigation (such as the regular spraying of access roads) must be considered.

4.2.4 Litter
The ecological impacts of windblown litter should be fully considered by EcIA. The contamination of sensitive habitats as a result of litter-blow is unlikely, as most litter is inert. The greatest danger is likely to be the entanglement or poisoning of

animals. Once again, this is particularly relevant where rare species are identified downwind of the site. If such species are legally protected there may be legal implications, and appropriate mitigation should be proposed in such cases.

4.2.5 Noise
Noise from landfill operations can be substantial. As well as affecting local residents, local ecosystems can also be affected by noise. For example, birds have been found to breed at much lower densities close to busy roads; noise is the most likely factor responsible for this, probably as a result of distorting male song (Reijnen et al., 1995). The existence of high densities of breeding birds close to a site, as may be present in scrub or woodland for example, or the presence of rare species should therefore be identified and the extent of impacts fully considered by EcIA.

4.2.6 Landfill gas and leachate
At modern sites, which are carefully engineered to control pollution, ecological impacts from the discharge of landfill gas and leachate are likely to be minimal. At sites where it is planned to operate landfill gas flares, potential ecological impacts, e.g. on birds in flight, may need to be considered, although such impacts are likely to be limited in extent.

4.2.7 Additional ecological impacts
Watercourses are particularly susceptible to impacts at potential landfill sites. Streams or other watercourses cannot generally be retained where they flow through sites and the requirement for streams to be diverted or culverted can have substantial impacts on vegetation and wildlife species present, not just for the length of the section affected but also downstream due to possible alterations to flow patterns. Note that culverting cannot be recommended ecologically due to loss of habitat and may not be permitted by the EA for pollution prevention reasons. Groundwater levels may also be affected by landfill development; any alterations that make a site wetter or drier are liable to have substantial effects on habitats and species. This will be of particular concern where habitats or species of particular ecological interest are identified on or adjacent to a site. Such impacts must therefore be fully considered during the EcIA.

4.3 Potential impacts on ecosystems following restoration
The restored landfill site typically comprises a domed landform, covered by a low-permeability cap below the surface

soil layer (see Section D for further detail). Such a landform is likely to substantially alter local drainage patterns and may also impact upon other factors such as local microclimates. Changes to key environmental processes in this manner, after landfilling has been completed, can have major impacts upon habitats and species, particularly where habitats of high value lie adjacent to the site. Such impacts are just as important as those that take place during construction and operation; consequently, the likely ecological impacts of the proposed final landform on areas adjacent to the site must be assessed as part of the initial EcIA. Such an assessment is necessary at the outset of site planning and design, even though impacts may not take place for several years, in order that appropriate mitigation or alterations to site design can take place in good time to prevent damaging impacts occurring.

4.4 Opportunities for mitigation at landfill sites
Most mitigation options available at landfill sites are similar to those that might be used in a range of other development types where mitigation for ecological impacts is required. The most common mitigation measures were broadly outlined in the previous chapter; the following paragraphs concentrate primarily on mitigative features that might be especially relevant at landfill sites.

4.4.1 Retention of key habitats of conservation value
Habitats or species of particular importance identified by the EcIA (e.g. designated sites, priority habitats listed by the Habitats Directive or habitats holding protected or red data book species) should be retained in situ wherever possible. This is made much simpler when EcIA is carried out at the outset of the site design process allowing the retention of such features to be incorporated into the initial site design. Great care must be taken to ensure that retained areas are not inadvertently damaged through site operations either directly (for example by vehicle movements or soil storage) or indirectly (for example by dust, litter or noise). Damage can be avoided through simple techniques such as the fencing of important areas and thorough briefing of staff; where appropriate, such protective measures should be suggested as part of the EcIA. The EcIA should also make provision for monitoring to ensure compliance, which may include for example the provision of an ecological clerk of works.

Table B.4.1. Summary of potential impacts on ecosystems, specific to landfill site developments, that should be fully considered during an Ecological Impact Assessment

Source of potential impact	Type of site affected	Description of potential impact	Habitats at particular risk	Potential area affected
Scavenging birds (gulls & corvids)	Sites accepting putrescible waste	Increase in predation of e.g. rare ground nesting birds	Habitats holding rare ground-nesting birds e.g. gravel pits, beaches, etc.	Wetland sites within c.10 km of site / along entire length of gulls roost flight-lines (up to 50 km)
		Nutrient enrichment of sites frequently used for bathing / roosting by large numbers of gulls	Nutrient-sensitive habitats e.g. chalk/acid grassland, heathland, water bodies, etc.	Within c.1 km of site
Other pest species e.g. rats	Sites accepting putrescible waste	Increase in predation of rare species	Habitats holding rare or protected species e.g. water vole, slow-worm, etc.	Within c.1km of site
Dust	All sites	Contamination of sensitive habitats	Several habitats, particularly woodland. Special attention should be paid to rare habitats close to the site	Within c.1 km of site, particularly downwind of prevailing wind direction
Litter	All sites, but particularly sites accepting controlled waste.	Contamination of sensitive habitats (n.b. impacts likely to be low at most sites)	Certain wetlands, grasslands, etc; special attention should be paid to rare habitats close to the site	Within c.1 km of site, particularly downwind of prevailing wind direction
		Entanglement & poisoning of animal species	All sites – particularly where rare species identified close to site	Within c.1 km of site, particularly downwind of prevailing wind direction
Noise	All sites	Damaging effect on breeding bird populations	Habitats holding high density of breeding birds or populations of rare bird species	Within c.1 km of site. Greatest impact within 200m of noise source
Alterations to watercourses	All sites	Loss of habitat	Wetlands and riparian habitats	Within site boundary
		Damaging effects downstream of site, e.g. siltation, erosion, etc.	Wetlands and riparian habitats	Up to several km downstream of site, especially on high volume watercourses
Alterations to groundwater regime	All sites	Changes / damage to sensitive habitats and species through either raising or lowering of water table	Rare habitats are of particular concern	Within water catchment (possibly very wide area)
Changes to local conditions following restoration	All sites	Changes / damage to local ecosystems as result of changes in surface runoff, topography, microclimate, etc.	Particularly rare habitats where even slight changes to key processes may cause great damage	Within 1 km of site or several km downstream on watercourses

Where ecologically significant areas are retained they should be incorporated into the final habitat creation scheme wherever possible. Sensitive restoration can benefit the retained area, and colonisation of created habitats will be far more rapid if an area of primary habitat is retained from the outset (see Section E for more detail on the benefits of habitat retention).

4.4.2 Specific impact reduction measures

Many standard impact reduction measures, such as noise screens, are not specific to landfill and are therefore not covered here. Measures to control scavenging birds are more or less specific to landfill sites, and should be strongly considered at sites where ecological impacts resulting from high gull populations are potentially large. Bird control may also be required to mitigate for other potential impacts, although measures employed to reduce impacts from scavenging birds can themselves have negative impacts, both on humans and on wildlife. Detailed information on the complete range of bird control methods is given in Section C.3.

Control of other pest species is also strongly recommended at sites where ecological impacts from such species are expected to be high. Note that the pest control programmes themselves can also impact upon other wildlife if not carried out with great care; for example, poisoned bait must not be placed where it may affect other species such as water vole. See Section C for further detail about the control of a range of potential pest species.

4.4.3 Translocation

The nature of landfill site development, particularly on sites where operations and restoration are phased, does present a number of opportunities for translocation, both for individual species and for entire habitats. However, translocation will not be a viable option in many circumstances, and should therefore only be considered as a last resort, once all alternative mitigation options have been ruled out.

On many phased landfill sites it may be possible for some habitats or species to be translocated from un-worked areas to areas already restored. Note that great care is necessary to ensure that translocated species or communities will survive on newly restored land. Conditions such as drainage, slope and soil structure are likely to be greatly altered on restored landfill (see Section D), and the effects of these upon

translocated vegetation must be fully considered before translocation takes place. For species translocations, it must be ensured that restored habitats have reached a suitable stage of maturity to support the species concerned. Whilst some species may be relocated successfully in relatively new habitats, others (e.g. most reptile species) may require several years of habitat development before conditions are suitable for their release. Translocations must also ensure that a large enough quantity of material or number of individuals is moved to ensure that a viable habitat or population remains. Furthermore it should be noted that translocation is not possible for many habitats and species. Translocations should never be carried out onto restored areas where there is any possibility of remedial work on pollution control systems being required.

4.4.4 Site restoration / habitat creation

Landfill site restoration can in many cases provide an excellent opportunity to mitigate for ecological interest lost or damaged during site development. Whilst habitats and species of the greatest importance should always be retained, sites supporting habitats or species of lower priority may be candidates for a programme of habitat creation as a mitigation measure.

It is therefore the role of the EcIA to recommend habitat creation measures at all sites where ecologically important areas are to be lost or damaged during development. Restoration may also be proposed that extends areas of habitat adjacent to the site in mitigation for potential damage during landfill operation. Once again it is the role of EcIA to make such proposals, based upon ecological information from the area surrounding the site. Note that habitat creation may be a viable after-use even where there is no need for it as mitigation, i.e. for sites with minimal ecological interest. For further information on habitat creation at landfill sites see Section F.

4.4.5 Compensation

The creation of new habitats, or the management for conservation of existing habitats, beyond the actual impact area of a development is now a frequently used form of mitigation for damaged or destroyed habitats at a range of sites, including landfills. This book is aimed primarily at habitat creation on restored landfill, and whilst the majority of the techniques described in Section F are also relevant to non-landfill environments,

it is suggested that the reader also consults alternative texts for comprehensive information on habitat creation and management (e.g. Buckley & Knight (1989), Baines & Smart (1991), Andrews & Rebane (1994), RSPB/NRA/RNSC (1994), Merritt (1994), Sutherland & Hill (1995), RSPB/EN/ITE (1997) and Gilbert & Anderson (1998)).

4.5 Ecological information and the restoration of old sites

At most old landfill sites the existence of an EcIA or equivalent is extremely unlikely. However, assessments should be carried out at all old sites prior to habitat creation works, following the same principles employed for EcIA at modern sites, despite the fact that for planning purposes old landfill sites are usually labeled as 'brownfield sites' for which it is commonly perceived that EcIA is not necessary. Even on partly restored landfill sites there is often good potential for ecologically important habitats to have developed, particularly on poorly restored sites where settlement may have created interesting wetland habitats or where the site has been left abandoned and undisturbed for some time. Indeed, the longer a site has been left undisturbed, the greater the chances that habitats or species of value may be present.

Where ecological interest is identified at old landfill sites it should be incorporated into the restoration designs wherever possible. The failure to carry out appropriate ecological assessments prior to habitat creation could result in loss or damage to existing habitats that may outweigh the benefits of creating new ones.

SECTION C

Wildlife management on operational landfill sites

1 Background & introduction

Wildlife-related issues at operational landfill sites involve two main issues:

1. Impacts from undesirable species attracted to landfill sites during their operational phase.

Such impacts are generally caused by large populations of:
- Birds (Section C.2)
- Rodents (Section C.3)
- Insects (Section C.4)

The greatest impacts, and often the hardest to control, usually result from flocks of birds attracted to large amounts of biodegradable waste. Much of this chapter is therefore devoted to birds on landfill sites and ways of reducing the problems they cause. A summary of undesirable species most commonly attracted to landfill is given in Figure C.1.1.

2. Impacts upon sensitive wildlife habitats.

Important wildlife habitats both on and adjacent to sites should be identified during the Ecological Impact Assessment (EcIA). If such habitats are present, site-specific management techniques to minimise impacts, such as excessive noise and dust during the operation of the site, should be employed. This issue was covered in full in Section B.

1.1 Species attracted to landfill sites

1.1.1 Birds

Several bird species are often found at operational landfill sites in large numbers. The commonest species are gulls; in addition to feeding on landfills, they also tend to use the large expanses of bare ground associated with landfill sites for 'loafing' and social activities. Although gulls are commonly perceived as coastal birds, they are now found in substantial numbers inland across almost all of the UK. Other species attracted to landfills include a range of corvids (crows, rooks, etc.), starlings and other small birds such as pied wagtails which feed on insects.

1.1.2 Rodents

The brown rat *Rattus norvegicus* is the only species of rodent that is common at landfill sites. Consequently, attention in this chapter is focussed on issues relating to rats at landfill sites and the means of controlling them. Other rodent species can occur at landfill sites (e.g. house mouse) but these are not usually directly associated with waste.

1.1.3 Insects

The tendency of many species of fly to lay their eggs in rotting organic matter can lead to large infestations at and around landfill sites at which large quantities of organic waste are deposited. The commonest pest species associated with landfills include the housefly *Musca domestica* and blowflies such as bluebottle *Calliphora vicina* and greenbottle *Lucilia sericata*. Other insect pests known to breed at some landfill sites include the oriental cockroach *Blatta orientalis* and house cricket *Acheta domesticus*.

1.2 Wildlife management issues at landfill sites

The major potential problem resulting from the presence of large numbers of birds at landfill sites is the increased risk of bird-strike – the potentially lethal collision between birds and aircraft taking off or landing at nearby airfields. Other potential problems include concerns over human health, implications for amenity of local residents and possible detrimental effects on sensitive wildlife habitats nearby. Rodents and insects can impact upon the health and amenity of humans living close to landfill sites. These impacts can be exacerbated by the ability of both rats and flies to reproduce very quickly; small populations have the potential to become major infestations within a relatively short period of time.

1.2.1 Bird control

The number of birds attracted to individual sites, and hence the scale of potential impacts, can vary in response to a wide range of factors. Even where large numbers of birds are present their impact on issues such as aircraft safety and local amenity is also dependent on a range of factors. The potential problems arising from large bird populations at landfill sites are discussed in Section C.2.1. Detailed information on factors affecting bird numbers at individual sites and guidelines for assessment of the extent of impacts is given in Sections C.2.2 and C.2.3.

On sites where the impacts of bird populations are perceived to be serious, it is desirable to reduce the number of birds present or even eliminate bird populations entirely. A number of different methods exist to deter birds from using landfill sites; these methods differ greatly in their effectiveness. In addition, certain methods may be successful at one site but not at another. At sites where impacts from birds are high, clear objectives for what bird control is designed to achieve must be set. Where necessary, an appropriate programme of bird control should be introduced. Guidance on setting objectives for bird control, an assessment of the effectiveness of a range of control techniques and guidance on best practice for these are given in Sections C.2.4-C.2.7. The results of an independent study carried out by Ecoscope Applied Ecologists testing the effectiveness of a number of different bird control techniques are presented in Appendix 1. Central Sciences Laboratory (CSL) are also currently carrying out a project to determine the effectiveness of bird control techniques. A discussion of progress to date can be found in Baxter (1999).

1.2.2 Rodent and insect control

Methods used to control rodents and insects at landfill sites are generally similar to those employed at a range of other sites, with certain adaptations to account for the large scale of problems at landfill sites. Potential issues arising from rodent and insect populations and standard control methods are outlined in Sections C.4 and C.5.

concern is understandable.

With respect to potential impacts on drinking water, impacts will be highest at inland sites where reservoirs are used as overnight roosts. Site location studies for a landfill should therefore assess, at the EIA stage, the distribution, extent and range of waterbodies greater than 5 ha in size, for proposed landfills which will accept domestic waste.

Should further evidence to link gulls and human health problems come to light, it may be prudent to exclude gulls that utilise reservoirs from feeding at landfill sites, although the cost of total deterrence at what would be the majority of British sites would be extremely high.

2.2.3 Amenity impacts

Where residential areas are situated close to landfill sites, large numbers of birds can have a number of negative impacts on amenity, including:

- Bird droppings fouling nearby gardens (particularly washing on clothes lines), buildings and cars (paintwork can be damaged in this way).
- The dropping of waste by birds over nearby residential or amenity areas, leading to concerns over health, an increase in litter, and items such as tin cans causing damage to livestock.
- Negative impacts on visual amenity. Large flocks of circling birds, particularly gulls, are generally considered undesirable. They also provide a reminder of the presence of the landfill, even where the landfill itself is well screened.
- High noise levels.

Often, however, problems are perceived as being more acute than they actually become in reality.

Assessing the magnitude of potential impacts

Where housing is located within 1 km of a landfill site, the impact of gulls on amenity is likely to be high. Where housing is located within 1-2 km of a site, the impact of gulls will be lower although the impact may still be moderate if gulls regularly loaf off-site in areas between the site and the housing. Moderate impacts may also occur where daily flight-lines to and from roost / breeding sites pass directly over nearby housing. For most sites further than 1 km from housing, impacts from gulls upon amenity will be low.

Amenity may also be affected by the presence of corvids and starlings within the immediate vicinity of a site. Beyond

that distance, however, the tendency of these species to disperse evenly means that impacts on amenity are likely to be minimal.

Attention should also be paid to impacts upon amenity in parks or areas of public open space within the vicinity of the site.

2.2.4 Impacts on nearby habitats and species of conservation importance

A large increase in the local bird population, especially gulls and crows, due to the presence of a landfill may cause the following problems:

- An increase in predation, especially of eggs and young of nearby breeding birds. This could have major impacts on rare bird species, particularly in open or wetland habitats. Methods of bird control at the landfill site may also need to be adjusted to avoid impacting on birds outside the landfill site.
- Sensitive, nutrient-poor habitats could be damaged by increased use by birds. For example, large quantities of droppings can cause nutrient enrichment and the consequent loss of rare species. Similarly, the creation of habitats requiring nutrient-poor soils on completed phases of landfill could

be compromised by the presence of large numbers of birds attracted to operational areas. Indeed, newly restored areas, with large expanses of bare ground and low vegetation, are frequently used by gulls for 'loafing'.

Assessing the magnitude of potential impacts

Important habitats and species (such as those listed under Annexes I and II of the EU Habitats Directive) within the area surrounding a site should be identified as part of an initial Ecological Impact Assessment (see Section B). In particular, attention should focus on identifying sites which support colonies of rare breeding birds (e.g. for estuary sites or inland wetland reserves, species such as avocet and black-tailed godwit may be affected) and sites where the conservation interest is directly related to low soil or water nutrient levels.

An increase in the number of gulls attracted to a landfill can have an impact within a wide surrounding area; consideration of an area within 10 km of the site is suggested. Any sensitive habitats located along the usual flight lines to and from likely roost / breeding sites should also be identified as these may be affected by birds en route to and from the site.

POTENTIAL BIRD PROBLEMS AND IMPACTS AT OPERATIONAL LANDFILL SITES

SUMMARY

- All landfill sites where food waste is accepted can attract scavenging birds in large numbers. Even in areas where numbers of such birds are low at present, large numbers will enter almost all areas in the UK as a direct result of a landfill site opening if suitable control measures are not implemented.
- Largest numbers of birds will be attracted to the largest landfill sites, although numbers are not thought to be directly related to the quantity of waste accepted. Not all sites will retain birds all year round with high numbers of gulls in summer generally only found at sites near the coast (also some inland sites in northern Britain).
- Most impacts are caused by the presence of large numbers of gulls. With respect to air safety, gulls create a particular hazard due to their tendency to rise high in the air on thermals above sites, the long distance they are prepared to fly between feeding and roost or breeding sites, especially where airfields are located in between roosts and landfill sites and the large size of flocks at many sites. Corvids and starlings generally cause fewer problems although impacts can be high at certain sites.
- For sites within 13 km of airfields, the extent of bird-related impacts depends upon distance from the runway / aircraft flightpath, the number of birds present and the location of birds' flight lines to and from roost sites.
- Impacts upon amenity are likely to be high where sites are located within 1km of housing, or for a greater distance from the site if gull loafing areas are situated between the site and housing.
- Impacts upon certain habitats of conservation importance are possible within a large radius around the site and along the entire length of potential flight lines to and from gull roosts or breeding sites.

At sites where gull numbers are low during the summer months, impacts on breeding birds are likely to be low. However, at sites with large summer gull populations, the presence of rare species (especially wildfowl, waders or terns) within the surrounding area or along likely flight-lines implies that impacts are potentially possible. Impacts from large numbers of corvids are also possible where certain rare breeding bird species are present, although within a smaller area surrounding the site than that affected by gulls.

Impacts on habitats may be high where sensitive nutrient-poor habitats lie immediately adjacent to the site. Some wetland habitats may also be affected in a similar way. Impacts on wetland sites are likely to be high where such sites lie within a few kilometres of a site or below a likely flight-line to and from a potential roost when they may be used by gulls for bathing.

2.3 Assessment of the effectiveness of techniques used to deter birds from operational landfill sites

2.3.1 Setting objectives for bird control

Bird control is likely to be necessary when potential impacts resulting from large bird numbers are high. In such cases a bird control programme may be made a condition of the site being allowed to operate, or may be undertaken voluntarily by the site operator.

If a bird control programme is to be introduced it is extremely important that clear, targeted objectives are set for it. Objectives must be set that specify a measurable end-result for bird control operations, for example a complete elimination of a particular species from the site during operational hours. Monitoring and subsequent enforcement of the effectiveness of a bird control programme can then be set against measurable objectives. Objectives need not specify methods of bird control to be used, but should define the desired end result of bird control, i.e. the long-term effect on numbers of scavenging birds.

At most sites one of the following objectives should be set for a bird control programme (modifications to these or objectives tailored to individual sites may be acceptable depending on individual site factors):

1. **Total deterrence of birds from the site and the surrounding area**
2. **Total deterrence of birds from feeding on waste at the site**
3. **No bird control**

The first objective is likely to be imposed only at sites with potential bird-strike risk, whilst the second is more likely in areas with potential amenity or habitat concerns – deterrence of birds from feeding at the site will inevitably also lead to a major reduction in bird numbers in the surrounding area. It might be argued that at many sites the cost of intensive bird control is not justified in relation to the magnitude of impacts. Where this is the case it is probably more cost-effective not to operate any bird control rather than attempt to deter birds using a variety of low-input, relatively low-cost devices operated by site staff (as occurs at a substantial number of sites at present) which in the long term will simply not be effective. Note that objective 3 should of course be subject to periodic review with respect to changes in the magnitude of impacts.

Photo: Duncan Watson

Gulls can be attracted to operational landfill sites in large numbers.

Figure C.1.1. Common Pest species on landfill sites

Great black-backed gull
Larus marinus

Photo: Chris Gomersall

Most common in coastal areas, also inland in northern England and around major conurbations. Rarely the most numerous gull species on landfill sites. Impact high where it does occur in large numbers due to large size.

Lesser black-backed gull
Larus fuscus

Photo: Chris Gomersall

Most common in southern half of Britain during winter, although breeds further north. Most common large gull on landfill sites in inland areas where it occurs. Species of conservation importance due to high proportion (>20%) of European population present in Britain.

Herring gull
Larus argentatus

Photo: Chris Gomersall

Most common around coast although present throughout Britain in smaller numbers during winter. Frequently the commonest gull species at landfills in coastal areas. Species of conservation importance due to moderate decline in breeding population over last 25 years.

Black-headed gull
Larus ridibundus

Photo: Chris Gomersall

Present throughout most of Britain. Usually the commonest gull species at landfills in inland areas, particularly in the southern half of Britain. Impacts often lower than for large gulls due to smaller size, although frequently present in very large numbers.

Rook
Corvus frugilegus

Photo: Chris Gomersall

Common throughout much of Britain. Can be present in large numbers at landfills, often outside operational hours. Nests in colonies, which are frequently found in trees close to landfill sites.

Carrion crow
Corvus corone

Photo: Chris Gomersall

Common throughout Britain. Like rook can be present in large numbers at landfills, often outside operational hours. Strongly territorial and therefore less likely to breed in large numbers close to sites.

Starling
Sturnus vulgaris

Photo: Chris Gomersall

Common throughout Britain. Feeds at landfill sites throughout operational hours and often unresponsive to bird control. Impacts greatest from large, dense flocks formed close to roost sites. Species of conservation importance due to extensive decline in breeding population over last 25 years.

Brown rat
Rattus norvegicus

Photo: Mark Lucas/Windrush

Widespread throughout Britain. Likely to be found at any landfill site where food waste is present where burrows are constructed in bunds and banks surrounding the operational cells. Persistent pest where it occurs around human habitation therefore impacts potentially great where landfills sited close to housing.

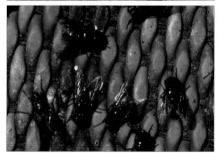

House fly
Musca domestica

Photo: Alan Petty/Windrush

Widespread and abundant throughout Britain. Breeds in rotting organic matter and therefore present at most landfill sites. Large numbers can have high impacts on houses in the surrounding area.

Bluebottle
Calliphora vicina

Photo: John Gardner/Windrush

Common throughout Britain. Breeds in rotting animal matter. Larvae are frequently brought into landfills within incoming waste.

Photo: David Hill

Gulls feeding on an operational landfill site.

2.3.2 Changes required to the existing situation

At present, objectives (as set out in planning or licence conditions) are rarely specific. For example, objectives such as 'methods to control numbers of birds should be employed' are common (taken from Environment Agency (1999) guidance on setting licence conditions). Such an objective does not make it clear what constitutes success. They are easily misunderstood and impossible to enforce. Objectives also frequently do not aim high enough. Bird control can be very effective and objectives 1 and 2 **can** be achieved in practice (see C.2.4). At present this is not widely appreciated by operators and regulators across the industry.

Bird control is often regarded as rather unimportant by site operators, with some semblance of control carried out simply to appease local residents or inspectors. Once again this may be based on a lack of appreciation of how successful bird control can be. If potential impacts are high enough that bird control is considered necessary, a minimum of objective 2 above must be set. If impacts are low there is probably no need for bird control. Piecemeal, half-hearted attempts at bird control will seldom be effective.

2.3.3 Statutory requirements for bird control

A bird control programme can be imposed at sites by:

1. CAA / MoD for sites within 8 miles of specified airports or bases. They have:
- powers to impose total exclusion of birds (i.e. by netting), total deterrence of birds from dawn until dusk or both together; and
- powers also to recommend refusal of the site application altogether, if even the extremely slim risk of simultaneous failure of bird exclusion and bird deterrence is considered too great a threat to air safety. In such circumstances, the local planning authority is unlikely to recommend a granting of permission since they would not be prepared to take the health and safety risk.

2. Planning Authorities. These have:
- powers to impose a bird control programme where expected impacts on amenity are high or where there is an unacceptable environmental health risk; and
- powers to impose bird control conditions with respect to potential impacts on sensitive wildlife habitats.

In most cases it is the responsibility of the planning authority to set specific, clearly understood objectives for bird control and to ensure enforcement.

3. Environment Agency / Scottish Environmental Protection Agency. They may:
- set bird control conditions in the site licence. The latest consultation draft of the Library of Licence Conditions (Environment Agency, 1999) specifies that *"preventive measures and controls should be provided where the permitted waste types and nature of activities are likely to attract birds."* However, this is not a specific objective. It would be preferable if one of the objectives specified in Section 2.3.1 were set in the site licence.

Where well-defined objectives are set that involve bird control it is the responsibility of the EA/SEPA to ensure that they are met. At present, standards of enforcement across the country are highly variable from region to region.

2.3.4 Minimisation of bird numbers through good operational practice

If birds are likely to be a problem it is essential that feeding opportunities and areas where birds can loaf or bathe are kept to a minimum through a range of site management practices. Examples of good practice that can help to deter birds include:
- Daily cover of exposed food waste with a layer of inert material. This reduces the available quantity of food for birds such as gulls. This is standard practice at all UK sites.
- Minimisation of the area of exposed waste during site operation. It has been shown that large gulls prefer feeding on large areas of exposed waste (Horton *et al.*, 1983); reducing this area can therefore reduce the site's attractiveness to large gulls.
- Minimising areas of bare ground reduces opportunities for 'loafing' and therefore can reduce the overall number of birds on site. Similarly, management of restored areas to allow grass to grow long can reduce bird numbers; gulls in particular prefer short grass for 'loafing'.

2.3.5 Limitations of site management practices as methods of reducing bird numbers

Daily cover of waste with inert materials does not prevent gulls from feeding on exposed waste during the day. It also fails to prevent corvids from feeding; these

species feed by probing into earth. Where cover is not thick enough, which can occur at many sites where large quantities of cover materials are not available, gulls may also be able to feed on areas of covered waste. Similarly, food waste can be brought to the surface by vehicle movements across areas of covered waste, also presenting feeding opportunities.

Operational constraints mean that in many instances it is impossible not to leave large areas of bare ground as areas are progressively excavated for future landfilling and restored once filling has been completed.

The examples of good site practice outlined in C.2.3.4 should be operated at all sites. However, at sites where impacts from birds are likely to be high, a programme of bird control will also be necessary.

2.4 Assessment of methods used to control birds at landfill sites

Birds will be attracted to all landfill sites accepting food wastes. The attraction of landfills is so high that birds are willing to take greater risks and expend more energy obtaining food than they would at other sites. They may also be willing to wait around for long periods for the chance of getting access to food. Birds are therefore unaffected by many common scaring methods and quickly habituate to others. Furthermore, if constant vigilance is not maintained, large numbers of birds may descend on a site at a moment's notice. However, despite these problems bird control can be effective at most sites if operated to the highest standards. Techniques used can be divided into the following categories:
- Methods which exclude birds from the site.
- Active deterrence:
  - Aggressive techniques e.g. shooting and falconry.
  - Disturbance techniques e.g. noise stimuli and recorded distress calls.
- Passive deterrence e.g. kites, scarecrows and aerial spinners

The following section assesses the effectiveness of every major method and technique in use on landfills in the UK today, and provides guidelines for best practice. Information used in formulating the guidance both for individual techniques and combinations of techniques has been assimilated from:
- literature reviews and scientific studies both published and unpublished;

Table C.2.1. Summary of commonly used bird control methods.

Category	Method	Main advantages	Main disadvantages
Exclusion methods (C.2.5.1)	Netting	Total elimination of birds possible if operated to a high standard.	Very high construction and operating costs, particularly for the large structures necessary to operate effectively.
Active methods – aggressive (C.2.5.2)	Shooting	Reduces habituation to standard disturbance techniques.	Safety, publicity, licensing and conservation implications.
	Falconry	Continuous coverage to a high operational standard can result in a complete elimination of birds.	High operational costs (although several times lower than netting costs). Weather limitations require occasional use of supporting methods.
Active methods – disturbance (C.2.5.3)	Noise stimuli	Relatively inexpensive (although required to be operated at high intensity to be effective).	Habituation likely to all methods. Potential nuisance implications due to noise.
	Recorded distress calls	Relatively inexpensive (although required to be operated at high intensity to be effective).	Habituation likely. Unclear if effective on very large numbers of birds at large landfill sites.
Passive methods (C.2.5.4)	Kites	Inexpensive (although frequent movement required), quiet.	Habituation occurs very quickly. Weather limits use.

- independent trials of a range of bird control methods carried out by Ecoscope Applied Ecologists (see Appendix 1);
- consultation with a range of experts and practitioners in the field.

The methods are summarised in Table C.2.1.

2.4.1 Exclusion methods
Netting
Principles
The principles of using netting are simple in that all exposed waste is tipped and compacted within a large netted area that prevents birds from getting access to food. Birds quickly learn that food is not available at the site and leave the area.

Various systems exist; entire operational cells can be netted and worked until landfilling is completed and pre-restoration works carried out, before the net is taken down and moved to cover the next operational cell. Other systems cover a smaller area and are moved on rails to cover new areas when required.

With both systems, doors must be opened to let waste lorries in, and shut immediately to keep birds out. If operated to high standards, netting is scientifically proven to exclude birds from landfill sites (CSL, 1998).

Best Practice
Netting of an entire operational cell is the best method, with waste covered with a thick layer of inert materials before the net is removed. Two nets will be required in order that landfilling can begin immediately in the new cell once completed in the old one as nets can take up to four weeks to deconstruct and install. Constant checks must be made for damage, and standards of door operation must be very high. This should be supported by strict enforcement and appropriate penalties for poor practice.

An example of the sort of structure required is that in place at Ugley Landfill Site in Essex. Each cell is enclosed by 27,000 m² of netting suspended from eight steel pylons, each weighing 13 tonnes. The netting is 30m high, enabling all work on a cell to be completed without moving the net. This system has been 100% successful in deterring birds since its installation in 1997.

Limitations
Poor operational practice is a major limitation. Examples include net doors left open overnight and food waste tipped outside the net whilst loads are waiting to enter. Nets can also tear or collapse in high winds or under the weight of snow. Birds will quickly exploit any breakage or slip in standards.

Smaller nets do not enclose areas of covered waste, which can be attractive to feeding corvids or even gulls if food waste is brought to the surface by excessive vehicle movements.

Other considerations
Use of netting is extremely costly. Construction and installation costs can be in the region of several hundred thousand pounds (see Table C.2.2), and running costs are also very high. It is therefore only practicable at sites where planning applications would otherwise be turned down, for example those near airports. An additional benefit of netting is the elimination of windblown litter; sites can therefore remain open on days when they might otherwise be forced to close due to high winds. Smaller, low-cost netting systems primarily designed for

litter control are generally not 100% effective in meeting bird control objectives.

Netting – recommendations for use

When operated to the highest standards, a complete exclusion of birds is possible.

Netting is therefore suitable for high-risk sites such as those near airports. However, a structure too small in scale or one slip in operating standards could attract birds.

Operation must therefore be of the highest standard with strict enforcement and stiff penalties, possibly including site closure, for incidents of failure.

Even with such systems in place it is not certain that the CAA or MoD will accept applications for sites in areas extremely close to airfields.

Falcons used for bird control at a landfill site.

Photo: Khyber Associates

2.4.2 Active methods – aggressive techniques

Shooting

Principles

It is a common misconception that shooting can actually eliminate birds from an area, but this is not in fact the case. Firstly it is logistically impossible to shoot thousands of birds, and secondly, birds are highly mobile and those killed would quickly be replaced by others from elsewhere.

However, the periodic use of shooting can reinforce the effect of other deterrents in letting birds know that they can come to harm at landfill sites and hence reduce habituation to non-lethal methods.

Best Practice

If shooting is to be used in conjunction with other methods it is best carried out very infrequently, i.e. every few months, for no more than one or two days at a time. On each occasion no more than one or two birds need to be shot – the intention is purely to remind birds of the threat.

Limitations

Shooting alone will never eliminate birds from a site. There are also serious safety implications for shooting at busy landfill sites and it is therefore strictly licensed.

Only certain species are permitted to be shot under legislation in the 1981 Wildlife & Countryside Act. These include all common corvids but only certain species of gull, notably herring, lesser black-backed and great black-backed gulls. Black-headed gull, the most common

species on many sites, may not be killed at any time. Furthermore, the shooting of large numbers of herring and lesser black-backed gulls cannot currently be recommended for conservation reasons; both species are listed on the Amber List of Birds of Conservation Concern (Gibbons *et al.*, 1996). Herring gull has declined in numbers by over 25% in the last 25 years whilst Britain holds more than a fifth of the European population of lesser black-backed gull.

Other considerations

Bad publicity can occur as a result of shooting birds. This is an important consideration especially where bird control is implemented to reduce impacts on amenity.

Other culling techniques such as nest removal may be considered in extreme situations where corvids associated with a landfill pose a threat to rare species breeding nearby.

Shooting – recommendations for use

Shooting may be used infrequently on certain sites in order to reduce habituation to disturbance techniques normally used at the site.

However, shooting must be strictly controlled and carried out only by licensed persons.

Falconry

Principles

Flying trained birds of prey over a landfill site induces fear amongst other birds

present, causing them to leave the site. Continued regular flying keeps them away. Provided species that actually hunt birds are used, i.e. falcons such as Peregrine, Lanner and Saker, their mere presence in the air is usually enough to deter birds from using the site, although birds are inevitably caught from time to time. If operated to a high standard, the use of birds of prey is without doubt (netting excluded) the most effective single method of bird control in use at landfill sites. Its major advantage, in addition to its effectiveness in clearing birds from a site, is that because the threat to birds' well being is real it does not suffer from habituation. Note that falconry should always be carried out by a trained operator.

Best Practice

Success can vary depending on the species used. Peregrine, saker and lanner falcons have all been used to good effect, as have hybrids that combine the best attributes of each. Use of other raptor species is not recommended. Whichever species are used, operators must hold a licence issued by the DETR before flying raptors at a landfill site.

Continuous coverage is required, as falcons do not provide a long-lasting deterrent. Gaps as short as a day may result in birds returning to the site. Coverage may be from dawn until dusk or simply during operational hours depending on the objective for bird control. For an average site a minimum of three birds is required each of which should be flown up to five or six times a day.

Due to the limitations described below, supporting methods should be used to cover for periods when falcons cannot be used.

Limitations
Poor weather reduces the effectiveness of falconry. In heavy rain or strong winds the birds can fly but take a long time to recover so cannot provide consistent coverage throughout the day. Also, when birds occasionally make a kill it can result in a short period of time with no bird control coverage whilst the falconer collects the bird. In both cases a supporting control method may be required to retain continuous coverage.

Several other perceived problems associated with falconry such as loss of birds, periods of inactivity due to moult and disturbance to rare species in the surrounding area will almost always only happen as a result of poor standards of operational practice. Loss of birds can be prevented by high standards of falconry, periods of inactivity can be avoided by having a number of operating birds available and effects on other species can be eliminated simply by not flying the birds over sensitive areas. Other examples of poor results can also be put down to poor practice, for example the use of the wrong raptor species or infrequent flying due to an operator not having enough birds.

Other considerations
The cost of operating bird control based on falconry is high in comparison with most other control methods, being around £20-30,000 per annum (see Table C.2.2). However, this is still well below the cost of

Falconry in progress at a landfill site.

Photo: Khyber Associates

operating a netting system. Another consideration is that falconry can provide good publicity for a site operator, in contrast with some of the other bird control methods, which can be perceived as a nuisance.

2.4.3 Active methods – disturbance techniques
Noise Stimuli
Principles
Noise-based bird-scaring techniques work on the principle that birds don't know if unfamiliar noises can be harmful to them and therefore instinctively avoid them. The more intensive the noise, the greater the disturbance caused to the birds.

A variety of noise-based techniques to scare birds are in common use at landfill sites. These include:
● Shell crackers (also known as bird-scarer cartridges)
● Bird-scarer rockets
● Blanks cartridges
● Rope bangers
● Gas cannons

Best Practice
Noise stimuli alone are unlikely to be able to deter birds from a site and surrounding area. However, it has been shown (see Example 3 on page 35) that intensive use of various combinations of noise stimuli can effectively deter birds from feeding and dramatically reduce numbers around a site (note that recorded distress calls were also used in this case). Best practice for each method is as follows:

Shell crackers typically comprise a projectile containing an explosive charge and delay fuse fired from a modified starting pistol. They are effective because the explosion occurs in the air, close to the birds, exploiting the instinctive fear that birds have of avian predators above them.

They should be used only when required to disperse flocks of birds (excessive use will speed up habituation, and cartridges are also relatively costly). Cartridges should be fired at a 45° angle to the side or behind the flock and never be fired into a flock as this results in birds scattering into smaller groups which can subsequently be harder to disperse. There are several important safety considerations and they should therefore only be used by licensed, specially trained operators.

Rockets have a similar effect to shell crackers in that explosions occur in the air. Like shell crackers they should also be used sparingly to delay habituation (they are also relatively costly).

Blanks cartridges are usually fired from a pistol. They can be effective in dispersing small numbers of birds, especially those prospecting the site, and should therefore be used immediately when small numbers of birds appear over the site. However, they should also be used only when required, in order to delay habituation.

Rope bangers comprise a number of explosive charges located along a slow burning fuse. They produce bangs at infrequent intervals. Ropes should be

---

Falconry – recommendations for use

Falconry, used in combination with supporting methods can effectively deter birds from using a site. Where there are no constraints on operation, falconry also has a significant impact on birds using the surrounding area. It must however, be operated more or less continuously and to consistently high standards to keep birds away.

To ensure high standards the performance of bird control contractors should be regularly monitored and high standards enforced. Enforcement should be the responsibility of EA/SEPA.

---

placed in several locations around the site, covering both feeding and loafing areas.

Habituation to this method is rapid; it should therefore only be used in combination with other methods, and never used continuously.

Gas cannons emit an explosion or explosions at regular intervals. They should only be used in combination with other methods as habituation is very quick. They may be particularly useful to cover for short periods when other methods are not being employed. The position of the cannon(s) should also be changed frequently to delay habituation as much as possible.

Limitations
The major limitation of noise-based techniques is that birds soon become habituated to them. To reduce habituation, methods should be:
- used as infrequently as possible;
- intensive (i.e. as loud as possible);
- brief;
- variable in sound, location or appearance; and
- non-localised / difficult to locate.

Stationary devices such as gas cannons and bangers are therefore especially susceptible to habituation, even if equipment is moved frequently.

Other considerations
At sites close to housing or other noise-sensitive areas, constant use can be worse for public relations than the gulls themselves. In an extreme scenario, a site operator may be served with a nuisance order. The magnitude of potential noise impacts from bird control therefore requires assessment on a site-specific basis at an early stage in the design of a bird control programme.

Noise stimuli could also potentially cause disturbance to wildlife species present in habitats adjacent to the site, although cartridges and other measures which create 'bangs' will also be habituated to by birds in adjacent habitats. This is because, unlike a hunter with a shotgun, this method does not involve a person walking about shooting. Hunting is known to have a considerable disturbance effect on birds, especially waterfowl, reducing densities to almost zero. There are many examples of the huge preference for overwintering refuge areas by waterfowl in comparison to areas shot over, particularly along estuary foreshore habitats and wetland sites such as on the Ouse Washes. Where the

source of the disturbance is reinforced by the presence of people, habituation rarely occurs. As above, potential impacts require assessment at an early stage in the design of a bird control programme.

All noise-based bird-scaring equipment is relatively cheap, although it is necessary to employ a specialist member of staff to ensure their effective use.

Noise stimuli – recommendations for use

Best practice for all noise stimuli involves the use of combinations of the above methods with frequent variations.

Successful deterrence is possible, but requires constant vigilance and rapid response to bird activity. It therefore needs specialist, dedicated staff.

In practice, noise stimuli methods are best used in combination with other bird control techniques.

Recorded Distress Calls
Principles
Many bird species (including most gulls, crows and starlings) emit a distinct distress call when captured by a predator. On hearing distress calls, flocks of birds tend to behave in a characteristic manner, taking flight then circling over the call source searching for the predator, trying to drive it away and then dispersing, usually well away from their original location.

In theory, the reaction of birds to recorded distress calls is similar, except that the predator is not there to be located; fearing danger, birds will depart from the area.

The use of recorded distress calls is now the recommended method for dispersing birds from aerodromes (CAA, 1998). However, success at aerodromes cannot necessarily be extrapolated to landfill sites, which are much more attractive to birds and therefore make the birds harder to scare away. Research carried out during this study (see Appendix 1) was unable to prove the extent to which recorded distress calls are effective at landfill sites. Further research is currently underway; a discussion of progress to date can be found in Baxter (1999).

Best Practice
For any bird control objective, the sole use of recorded distress calls cannot be guaranteed to be effective. However, use of the method in combination with other methods is perfectly reasonable and where used, methods of best practice are as follows:

Digitally recorded systems should be used. These give better sound quality, faster response to the presence of birds and quicker switching between calls in comparison with tape-based systems. Equipment should contain calls for all species common at an individual site. When used on a mixed flock the call of the commonest species should be used first; if they disperse other species are likely to follow. This requires basic species identification skills.

Broadcasts should be approximately 90 seconds in length, allowing birds time to approach and circle. They should take place from a stationary vehicle within 200m of the target flock, a specially devoted vehicle such as a landrover will therefore usually be required. Broadcasts are far less effective when made on foot or from a moving vehicle – habituation may also be speeded up.

Other bird control methods must not be used during a broadcast as this merely creates confusion. Departure in response to a distress call broadcast can be slow and may be speeded up by use of artificial noise stimuli but only once the broadcast has ended.

Once gulls have been cleared from the site, the equipment should be used whenever small numbers of birds reappear – small numbers can quickly become large flocks, which are much more difficult to remove. Effective use therefore necessarily requires constant vigilance from a member of staff specially devoted to bird control. Additional use is not recommended in order to delay habituation.

Limitations
Habituation does occur in practice. This is especially likely to be true of fixed, pole-mounted systems, which emit recordings at random intervals.

It is also unclear whether the method has the desired effect at larger landfill sites with large numbers of birds. Gulls have been observed to simply fly away to nearby loafing areas upon playback of distress calls and return shortly after. This may be due to habituation, although poor operating standards may play a part.

Other considerations
Noise from equipment may create a nuisance to nearby residences. Impacts are unlikely to be as great as those from use of artificial noise stimuli, although an assessment of potential impacts will be required at an early stage.

Operational costs are relatively low once equipment has been purchased although as with other methods effective use requires the employment of staff devoted to bird control.

2.4.4 Passive methods – disturbance techniques

Kites

Principles
The flying of kites at landfill sites is designed to exploit the instinctive fear that birds have of airborne objects, particularly those which look like avian predators. Two different types exist, standard kites which require wind to fly (although they can be tethered to tall poles) and 'Helikites', which combine a kite with a helium-filled balloon. Both types are available in designs mimicking the shape of a bird of prey.

Best Practice
To prevent habituation, kites must be moved frequently, every couple of hours if necessary with more than one kite used if more than just a very small area is to be covered. Furthermore, different types of kite will be required if coverage is to be maintained in different weather conditions.

Realistically therefore, kites can only be used as a very short-term measure in support of other methods. Practical uses include cover during short periods when other methods cannot be employed.

Limitations
The principal limitation of kites as a bird control technique is habituation. Used alone, this can occur within hours, and at best within a few days. This limits use to nothing more than a short-term measure.

Each type of kite is also heavily reliant on the weather with regard to its performance. The standard type of kite requires wind in order to fly, whilst a 'Helikite' is brought down by winds much greater than Force 4. Both types struggle to fly in heavy rain.

Other considerations
Kites are relatively cheap (see Table C.2.2). They are also silent and thus do not attract complaints like some other methods.

Other passive techniques
Other passive techniques in use include scarecrows, both fixed and revolving, peaceful pyramids and aerial spinners. All are designed to exploit birds' fear of unusual objects and colours. However, in the landfill environment habituation to all such methods is rapid. None of these methods can therefore be recommended for use at landfill sites.

Table C.2.2. Comparison of approximate costs of a range of bird control techniques

Technique	Approximate cost*	Other comments
Netting	£500,000 (construction and installation)	Subsequent costs including those arising from movement of netting structures from cell to cell are also very high (several £'000 pa).
Falconry	£20,000 – £30,000 p.a.	Costs vary depending on level of coverage required. Figure includes supporting methods and all staff costs.
Recorded distress calls	£500-£3000	Cost of equipment ranges from £500 for the cheapest hand-held system to £3000 for the best vehicle-mounted system. Maintenance costs thereafter are low.
Rockets / shell crackers	c£20 for 10	10 rockets/shells may last for between 2-5 days depending on supporting measures in use.
Blanks pistol & cartridges	£100	Cost includes pistol plus 1000 cartridges, which should last several weeks.
Gas cannon	£400-£600	Maintenance costs are relatively low.
Standard bird scaring kite	£30	Pole for use in low winds costs a further £80.
Helikite	£180	Cost includes kite and initial helium supply. Running costs are low thereafter.

* Note that figures given represent only a very general guide. Note also that with the exception of falconry costs given do not include costs of employing staff or specialist manpower to operate bird control. Specially devoted staff are of course essential for the long-term effectiveness of any bird control programme.

2.5 Use of combinations of bird control techniques

The use of a combination of techniques is probably essential in achieving successful bird control. Using a combination of methods has the following advantages:

- Habituation to a single method is prevented.
- The combined effect of two or more methods can be greater than each method used individually.
- The limitations of each method are covered by the use of others.

Three examples of where a combination of techniques successfully deterred gulls from using sites are given overleaf.

2.6 General principles of introducing a bird control programme

Whatever combination of methods is chosen, the following general principles should be followed in order for bird control to be successful and meet objectives:

- High standards of operational practice are essential. Successful bird control requires constant vigilance and rapid reaction to birds' activity. The employment of a specialist person or persons to carry out bird control is therefore most important. Staff motivation is important and bird control staff should not be given other duties. It is also important that any absences in bird control staff are covered – bird control must be continuous to be effective.
- Flexibility is essential. Techniques must be able to be varied at short notice if certain combinations become less effective. Additionally, supporting measures to cover for periods when certain methods cannot be used must be available.

Anything less than the highest operating standards and total flexibility will almost certainly lead to ineffective bird control in the long term.

2.6.1 Choice of bird control methods in relation to site-specific objectives

Total deterrence from site and surrounding area

For this objective a netting solution may be required by the CAA or the MoD. However, this objective could also be met satisfactorily at a number of sites by a combination of other bird control methods with the emphasis on falconry, if carried out to the highest operating standards from dawn to dusk seven days a week.

Effectiveness may be reduced on very

large sites, sites where bird controllers cannot access all areas and sites which have been operational for some time without bird control. However, at many sites bird control can provide an equally successful and much more cost-effective alternative to netting. Locating new sites in very close proximity to airports may still have to be avoided, but otherwise the only realistic concerns of the statutory authorities involve failures in coverage. These fears can be allayed by strict regulation including appropriate penalties for poor standards.

BIRD CONTROL AT LANDFILL SITES

SUMMARY

- Birds can be effectively deterred from feeding at landfill sites. It is also possible to exclude birds from the surrounding area although the extent to which this is possible depends upon the level of coverage, methods used and a number of site-specific factors.
- Where expected impacts from birds are high and bird control is considered necessary, clear, targeted objectives for a programme of bird deterrence must be set. These should not specify the methods to be used but rather set targets that enable the effectiveness of bird control to be assessed and enforced. At most sites one of the following objectives should be set:
  1. Total deterrence of birds from the site and the surrounding area
  2. Total deterrence of birds from feeding on waste at the site (as a direct consequence bird numbers in the surrounding area will be substantially reduced)
  3. No bird control (with periodic review)
- At sites where the scale of potential impacts does not justify the high costs of an intensive bird control programme, it may be more cost-effective to have no bird control than to operate piecemeal low-input bird scarers which are likely to be ineffective in the long term.
- In all cases deterrence is most successful through use of a combination of bird control methods. Combinations including falconry are most effective, although other combinations may be almost as effective if used intensively.
- Whichever methods are used, intensive coverage is required for bird control to be effective. Constant vigilance must be maintained and reaction to changes in bird activity must be immediate. As a result specialist staff or contractors, fully trained in a range of techniques and devoted solely to bird control must be employed. Anything less intensive will be ineffective in the long term.
- Netting of sites is scientifically proven to deter birds from landfill sites, if operated to the highest standards. However it is extremely expensive to operate. For sites close to airfields the operation of a dawn to dusk bird control programme, based on falconry supported by other methods should be able, where bird control operation is not subject to constraints, to provide a viable and much more cost-effective alternative to netting. To be viable in such situations the highest operational standards must be maintained supported by the establishment of strict regulation and enforcement with appropriately severe penalties.
- At present however the Civil Aviation Authority and Ministry of Defence are cautious about allowing applications to proceed on the condition of bird control alone being imposed. Particular concerns exist over the likelihood of occasional failures in bird control as a result of unforeseen or unavoidable circumstances. Further studies, empirically testing the effectiveness of dawn to dusk bird control at a range of sites, over long time periods may therefore be required before bird control is viewed by the statutory authorities as a satisfactory way of reducing bird-strike risk to acceptable levels. The main debate concerns the number of birds of different species which constitutes a risk. In the absence of a lack of a risk assessment set against background population levels, the CAA have simply advocated a 'total exclusion' policy. However, this places a significant burden on waste management companies since netting is very expensive.

Examples of the use of a combination of bird control techniques

Example 1	
Site name	Salt Ayre Landfill Site, near Lancaster.
Site details	Site regularly used by up to 3,500 large gulls throughout the summer. Study carried out during July and August to assess the effects of bird control (Natural Environmental Consultants, 1995b).
Control techniques used	Dawn to dusk bird control for six weeks using falcons, supported by kites, rockets, blanks cartridges and recorded distress calls.
Effect on bird populations	Numbers fell from 3,500 to below 1000 within a few days. By the end of week six total of 176 gulls counted in the area surrounding the site. No gulls were observed feeding on exposed waste throughout the study. Gull numbers may have been reduced further had bird controllers not been prevented from operating around some nearby buildings. Gull numbers returned to around 3000 within 4 days of bird control ending.
Conclusion	Possible to completely deter gulls from using a coastal landfill site. Possible to reduce gulls in the surrounding area to 10% of their former numbers within six weeks.

Example 2	
Site name	Midgeland Farm Landfill Site, Blackpool.
Site details	Over 4000 gulls regularly present prior to bird control. Results of two years of bird control presented (Leslie, 1984).
Control techniques used	Varying combinations of gas cannon, rope bangers, recorded distress calls (n.b. early version), shell crackers and blanks cartridges. Carried out from dawn to dusk, Monday to Saturday (site closed Sunday). Live ammunition was used periodically.
Effect on bird populations	Site and surrounding area effectively kept clear of gulls. Birds returned periodically but were always successfully scared away.
Conclusion	Bird control using a range of disturbance techniques can be successful. High standards of operation were essential throughout with two dedicated members of staff employed specifically to control birds.

Example 3	
Site name	Masons Landfill Site, Great Blakenham, Suffolk.
Site details	Bird control carried out due to site licence requirement. Bird numbers compared with control site 20 miles away for eight-week winter period (Natural Environmental Consultants, 1995a).
Control techniques used	Bird control in place throughout operational hours. Falcons preferred method, supported by blanks cartridges, kites and rockets.
Effect on bird populations	No birds feeding on site during bird control. Between 100 and 1000 within 3 km of site, but mainly on flooded gravel pits. Numbers in vicinity of control site averaged 2500 throughout. When bird control suspended at Masons bird numbers rose to 2500 within ten days – no effect on numbers at control site.
Conclusion	Bird control based around falcons effectively deterred birds from using the site during operational hours. Numbers in the vicinity were reduced almost to background levels.

Deterrence from feeding on the site

This objective can be met by a range of bird control method combinations. However, the general principles above must be followed and operators must be prepared to change methods if those in use prove to be ineffective. Once again strict regulation should result in improved standards of operation.

Part-time use of any bird control methods cannot be expected to achieve any objectives that require effective deterrence of birds. Therefore unless high impacts demand bird control, it may be more cost-effective to not carry out bird control at all.

3 Rodent-related issues and methods of control

This section provides an overview of the major **potential** issues arising from large populations of rats attracted to operational landfill sites and the methods which can be employed to prevent these issues from becoming problematic. Note that it is possible that additional site-specific issues not covered may occur at certain sites.

Standard operational procedures are designed to control many of these potential problems, and can be effective. For example, daily cover and compaction will make the site less attractive as a habitat for rats.

3.1 Potential impacts arising from rat populations at landfill sites

Brown rats do not usually live in landfill waste itself, although they can do so where it has been insufficiently consolidated (ADAS, 1985). However, rats feed on the waste, building their burrows in surrounding earth mounds and bunds. They become sexually mature at the age of about three months, after which a female can produce a litter of 7-8 young every 3-4 weeks for up to a year. A small population therefore has the potential become a major infestation over a relatively short period of time. When populations increase in this way, large numbers of animals tend to disperse into the surrounding area. Consequently, rats associated with landfill sites can potentially have major impacts on the surrounding land and housing. The major issues arising from such dispersal are given below.

3.1.1 Human health impacts

The most common disease carried by rats in the UK is the potentially fatal Leptospirosis (Weil's Disease), which is carried by up to 30% of rats. However, it can only be transmitted through contact with contaminated water or direct contact with rats carrying the disease. An increased incidence of the disease in humans as a direct consequence of a landfill site is therefore only likely where water bodies used by humans lie adjacent to the site. Perhaps the major threat to human health from large rat populations on landfill is through cross-contamination of food with bacteria present in rotting waste. Where rats migrate from a landfill to nearby farms or housing and make contact with food sources, contamination with bacteria such as Salmonellosis and parasites such as ringworm, tapeworm and various mites can occur. Impacts are

likely to be greatest in winter when rats may move into residential areas seeking warmth, or when quantities of available food at the landfill fall suddenly, following site closure for example.

3.1.2 Impacts on crops and structures

Rats can cause severe damage to agricultural crops; fields adjacent to large rat populations at a landfill site are therefore particularly at risk. Rats can also cause damage to structures such as buildings, pipes and cables by gnawing holes through them. Such impacts are likely to be high if large rat populations occur at landfill sites close to residential areas. There is also the potential for pollution control systems on sites themselves to be damaged in this way, particularly on phased sites where pollution control infrastructure may be located close to operational areas. Additionally the effectiveness of capping systems could potentially be compromised by the burrowing activities of rodents.

3.1.3 Amenity impacts

Health considerations aside, the presence of rats around housing is likely to be very unpopular and presents a considerable loss of amenity to residents. As with health issues, problems are likely to be most acute in winter when rats are more prone to enter buildings.

3.1.4 Impacts on nearby habitats and species of conservation importance

A large rat population could impact upon a number of wildlife species nearby through predation. Ground-nesting birds such as waders and terns are potentially likely to be affected by predation of eggs or young whilst reptiles such as slow-worm and other lizard species could be susceptible to rat predation. Predation could also affect nearby amphibian populations.

3.2 Control of rodent pest species

For sites in close proximity to housing or arable farmland, the undesirable impacts of a large rodent population associated with a landfill are likely to be high. Negative impacts are also likely for other sites due to the potential for damage to pollution control infrastructure combined with health and safety issues for site staff. It is therefore recommended that a permanent rodent control programme should be operated at all sites accepting food waste.

All waste management licences should contain a condition relating to pest control. Rodent control can also be included as a planning condition on environmental health grounds. The latest consultation draft of the Library of Licence Conditions (Environment Agency, 1999) specifies the objective 'to control and eliminate pest infestation so as to prevent harm to human health and serious detriment to the amenities of the locality'. This implies that pest control may not be necessary at particularly isolated sites. However, it is our recommendation that permanent control of rat populations should be implemented at all landfill sites where food waste is accepted with the effectiveness of such programmes strictly monitored by EA/SEPA.

The following paragraphs outline the standard techniques used to control rat populations at landfill sites. Clearance of an infestation may require intensive treatment for up to a month which should then be followed by less intensive treatment over an indefinite period to prevent numbers from building up again. At all sites, even where rat populations are currently low or non-existent, continuous low intensity control programmes should be operated to avoid the occurrence of infestation. In all cases, site-specific advice should be sought, either from the local authority environmental health department, the local Ministry of Agriculture, Fisheries and Food (MAFF) service centre or from a specialist pest control company. In many cases it may be advisable to employ a specialist pest control company to control rodent populations at a site indefinitely. Sites with rodent problems caused by species other than rats should consult with their local MAFF service centre.

3.2.1 Operational practice
Good operational practice, for example the efficient compaction of waste and daily covering with a layer of inert material, can help to reduce rodent problems. However, even where such practices are carried out well there is still the potential for rodent infestation at almost all sites accepting food waste.

3.2.2 Site survey
This is an essential first step in any control programme. Areas used by rats for feeding, breeding and travelling between areas should all be noted and potential locations for bait application identified. Signs of other animals present (if any) should also be recorded and their location incorporated into a control programme strategy to avoid inadvertently poisoning other species. Site survey must be carried out by an experienced professional – poor survey is a frequent cause of control programme failure.

3.2.3 Methods of control
Anticoagulants
Use of slow-working anticoagulant poisons is the recommended and most cost-effective method of removing rats from a site. Poisons are mixed with bait and, if eaten regularly, should kill all rats within a two-week period. Methods of application are covered below. Substances that can be used include Warfarin, Coumatetralyl, Chlorophacinone, Diphacinone, Bromadiolone and Difenacoum. Note that rats in some areas are resistant to certain poisons (see Section 3.2.5). Note also that the substances Brodifacoum and Flocoumafen are only to be used indoors and must therefore not be used on landfills.

Acute poisons
These are not recommended for use on landfill sites as they tend to be less effective than anti-coagulants and their use can be very dangerous.

Traps
Use of traps to control a large rodent population on an active landfill site is much less effective than use of anti-coagulants and is therefore not recommended.

3.2.4 Application techniques
Anticoagulant poisons must be mixed with food (usually some form of cereal) to act as bait. Poisons can be bought ready-mixed or as solid or liquid concentrates which require mixing. Note that the sale of concentrates is strictly controlled and that these should only be used by pest control specialists. For control programmes designed to eliminate infestations of rats, bait should be placed in suitable containers at sites identified during the site survey (see above) and replenished continuously. Once bait stops being taken it can be assumed that the poison has worked and the rats have been killed. Note that rats may be very cautious about taking bait from unfamiliar containers due to a strong new object reaction (neophobia). Consequently it can take at least ten days for rats to start to take bait.

The most common reasons for the failure of a rat control operation, in addition to poor site survey are inadequate placement of bait and failure to replenish bait frequently enough. A firm commitment to controlling the problem effectively is therefore essential.

For prevention programmes, bait should be placed in containers around the perimeter of the site at approximately 25m intervals and replenished, if necessary, every two to three weeks. In this way the presence of any prospective new rats can be identified and controlled. Once again a definite commitment is needed to ensure bait stocks are adequately replenished and that any new signs of rodent activity are identified at an early stage.

3.2.5 Other considerations
Genetic resistance to certain anticoagulants is increasingly common in some areas, notably the England / Wales border around Shropshire and in the south of England particularly Berkshire, Hampshire, Wiltshire, Sussex, Surrey, Kent and Essex. In such areas resistance will be apparent when bait continues to be taken indefinitely. In such situations, use of an alternative substance is suggested (e.g. Difenacoum or Calciferol). Professional pest controllers should be aware of resistance levels in their local area and use appropriate anticoagulants.

Safety is an important consideration at all stages in a pest control programme. Poisons and dead rodents must be handled with caution and disposed of carefully. In addition the manufacturer's instructions must always be followed carefully, especially with regard to quantities of substances used.

It is also important to ensure that poisons do not affect other animals that may be present in the vicinity of a site. Signs of other animals should be recorded during the initial site survey (see above) and precautions taken to guard against their being poisoned inadvertently, e.g. not placing baits close to areas where other animal species are known to be present. Killing of certain animal species may lead to operators being in contravention of the Wildlife and Countryside Act 1981.

Costs of implementing a rodent control programme vary depending on a number of individual site factors. As a general guide, the costs of employing a contractor to clear a large infestation are likely to be in the region of £5000. However, the cost of operating a long-term preventative programme is likely to be far less; in the region of £3000 per

SECTION D

Background to landfill site restoration

1 Introduction

Restored landfill sites present a unique environment for habitat creation. Consequently, techniques for creating habitats in other environments such as former agricultural land or disused mineral workings can often not be translated directly onto restored landfill sites. It is therefore fundamental for all habitat creation planners and practitioners to have a good understanding of the basic principles of landfill site restoration and the specific constraints that may be imposed upon habitat creation schemes.

The following sections provide an outline of the key processes in landfill site restoration and explain how the nature of the restored landfill environment can affect habitat creation. Although consultation between restoration engineers and those involved in habitat creation is essential, habitat creation practitioners are unlikely to be directly involved in the precise design of engineering systems and restoration. The reader should therefore consult alternative references for further detail on this subject (e.g. Environment Agency, in prep.).

Section D.2 outlines the different engineering systems required at landfill sites. For the purposes of this manual the definition of engineering systems covers all environmental protection works including landfill capping and the extraction of landfill gas and leachate. Whilst engineering systems do not fall within the strict definition of restoration (see below), they are an integral feature of any restored site and can have a major effect on habitat creation.

Section D.3 outlines the fundamental processes of site restoration. For the purposes of this manual, restoration is defined as "the process that returns a landfill site to a condition suitable for its after-use: restoration includes soil handling and replacement, as well as design, initial landscaping works, interim restoration and aftercare" (Environment Agency, in prep.). Aftercare, particularly with respect to habitats of nature conservation interest, is covered in Sections E & F.

Section D.4 emphasizes the importance of integrating restoration with operations and site engineering systems. The concept of interim restoration, whereby sites are partially restored during the period whilst maintenance and remediation works on engineering systems are likely prior to full restoration, is also introduced. Interim restoration is now recommended practice (Environment Agency, in prep.).

Section D.5 summarises a number of constraints upon habitat creation on landfill sites. Although habitat creation is always site-specific, a number of the most commonly encountered difficulties faced during habitat creation at landfill sites are covered here.

1.1 The importance of waste type to restoration

The type of engineering systems required and restoration design are strongly dependent on the type of waste accepted by a site. For example:

- sites that have accepted only relatively inert wastes (e.g. excavation or demolition wastes and building rubble) require relatively basic engineering systems and are subject to far fewer constraints upon restoration design. Habitat creation is therefore much more straightforward and open to a much wider range of possibilities on these sites.
- Sites that have accepted controlled wastes require complex engineering to control pollution and are also subject to a number of constraints on restoration design. Several limitations on habitat creation exist on these sites.

The guidance in this manual is primarily aimed at sites which have accepted a certain degree of controlled wastes. However, the basic principles for habitat creation at such sites can also be extended to sites that have taken only inert wastes with far fewer limitations on what can be achieved.

1.2 Restoration at older closed landfill sites

The guidance in this manual is primarily aimed at modern sites, which are subject to strict regulations concerning restoration and environmental protection. However, there are a large number of old sites across the country, many only partially restored, that may be ideal candidates for habitat creation. Figures for the total number of old sites across the UK as a whole are not available. However an indication of the area of land taken up by old landfills is provided by the Mersey Forest in the north-west of England; in that area alone there are at least 1200 hectares of derelict former landfill (Mersey Forest and Red Rose Forest Partnership, 1999).

At many older sites restoration can be very poor by today's standards with some sites having only a thin cap and minimal pollution control whilst others may have no cap and no pollution control at all. Constraints on habitat creation are therefore quite different at such sites, and the direct effects of landfill gas and leachate are more apparent. The restoration of old landfill sites is covered briefly in Section D.3.

2 Landfill engineering systems

2.1 Introduction

Landfill engineering systems are not strictly part of the restoration process. However, the installation and maintenance of such systems primarily takes place after landfilling operations have ceased, i.e. at the same time as restoration. Consequently, there are a great number of interactions between engineering systems and site restoration. A basic knowledge of landfill engineering systems therefore is fundamental to understanding the constraints upon habitat creation that exist within the landfill environment.

Landfill engineering systems can basically be summarised as:

- An impermeable basal seal or liner
- The landfill cap
- The landfill gas control system
- The leachate control and extraction system

2.2 The landfill cap

The landfill cap is the term given to the layer of low-permeability material placed directly on top of the waste following the completion of landfilling operations. The objectives of the cap are to:

- reduce the infiltration of rainwater into the waste and hence control leachate production;
- control the migration of landfill gas; and
- isolate the waste from restoration materials.

The cap is usually made up of high-density clay (recommended thickness of 1m and bulk density of between 1.8-1.9 g/cm^3), although synthetic materials including geotextiles such as HDPE are being increasingly used at modern sites. The cap is designed to join up with the basal liner to ensure that the waste is completely sealed. Landfill gas migration and leachate breakout are therefore controlled, preventing pollution from occurring beyond the landfill site boundary. The cap itself is finally covered by a soil layer, which in addition to providing a growing medium for vegetation, acts as a protective layer for the cap. Without the soil layer the clay cap would be prone to desiccation and cracking in prolonged spells of dry weather. Damage to the cap may lead to the uncontrolled escape of landfill gas and the loss of control over leachate production.

2.3 Landfill gas control and extraction

Gas control systems vary in extent and design according to a number of factors such as the type and quantity of waste accepted. At most large sites where controlled wastes have been accepted, gas will be actively extracted and either flared or, as at an increasing number of sites, used to generate electricity. At smaller sites or sites that have accepted relatively inert wastes, gas control may simply be passive, whereby migrating gas is vented to the atmosphere via a number of collection trenches within the fill.

Active gas control systems may include a series of monitoring boreholes beyond the filled area to detect uncontrolled migration; a number of vertical collection wells connected by a network of horizontal pipes to a gas compound; a gas treatment plant possibly including a waste-to-energy facility; and a number of dewatering points to remove condensate from the gas (see Figure A.1.1). On sites where gas production is high, systems may require collection wells at least every 50 m and a network of pipes extending for several kilometres. Furthermore, many decades may have to elapse before stabilisation of the waste is achieved, so gas control systems may have to remain in place almost indefinitely. The implications for site restoration arising from such extensive infrastructure are therefore potentially enormous.

The major implications for habitat creation from gas control systems relate primarily to the requirement for large-scale infrastructure. A network of wells and pipes can seriously limit the potential for creating some habitat types (woodlands and wetlands in particular), partly due to the need for maintaining access to the wells. However, careful consultation between pollution control engineers and habitat creation designers should enable schemes to be designed that overcome many of these problems. Further difficulties may be caused by damage to gas control systems through settlement (see Section D.2.5). If settlement causes damage, remedial works will be required which may cause damage to restored areas both directly and through factors such as soil compaction caused by vehicles.

2.4 Leachate collection and extraction

Leachate is generally collected from sites via pumping from a number of vertical collection wells within the fill. Where necessary, any excess leachate is either treated on site prior to discharge, pumped to an off-site facility such as a local sewage treatment works or removed by tanker. On many sites a number of temporary storage lagoons are also used.

The infrastructure required for a leachate collection system is by no means as large as that required for gas extraction. Additionally, vertical leachate collection wells are usually installed when landfilling commences, and impacts upon habitat creation are usually much smaller. Furthermore, the efficiency of leachate collection systems is less likely to be compromised by settlement than that of gas systems, and hence potential implications for habitat creation from the need for remediation works are also likely to be small.

A typical active landfill gas extraction plant.

2.5 Possible effects of settlement

Settlement occurs most rapidly during the peak period of biodegradation when landfill gas and leachate production are at a maximum. Most settlement takes place during the first five years after capping; rates of settlement after this initial period are generally negligible, although settlement can continue for several more years.

Potential effects of rapid settlement on the landfill cap include stress damage and cracking to the cap structure. Damage is most likely to occur where differential settlement has taken place (where settlement rates vary between adjacent areas due to differences in factors such as waste composition and time since capping). Serious damage to the integrity of the cap is likely to require excavation of the soil layer (including any created habitats) and repair or replacement of the affected cap area. Even if careful replacement of the soil takes place following remediation works, damage to any habitat creation that has taken place is inevitable.

Potential effects of rapid settlement on landfill gas and leachate control systems include the deformation of collection wells, settling of horizontal pipework (which for gas systems can lead to blockages caused by condensate) and the distortion of pipe connections. Again, impacts are likely to be greatest where differential settlement takes place, and remediation works may be necessary in such circumstances, with consequent serious effects on created habitats.

To counter the potentially damaging effects of engineering system remediation work upon newly created habitats, a period of interim restoration is now recommended. This concept is discussed more fully in section D.4.

3 Landfill site restoration

3.1 Landform and drainage design

Most landfill sites may incorporate an element of 'land-raising', whereby the final landform is raised above the initial profile of the land, resulting in the familiar domed profile of many former landfill sites. Such a raised profile has three main functions:

- to facilitate surface water drainage and hence minimise the amount of water infiltrating the waste;
- to maximise the void space (the largest possible void space is essential to the economic viability of a site); and
- to allow for settlement.

The nature of the final landform must be fully considered at the design stage if habitat creation is to be successful.

3.1.1 Drainage

Drainage patterns are site-specific, dependent on a range of factors such as soil conditions and annual rainfall patterns. Important issues addressed during restoration design include:

- Rates of discharge into local watercourses – rapid discharge into existing watercourses should be avoided. The construction of balancing ponds may be required, providing the opportunity to combine drainage requirements with habitat creation objectives (see F.5 for further information on wetland design).
- Prevention of erosion – soil erosion reduces the protection for engineering systems. The potential for erosion can be reduced by high standards of soil handling (see F.1.6) and early establishment of vegetation, but may still take place on many sites with slopes steeper than 1 in 10.
- Prevention of waterlogging – to reduce the chance of water infiltrating the cap, the soil above the cap should not be allowed to become waterlogged. Waterlogging is likely to occur on relatively impermeable soils where the gradient is insufficient to allow natural drainage.
- Retention of sufficient water for vegetation growth – it is important to ensure that soil at the top of slopes does not become too dry to support vegetation.
- The effects of water run-off on adjacent land and buildings – it is

important that adjacent land is not placed at an increased risk of flooding as a result of water movements off the landfill cap.

Due to the presence of the low-permeability landfill cap below the soil surface, drainage must take place laterally, either over the surface or through the soil. Surface drainage is generally undesirable as it can cause soil erosion; slope gradients must be sufficient to promote natural drainage of water through the soil layer. This is largely dependent on soil type and structure, and at sites where soils are relatively impermeable or where soils have become compacted during restoration, the installation of underdrainage may be required. To prevent disruption to created habitats, underdrainage should be installed prior to restoration, although this renders it susceptible to damage from settlement. A further case for interim restoration (Section D.4) may be argued in such circumstances.

3.1.2 Slopes

Slope gradients must be steep enough to promote natural drainage but not so steep as to compromise site operations and after-use or so that the final landform does not blend in with the surrounding landscape. To allow successful drainage, a minimum slope of 1 in 25 is recommended for all capped landfill sites, increasing to 1 in 15 at sites in areas of high rainfall or where soils are relatively impermeable (Environment Agency, in prep.).

The anticipated effects of settlement must be taken into account when designing slope gradients, hence the use of pre-settlement contours and 'overtipping' to allow for the reduction of gradients during settlement.

3.1.3 Landscape design

Landscape design must try to reduce the visual impact of the site, both during operation through the use of screening, and in the long term through the integration of landform design into the local landscape.

Initial landscaping may include bank construction and tree planting to screen the site during operation. It is essential that these works are integrated into the final site restoration design, particularly where habitat creation is planned, as they represent an early opportunity to begin the habitat creation process. Woodland planting carried out for screening purposes could add valuable structural diversity to woodland creation during final restoration. Consideration should also be given to retaining features of ecological interest within the initial landscaping designs for the site.

Where habitat creation is planned, communication between landform designers and habitat creation designers is essential to ensure that the landscape design is suitable for the proposed habitat creation project.

3.2 Soils

The provision of suitable soil conditions is essential for successful habitat creation. Detailed guidance on the provision of suitable soils is given in F.1.

3.3 Aftercare

The term aftercare refers to the establishment of the after-use and the management required to maintain the after-use in the period following site closure. Most modern sites are obliged by planning conditions to carry out management for a five-year aftercare period following completion of restoration works. With respect to habitat creation, aftercare includes the establishment of the specified habitat and the initiation of management that may be required to maintain the conservation interest of that habitat in the long-term. Works which are essential to allow the habitat to be created must be included as aftercare conditions on the planning permission. Activities required to maintain the habitat beyond this period will need to be addressed separately (see below).

3.4 Long-term management

The maintenance of conservation interest at most sites will require management beyond the end of the statutory five-year aftercare period. It is therefore essential that management requirements are fully considered at the outset of habitat design, and appropriate mechanisms established to maintain appropriate management in the long term if required. The planning authority cannot legally impose an aftercare period of more than five years, although the site operator may voluntarily carry out beneficial works beyond the aftercare period if they wish. This, however, is not likely, and mechanisms to allow work to continue for a longer period will generally have to be secured through another route, for example through the use of legally binding Section 106 agreements secured under the 1990 Town & Country Planning Act (in England and Wales). This is particularly important for woodland creation (section F.3), unless

natural colonisation of woodland is used as the creation method, since a functioning woodland ecosystem takes substantially longer than 5 years to develop. Other habitats also require long-term management; otherwise, the process of succession will result in grassland (section F.2) and heathland (section F.4) developing into woodland.

Activities necessary to maintain habitats in the long term should ideally be incorporated into a management plan for the site, with the implementation of the management plan forming part of the Section 106 agreement. This should be signed as a pre-requisite to the planning permission. The management plan and agreement should also consider who should carry out long-term management works (e.g. site operator, contractors, local conservation groups or local Wildlife Trust) and how the works are to be funded.

3.5 Restoration of old sites

Restoration standards at sites closed before 1990 are highly variable. Many old sites have no engineering systems at all, and even where engineering systems were installed the standards usually fall short of those required at modern sites. The depth of soil cover is also highly variable - at some sites the waste is less than 20 cm below the surface. Aftercare standards also vary widely; many sites remain virtually derelict, whereas important wildlife habitat has been created at some sites (see Stadt Moers case study 9). More rarely, important ecological habitat has developed naturally at some sites.

Restoration of old sites first requires a full assessment of site conditions. Whilst the techniques for habitat creation on old sites are similar to those given in Section F, full details on site assessment are beyond the scope of this manual. An excellent example of an approach to assessing old landfill sites is provided by the 'Staged Pathway' approach developed for assessment of sites for potential community woodland use (Mersey Forest and Red Rose Forest Partnership, 1999).

The large number of derelict former landfill sites provides a great opportunity for habitat creation. Unfortunately, funding is a major limitation to such works; planning obligations have long since ended at many sites, and the cost of habitat improvements must therefore be met by external sources. Note that although some funding may be available through initiatives such as the Community Forest or the Woodland Grant Scheme, conditions attached to such funding can greatly restrict the types of habitat that can be created. Further potential limitations on habitat creation at old landfill sites are outlined briefly below:

- Uncontrolled landfill gas and leachate production may impact directly on habitat creation (see section D.5).
- On-site soil resources are likely to be limited. External sources of soil or soil-forming materials must therefore be sought (see section F.1).
- Designers must work around the existing landform; changes to the landform are unlikely to be feasible.
- There is less scope for consultation with pollution control engineers than at well-planned modern sites. Designers must therefore work around existing systems.

Photo: Melvyn Foxton

Landfill site restoration taking place. The photograph demonstrates the restriction of traffic movements to parts of the site away from previously laid soil.

4 Integration of restoration with operations and engineering systems

4.1   Introduction

The integration of habitat creation design with other stages in landfill site development is essential to ensure successful habitat creation at landfill sites. This section therefore provides a brief outline of:

- the phasing of restoration and aftercare;
- the integration of restoration and aftercare with the installation and maintenance of pollution control infrastructure; and
- The concept of interim restoration.

4.2   Phased restoration

Phased restoration, whereby areas of the site are sequentially restored immediately after completion of operational activities, is now common practice at modern landfill sites.

Phased restoration has a number of advantages, including:

- Habitats created on early phases have more time to develop before site operations cease. Phased restoration may therefore help to speed up habitat development on later phases as species already present on the early phases can colonise later phases.
- Soil for the restoration of one phase may be transported directly from the excavation of a another, reducing the need for storing soil.
- Restored early phases can be used to screen later phases and consequently reduce environmental impacts on the surrounding area.
- Early restoration is a good public relations tool, helping to convince local communities that the site will be returned to a beneficial after-use.

Despite the advantages of phased restoration it is essential that potential negative impacts from operational activities on newly restored areas are fully taken into consideration, particularly where sensitive habitats have been created (see section D.5).

4.3   Integration of restoration with pollution control systems

As stressed in section D.2, the sheer number of collection wells and monitoring points and the length of pipework required for pollution control systems can have considerable implications for the design of habitat creation on landfill sites. The impacts of infrastructure and the associated long-term requirement for access can be minimised by detailed consultation between habitat creation designers and pollution engineers. For example, monitoring points can be located along woodland rides or along hedgerows, and ponds can be situated away from pipes.

Potentially the largest impacts upon habitat creation from pollution control systems are those resulting from remedial work required due to damage to infrastructure from settlement. On sites where settlement is expected to be substantial it may therefore be better to delay habitat creation until the majority of settlement has taken place. At such sites a period of interim restoration is recommended (see below) during which remedial works to pollution control systems are carried out, prior to habitat creation works taking place.

4.4   Interim restoration

4.4.1   Concepts and processes

Interim restoration, whereby a temporary grass sward is established on a shallow layer of subsoil following capping, is intended to reduce damage to the final restoration of a site from remedial works to engineering systems that are required as a result of settlement. This is now recommended by government guidance in the forthcoming Waste Management Paper 26e (Environment Agency, in prep.), although it has yet to be fully embraced by all Waste Planning Authorities.

The process of interim restoration begins with the placement of up to 500mm of subsoil or soil-forming material over the cap. Pollution control systems are installed within this layer. A temporary cover of vigorous grass species is sown to prevent erosion, reduce infiltration and improve the visual appearance of the site. Any necessary remedial works can be carried out without damaging the final restoration. Once the majority of settlement has taken place (usually after 2-5 years), the final restoration can proceed, following the placement of an additional layer of soil on top of the interim restoration layer.

Interim restoration is not necessary at all sites. Sites accepting mainly inert wastes will not require interim restoration, as settlement rates are likely to be low. Even at sites that have received predominantly biodegradable wastes, interim restoration is unlikely to be necessary across the whole site. For example, areas around the site perimeter are unlikely to be affected by settlement. Sloping areas are also less likely to be affected by settlement than flat areas and are therefore less likely to require interim restoration. Interim restoration is most commonly employed at sites where a high standard of soil quality is required (i.e. sites restored to an agricultural after-use). However, it may play a part at many sites where habitat creation is planned.

The advantages of interim restoration are clear. It provides a much higher standard of final restoration and can also be much more cost-effective on sites where high rates of settlement are expected. However, interim restoration delays final site restoration and may therefore prolong the impact on local amenity. It should not therefore be considered as a standard requirement for all sites.

For further details on interim restoration concepts and processes, refer to WMP26e (Environment Agency, in prep.).

4.4.2   Interim restoration as part of habitat creation

As mentioned above, interim restoration is primarily intended for sites that are to be returned to an agricultural after-use, where the maintenance of good quality soil is vital. It should also be carried out at all sites where considerable settlement is anticipated and tree planting is planned, which may include a number of habitat creation sites. Wholescale tree loss could occur if remedial works to pollution control systems are necessary in areas planted with trees.

It has been suggested that interim restoration is unnecessary for creating certain habitat types. For example, grassland can be planted directly onto subsoil or soil-forming materials, which are likely to sustain less damage than highly fertile topsoil during comparable remedial works. However, great care during remedial works would be necessary to avoid undue damage to the habitat. Repair works on created habitats following disruption are also likely to result in reduced habitat quality due to factors such as soil compaction. The possibility of habitat creation after-uses being regarded as less important than other after-uses, with less care consequently taken during remedial works, must be avoided at all costs. The need for interim restoration should therefore be strongly considered as part of any habitat creation scheme.

5 Constraints imposed on habitat creation by the restored landfill environment

The restored landfill environment presents a number of constraints on habitat creation projects. Many of these constraints are common to habitat creation schemes at a wide variety of sites, but some relate specifically to landfill sites. This section summarises the constraints upon successful habitat creation presented by the restoration processes discussed in Sections D.1-4.

5.1 Major constraints upon habitat creation

5.1.1 Soils

Availability of suitable soil is **the** major limitation on successful habitat creation at landfill sites. Habitat creation at landfill sites also frequently encounters problems due to a lack of on-site soil resources and the subsequent need to import soil from elsewhere.

Detailed guidance on the provision of soil for habitat creation is given in Section F.1.

5.1.2 Pollution and the products of biodegradation

At old sites, or sites where engineering standards are poor, the products of biodegradation (landfill gas, leachate and heat) can directly affect the standard of habitat creation. If uncontrolled, the migration of landfill gas can kill vegetation through the replacement of soil oxygen with methane and the toxic effects of high carbon dioxide levels. Such effects are usually apparent as distinct areas of bare ground centred on landfill gas 'hotspots'. Leachate rarely affects habitat creation to the same extent, although where breakouts do occur they tend to be characterised by a flush of lush, tall vegetation promoted by greatly increased nutrient levels. Heat generated by biodegradation can also directly affect habitat creation. Effects are particularly noticeable where the cap or overlying soil layer is thin (effects should be less common at well-engineered modern sites) and are characterised by vegetation die-back due to drought stress in areas where soil moisture has evaporated.

At modern sites, direct impacts from landfill gas, leachate and heat are unlikely due to the presence of environmental protection systems. At such sites the principal constraint on habitat creation is the scale of the engineering systems installed to control and extract gas and leachate. Gas systems form the main constraint as they can comprise several kilometres of piping with numerous wells and boreholes. As well as access to monitoring points, access to the entire system may be required during the first few years after site closure to allow for corrections to the system to take account of settlement. Tree planting is therefore not recommended over pipes or access routes, and habitat design must be carefully integrated with the gas control system. Other habitats are also likely to be affected in a similar manner.

5.1.3 Landform and drainage

The final landform at landfill sites is usually designed to promote effective site drainage; this generally entails a sloping profile. Although habitat creation designers can and should have an input to landform design, the basic requirements cannot be altered. Consequently, it is generally not possible to create habitats that require large, flat areas or those which require a soil profile which is wet for part or all of the year. This effectively rules out large-scale creation of wetland habitats on landfill caps. In any case, the creation of wetland habitats above the fill at landfill sites is not recommended due to the increased risk of stress to the cap and water infiltration into the fill.

The highly specific drainage regime produced by the presence of a landfill cap must be carefully considered at the design stage in any habitat creation project. Habitats such as chalk grassland and dry lowland heath are predominantly situated on free-draining soils and may therefore be difficult to re-create on landfill sites where the cap forms a low-permeability layer at a much shallower depth than is usual. It is therefore essential that drainage is fully considered if attempting to create these or any similar habitats on landfill sites.

Table D.5.1. Constraints on the creation of particular habitat types imposed by the landfill environment	
Habitat type	**Example of constraints faced**
Wetland	– Wetland creation is not recommended over the fill due to potential implications for environmental protection systems. – Sloping landforms and improved drainage are generally unsuitable for wetland creation, except around the site periphery.
Woodland	– Trees should not be planted over pollution control infrastructure, particularly whilst settlement is still likely. Access to monitoring points must also be maintained for several years - woodland design must take account of this. – A minimum depth of 1.5 m soil over the cap is recommended for tree planting in order to protect the cap. This may create difficulties at sites where soil availability is limited. – Several species will not grow well in the poorly structured soils present in the early stages of restoration. Choice of species is therefore initially restricted to pioneer species, with other species planted in later years. The length of the aftercare requirement is consequently increased.
Grassland	– Soils used in restoration are often too fertile and several wildflower species are consequently out-competed by more vigorous species.
Heathland	– Soil fertility and pH must be exactly right for successful heathland generation. This is difficult to achieve where a mixture of soils are used in restoration. – The effect of the landfill cap on drainage must be fully considered prior to the creation of heathland habitats.

5.2 Specific constraints upon the creation of different habitat types

Creation of particular habitat types is likely to face a number of specific constraints in addition to the general constraints discussed above. Examples for a range of habitat types on landfill sites are summarised in Table D.5.1.

5.3 Additional considerations – phased restoration

At most large landfill sites where restoration is phased, the continuation of landfilling in operational areas can present constraints on the effectiveness of habitat creation in areas where filling has been completed. The following factors resulting from landfill site operation may damage created habitats:

- Soil compaction from vehicle movements – vehicles must therefore be kept well away from restored areas.

- Contaminated surface water runoff – care must be taken to ensure that water draining onto restored areas does not come from operational areas, tracks and roads or from areas restored to a different after-use. Runoff from an area restored to agriculture may be rich in nutrients, and could have severely damaging effects if allowed to enter nutrient-sensitive habitats such as heathland or species-rich grassland.

- Windblown litter – measures should be taken to avoid contamination of habitats by windblown litter and dust.

- Gull droppings – consideration must be given to the effects on nutrient-sensitive habitats of large quantities of gull droppings. Gulls are attracted to landfill sites by large quantities of food waste. They are also attracted to newly restored grassland, heathland and wetlands where they spend their time loafing and bathing. The potentially damaging effects from droppings must not be under-estimated (See Section C.2 for further details on the management of gulls at operational landfill sites).

SECTION E

Habitat creation on landfill sites

1 Choice of after-use

1.1 Introduction

It is essential for the continued public acceptability of the waste management industry that, following restoration, landfill developments are able to demonstrate a beneficial after-use. There are a number of choices of beneficial after-uses, of which habitat creation is one. This section summarises the various after-use options available to site developers and considers their advantages and disadvantages.

1.2 Alternatives for the after-use of landfill sites

A summary of the advantages and disadvantages of the main alternatives to habitat creation as after-uses at landfill sites is outlined in Table E.1.1.

In accordance with government guidance in Waste Management Paper 26e (Environment Agency, in prep.), landfill site after-uses can be broadly divided into five categories, as detailed below.

1.2.1 Agriculture

Agriculture has long been the most common after-use for landfill sites. This is usually because agriculture formed the original land-use at the site, although safety concerns over alternatives and a lack of political will to restore to other after-uses may also have contributed in the past.

Restoration to low-maintenance grassland for livestock grazing is most common, although restoration to arable agriculture is technically feasible and has been carried out at a number of sites.

1.2.2 Forestry

Trees are commonly incorporated into most site restoration schemes to a certain extent, if only for screening and landscaping purposes. Actual woodland after-uses can be categorised as:
- commercial forestry – for timber;
- amenity woodland – e.g. the Community Forest Initiative, which aims to create woodland in 12 designated Community Forests in

England with a combination of objectives including commercial forestry, landscape improvement, wildlife habitat provision and public access and recreation; and
- woodland habitat creation.

In the past, forestry after-uses were not recommended for landfill sites due to fears about potential damage to the integrity of pollution control systems. However, recent research (e.g. Dobson & Moffat, 1993; Bending & Moffat, 1997) has shown that tree planting on landfill sites is viable, provided certain restoration standards are met (See Table F.1.1 and Section F.3).

1.2.3 Amenity

A variety of amenity after-uses for landfill sites are possible, which in urban areas in particular, may help contribute to development plan targets. Examples of amenity after-uses include both formal after-uses, such as sports pitches and children's play areas and informal after-uses such as amenity grassland and country parks.

1.2.4 Nature conservation

Nature conservation after-uses form the main subject of this section of the manual. Whilst use of an entire site for habitat creation is likely to provide the maximum benefits to biodiversity, the incorporation of habitat creation into alternative after-uses may be more practical at some sites (see Stadt Moers case study number 9).

1.2.5 Hard after-uses

Hard end-uses such as buildings, car parks, etc. are generally not suitable for landfill sites (Environment Agency, in prep.). This is particularly the case at sites which have accepted biodegradable wastes; constraints upon development include the unstable nature of the ground due to settlement, the potential for gas generation and the long-term access and monitoring requirements for pollution control systems.

1.3 Factors affecting choice of after-use

1.3.1 Development plan requirements

A number of development plan policies at various levels of the planning system may influence the choice of after-use at landfill sites, depending on the nature of the policies and site location. The following examples illustrate development plan policies that might affect the choice of after-use at landfill sites:
- Priority habitats and species should be identified by development plans. If these occur in the vicinity of a site, habitat creation that contributes to relevant development plan targets may be required. Likewise, sustainable development policy objectives may require that biodiversity lost to landfill development is replaced through habitat creation.
- Development plan policies promoting increases in public open space may be relevant to an amenity after-use being selected at certain sites, particularly in urban areas.
- High-grade agricultural land should be identified in development plans in conjunction with policies for that land which ensures that the potential for food production is retained. Agricultural restoration may therefore be required at sites on such land, although development plans may contain policies to reduce the quantity of agricultural land in production and thus promote alternative after-uses for landfill sites.
- Many development plans contain some kind of woodland strategy, which may promote the creation of woodland in particular areas. Development plans within any of the 12 Community Forests will definitely contain objectives for woodland creation and these may be relevant to landfill sites in certain areas.

1.3.2 Surrounding land use

The land-use in the area surrounding the site can have a large bearing on the type

Table E.1.1 Advantages and disadvantages of alternatives to habitat creation as an after-use at landfill sites

After-use	Advantages	Disadvantages
Agriculture	Likely to be acceptable both in landscape terms and to local communities. Income-generating. Government policies to safeguard the "best and most versatile" agricultural land effectively require sites on high-grade agricultural land to be restored to agriculture.	Current political climate moving towards reducing food production and taking land out of agricultural production. Good quality topsoil necessary, leading to high establishment costs. Management costs also high. Efficiency of arable/productive grassland after-uses likely to be severely compromised by access and maintenance requirements of pollution control systems. Sites in urban areas may be subject to vandalism, damage to livestock, etc.
Forestry	Less demanding on soil resources than agriculture and therefore potentially less expensive. In urban areas, forestry after-use may help meet Community Forest targets. Commercial forestry income-generating.	Restored landfill sites provide a harsh environment for tree growth therefore growth rates may be poor (especially relevant to commercial forestry). Tree planting may have to be delayed for several years following restoration to prevent disruption from remediation works due to settlement. Pollution control access requirements will reduce potential size of forestry blocks, possibly to non-commercially viable levels.
Amenity	High quality soil resources often not required therefore low establishment costs. Informal amenity less likely to be affected by pollution control infrastructure requirements than other after-uses. High demand for public open space in most urban development plans. Amenity after-uses can be incorporated with other after-uses such as nature conservation and forestry.	Non-income-generating, therefore provision must be made for ongoing management costs. Pollution potential may have implications for public access. Lower demand for public open space in most rural development plans. Settlement problems at sites that have taken biodegradable wastes make such sites unsuitable for formal amenity after-uses such as sports pitches.

of after-use proposed, as illustrated by the following examples:

- The existence of certain habitat types in the area surrounding a site is likely to present a much better opportunity for habitat creation to make a tangible contribution to BAP objectives and targets than where sites are surrounded by land of little ecological interest. Existing habitats can be enlarged or linked, increasing their conservation value, and a higher standard of habitat creation may also be achieved.
- Whether a site is in a rural or urban area can influence after-use. Amenity after-uses are likely to be more appropriate in areas with a large population than in remote rural areas. Agriculture, forestry and nature conservation may be better choices of after-use in rural areas.
- Proposed after-use must aim to complement the surrounding landscape, particularly in rural areas. The design of landscape features such as hedgerows and walls can also be very important.

1.3.3 Technical aspects

Various site characteristics such as available soil resources, restoration gradients and requirements for gas and leachate control (dependent on waste type accepted) can play a large part in determining the type of after-use that is technically feasible. Implications for the choice of after-use include the following:

- A lack of topsoil for restoration effectively precludes an agricultural after-use unless large quantities of soil are imported, which is prohibitively expensive. However, most nature conservation and informal amenity after-uses (including amenity woodland) can be established on subsoil or soil-forming material, making them a much more viable alternative in such cases.
- Commercial forestry and intensive agriculture are likely to be unsuitable at sites with a large pollution control infrastructure due to the increased management costs of cultivating around collection wells, boreholes and pipework. Nature conservation

and informal amenity after-uses are usually far less constrained by pollution control infrastructure and are therefore a more attractive option at such sites.

1.3.4 Economic aspects

Economic aspects affecting the choice of after-use include establishment costs, costs of ongoing management and maintenance, and whether or not such costs can be offset by income generated following restoration. The following examples illustrate how such factors may affect the choice of specific after-uses:

- Intensive agricultural after-uses tend to have high establishment costs and high maintenance costs. However, such costs may be offset to a certain degree by the potential income to be earned from food production.
- Habitat creation and many informal amenity uses have relatively low establishment and management costs and may therefore appear attractive on economic grounds. However, the requirement for

ongoing management must be fully considered as such after-uses have little potential for income generation. Nevertheless, this long-term commitment should not deter site operators from choosing a habitat creation after-use, as long-term management costs may be met by other means. For example, site restoration for a nature conservation after-use may be substantially cheaper than restoration for another use such as agriculture – conservation after-uses generally do not require large amounts of expensive topsoil. The money saved could therefore be allocated for long-term management.

1.3.5 Requirements of other interest groups

A number of interest groups may have a view on the choice of after-use at specific sites, ranging from the landowner and the local community to statutory consultees on planning applications such as the MAFF, the Forestry Commission and English Nature. All should be consulted for their views during the habitat creation design process, although the final choice of after-use must still be consistent with development plan policies.

2 Habitat creation after-use

2.1 Introduction

The rather fuzzy concept of a "nature conservation" after-use is frequently referred to in a range of literature relating to landfill site restoration and aftercare. However, at a practical level a number of different types of habitat creation exist and it is important for each to be recognized, as certain types will be more appropriate than others at different sites.

The degree of appropriateness of a particular type of habitat creation at a particular site is dependent on a number of factors. These factors include:

● the nature conservation importance of the site and surrounding area – this should be identified by the site EcIA;

● Biodiversity Action Plan (BAP) targets for habitats and species relevant to the site and surrounding area;

● local development plan policies; and

● site characteristics (including size, fill composition and soil resources).

This section provides an outline of the reasons for habitat creation, its benefits and a brief description of the different types of habitat creation that may be carried out at landfill sites.

2.1.1 Definitions

Definitions of habitat restoration and creation in the existing literature are often inconsistent. Parker (1995) defines habitat *restoration* as 'the restoration of existing degraded semi-natural vegetation'. Lewis (1990) defines habitat *restoration* as returning a site from a disturbed or totally altered condition to a previously existing state. Habitat *creation* is defined by Lewis as the conversion of a habitat into another habitat which has never previously existed on the site, whereas Parker (1995) defines habitat *creation* as 'the construction of interesting and attractive ecological communities on sites which currently support little nature conservation interest'. According to Lewis, Parker's definition of habitat restoration would be termed habitat *enhancement*.

Using Lewis's definitions, it follows that planting a woodland on a landfill that was originally wooded is habitat *restoration*, whereas planting a woodland on a site which was previously grassland or heathland would be habitat *creation*. However, this book uses the term 'habitat creation' to refer to the establishment of habitats on a restored landfill site, regardless of the previous land-use. This is firstly for simplicity, and secondly to

avoid confusion with the term 'restoration' used in a landfill context to refer to the process that returns a landfill site to a condition suitable for an after-use (Environment Agency, in prep.). See Section A.1.4 for key definitions used in this book, and also the glossary for a fuller list. See also Anderson (1995) for a review of ecological restoration and creation.

2.2 Reasons for creating habitats

The countryside of Britain contains a wealth of different habitat types. The landscape we see today is the cumulative result of the impact of generations of people using natural resources in a variety of ways to support themselves (e.g. stock husbandry, crop planting and firewood / timber cutting). In the past, the majority of lowland Britain was covered in natural woodland (although the dominant vegetation above the treeline in upland areas was dwarf-shrub heath) (Rackham, 1994). The increasing influence of humans on the landscape over many years resulted in the almost complete transformation of the countryside from natural to semi-natural habitats. For example, woodland was cleared to plant crops (creating arable fields) or to graze stock (creating grasslands). Very few examples of wholly natural vegetation remain; scattered remnants of Caledonian pine forest in Scotland, montane heaths, raised and blanket bog, some wet woodlands and some maritime habitats such as saltmarsh are perhaps the closest to natural forms of vegetation that still exist in this country.

Semi-natural habitats can be categorised into broad habitat types: grassland, woodland, heathland / moorland, wetland and arable. Arable habitats (and some examples of the other habitat types) can be viewed as artificial. Intensification of agricultural practices since the 1940s has resulted in a dramatic decline in the extent of semi-natural habitats and populations of associated species.

Despite being far removed in character from natural habitats, semi-natural habitats have accumulated or retained nature conservation value. The rate of change from natural to semi-natural habitats was slow enough to permit species to adapt, and the management of semi-natural habitats permitted a range of species to coexist. The difference between semi-natural habitats and artificial or intensively managed habitats, and the reason why the latter have such a reduced value to wildlife, is partly due to the relative newness of these habitats in evolutionary terms. However, the difference is mainly due to the increased control of species perceived by landowners to be undesirable (i.e. weeds and insect pests) with pesticides, and to recent rapid changes in management practices which have occurred too quickly for species to adapt. In summary, the potential for wildlife to coexist with the management of the countryside by humans for humans is now greatly reduced.

When it is considered that large areas of semi-natural habitats are disappearing through destruction and intensive management, coupled with the fact that the replacement habitat is poorly suited for wildlife, the case for the preservation of existing semi-natural habitat and the creation of additional areas becomes strong. There will be instances where semi-natural habitats will have to be destroyed, but in such cases their replacement is also essential. This is recognised by WPAs where landfill development results in the destruction of semi-natural habitat; they no longer permit restoration proposals entailing the creation of simplistic artificial habitats, but instead demand higher standards and the creation of habitats of value to wildlife.

It can be argued that semi-natural habitats, like natural habitats, are virtually non-recreatable. An ancient woodland, for example, will have been continuously wooded for many centuries, and there are likely to be thousands of species of flowering plants, mosses, lichens, invertebrates, birds and mammals which have colonised and established without human assistance. The creation of a woodland habitat by physically collecting and moving these species from one site to another would be logistically impossible, and in any case the conditions under which the ancient woodland developed are likely to be different from the conditions occurring now. Any attempt at habitat creation will almost always result in an inferior version of the original. Habitat creation should, therefore, never be offered as a substitute for the conservation of existing habitats. Apart from the inevitable loss of species diversity in a created or translocated habitat, the continuity of a site is also lost, and with it an important intrinsic value of the site. However, this does not imply that habitat creation has no value, only that creation on one site is not an adequate substitute for destruction on another. Habitat creation can play a valuable role in mitigation for adverse environmental impacts of development, and can help to lessen or reverse the decline of semi-natural habitat extent.

2.3 Benefits of habitat creation

In nature conservation terms, the principal benefit of habitat creation at landfill sites is its contribution to biodiversity conservation. At many sites, it is possible to create habitats that contribute directly to Biodiversity Action Plan targets for priority habitats and species. Even at sites where a direct contribution to BAP targets is not possible, habitat creation will always be able to benefit biodiversity in some way and in so doing may also help to meet Local Agenda 21 commitments to sustainable development.

The ability to demonstrate a beneficial after-use to both the WPA and the local community is essential, not only for the acceptance of the site in question but for the public and planning perception of site restoration and the industry as a whole (Simmons, 1992a). Habitat creation is highly likely to be viewed as a beneficial after-use by both the WPA and the local community, perhaps more so than some alternative after-uses, and may therefore provide an attractive after-use option in both planning and public relations terms.

Compared with agriculture, forestry and formal amenity after-uses, habitat creation has the potential to be much more cost-effective. Most habitats can be created without the need for topsoil, which considerably reduces costs, particularly where topsoil is not available on site. Management and maintenance costs can also be considerably lower than for alternative after-uses; a species-rich hay meadow may only require mowing once a year, compared with several times a year for many amenity grasslands. On economic grounds alone, habitat creation can therefore be a very attractive option for site operators.

Constraints on alternative after-uses can also make habitat creation an attractive after-use option. For example, some agricultural and forestry after-uses are severely constrained by the scale of pollution control infrastructure required on sites that have accepted controlled wastes and where extensive infrastructure reduces available space and increases management costs. Most habitat creation after-uses are less constrained by such infrastructure. Other constraints such as the fall in demand for agricultural production and the requirement for a delay in tree planting on sites subject to settlement also increase the attractiveness of habitat creation as an after-use choice.

One common argument against habitat creation as an after-use is that it imposes a long-term financial commitment on the site operator to manage the site. Whilst this is partially true in that almost all created habitats will require some form of ongoing management to retain their conservation value, it may be possible to set up management agreements with, for example local Wildlife Trusts and use the money saved by, for example, not having to import topsoil for site restoration, to fund long-term management (see E.1.3.4). Furthermore, the funding for such agreements may not have to be met by the site operator – in the long term, alternative funding sources may be sought such as environmental trust funds or grants.

Whilst the promotion of habitat creation is fundamental to this manual, it is acknowledged that arguments in favour of alternative after-uses may be stronger at a number of sites. However, there will almost certainly be a case for an ecologically sensitive component to any creation scheme. For example, habitat creation may be included as part of an informal amenity after-use or as hedgerows, field margins and copses included within agricultural restoration. Woodland creation can also be made more ecologically sensitive simply by careful consideration of species planted and planting designs. Habitat creation may also be carried out in combination with a range of engineering requirements; for example, the creation of balancing ponds away from the landfill cap may help to fulfil drainage requirements whilst also having conservation benefits. In some areas, ponds can provide habitat for priority species such as great crested newt (see Maw Green case study number 6), and therefore contribute directly to BAP targets.

In summary, all landfill sites have the potential to contribute to biodiversity conservation after restoration, from complex habitat creation to the simple creation of a wildflower meadow in the corner of a public park. It is therefore the responsibility of all involved, from site operators and planners to ecologists and conservationists, to ensure that opportunities are taken and that the potential of the landfill industry to contribute to biodiversity conservation is fully realised.

2.4 Types of habitat creation

2.4.1 Habitat creation that contributes to BAP targets for habitats and species

Habitat creation at restored landfill sites may be able to contribute directly to targets for priority habitats or species at either a UK or Local BAP level. National objectives and targets have been set for 38 habitats and roughly 400 species, several of which involve the creation of new areas of habitat. Targets that apply to particular geographical areas should now be incorporated into local development plans and should therefore be easily identified at the project planning stage. Additional targets often exist for habitats and species at a local level, which once again may include targets relating to the creation of new habitats. Further information on BAPs and BAP targets is provided in Section E.3.2.

It must be stressed that a large number of BAP targets for priority habitats and species will not be relevant to the restoration of landfill sites. For example, BAP targets relevant to a particular area may not include targets for habitat creation if the important habitats in that area cannot physically be re-created. Alternatively, habitat creation targets may exist but relate to habitats that cannot be created in the restored landfill environment. For example, the creation of wetland habitats is not recommended at sites that have received biodegradable wastes (Environment Agency, in prep.). Also, some sites may also be too small to enable habitat creation on a scale able to meet BAP targets; for example, new reedbeds must be at least 20 ha in size to contribute to national BAP targets.

Additionally, whilst a created habitat may in principle be suitable for supporting rare species, it is unlikely that rare species will colonise the site in the short term; the occurrence of rare species at the site should not be expected. However, over time, and given appropriate management, it is possible that suitable conditions will develop to allow rare species to colonise.

Habitat creation will always be able to contribute to biodiversity conservation even if targets for specific habitats and species cannot be met. The next sections outline ways in which this can be done.

2.4.2 The creation of buffer or linking habitat

Habitat fragmentation exacerbates the effects of habitat loss, and is a key reason for the decline of associated species. For example, silver-studded blue butterflies have declined following fragmentation of lowland heathland, as the distances between remnant fragments became too great to allow individuals to disperse, resulting in increased local extinctions.

Fragmentation can be reversed by increasing biodiversity on intervening land through land management and/or habitat creation (ALGE & the South West Biodiversity Initiative, 1998).

Habitat creation at landfill sites may therefore be able to reduce fragmentation, principally through the creation of buffer or linking habitat (see Box E.2.1). Such habitat creation is likely to be most appropriate for:

- sites where BAP priority habitats exist in adjacent areas; and
- habitats that are technically difficult to re-create.

It must be accepted that true creation of many habitats, particularly those that have developed over hundreds of years, is often impossible. For such habitats, it may be more appropriate to create an area of buffer or linking habitat rather than to attempt to create areas of the habitat itself. Indeed, a number of BAP targets involve the creation of buffer habitat or the creation of habitat which links priority sites.

2.4.3 "Political" habitat creation

The types of habitat creation described in Section E.2.4.1-2 are only likely to be appropriate in certain circumstances, i.e. where habitats of conservation importance are located close to the site or where there is an opportunity to contribute directly to BAP targets for habitats and species.

These circumstances will generally not apply to the majority of landfill sites; a different type of habitat creation is likely to be more appropriate in such cases.

"Political" habitat creation was described by Baines (1989) as the creation of simple habitats with immediate popular appeal, which have the prime function of education and making wildlife accessible to a larger number of people, particularly in urban

areas. These objectives are certainly valid, but it is also true that such habitat creation can also contribute to biodiversity conservation. However, the distinction should be made between 'habitats created solely for amenity purposes and those which are re-created for ecological purposes' (Newbold, 1989).

This type of habitat creation may involve the creation of habitats such as wildflower meadows, ponds, scrub and woodlands, which if created following the best practice guidelines presented in this book will undoubtedly provide habitat for a wide range of more common species. Although this type of habitat creation may not benefit the conservation of rare habitats and species, it will benefit the conservation of biodiversity as a whole. Indeed, the conservation of so-called 'common' species is a central theme of the UK Biodiversity Action Plan, in addition to the plans for priority habitats and species.

The location of a large number of landfill sites within predominantly urban areas provides an excellent opportunity for habitat creation of this type to be used as part of an environmental educational strategy and may also contribute to additional development plan targets such as the provision of "urban wild space". There is also a great opportunity for habitat creation of this type to be combined with other after-uses such as public open space.

2.4.4 Strategic and opportunistic habitat creation

Habitat creation may be further divided into strategic and opportunistic habitat creation (ALGE & the South West Biodiversity Initiative, 1998).

Box E.2.1. Buffer and linking habitat

Buffer habitat – habitat immediately adjacent to similar but ecologically more important habitat. Although not of the same quality, buffer habitat increases the value of adjacent habitat by increasing its size, protecting it from other land-use impacts and allowing more migration of species. An example of the principle is the provision of new grassland adjacent to an ancient species-rich meadow. Whilst the diversity of the new grassland is unlikely to match that of the adjacent meadow, its mere presence should greatly benefit the biodiversity of the existing meadow, and colonisation of the new grassland should occur gradually over time, potentially increasing the populations of a number of rare species.

Linking habitat – habitat creating a continuous link or "stepping stone" between two similar areas of ecologically important habitat that facilitates greater migration of species between the two sites. The creation of hedgerows or copses between two areas of ancient woodland is a good example of this principle.

Buffer or linking habitat may not in itself be of high ecological value but its provision can greatly increase the value of the habitats it is buffering or linking.

Strategic habitat creation targets priority habitats and species in pre-determined areas most suited to creation of particular habitat types. The habitat creation types covered in section E.2.4.1 to section E.2.4.2 could be categorised in this way and are therefore of most relevance to landfill sites located within such strategic areas (which should be identified in development plans).

Opportunistic habitat creation occurs where sites become available for habitat creation outside these pre-determined strategic areas. Most landfill developments are likely to fall into this category and in such cases it is important that habitats appropriate to the location of the site are created, following guidance given in Local BAPs and Natural Area profiles and using EcIA information in order for the benefits for biodiversity to be maximised.

3 Habitat creation – general guidelines

3.1 Introduction

Choosing the most appropriate type of habitat creation for an individual site is vital if conservation benefits are to be maximised.

Parker (1995) states that the initial stages of habitat creation involve two crucial parts. These can be set out as follows:

1. Setting clear objectives
2. Choosing the right site and appropriate habitat

The habitat chosen for creation should be appropriate to the surrounding landscape, existing semi-natural habitats and historical land use. The habitat should occur naturally in the locality and should be appropriate given the local soil type and climate. For example, one should not attempt to create heathland on calcareous soil, or upland oakwood in the lowlands. If it is decided that grassland is to be created, a decision is required regarding the type of grassland (i.e. acid, neutral or calcareous), and the management regime (i.e. if neutral grassland is appropriate, will it be managed as a hay meadow or permanent pasture?). These decisions will affect the choice of species used to create the habitat. The exact location of the habitat on the landfill is also important; for example, wetlands should not be positioned over the fill, but can be situated around the edge of the cap so that they can intercept runoff.

Good planning, monitoring and aftercare are fundamental parts of habitat creation; habitat creation failure is often due to deficiencies in these aspects of the process.

Common causes of habitat creation failure as listed by Parker (1995) are:

- insufficient planning and imprecise objectives;
- overly ambitious projects which demand a greater amount of resources than are available;
- too little attention paid to the appropriateness of the habitat to the existing soil;
- failing to address the need for aftercare and management at the planning stage (these may have to extend for an indefinite period); and
- inadequate site monitoring being unable to determine whether the project is achieving its objectives.

Mitchley *et al.* (1998) set out clear monitoring objectives for a range of habitat types specifically designed for habitat creation schemes.

3.1.1 Setting clear objectives

The first and most important question that should be asked is **what is the desired end result?** Given that it is not possible to create an exact replicate of a semi-natural habitat instantaneously, one should follow ecologically sound guidelines to create the appropriate conditions to permit nature to do the rest.

Habitat creation must start with an idea of the final product in mind from the outset. **The ideal is the replication of a semi-natural habitat of conservation value.** This therefore excludes artificial habitats and those representative of degraded semi-natural habitats, but encompasses grasslands, heathlands, woodlands and wetlands. Maritime habitats with a saline influence such as saltmarsh are excluded from this manual as they are extremely unlikely to be relevant to landfill restoration.

3.1.2 Choosing the appropriate habitat

In order to refine the objectives of habitat creation and to obtain a working model upon which to base habitat creation, an accurate description of semi-natural habitats is required. This is provided by the National Vegetation Classification (NVC) system (Rodwell, 1991 *et seq.*). The NVC is a working classification of semi-natural habitats occurring in Britain, and is described in more detail in Section E.3.2.7.

The basis of habitat creation is the introduction of vegetation. Although it is possible to go further and introduce other species groups such as invertebrates, this is only possible if these species are removed from another site. This will result in the impoverishment of the donor site, and should not therefore be considered unless the donor site is being destroyed for other reasons. Habitat creation should in general only be concerned with vegetation, and other species should be left to colonise naturally. There are minor exceptions to this rule; the introduction of frogspawn or caterpillars will in most cases be acceptable, providing that a substantial quantity is left at the donor site. The translocation of species and / or habitats is risky; thorough guidance should be sought from a professional ecologist and the statutory nature Conservation agencies before translocation is carried out, and one should be mindful of the fact that a special licence is required to translocate many species. NCC (1990b) sets out the NCC policy on species translocation.

Where the destruction of high nature conservation value habitat is inevitable, habitat translocation can be used as one method of mitigation provided that it is used in conjunction with other habitat creation methods as back-up. Additional habitat creation is necessary because it is very difficult to ensure that the donor and receptor site match in ecological terms, and hence difficult to maintain the species composition of translocated habitats. Thorough planning and monitoring of the project is essential (Bullock, 1998), and attempts should be made to rectify unforeseen post-translocation problems.

The creation of an appropriate NVC community type (excluding any non-native species which may be present) should form the goal of a habitat creation scheme designed to benefit nature conservation.

3.2 Selecting habitat type, community type and species

3.2.1 Sources of information

Any existing ecological interest at a site should be identified during the Ecological Impact Assessment (EcIA) process (see Section B). The following other sources of information should also be consulted during the site planning process (in addition to carrying out a full EcIA):

- UK Biodiversity Action Plan
- Relevant Local Biodiversity Action Plans
- Relevant Natural Area Profile(s) (England only)

3.2.2 EcIA information

The value of EcIA to habitat creation design depends on the level of ecological interest present at the site. At sites where there is existing ecological interest, re-creation of this interest should often form the basis for habitat creation design. However, at sites where little ecological interest exists, EcIA is likely to be less valuable to habitat creation design, although there may still be important site-specific information within the EcIA that could be incorporated into site design to increase the quality of habitat creation. Alternative sources of information such as local BAPs or the relevant Natural Area Profile are likely to prove equally important at these sites.

Sites with existing ecological interest

At sites where existing ecological interest is identified, information from the EcIA should form the basis of habitat creation design. In such cases the restoration of the habitats identified at the outset, where technically possible, will almost always be the most appropriate type of habitat creation. Information in the EcIA may also be able to improve the end result, for example through the retention

of key habitat features (even if only in small or peripheral areas). Box E.3.1 describes a number of examples of how information contained in an EcIA may benefit habitat creation.

It will not always be technically possible to re-create habitats present prior to development of landfill sites; for example, wetlands must not be created over biodegradable fill. However, alternative recommendations for potentially suitable habitat creation schemes should be made in the mitigation section of the EcIA. Ecological information will still be valuable; key areas can be identified for retention, and habitat creation designed

around such areas. Information on site-specific characteristics such as soil type and climate may also assist in choosing suitable habitat types. Note that alternative information such as local BAPs and Natural Area Profiles (Sections E.3.2.3-3.2.5) should also be consulted.

Sites with little ecological interest

For many types of development, including landfill, the identification of important habitats in the area surrounding a potential development, in addition to the site itself, should be an integral part of EcIA (see Section B). Consequently, even where little existing ecological information

---

Box E.3.1. Opportunities for EcIA to benefit habitat creation

Retention of key habitats

Areas of habitat retained throughout site operation can add to the success of habitat creation, particularly if integrated into the creation of similar habitats. Retained habitats can increase the speed of colonisation or provide a source of material (e.g. plant seeds or cuttings) to assist the establishment of vegetation on other areas. Such processes can benefit habitat creation by lowering costs, speeding up habitat development and ensuring that the local gene pool of species is conserved. It is the role of the EcIA to suggest the retention of habitat, even if only in very small areas or on the periphery of the site. Failure to retain areas of ecological interest may result in the loss of a great opportunity to improve habitat creation.

Careful phasing of operations to benefit creation

Even on sites where it is not planned to retain habitats, the careful incorporation of ecological information into the design and phasing of operation and restoration can provide great benefits to habitat creation. For example, material from existing habitats of interest can be harvested in advance of development and used in the establishment of vegetation on areas where landfilling has been completed. This does not necessarily imply full-scale translocation, but could simply involve the use of seeds, litter, cuttings, etc. in the creation of similar habitats. Note that the benefits of such techniques can only be realised if the planning of habitat creation and site design is integrated with ecological information and carried out at the earliest possible opportunity.

Choice of appropriate alternative habitats

Certain habitats are very difficult if not impossible to re-create. For example, the retention of rock faces (which may have considerable ecological interest) at a limestone quarry landfill site may conflict with the maximisation of landfill void space. However, by identifying such features before the site is developed it should be possible to incorporate ecological information into habitat creation plans to ensure that the site is restored to an appropriate compensatory after-use. In the case above, for example, it might be appropriate to create limestone grassland.

Integration of creation with habitats in the surrounding area

Identification of ecologically important features in the area surrounding a landfill site should be an integral part of EcIA. This information is essential to ensure that habitat creation is appropriate to the local area. For example, habitat creation may include the extension of adjacent woodland onto the restored site – the creation of buffer habitat adjacent to an existing woodland is likely to be of much greater ecological value than the creation of an isolated woodland block of similar size. Habitat creation that links adjacent blocks of habitat may also increase the conservation value of habitat creation. As in the above examples, it may also be possible to utilise adjacent habitats as 'nursery sites' for restored areas (i.e. as a source of seeds or cuttings).

is identified on the site itself, EcIA information may still be fundamental to the design of habitat creation where important habitats are identified close to a site. In such cases, the most appropriate habitat creation will almost certainly involve the adjacent habitats in some way; it may be possible to create an area of buffer habitat or provide a link between two blocks of similar habitat. In some cases it may even be possible to directly contribute to BAP targets for habitats or species.

Even for sites with no ecological interest and no nearby important habitats, EcIA may still be useful to habitat creation designers by providing an indication of site conditions and suggesting potentially suitable habitat creation schemes. However, alternative sources of information should be consulted in such situations (Sections E.3.2.3-3.2.5).

Existing or old sites

Where habitat creation is being considered at old landfill sites, some form of ecological assessment (if not a full EcIA) is highly recommended prior to restoration works taking place. In this case its main function will be to identify interesting habitats or species that may have developed or colonised since site closure. Features of interest should be incorporated into creation designs if possible, although note that wetlands (which often develop on old sites as a result of differential settlement) may compromise remedial engineering works, and it may not be possible to retain them. Note that some old landfills where ecologically interesting habitats have developed may also have safety hazards which must be dealt with at the expense of the habitat e.g. exposed hazardous materials.

EcIA may also identify habitats of conservation importance in the area surrounding an old landfill site and in this case, as at new sites, restoration that integrates habitat creation with existing habitats of importance should be carried out wherever possible.

Even at existing operational sites at which an EcIA was not prepared, it can be worthwhile carrying out some form of ecological assessment. Unusual habitats and species can exist within an operational landfill site and may, if identified in time, be incorporated into a review of creation design. There is also scope to review creation proposals, particularly where important habitats or species are identified adjacent to the site.

3.2.3 UK Biodiversity Action Plan (UK BAP)

The UK BAP (Anon., 1994) was published by the Government in 1994, in response to commitments following the signing of the Convention on Biological Diversity at the 1992 Rio Earth Summit. The UK Steering Group Report (Anon., 1995), identified 38 priority habitats and around 400 priority species for which detailed conservation action plans should be prepared, most of which have now been published. These habitats and species represent the most important habitats and species in the UK and those most in need of conservation action. In addition, Tranche 2 of the Action Plans was published in 1998 (Anon., 1998).

Each action plan sets out a number of key objectives and targets for the conservation of each habitat or species. Targets are set for several habitats and species relating to the restoration or creation of new habitat. Habitat creation on landfill sites may be able to make a significant contribution to these targets.

Contribution to national targets for some habitats or species will not be appropriate across the whole of the UK. For habitat creation to be appropriate to a specific area, consultation with sources of guidance that are targeted directly at local areas is essential (see Sections E.3.2.4-3.2.5).

3.2.4 Local Biodiversity Action Plans (Local BAPs)

Local BAPs are a key mechanism for achieving national BAP targets for habitats and species. A local BAP should highlight national priority habitats and species most relevant to the local area and specify clear targets for conservation action. Additional habitats and species that are particularly important in a local context should also be highlighted and similar objectives and targets set. Specific areas where the creation of new habitats is most appropriate should be clearly defined through this framework.

For habitat creation planners, consulting the local BAP is essential if benefits to biodiversity conservation are to be maximised. Indeed, the local BAP is actually likely to be of much greater direct relevance than the national BAP to specific sites, as it will only include national BAP targets that are directly relevant to the local area. Furthermore, for the majority of landfill sites, where contribution to national targets is not possible, the provision of targets for habitats and species of importance at a local scale may provide additional opportunities to benefit biodiversity.

Local BAPs exist at a variety of scales.

A local BAP should be published or in preparation at the county or local authority level over most of the UK, and these will be supplemented in many areas by BAPs targeted at specific regions such as National Parks or distinct geographical areas. For example, a local BAP has been produced for the Isle of Purbeck in Dorset in addition to the county level plan in preparation.

Unfortunately, Local BAPs have not yet been produced for the whole of the UK at the time of publication. This is due in part to there being no statutory requirement for their production, and their preparation is consequently dependent to a large extent upon voluntary organisations. However, a draft version should be available in most areas, even where a local BAP has not yet been published. At the very least, a list of priority habitats and species with specified objectives and targets should be available. In the absence of a local BAP (or in addition to it if one has been published), the relevant Natural Area profile should prove very useful (Section E.3.2.5). Note that Natural Areas have only been defined in England and do not apply to Scotland, Wales or Northern Ireland.

3.2.5 Natural Area profiles

The Natural Areas concept involves the division of England into 120 natural areas, identified with reference to ecological and physical characteristics (geology, soils, climate, etc.) rather than political boundaries. Natural Areas are intended to inform the planning process of the most relevant nature conservation issues and concerns in an ecologically and physically coherent area, both through and in addition to local BAPs.

With respect to habitat creation at landfill sites, the Natural Area concept specifically aims to focus conservation effort (including habitat creation) on the right targets for a particular area. This should therefore enable consistent choices to be made throughout England ensuring that targets set at a local level are fully consistent with those set at a national level.

English Nature has produced a profile of each Natural Area. Although the exact format varies, all should contain the following:

- a description of key habitats and species within the Natural Area, with general objectives and targets for the conservation of each; and
- key objectives for conservation in the Natural Area, each of which may be made up of a number of component parts.

Each profile should be fully consistent with national targets for habitats and species with the aim of allocating each national BAP target to the most appropriate Natural Areas. The relevant Natural Area profile is therefore a key source of information to consult during the habitat creation planning process, either in addition to or in conjunction with the local BAP.

3.2.6 Case study illustrating sources of information available for habitat creation planning

The case study below aims to illustrate the types of guidance available to anyone involved in planning habitat creation at landfill sites, in this case within the county of Dorset.

Note that the principal role of the information shown is to highlight opportunities to contribute to national and local conservation targets in the case study region. Published objectives and targets may not actually be achievable at certain sites; site-specific information (such as that provided by EcIA) is also essential.

CASE STUDY: GUIDANCE AVAILABLE TO HABITAT CREATION PLANNERS AT LANDFILL SITES IN DORSET

Local BAPs
- There is currently no published BAP for Dorset.
- The Dorset Biodiversity Initiative has selected 13 priority habitats and species in addition to habitats / species for which national projects exist in the county.
- A BAP has been produced for the Purbeck Area (Barnes, 1997).

Natural Area Profiles
There are four natural areas covering the county of Dorset: Dorset Heaths, South Wessex Downs, Wessex Vales, and Isles of Portland & Purbeck

Conservation objectives & targets of potential relevance to landfill sites in Dorset

Local BAP Targets
- *Dorset Biodiversity Initiative*
  Of the 13 priority habitats and species most are unlikely to be relevant to landfill site creation. Projects to which landfill site creation may be able to contribute are shown below:

Habitat / species	Targets potentially relevant to landfill restoration
Great crested newt	To liaise with landowners and create suitable habitats through pond management

- *Purbeck BAP*
  Habitats identified by the Purbeck BAP with targets to which landfill restoration may be able to contribute are shown below:

Habitat	Targets potentially relevant to landfill restoration
Lowland heathland	Re-establish 970 ha of heathland within the BAP area (750 ha from forestry and 220 ha from other land uses) with a view to linkage and creation of large blocks of habitat
Broad-leaved woodland	Where appropriate enlarge existing woods
Calcareous grassland	Identify areas suitable for re-establishment and linkage and initiate re-establishment programme

Targets relevant to Natural Areas
Although the relevant Natural Area profiles contain similar information, they vary somewhat in style and these differences are reflected in the information presented here. For the purposes of this case study, objectives and targets have been extracted from both the sections relating to habitats and species and the sections covering conservation objectives. Those considered most likely to be relevant to landfill sites are presented.

- *Dorset Heaths Natural Area*
  Key habitats and conservation objectives that may be relevant to landfill site restoration in the natural area are shown below:

Lowland Heathland	
Importance in Natural Area	The Natural Area is of outstanding importance for lowland heathland
Targets potentially relevant to landfill restoration	Re-establish 6000 ha of heathland by 2005 (national BAP target) Take opportunities to re-create heaths so as to relieve pressures on existing heaths, minimise edge effects and maximise linkage. (Natural Area objective)

BAP priority species found in the Natural Area include great crested newt. There may therefore be scope for relevant habitat creation at landfill sites in such areas.

- *Wessex Vales Natural Area*
  Key habitats and conservation objectives that may be relevant to landfill site restoration in the natural area are shown below:

Lowland neutral grassland	
Importance in Natural Area	Natural Area contains a high proportion of the region's unimproved neutral grassland
Targets potentially relevant to landfill restoration	Attempt to re-establish 500ha by 2010 (national BAP target)
Lowland Heathland	
Importance in Natural Area	Locally distributed within natural area
Targets potentially relevant to landfill restoration	Re-establish 6000 ha of heathland by 2005 (national BAP target)
Habitat corridors	
Targets potentially relevant to landfill restoration	Encourage the creation and maintenance of corridors such as field margins and copses on agriculturally improved land

CASE STUDY continued

The Profile also identifies the presence of great crested newts within the natural area, and there may therefore be scope for habitat creation to benefit this species.

- *South Wessex Downs Natural Area*
  Key habitats and conservation objectives that may be relevant to landfill site restoration in the natural area are shown below:

Chalk grassland	
Importance in Natural Area	Dominant semi-natural habitat Natural Area contains >60% of UK chalk grassland
Targets potentially relevant to landfill restoration	Extend chalk grassland and link existing sites by restoration and re-creation in appropriate areas

Broadleaved and yew woodland	
Importance in Natural Area	Natural Area has relatively high importance for ancient semi-natural woodland
Targets potentially relevant to landfill restoration	Extend and link woodland habitats to reduce fragmentation of ancient woodland: promote natural regeneration or appropriate planting in appropriate sites

Acid and Neutral grassland	
Importance in Natural Area	Only occupy a small area but formerly key component in the range of chalk-associated habitats
Targets potentially relevant to landfill restoration	Re-create habitats where appropriate, preferably adjacent to existing semi-natural habitats in order to reduce habitat fragmentation

Other targets
Carry out relevant research to understand ecosystems as basis for habitat and species conservation, restoration and re-creation/re-establishment

- *Isles of Portland & Purbeck Natural Area*
  Key habitats and conservation objectives that may be relevant to landfill site restoration in the natural area are shown below:

Calcareous grassland	
Importance in Natural Area	Most extensive semi-natural habitat in the natural area
Targets potentially relevant to landfill restoration	Restore selected areas of degraded calcareous grassland by buffering and linking sites

Implications for landfill developments in Dorset

There are at least 9 landfill sites in Dorset (Aspinwall & Co., 1998). The implications for habitat creation at landfill sites located in each natural area are outlined below.

- *Dorset Heaths*
  Five sites, covering a total area of 125 ha, are located within the Dorset Heaths Natural Area. Restoration of all these sites to heathland is likely to be the most appropriate after-use, with the potential to make a major contribution to BAP targets.
  There may also be scope to create habitat for great crested newts at sites within the Natural Area if the location is suitable. Reference to site-specific information is required.

- *Wessex Vales*
  Two sites are located within the Wessex Vales Natural Area in Dorset. It may be desirable to create neutral grassland or heathland on these sites, although EcIA information is necessary to confirm this. If neither of the sites are located in suitable areas for this, the creation of corridors and copses within an otherwise agricultural restoration may provide the greatest realistic benefit to biodiversity.
  Great crested newts are found in the Natural Area and there may therefore be scope for pond creation in line with the Dorset Biodiversity Initiative targets.

- *South Wessex Downs*
  Only one Dorset landfill site is located within this Natural Area. Options for habitat creation at the site are very much dependent on its location and proximity to areas of the priority habitats, which is not known. However, if close to any of the priority habitats listed, appropriate habitat creation could certainly contribute to targets through the creation of linking habitat and the extension of existing sites. Such a scheme could also contribute to research into habitat re-creation techniques – another natural area objective.

- *Isles of Portland and Purbeck*
  Only one controlled waste landfill site is located in this Natural Area, although it is known that a number of further sites, mostly taking inert wastes, are located on Portland. The most appropriate form of habitat creation at this site is likely to be the creation of calcareous grassland, which could contribute to re-establishment targets in the Purbeck BAP. Once again the extent of the contribution is dependent on the site's location in relation to areas of existing grassland – this information should be included within an EcIA for the site.

3.2.7 Selection of communities and species

Once an appropriate broad habitat type for creation has been selected, the second stage is to select the appropriate community type (e.g. wet grassland, neutral grassland, acid grassland). For this stage, attention must be paid to site characteristics, particularly soil pH. This will determine which species can survive on the site and thus the community type which can be created. If local and naturally occurring materials are used for initial restoration, creation of local habitat types will not be too difficult to achieve.

However, at some landfill sites, locally-occurring restoration materials may not be available. This therefore requires the use of imported soils or soil forming materials (Section F.1.2.4) which may create a different combination of environmental factors to those under which semi-natural habitats would normally occur. In such cases, the use of nurse species (Section F.1.6.2) may be required to create suitable conditions for the creation of a particular community type.

For instance, official advice states that 1.5 m depth of soil must be provided over a clay cap if woodland is planned on a landfill site (Environment Agency, in prep.). It is unlikely that enough soil will be available to cover an entire site to a depth of 1.5 m, and soil forming materials may therefore have to be used. Many of these are highly infertile when immature, and characteristic woodland trees may well not survive on such substrates. To overcome this problem, stress-tolerant nurse species should be used that ameliorate and condition the soil. However, many of the best nurse species are alien to the British flora (e.g. grey alder). This is due to the fact that the conditions occurring on a landfill site restored with soil forming materials have a greater resemblance to Mediterranean dry soil habitats than those suitable for British species.

Using alien species is contrary to the fundamental principles of habitat creation. However, an alien species can perform the valuable function of speeding up the natural weathering process of the rooting material and hastening habitat development. If there is no indigenous species capable of performing this function, the introduction of alien species can be justified, provided that the species do not persist on a permanent basis.

A firm commitment to appropriate long-term management must be made.

The nature of the management should be identical to the traditional management regime under which that specific community developed, i.e. a hay meadow should be managed as a hay meadow and not used for permanent grazing. Failure to adopt the correct management for the required NVC community will result in the loss of many species, and the created habitat will bear little resemblance to the desired community.

Species selection

When the appropriate community type has been selected, the species to be introduced can be obtained from the constancy tables of NVC communities given in the various NVC volumes (Rodwell, 1991 *et seq.*). See Box E.3.2 for more information.

An attempt to create an exact replicate of an NVC type could prove costly, especially if there is no local seed source (see Box E.3.3). Probably the best alternative in the absence of a local seed source is to purchase seed from a commercial supplier. Species should be purchased individually rather than bought in a ready-made seed mix to ensure that the species sown are adapted to the site and that only the desired species are introduced.

If the NVC cannot be used as a template for the species to be introduced (i.e. if the conditions on the site are different to those under which NVC communities would naturally develop), an NVC community can still be used as a framework. The choice of species would need to be altered to suit the constraints of the landfill site. Local sites of nature conservation interest can be used as a template from which to compile a species list and copy the management employed.

In all cases, and regardless of whether an existing site or an NVC description of a habitat is used as a model for the habitat to be created, it is essential that detailed ecological advice is sought at the outset on both the type of habitat to be created, the species to be included and the most appropriate long-term management for that habitat.

Guidelines have been developed for the selection of species to be used as a seed source or included within a seed mix (Wells *et al.,* 1981). These guidelines can be used to assist the selection of species for any habitat type, and if followed will result in the creation of a habitat with the maximum inherent nature conservation value.

(i) Species should be regular members of that habitat (i.e. not rare or only occasionally associated).

(ii) They should be relatively abundant in a variety of types of that habitat, preferably with a wide distribution in the British Isles and be a native member of the British flora.

(iii) They should be perennial, preferably long-lived and with an effective means of vegetative spread.

(iv) A high proportion of the species used should have colourful flowers, and these should preferably be attractive to insects.

(v) Highly competitive and invasive species known to form single-species stands in the wild should be avoided.

(vi) The seed should have a high percentage germination over a range of temperatures and should not have dormancy problems or special requirements (see Section F.2.4.2).

It should be borne in mind that natural habitats comprise a range of plants from a variety of different groups such as trees, shrubs, grasses, sedges, herbs and rushes. Relevant species from all these groups should be included (although sedges and rushes are not widely available). The greater the diversity of plants, the greater the resultant diversity of animals associated with the habitat. Alien species support far fewer insects than native species, so a bias towards native species will have greater overall biodiversity benefit. For example, the native pedunculate oak supports 284 invertebrate species whereas the alien sycamore supports only 15 (Baines & Smart, 1991). A variety of colours and heights also increases visual attractiveness and is more likely to produce year-round interest (Wells et al., 1981). Lists of common species associated with the various habitats are given in Sections F.2-6. An important point to note is that a seed mix for a habitat need not contain a large number of species. The selection of a limited number of species that are well suited to the site should be sufficient to start the process of habitat development. Provided that the habitat is managed carefully (i.e. colonisation niches are present and fertility levels do not become to high), species diversity should eventually increase through natural colonisation.

Box E.3.2. The National Vegetation Classification system (NVC)

The NVC provides a comprehensive and systematic catalogue and description of the plant communities of Britain. It relates these vegetation types to the environmental conditions and management practices that shape the vegetation, and indicates trends that may occur due to natural processes and changes in management. It is designed to be a working tool for conservation agencies, land managers and anyone concerned with the diversity and management of British vegetation.

The NVC covers all natural, semi-natural and the major artificial habitats in Britain, and is presented in five volumes: woodland and scrub, grassland and montane, heath and mire, aquatic, swamp and fen, and coastal and open (disturbed) vegetation types (Rodwell, 1991 *et seq.*).

Each broad habitat type is divided into a range of vegetation communities. For example, grasslands are split into 48 vegetation communities. Each community is a readily identifiable assemblage of species which arises wherever the same environmental factors (e.g. soil pH, water levels) and management regimes occur.

Many communities are further divided into sub-communities and variants depending on the presence of species peculiar to a subcommunity (termed preferential species). These sub-communities often evolve through slight differences in environmental factors or management regimes.

The use of the NVC in habitat creation

Throughout this book it is recommended that habitat creation should aim to create a known NVC type (i.e. a naturally occurring species assemblage) rather than a selection of species which would not naturally be found together. The range of potential NVC communities can appear to be overwhelming, and advice is therefore given in the habitat-specific sections of this book (F.2-5) on how to select an appropriate NVC type. Advice is also given on how to select species from a chosen NVC type, primarily based on floristic tables. The use of floristic tables to select the most appropriate species is described below.

Other uses of the NVC

The NVC has other applications in the context of habitat creation. It can yield:

- appropriate vegetation types and species assemblages for a given location (some NVC communities are geographically   restricted, and it would be inappropriate to create these outside their natural range);

- information on management regimes and practices necessary to maintain a given NVC community; and
- information on changes to that are likely to occur to unmanaged vegetation or the effects of various management regimes.

NVC surveys

To determine an NVC community, five representative samples are taken within a homogeneous stand of vegetation. The samples are usually square quadrats, their size reflecting the scale of the vegetation (e.g. grassland is surveyed with 2 m x 2 m quadrats, whereas woodland canopy is surveyed with 50 m x 50 m quadrats). The percentage cover of each species within a quadrat is recorded, and the frequency of each species is calculated from its occurrence in the five samples. This data is then tabulated to form floristic tables, described in more detail below.

For more information on the use of frequency and cover estimates for botanical recording, consult Kent & Coker (1992) and Shimwell (1971). For more detail on the NVC, see Rodwell (1991 *et seq.*).

Floristic tables

An integral part of each NVC community description is the floristic table. This lists all the species that are associated with a community type, presented as a table divided into blocks of constant, preferential and associated species. These tables also provide the range of frequency and abundance scores associated with each species for each community and subcommunity.

Woodland and scrub community tables are structured slightly differently due to the three-dimensional structure of the canopy, shrub and field layers. For these communities, trees and shrubs are presented in a separate table from the field layer.

Not all species listed in the NVC are native. Non-native trees and shrubs are commonly planted in British woodlands, and in many cases have become characteristic members of vegetation communities. The NVC is a classification of existing habitats, and thus reflects historic and current management techniques. Only native species should be included in the species list for habitat creation.

The structure of an NVC floristic table

	Subcommunity a	Subcommunity b	Summary of all species records
Constant Species	Frequency and DOMIN range	Frequency and DOMIN range	Frequency and DOMIN range
Preferential species for subcommunity a	Frequency and DOMIN range	Frequency and DOMIN range	Frequency and DOMIN range
Preferential species for subcommunity b	Frequency and DOMIN range	Frequency and DOMIN range	Frequency and DOMIN range
Associate species	Frequency and DOMIN range	Frequency and DOMIN range	Frequency and DOMIN range

Constant species

Constant species are the core species that occur frequently in a vegetation assemblage. Frequency is a measure of how often a species is found within any number of representative samples of the community type. Each species is assigned to one of five constancy classes denoted by the roman numerals: I-V, with the most frequent species assigned to constancy class V (see below). The constant (core) species for a community are those species that are found in 80 to 100% of samples (constancy classes IV or V).

NVC constancy classes

Constancy class	Percentage of samples in which a species occurs
V	81-100 % (Constant species)
IV	61-80 % (Constant species)
III	41-60 % (Common species)
II	21-40 % (Occasional species)
I	1-20 % (Scarce species)

Constant species are the 'backbone' of NVC communities and are therefore of great importance for habitat creation. Use of these constant species helps to ensure that the created habitat is similar in species composition to a natural or semi-natural habitat. Where possible, all the constant species should be included. If one is unavailable, it is preferable to omit the species from the mix entirely rather than attempting to use another species as a substitute.

The proportion (or abundance) of each species in the community is also important. The NVC discriminates between frequent and abundant species and frequent species which occur in small quantities. Abundance is measured using percentage cover and expressed using the DOMIN scale (see below). The NVC indicates the range of abundance for each species within a vegetation assemblage. This abundance range should be used to estimate the proportions of each species in the final species mix for habitat creation. It is likely that specialist advice will be required to translate proportions expressed in terms of percentage cover into weight of seed per hectare or percentage of species seed per kg of seed mix.

Domin scale	Equivalent percentage cover
10	91 - 100%
9	76 - 90%
8	51 - 75%
7	34 - 50%
6	26 - 33%
5	11 - 25%
4	4 - 10%
3	<4% - frequent
2	<4% - occasional
1	<4% - rare
+	Insignificant – normally 1 - 2 individuals with no measurable cover

Preferential species

Preferential species are used to determine which subcommunity is present. For example, a species may only be associated with one of several sub-communities, or may be much more frequent in one subcommunity.

The preferential species of a subcommunity can be used as optional species in the design of a species mix, enabling the species mix to be a more realistic representation of a particular subcommunity. This might be particularly relevant in areas where a particular subcommunity is prevalent.

Associate species

Associate species are those that are part of the community but with low abundance and irregular occurrence. These species do not necessarily have to be included in a seed mix as they contribute little to the overall structure of the community being created.

Box E.3.3. Native provenance

The importance of using only native species in habitat creation schemes cannot be over-emphasised. Alien species can be very invasive, as has been demonstrated by several notorious examples including Himalayan balsam (*Impatiens glandulifera*), New Zealand pygmyweed (*Crassula helmsii*), Canadian pondweed (*Elodea canadensis*) and Japanese knotweed (*Fallopia japonica*).

Species native to Britain are also likely to be native to other parts of Europe. However, British species have been isolated from mainland European stock for up to 4 million years (Gilbert & Anderson, 1998), and strains of the same species from different areas are genetically distinct from one another. This genetic variation may manifest itself physically through characteristics such as leaf size, bud burst timing or degree of frost tolerance. These different strains resulting from different climatic or locational influences are termed ecotypes.

To maintain within-species genetic diversity, it is desirable that European ecotypes are not introduced to Britain. The possible consequences of such introductions are:

- the direct replacement of British ecotypes by European ones with a consequent reduction of the diversity and uniqueness of the British flora.
- the pollination of British strains by European ones, again leading to a reduction in genetic diversity; and
- hybridisation between closely related species, again reducing diversity.

Planting non-native species or strains can also reduce the conservation value of habitat creation. For example, if the flowering time of a non-native strain differs from the native strain, there may be effects on butterflies that time their emergence to coincide with flowering. This could then have knock-on effects on other species. The planting of non-native strains should therefore be avoided.

Local provenance

Genetic variation within species also exists on a much smaller scale than that of countries. Various ecotypes of a substantial number of species exist within Britain. These local populations develop in response to local conditions such as climate and altitude. If non-local strains are planted in an area where local ecotypes exist, the genetic diversity of the local forms may be diluted or lost. The conservation of biodiversity at the genetic level, as well as the species level, is a central aim of the UK Biodiversity Action Plan.

Rare species and natural distributions

There is a need to distinguish between species that are naturally rare because they possess very specific habitat requirements, and those that are rare due to the widespread loss of their characteristic habitat. Regardless of the reason for rarity, the planting of rare species is generally not recommended. There are many reasons for this, but briefly, a small population is more vulnerable to genetic depletion than a larger one. The genetic integrity of wild individuals is threatened if widespread planting of commercially cloned individuals is carried out. Furthermore, increasing a dwindling population is a complex procedure and not within the remit of general habitat creation. Our ecological knowledge of rare species and the reasons why they are rare

is often poor. Introductions would not be guaranteed to succeed, and therefore constitute a waste of resources (Soutar & Peterken, 1989).

The vast majority of species are not ubiquitous, and their distributions are governed by factors such as climate and soil type. Planting species outside their natural ranges erodes the local and regional character and composition of habitats. Finally, species distributions are of scientific interest; the artificial expansion of ranges confuses scientific research and also conflicts with the fundamental principles of nature conservation.

The Forestry Commission recommends that only local stock should be used in new planting and that detailed records should be kept of the seed source. To ensure local provenance, they further recommend that the seed should be collected from semi-natural stands no further than 10 miles away from where the stock is to be planted.
It is <u>essential</u> to obtain local provenance stock of the following species: Scots pine (*Pinus sylvestris*), alder (*Alnus glutinosa*) and aspen (*Populus tremula*).

In terms of best practice, the following woody species should not be planted in a habitat creation scheme (Gilbert & Anderson, 1998). They are unsuitable for planting either because wild individuals are at risk from genetic contamination, or because their natural distribution is limited.

Juniper *Juniperus communis*
Midland hawthorn *Crategeus laevigata*
Whitebeam *Sorbus aria*
Black poplar *Populus nigra*
Small-leaved lime *Tilia cordata*
Yew *Taxus baccata*
Large-leaved lime *Tilia platyphyllos*
Plymouth pear *Pyrus cordata*
Wild service tree *Sorbus torminalis*
Box *Buxus sempervirens*

Virtually all of the British native grasses have been genetically altered. As a result there are very few pure grass species left in the wild, as most have been affected by cross-pollination with altered strains (Flora Locale, 1999). It is therefore generally not feasible to obtain grass seed of local provenance. The best practice is to use commercially available seed, and direct resources towards obtaining local provenance herb species.

In recent years, the seeds of several native herb species used in wildflower seed mixes have been derived from cultivated agricultural varieties rather than the wild forms. These varieties are often substantially larger and more aggressive, and tend to dominate the sward unless frequently managed. Cultivars may not survive on infertile soil, whereas the wild forms are more likely to succeed. Cultivated forms are also often lacking in nectar; bumblebees cannot feed on cultivars of red clover (Flora Locale, 1999). It is therefore important that only wild forms of herbs are included in seed mixes rather than cultivated fodder varieties.

A selection of species widely included in 'wildflower' mixes that are actually aggressive agricultural strains is given below (Akeroyd, 1994).

Agricultural strains of herb species commonly included in wildflower seed mixes

Alsike clover *Trifolium hybridum*
Oxeye daisy *Leucanthemum vulgare*
Bird's-foot trefoil *Lotus corniculatus*
Red clover *Trifolium pratense*
Black medick *Medicago lupulina*
Sainfoin *Onobrychis viciifolia*
Corn marigold *Chrysanthemum segetum*
Salad burnet *Sanguisorba minor*
Kidney vetch *Anthyllis vulneraria*
White clover *Trifolium repens*
Lesser trefoil *Trifolium dubium*
Yarrow *Achillea millefolium*

Summary of best practice

Ideally, the contract specification for habitat creation should stipulate that all plant material must be:

1. of native origin;
2. (for herbs) of local provenance;
3. (for herbs) of wild strains (not cultivated varieties);
4. (for grasses) of an appropriate cultivated variety (i.e. not an aggressive cultivar) or a wild form; and
5. restricted to common and widespread species within their natural ranges.

If the habitat creation scheme is adjacent to a site of nature conservation importance, or an existing semi-natural site is to be expanded, the most important consideration is to protect the integrity of the existing habitat by using plants of local provenance.

The most appropriate method to achieve this would be to allow the site to vegetate by natural colonisation. However, the rapid establishment of vegetation is required on landfill sites, and the best option is therefore to establish vegetation by using seed harvested from adjacent or nearby sites of conservation interest. This avoids the need to purchase commercial seed that, even with the best intentions, may be contaminated with agriculturally manipulated strains or alien genetic stock.

If the habitat creation scheme is greater than 10 miles from a site of conservation importance, other methods of species introduction can be employed and it is acceptable to use stock of non-local provenance if local provenance stock is limited.

Practical problems

There are several practical problems regarding the use of local provenance stock. The first is availability. Many garden centres and nurseries sell genetically identical clones that have been propagated from a single stock plant (Flora Locale, 1999). Thus it is can be very difficult to obtain genetically diverse local stock unless the nursery has a practice of regularly collecting new stock from the wild. The number of nurseries supplying local stock is limited, and in general two seasons notice should be given to the nursery if large amounts of local stock are required. Ideally, a system such as that operated by the Forestry Commission should be used where seed stock is matched with the planting site and grown to order.

Due to its limited availability, local provenance stock is generally more expensive (although not always; seed harvested from a local meadow may be much cheaper than commercial seed). With compulsory competitive tendering, the contractor may substitute freely available non-local stock for local provenance stock even if local provenance is requested in the specification. This can be avoided by buying in the stock for the contractor to plant (Gilbert & Anderson, 1998).

Local provenance material is superior to commercial stock in that local plants are more likely to be adapted to local conditions. Although initially more expensive, the use of local stock will reap economic benefits in the long term, as the species are more likely to survive and flourish, thus avoiding the need for supplementary planting.

Recent developments

Forestry Commission

The Forestry Commission have developed a stock labelling system to enable the identification of locally sourced stock for planting of native trees and shrubs. The system is based upon local seed zones (Figure F.3.3 and Herbert *et al.* (1999)) and the labelling of seeds and plants with the zone within which they were collected. This initiative is relevant to all tree and woody shrub species native to Britain.

The system recognises a difference between local provenance and local origin. Provenance is the location where the reproductive material was collected, whereas the origin is where that genetic stock originated. These are likely to be the same for naturally colonised individuals, but will be different for planted stock.

There are four regions of provenance, numbered 10, 20, 30 and 40. These regions have been subdivided to give local seed zones using information on climate and geological variation. Elevation is also important; a threshold of 300 m is used to divide upland and lowland sites. A seed source should be selected from the seed zone containing the site (see also F.3.3.3).

Flora Locale

Flora Locale is a non-profit making organisation established to promote and enhance the conservation of native wild plant populations and plant communities. Their website www.naturebureau.co.uk/pages/floraloc/floraloc.htm is a good source of information and advice regarding many aspects of habitat creation. In particular, Flora Locale are working toward the establishment of a Code of Practice for collectors, suppliers and growers of native plants and seed, with the intention that this should become an industry standard for the specification, marketing and sale of native plant species. They are also currently working with the HTA to revise the system used for the specification of plant materials.

Factors affecting the suitability of species

The environmental conditions occurring at a site must match the ecological requirements of a species for it to be suitable for introduction. It is possible to alter some environmental conditions such as drainage or soil pH, but these alterations often prove very costly and may well only have a short-term effect Gilbert & Anderson (1998). Some conditions such as climate cannot be manipulated. The site should therefore dictate the choice of species to a great extent. The most important factors acting on the site can be described as '*determining factors*' and directly affect which species will survive. The main factors are:

- **Soil.** This is the most important factor, and particularly notable parameters are:
    - pH (acid, neutral or calcareous);
    - type (e.g. brown earth, sandy, loamy, clayey);
    - drainage (waterlogged or free draining);
    - nutrient levels (high, medium or low for both macronutrients – nitrogen, phosphorous and potassium – and micronutrients); and
    - depth.
- **Aspect** (south-facing etc.).
- **Climate.**
- **Geographical location** (north, south).

It is important to sample the soil used for site restoration to determine these characteristics. If soil originating from various sources has been imported on to the site, it is likely that variables such as pH and nutrient status will differ from place to place. Soil testing should therefore be conducted across the entire site.

In contrast, '*constraining factors*' are those that will act to prevent something taking place. For instance a lack of sufficient topsoil will preclude the creation of agricultural grassland over large areas (even if the soil that is available is suitable for the growth of the species necessary to create the grassland), as it is hard to adequately substitute topsoil structure and nutrient content. Constraining factors relevant to habitat creation on landfill are covered in Section D.5.2.

3.3 Habitat creation strategies

There are four strategies of habitat creation (Jones, 1990; Simmons, 1992b; Simmons, 1999). These are:

1. Non-intervention, allowing the vegetation to develop as a result of natural processes.

2. Allowing the natural development of vegetation with some management input.
3. Initial intervention followed by natural unmanaged development of the vegetation.
4. Full intervention and management to produce a target community.

Intervention is the planting or sowing of species, whereas management involves removing unwanted species or controlling the vigour of the vegetation to allow less aggressive species to remain part of the assemblage. The cost of habitat creation and the degree of technical input required increases from strategy 1 to 4, but the quality of the habitat creation is not necessarily proportional to the cost. What is proportional is the length of time involved between the habitat comprising a raw assemblage of species concentrated in one space and becoming a complex functioning community.

The slow and uncertain nature of habitat development associated with strategies 1 and 2 is likely to make them unsuitable in many landfill situations. If a site is left to vegetate naturally, soil erosion and increased rainwater infiltration are likely, which may have impacts on the integrity of the cap. The landscape implications of the site remaining unvegetated for a substantial period must also be considered.

Strategies 3 and 4 are more likely to be acceptable on landfill sites, although the exact strategy employed will be largely dependent on the nature of the habitat created. For example, strategy 3 will probably be suitable for the creation of most wetland habitats, which often require little on-going management. Conversely, strategy 4 is likely to be more suitable for habitats such as species-rich grassland or heathland for which a degree of on-going management is essential if their conservation interest is to be maintained.

3.4 Management

Management guidelines given in Section F.2-6 are general and based upon the management required to maintain desired vegetation communities. It is possible to manage a habitat for specific objectives such as enhancing the attractiveness of the habitat for butterflies or increasing populations of a rare species. However, it should be noted that management to benefit one species or group may often have adverse effects on other groups. For example, cutting a grassland for hay will benefit overall botanical diversity but could destroy valuable habitat for field

spiders. This illustrates the desirability of subdividing the site and catering for different groups by altering the management between each area.

Detailed guidance on habitat management is beyond the scope of this book. Consult the references in Box E.3.4 for more information. In addition, it is recommended that a qualified ecologist is consulted on such an important subject as the most appropriate method of management. Management should be closely linked to site monitoring; if the results of monitoring identifies an undesirable change in the species composition of the habitat, management should be used to rectify this change. Ecological advice will be required to interpret monitoring results and specify what remedial management (if any) is required. Guidance on monitoring created habitats is given in Mitchley *et al.* (2000).

Box E.3.4. Reference sources for habitat management.

Brooks (1984). *Woodlands: a practical handbook.*
Duffey *et al.* (1974). *Grassland ecology and wildlife management.*
English Nature and the Wildlife Trusts (1999). *The lowland grassland
 management handbook.*
Gilbert & Anderson (1998). *Habitat & creation and repair.*
Gimingham (1992). *The lowland heathland management handbook.*
Rowell (1988). *The peatland management handbook.*
RSPB/EN/ITE. *The wet grassland guide.*
RSPB/NRA/RSNC (1994). *The new rivers and wildlife handbook.*
Sutherland & Hill (1995). *Managing habitats for conservation.*
Warren & Fuller (1990). *Coppice woodlands: their management for wildlife.*
Watkins (1990). *Woodland management and conservation.*

SECTION F

Practical guidance on habitat creation

This section focuses on providing practical guidelines on the creation of habitats on landfill sites. Section F.1 provides an introduction to soils, one of the most critical aspects of any habitat creation scheme, and some of the key issues concerning the establishment of vegetation. Sections F.2 to F.6 deal with the creation of woodland, grassland, heathland, wetland and agricultural landscape features.

These sections briefly describe the objectives for creating habitats in terms of UK BAP targets and other objectives such as landscape amenity value. The habitat creation guidelines given in this chapter focus on creating habitats that approximate to semi-natural NVC communities which can in principle contribute towards national or local BAP targets for habitats or species. It is worth noting here that habitat creation should be viewed in a long-term context, and that one should not necessarily expect habitat creation on landfill to exhibit immediate results in terms of creating BAP priority habitats such as calcareous grassland. This in no way implies that habitat creation has no short-term conservation benefits, as the habitats created will benefit a range of species almost from the outset, even if the habitat does not initially resemble the desired NVC community. As described in Section E.2, the creation of buffer or linking habitat between areas of conservation importance will have direct benefit for the dispersal of mobile species. Furthermore, as the habitat develops over time, and providing that appropriate and adequate management is applied to that habitat, it is very likely that species will colonise from nearby areas, thereby increasing conservation value, and increasing the similarity of the created habitat to the desired semi-natural habitat. Aiming for the creation of semi-natural habitats from the outset of site restoration will maximise biodiversity benefits in the long term.

1 Soil and vegetation

This section is intended to be of practical assistance; however, the advice is of a general nature, and there may well be site-specific problems that are not addressed in sufficient detail. Professional advice should be sought if necessary, especially on matters such as soil amelioration or manipulation. Regular soil testing is essential to gain a baseline and assess the nature of the untreated soil, and also as a monitoring method in order to decide when habitat creation should commence.

1.1 Introduction to soils

1.1.1 The soil profile

In an undisturbed soil such as in an ancient woodland site that has never been ploughed, the soil forms distinct layers. These layers are termed *horizons*; a vertical section through the soil will reveal the various horizons that make up the soil profile. The *soil profile* extends from the parent material (usually bedrock) to the soil surface (often an organic litter layer).

The uppermmost layer is the O horizon, consisting of decomposed and decomposing organic matter. Below this is the A horizon, consisting of topsoil. This layer is generally characterised by a dark colour (indicating high organic matter and moisture content) and good crumbly structure.

The A horizon merges into the B horizon, the subsoil, which is less rich in organic materials and less fertile, and is usually beyond the rooting zone of vegetation.

The B horizon merges into the C horizon, the underlying parent material of the soil, which is often bedrock. The upper part of the C horizon is often considerably weathered, and merges gradually into unaltered rock.

1.1.2 Soil formation

Soil is formed from its parent material by the action of physical and chemical weathering. It is further influenced by biological and chemical processes acting within the soil profile such as the activity of soil organisms (e.g. bacteria and invertebrates such as earthworms) and chemical reactions such as oxidisation and reduction.

Physical weathering is the action of the forces of expansion and contraction induced by diurnal and seasonal temperature variations, causing rock to shatter over long periods. Chemical weathering is the dissolution and removal of rock minerals by water. Water is a natural solvent, and its ability to dissolve minerals is increased by the dissolution of carbon dioxide into rainwater, forming weak carbonic acid.

Soil consists of two main elements, a mineral fraction and an organic matter fraction, described briefly in Sections F.1.1.3 and F.1.1.4 below. For additional background information on soils, consult Halley (1982).

1.1.3 The mineral fraction

The mineral fraction is divided into three groups according to particle size: sand, silt and clay. Soils can also be classified according to mineral composition, but this is related to particle size. The size classes are:

- Sand: the largest particle size (60-2000 mm), largely inert and derived in chemically unaltered state from rock. Sandy soils are well drained, drought-prone and relatively infertile.
- Silt: particle size 2-60 mm. Silty soils are generally not fine enough to be very fertile and are also liable to waterlogging. They have intermediate properties between clay and sand.
- Clay: particle size less than 2 mm. Clay soils are frequently poorly drained but often very rich in nutrients. They can hold large amounts of water, although much of it is held in a form unavailable to plants. Clay soils are prone to drought and shrinkage during dry

weather (large cracks form in clay soils when they dry out).

Soils usually comprise a mixture of the three particles in varying proportions (Figure F.1.1). Loam is an ideal soil, consisting of equal amounts of sand, silt and clay. A sandy loam soil is required for habitats that cannot tolerate compaction (such as arable), or are likely to be subject to heavy use (such as amenity areas).

Soils with a high clay content are very susceptible to compaction if badly laid, and are therefore best avoided for most habitat creation schemes, particularly woodland, as they are generally poorly aerated and thus inhibit root growth (Dobson & Moffat, 1995b). Clay soils are, however, appropriate for wetland creation. Clay soils can be improved through the addition and mixing of sand.

Sandy soils can also be problematic as they are prone to drought, particularly if there is a high stone content. Where tree planting is planned, current guidance states that the maximum stone content of soil should be less than 40%, with few stones greater than 100 mm in size. (Moffat & Bending, 1992). The droughtiness of sandy soils can be alleviated by the addition of organic matter (see Section F.1.3.3).

Whether topsoil or subsoil is used for habitat creation, the soil texture standards adopted by the landscaping profession can be used as a guide. The recommended proportions of each of the soil particle types are 20-75% sand, 5-60% silt and 5-30% clay (British Standard BS 1377).

1.1.4 The organic matter fraction

Soil organic matter derives from material such decomposed roots and leaves. It contributes to the creation and stabilisation of soil structure, and contributes significantly to the amount of available nutrients within the soil and the water holding capacity (Simpson & Jefferson, 1996).

1.2 Recommended soil depth for habitat creation on landfill sites

Recommended minimum soil depths for different types of habitat creation on different types of landfill site are given in Table F.1.1.

If woodland is to be created, current official guidance states that 1.5 m of soil should be provided above a clay cap (1 m above a synthetic cap) to serve as an adequate rooting depth (Environment Agency, in prep.). Although certain habitats may well be able to survive and flourish on as little as 200 mm of soil, a depth of at least 500 mm – 1 m is required, depending on the nature of the buried waste and the cap/pollution control infrastructure.

On old landfill sites, a 1 m depth of soil / subsoil is needed in order to reduce the risk of contaminants in the fill coming to the surface (e.g. as a result of cultivation, frost heave or rabbit burrowing).

The provision of such soil depths across an entire landfill site requires a huge volume of soil. This requirement for soil resources presents one of the greatest challenges to landfill restoration and subsequent habitat creation, even at sites that have carefully conserved all on-site soil resources. Note however that the use of topsoil is likely to preclude the creation of many nature conservation after-uses due to its high level of fertility, and therefore large quantities of expensive topsoil will not generally be required.

The provision of sufficient soil resources may be addressed in one of the following ways:
1. restricting deep soil cover to certain areas;
2. using imported topsoil;
3. using subsoil; and
4. using materials that produce soil (soil forming materials).

Using subsoil (option 3) is generally the preferred option for habitat creation, although option 4 may be more practicable depending on available resources. The options are considered in further detail in Sections F.1.2.1-F.1.2.4 below.

Landfill sites (especially old sites) may fall within the remit of the Derelict Land Grant (DLG) to fund remedial works such as the importation and spreading of soil materials and planting and establishment of vegetation (Dobson & Moffat, 1995a).

1.2.1 Restricting deep soil cover to certain areas

To conserve available soil, a deep soil layer can be placed only where essential according to standard guidance (e.g. where trees are to be planted). This must be planned at the earliest possible stage, and the locations of various habitats to be created and the depths of soil they require should be considered. This enables the volume of soil needed for restoration and creation to be reduced compared with the volume required to cover the entire site to a depth of 1.5 m.

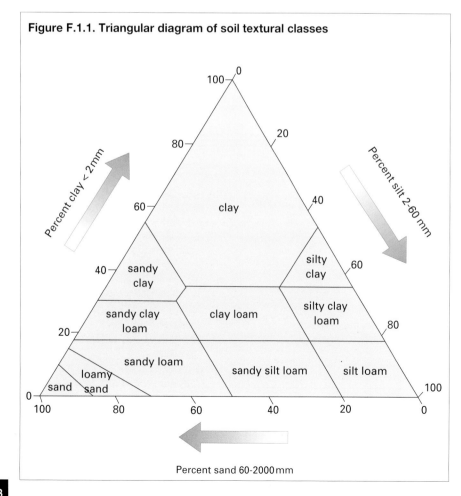

Figure F.1.1. Triangular diagram of soil textural classes

Percent clay < 2mm

Percent silt 2-60 mm

clay

sandy clay

silty clay

sandy clay loam

clay loam

silty clay loam

sandy loam

sandy silt loam

silt loam

loamy sand

sand

Percent sand 60-2000mm

Table F.1.1. Recommended minimum (settled) soil depths required for habitat creation (Environment Agency, in prep.)

After-use	Landfill type	Subsoil	Topsoil
Greenfield agricultural land (arable and productive grassland)	Capped with gas control	800 mm over the top of the gas pipes	200 mm[1]
Productive arable land (arable and productive grassland)	Inert waste	800 mm	200 mm[1]
Low productivity agricultural land (grazing)	Capped with gas control	350 mm over the top of the gas pipes, increased to 500 mm if topsoil is absent	150 mm[2]
	Inert waste	350-500 mm	150 mm[2]
Amenity/open space intensive use (may require drainage)	Capped with gas control	800 mm over the top of the gas pipes	150 mm
	Inert waste	500 mm	150 mm
Amenity / open space (low intensity use/no drainage)	Capped with gas control	500 mm over the top of the gas pipes	150 mm
	Inert waste	500 mm	150 mm
Nature conservation	Capped with gas control	500 mm subsoil	None
	Inert waste	500 mm subsoil	None
Woodland / tree planted areas	Clay cap with gas control	1.5 m subsoil	Not required
	Synthetic cap with gas control	1 m subsoil	Not required
	Inert waste	500 mm subsoil	Not required

1 – or pre-working depth whichever is greater
2 – not essential in upland grazing land

1.2.2 Use of imported topsoil

Topsoil is bulky, labour-intensive to collect and a valuable resource; it is therefore expensive to buy, collect, transport and lay. There may be an opportunity to siphon topsoil off with incoming waste during the active stages of landfill operations. However, topsoil mixed with waste is likely to be contaminated, and soil collected in this way also requires storage (see Section F.1.5) during the operational phase before it can be used.

It is important to note that topsoil is not the ideal substrate for the creation of many habitat types:

- Topsoil can be very fertile, particularly if it originates from an arable field. This will automatically preclude the creation of low-fertility habitat types such as heathland and species-rich grassland, and may well cause problems by encouraging aggressive species to dominate. Note that topsoil is not recommended for creation of nature conservation after-uses, and is not required for woodland (Table F.1.1).
- Topsoil originating from urban or

industrial locations may be contaminated with toxins. This will restrict the range of habitats which can be created; agriculture will not be possible and many species will not survive if the levels of toxins are too high. There is also a risk that the soil will contain rhizomes or seeds of alien species such as Japanese knotweed or buddleja.

The source of the topsoil will to a great extent dictate the nature of the habitat which should be created. Topsoil originating from semi-natural habitats is likely to contain an active seed and bud bank (as well as soil invertebrates, fungi etc.). If a habitat of nature conservation value is scheduled for destruction as part of the landfill development, it makes economic and ecological sense to make best use of this 'free' resource of plant propagules. Soil obtained from semi-natural habitats should therefore be used to create the same habitat as occurred on the donor site. It should be noted that this does in no way advocate the destruction of semi-natural habitats. However, if

destruction cannot be avoided then one should aim to use all the resources obtainable from the destroyed area as soon as possible to best effect.

1.2.3 Use of subsoil

Use of subsoil, either from on-site or imported from elsewhere, is often the best and most cost-effective way of providing a suitable substrate for habitat creation. Subsoil is the recommended substrate for creating nature conservation after-uses (see Table F.1.1).

There are several distinct advantages to using subsoil:

- subsoil does not generally contain an abundant seed bank; it is therefore mostly free of weeds, which reduces aftercare and management costs;
- subsoil is cheaper and easier to obtain than topsoil; and
- subsoil generally has low fertility and is therefore ideal as a base material for many nature conservation after-uses requiring infertile soils (check nutrient status with soil analysis – see Section F.1.4).

The main disadvantage of subsoil is that it lacks structure and is therefore prone to compaction, summer drought and winter waterlogging. Subsoil may therefore require amelioration before use, through the addition of organic matter (although avoid raising nutrient levels greatly).

1.2.4 Use of other materials that produce soil (soil forming materials)

If sufficient quantities of topsoil or subsoil are not available, it may be possible to make up the required depth using other materials as a soil substitute. There are a range of materials that are suitable, termed soil forming materials. Many of these materials are industrial waste products such as colliery shale, brick rubble, china clay waste, sands and gravels. These materials all require some amelioration before they can be used, but most can produce fertile well-structured soils given enough time and weathering. A recent review of the use of soil forming materials for land reclamation can be found in Bending et al. (1999).

The characteristics of materials that permit vegetative growth can be summarised as follows:

- They must form an absorbent substrate that retains water and oxygen. For a substrate to be able to retain water, particle size should be less than 2 mm. Water is held in the gaps between the particles; if they are too large, the water drains away quickly under the influence of gravity. A substrate which entirely consists of stones, cobbles or gravel is unsuitable. These materials can be used if mixed with finer material with particle size less than 2 mm. However, very fine material can also be problematic; poor aeration and

waterlogging can occur. This can be remedied by the addition of sand.

- They must permit root penetration; roots cannot easily penetrate dense material, and the substrate must therefore be uncompacted.
- They must supply adequate nutrients for plant growth (all plants require some nutrients, although low-fertility habitats such as heathlands need only very small amounts). The absence of toxic compounds is beneficial for most species, although some can tolerate higher levels of toxins than others.

The main disadvantages of the use of soil-forming materials are as follows:

- Soil formation occurs over a very long period; soil forming materials create raw and unweathered soils which will not resemble natural soils for many years.
- They do not possess the variation in particle size found in natural soils, and they are therefore lacking in structure and liable to compaction.
- They lack organic matter, a crucial element of soil, and are therefore often very infertile.

For plant growth on soil forming materials to be possible, the amount of organic matter must be increased. Organic matter supplies the four major plant nutrients: nitrogen, phosphorous, magnesium and potassium (macronutrients), the availability of which has been found to be the largest limiting factor on plant growth (Gough & Marrs, 1990; Bloomfield et al., 1982). Although nutrient content will increase naturally over time, as stress-tolerant plants colonise and contribute organic matter to the soil when they die,

this process takes years, and conditions will be unsuitable for many plant species in the interim. Organic matter can be introduced artificially, but a better alternative is to increase soil fertility by planting nitrogen-fixing leguminous species. These are capable of fixing more than 100 kg of nitrogen per hectare per year, but require inputs of lime and phosphorous to sustain growth (Bloomfield et al., 1982; Bradshaw, 1983; Bradshaw & Chadwick, 1980).

In addition to low fertility and poor structure, soil forming materials may also have other problems such as toxicity, high acidity (for example, pyrite weathers to form a highly acid substrate), and the capacity to heat up to high temperatures.

Minimum standards for soil forming materials acceptable for the establishment of woodland on landfill sites are given in Table F.1.2. Similar standards should be met by soil forming materials used for the creation of other habitats.

Woodland creation using paper mineral fibre as a soil forming material on Bidston Moss landfill site is described in Case Study 2.

Amelioration of soil forming materials
Soil ameliorants work by physically or chemically altering the nature of the soil forming material. Physical methods use inert substances to increase porosity, resistance to compaction and water retention. Suitable additives include natural materials such as sewage sludge, manure, leaf mould straw or bark (Ingelmo et al., 1998; see also Section F.1.3.3), or expensive artificial additives such as perlites or alginates – these can be obtained from a horticultural supplier along with details regarding their use. Chemical methods are used to manipulate soil fertility or release unavailable nutrients. Suitable additives may be gypsum, fertiliser or bulky organic material.

Table F.1.3 lists common soil forming materials and their physical and chemical characteristics. Table F.1.4 summarises appropriate methods for the amelioration of soils and soil forming materials.

Soil forming materials can be used effectively to bulk up available soil where it is in short supply, and in many cases relatively little amelioration is required for these materials to be used. Within the context of a landfill, it is not recommended that soil substitutes are used on their own; they should be well mixed and incorporated with true soil. Comprehensive information on restoring and revegetating materials frequently used as soil substitutes can be found in Bradshaw & Chadwick (1980).

Table F.1.2. Minimum standards for soil forming materials for woodland creation (Moffat & Bending, 1992)

Bulk density	<1.5 g cm-3 to at least 50 cm depth <1.7 g cm-3 to at least 1 m depth
Stoniness	<40% by volume. Few stones greater than 100 mm in size
pH	4.0–8.0
Electrical conductivity	<0.2 S m-1 (1:1 soil : water suspension)
Iron pyrite content	<0.05%
Heavy metal content	Not excessively over ICRCL (1987) threshold trigger concentrations
Organic contaminants	Not exceeding ICRCL (1987) action trigger concentrations

Table F.1.3. Physical and chemical properties of soil forming materials (Bradshaw, 1983)

Soil forming material	Physical characteristics			Chemical characteristics					
	Texture and structure	Stability	Water supply	Surface temperature	macro-nutrients	micro-nutrients	pH	Toxic materials	Salinity
Colliery spoil	d	d/a	d/a	a/3	d	a	d/a	a	a/2
Strip mining	d/a	d/a	c/a	a/3	d/a	a	d/a	a	a/2
Fly ash	c/a	a	a	a	d	a	1/3	2	a
Oil shale	c	d/a	c	a/2	d	a	c/a	a	a/1
Iron ore mining	d/a	c/a	b/a	a	c	a	a	a	a
Heavy metal wastes	d	d/a	c/a	a	d	a	d/a	1/3	a/3
China clay wastes	d	c	c	a	d	a	b	a	a
Acid rocks	d	a	c	a	c	a	b	a	a
Calcareous rocks	d	a	c	a	d	a	1	a	a
Sand and gravel	b/a	a	a	a	b/a	a	b/a	a	a
Coastal sands	c/a	d/a	b/a	a	d	a	a	a	a/1
Land from sea	c	a	a	a	c	a	a/1	a	3
Urban wastes	d/a	a	a	a	c	a	a	a/2	a
Roadsides	d/a	d	d	b/a	c	a	b/a	a	a/2

Deficiency: d=severe, c=moderate, b=slight, a=adequate   Excess: 1=slight, 2=moderate, 3=severe
(Relative to the establishment of a soil/plant ecosystem appropriate to the material. Variations in severity are due to variation in materials and situations.)

Table F.1.4. Methods of ameliorating deficiencies of soil forming materials (Bradshaw, 1983)

Attribute		Problem	Immediate treatment	Long-term treatment
Physical	Structure	Too compact	Rip or scarify	Vegetation
		Too open	Compact or cover with fine material	Vegetation
	Stability	Unstable	Stabiliser / mulch	Regrade / vegetation
	Moisture	Too wet	Drain	Drain
		Too dry	Organic mulch	Vegetation
Nutrients	Nutrient levels	Nitrogen	Fertiliser	Legumes
		Others	Fertiliser + lime	Legumes
Toxicity	pH	Too high	Pyritic waste or organic matter	Weathering
		Too low	Lime	Lime
	Heavy metals	Too high	Organic mulch or metal tolerant species	Metal tolerant species
	Salinity	Too high	Weathering or irrigation	Tolerant species

The use of soil forming materials with regard to planning applications

Soil forming materials and subsoil are strictly controlled wastes. Best practice is always to alert the planning authority at the earliest possible opportunity that soil forming materials may be used in site restoration and habitat creation. Stating that the amount to be used will be determined by availability will avoid restricting restoration to the use of specified quantities. The planning authority should also be made aware of the possible use of soil ameliorants such as composted green waste or poultry manure.

In practical terms, re-use of industrial by-products is a form of recycling and thus in principle should be encouraged. Provided that the full environmental consequences of the use of soil forming materials have been considered, and the necessity for their use is explained, there is little reason for the authority to object. However, if use of these materials has not been mentioned at the planning application stage, it is likely that an amendment to the planning consent will be required which could considerably delay proceedings. Therefore, to avoid this, mention must be made in the initial application.

McKendry (1996) states that many planning consents specify excessively high standards for topsoil which preclude the use of soil forming materials. He suggests that a more realistic specification should be based on the final soil after restoration, rather than assessing the individual materials before they are used. Thus, with careful mixing and amelioration, a wider variety of materials can be used whilst still retaining high finished product specifications either immediately following restoration or within a given time period.

1.3 Providing suitable conditions for habitat creation

The provision of suitable conditions for plant growth is essential for successful habitat creation on landfill sites. A summary of the conditions that must be suitable for the planned habitat is given below:

- Adequate rooting substrate depth – the minimum is fixed by official guidance (see Table F.1.1)
- Absence of compaction
- Correct level of fertility
- Acceptable pH
- Adequate moisture content (therefore good soil structure)
- Lack of waterlogging
- Lack of stones in the upper layer
- Adequate oxygen content

1.3.1 Compaction

Physical soil compaction is caused by pressure; long-term soil storage or virtually any amount of vehicle traffic will result in the soil becoming compacted. The effect of compaction is to compress soil particles and thus destroy soil structure by reducing soil volume and pore space and weakening the mechanical strength of the soil. Compacted soil does not retain water or air, or permit root penetration. Compaction by chemical processes is also possible (but far less common); for example, high levels of iron, aluminium and silicon can form a physical barrier in the soil which must be broken before any species can be planted.

Although virtually all soils are prone to compaction if subjected to sufficient pressure, the problem is more serious with clay-rich soils. Soil forming materials are prone to compaction due to the lack of organic matter and hence structure; they can become compacted under the influence of gravity alone (Willoughby & Moffat, 1996). They may therefore require the addition of other materials such as organic matter to prevent this from occurring.

Soil compactness is measured by Bulk Density (BD) in grammes per cubic centimetre. Normal soil has a BD of 1.0 whereas peat has a BD of 0.2. An ideal value is 1.2. If BD reaches 1.7 in a sandy soil and 1.5 in a clay soil, all root growth will be prevented (Dobson & Moffat, 1995b). Dobson & Moffat (1995b) outline a method for determining bulk density.

The best method of treating compaction is to avoid it in the first instance. This can be achieved by:

- ensuring that vehicle movement over all soils is minimised by restricting all traffic apart from caterpillar tracked machinery along designated haul routes, and immediately alleviating compaction in areas where the

Photo: Melvyn Foxton

Loosetipping and spreading of soil using low pressure tracked vehicles.

passage of traffic is unavoidable (for example haul route layouts see Environment Agency (in prep.));
- never working soil when it is wet; and
- always placing soil on site by loosetipping (see below).

Soil placement

The preparation and movement of the soil over the cap is a major element of the restoration phase. Due to the size and complexity of the operation and the necessity to minimise compaction and soil damage, the entire process should be carefully planned in advance. In particular, the location(s) of stored soil and soil substitutes should be marked on a plan with the destinations also shown. This should avoid unnecessary travel over laid soil. The timing of operations should also be planned in advance – soil placement should ideally take place during June – August (McKendry, 1996); soil movement can take place during May to September if rainfall is low. However, soil should not be moved when wet; moving wet soil can cause irreparable damage.

Placement of soil should be conducted by loosetipping using a dump truck working with an excavator that has a back-acter. Laid soil should be graded using a low ground pressure tracked bulldozer. Following placement and grading, the soil should be cultivated to produce a tilth (see below). Front loaders and box scrapers should not be used (Dobson & Moffat, 1995b; Environment Agency, in prep.).

If the soil is dry, it can be cultivated immediately after laying. Wet soil should be left until it has dried before cultivation. Unprotected soil is susceptible to erosion; if cultivation and sowing are likely to be delayed or interrupted by bad weather, it would be prudent to postpone the entire operation until it can proceed without interruption.

Alleviation of compaction

Physical compaction can be relieved by deep ploughing or ripping the soil to a depth of 90 cm. However, it is advised that the maximum depth of ripping should be set at at least 30 cm above the cap to avoid accidental damage to the cap. Deep cultivation should be conducted using a tracked bulldozer, as agricultural machinery is often not sufficiently powerful.

Winged tines are the best implement for loosening soil. This should be followed by discing or harrowing to break up clods and form a tilth (Willoughby & Moffat, 1996). If soil forming materials have been compacted by vehicle movements, cultivation may have to take place several

Photo: Valerie Hack

A wildflower grassland three years after planting. Note the numerous bare patches and restricted growth of the sward. This illustrates the potential problems caused by excessive soil compaction.

times if compaction is serious. Cultivation can bring stones to the surface; these should be removed if the area is to be used for amenity or the creation of grassland or heathland which will be managed by mowing. It is not necessary to remove stones if the created haitat will not be mown. For further details see Dobson & Moffat (1993).

It is essential that cultivation is conducted when at least the upper surface of the soil is friable (i.e. crumbly and not sticky) and not wet or excessively dry. In general, therefore, cultivation should only be conducted in autumn or spring (Willoughby & Moffat, 1996). Cultivation can also be used to mix organic and inorganic horizons, increase soil mineralisation (the release of nutrients), alter the physical properties of soil and control weeds (Willoughby & Moffat, 1996).

1.3.2 Waterlogging

Waterlogging is most common in soils with a high clay content. Creating a slope on the landfill surface and incorporating sand into the soil reduces the likelihood of waterlogging.The final contours of the site should take into account likely water movement and any risk posed to nearby land / properties by water flowing off-site.

Most plant species other than those adapted to survive in wetlands are killed by only a short period of exposure to saturated conditions. Frequent waterlogging can also increase the risk of trees being windthrown. However, areas

around the base of the cap that are prone to waterlogging are good candidates for wetland creation (see Section F.5).

1.3.3 Fertility

Semi-natural habitats require about 100 kg of available nitrogen per hectare per year in order to be self-supporting (i.e. not reliant on the application of nutrients for plant growth to be possible) (Bradshaw, 1983). This is a ballpark figure based on the requirements of poorly productive temperate ecosystems (the category in which British semi-natural habitats tend to fall); productive temperate ecosystems such as agricultural land-uses require around 200 kg N/ha/year (see Table F.1.5 for other nutrient requirements).

Recommended soil fertility levels for habitat creation

In order to provide guidance on fertility levels that are compatible with habitat creation, ADAS have developed an index of soil fertility for levels of extractable P, K and Mg (set out in British Standard 3882). The index is on a scale of 0 (low) to 9 (high). In general, an index of 0-4 is taken as suitable for habitat creation (Highways Agency, 1993). It should be remembered that the 'total nutrients' in the soil is not the same as 'total available nutrients'; nutrients may be present in the soil but in a form unavailable to plants.

The ADAS indices suitable for habitat creation and corresponding nutrient levels are given in Table F.1.6.

Table F.1.8. Nutrient content of soil conditioners and soil-forming materials (Bradshaw & Chadwick, 1980)

Material		Composition (%)				Special problems
		N	P	K	organic matter	
Soil conditioners	Farmyard manure	0.6	0.1	0.5	24	Can be toxic when applied directly on plants
	Pig slurry	0.2	0.1	0.2	3	High water content
	Poultry manure (broiler) (battery)	2.3 1.5	0.9 0.5	1.6 0.6	68 34	High levels of ammonia High levels of ammonia
	Sewage sludge (air dried)	2	0.3	0.2	45	Possible toxic metals and can have high water content
	Mushroom compost (dried)	2.8	0.2	0.8	95	None except high lime content
	Domestic refuse (municipal)	0.5	0.2	0.3	65	Miscellaneous objects
	Straw	0.5	0.1	0.8	95	Adverse C/N ratio
Soil-forming materials	Building rubble	0.05	1.8	2	0.5	Brick and pieces of masonry
	Colliery spoil	0.03	0.04	0.4	0	Possible high levels of pyrite causing acidity
	Pulverised fuel ash	0	0.05	2.2	0	High boron content

Earthworms

Earthworms have a very beneficial effect on soil; they mix the nutrient-rich top layers of the rooting substrate with nutrient-poor lower layers. Without this mixing, the top layers become very nutrient-rich but the lower layers remain infertile. Any opportunity to introduce earthworms to soil on a landfill should therefore be taken (Bradshaw, 1983), but such introductions should only be carried out when the soil is sufficiently well-developed; introducing earthworms into unsuitable soil conditions is unlikely to be successful.

Inorganic fertilisers

Inorganic fertilisers may be used in small amounts, but only in certain situations, and great care must be taken. They should not be used to raise the fertility dramatically (such as by several hundred kg / ha) over a short space of time (i.e. within three years); heavy applications of fertiliser increase soil salinity, which is fatal to most plants. For habitat creation schemes a very slow release fertiliser is preferred, to avoid the excessive growth of ruderal species by high nutrient levels. If inorganic fertiliser must be used, it is best used as a booster to plant growth at critical stages during development. It should not be added with seeds as it can inhibit germination, but should be added once the seedlings have

produced their second pair of first leaves. Fertiliser should not be added to bare soil; it will be leached through by water and therefore lost to the system.

1.3.4 Soil pH

pH is a measure of alkalinity or acidity, and is a very important soil parameter. Plants can grow in the approximate range 3.5-8.5; outside these limits, plants are very unlikely to survive. Species that can grow at the outer limits of this range are termed *stress tolerators* (Grime, 1979). The species characteristic of neutral woodlands, neutral grasslands etc. cannot tolerate pH values near these extremes, and require soil of a neutral pH. Interpretation of pH values is given below:

	<4.5	Strongly acid
	4.5-5.5	Moderately acid
pH	5.5-6.5	Slightly acid
	6.5-7.5	Neutral
	>7.5	Alkaline

If the soil is too acid, it is possible to raise the pH through the addition of lime (Gilbert & Anderson, 1998). However it should be noted that lime may well not have long-term effects; lime applications

will have to be repeated. It is most important that lime is mixed thoroughly with the soil; small pockets of pure lime can be toxic to plants. Liming is a traditional treatment of grasslands used to offset losses of calcium by leaching and cropping of herbage. Maintaining a constant pH also maintains grassland diversity, and is particularly important in areas with high rainfall and base-poor soils. At such sites, a soil test is recommended every 4 years to check if lime is needed (Simpson & Jefferson, 1996).

If the soil is too alkaline, it is worth first determining the cause of high pH. If it is due to the presence of calcium carbonate, leaching by rain will soon act to reduce the pH, avoiding the need for applications of costly additives. Otherwise, pH can be lowered through the addition of copper sulphate, sulphur or heather/bracken litter (Gilbert & Anderson, 1998).

1.3.5 Soil moisture content and structure

Organic matter makes up 2-5% of topsoil, and is the key to good soil structure. Soil forming materials derived from industrial wastes will not normally contain organic matter, and attempts should be made to increase the content to levels found within topsoil. Organic matter should be added to soil-forming materials as a matter of course, as its addition brings many

Case Study 1:

Beddingham Landfill, East Sussex
Translocation of chalk grassland

Site details

Site operator:	Viridor Waste Management Ltd.
Habitat created:	Chalk grassland
Area of habitat created:	2 ha
Existing nature conservation interest:	A small area of SSSI chalk grassland existed within the site boundary. Much of the land surrounding the site is also SSSI chalk grassland.

Site background

Beddingham landfill site is located on the site of a former chalk quarry. Due to complex engineering requirements, permission was sought to extend the existing landfill into an area of 2 ha of SSSI chalk grassland adjacent to the quarry. This was granted only on condition that the grassland was translocated to an alternative location within or adjacent to the site. An additional planning condition is that chalk grassland creation is incorporated into the restoration of the remainder of the site, which at present is still operational. The translocation was undertaken during 1991 and 1992.

Habitat creation objectives

The principal objective of the translocation was the complete retention of the conservation interest of the chalk grassland. Since the grassland was of high enough importance to afford it SSSI status, mitigation by other means (e.g.

creation of new grassland by seeding) was not considered to provide adequate compensation. Translocation also provided a means of conserving invertebrate populations on the grassland.

Choice of receptor site

The receptor site was carefully chosen to be of low initial conservation importance but to match the environmental conditions prevalent at the existing site as closely as possible. For logistical reasons the receptor site additionally had to be within a few hundred metres of the existing grassland. Consequently an area of non-SSSI grassland adjacent to the site was selected in which the bedrock, soil-type, aspect and topography were all identical to the donor site. The only environmental conditions that differed were altitude (the receptor site was 30 m lower than the donor site) and the number of rabbits (high at the donor site, low at the receptor).

Techniques used

Donor site
Grassland at the donor site was cut into 4 m x 2.4 m turves (a size determined by the bucket available for their transportation). To maintain the integrity of the site as far as possible, all turves were cut in a strictly controlled order to enable them to be placed in the same configuration at the receptor site. Turves were cut right to the bedrock (which was typically only 10-30 cm below the sward) to allow the entire soil profile to be moved. This greatly increased the probability of success.

Approximately 1 ha was translocated in the winter of 1991, and the remainder was moved in the winter of 1992. Translocation took place in the winter in order to avoid moving plants during the growing season.

Selective removal of turves was conducted so that any with a greatly reduced species diversity were not translocated, particularly those dominated by the aggressive species tor grass *(Brachypodium pinnatum)*.

Scattered shrubs were also present; the stems were cut to ground level and the roots were transferred with the turves.

Receptor site
Prior to the introduction of the turves, the entire soil profile was stripped down to the underlying bedrock and stockpiled at the edge of the site. The translocated turves were then placed directly onto the bedrock, in the same order in which they were removed. The soil stripped from the site was subsequently used to create long mounds alongside the site in an attempt to encourage rabbits. Rabbit grazing can be very important for the maintenance of species diversity on chalk grassland.

Photo: Duncan Watson

Classic chalk grassland species including chalk milkwort, common milkwort, glaucous sedge and rough hawkbit.

Photo: Duncan Watson

View of area of translocated chalk grassland (foreground).

Management and monitoring

With the exception of a sheep grazing trial in 1992 and a few attempts to mow the site within the first three years, management work has not been carried out at the receptor site since the translocation. This was partly due to the difficulty of obtaining grazing stock in the local area. Mowing is difficult due to the uneven nature of the ground, and is also likely to impact upon invertebrate populations through damage to structures such as ant-hills.

Ecological monitoring of the translocated area was carried out in each of the first three years following completion of the translocation, in order to allow its initial success to be evaluated. However, no monitoring has taken place since.

Preliminary results

In 1999 the vegetation exhibited marked differences across the site induced by the depth of soil translocated with the vegetation. The most species-rich area was that with the thinnest soil; the limited amount of nutrients available prevented the establishment of ruderal species. Here the sward is very short and probably very similar to its state before translocation.

Other areas show a reduced species diversity overall with a greater proportion of both competitive and ruderal species. Ruderal species are most likely to be present as a result of disturbance to the soil at the time of the translocation. Competitive species such as tor grass have been able to invade as a result of the lack of rabbit-grazing or other forms of management. These species now thrive at the expense of typical chalk grassland species.

At the time of the last monitoring study in 1995, species diversity was still high, and the translocation initially appeared to have been successful. However, species diversity in 1999 was reduced over much of the site, almost certainly as a result of a lack of management, and the conservation value of the site is currently much lower than prior to its translocation.

Suggested management

Species diversity and habitat quality could be maintained at the site by the instigation of regular management. It would be necessary to act quickly to prevent typical smaller chalk grassland species from dying out. Domestic livestock grazing is the best management option. In the years following translocation, the proportion of coarse grasses has greatly increased. These species tend to be unpalatable; livestock willing to graze coarse vegetation (e.g. goats) are required, at least initially. Sheep grazing could be implemented once the proportion of coarse grass species has been reduced.

The methods described here are presented purely as examples of landfill restoration and habitat creation techniques. They do not necessarily reflect the best practice standards contained within this book.

Case Study 2:

Bidston Moss, Merseyside
Woodland creation using mineral fibre as a soil forming material

Site details

Site operator:	Merseyside Waste Disposal Authority (MWDA)
Habitat created:	Principally woodland, with rides and larger meadow areas
Area of habitat created:	37 ha
Existing nature conservation interest:	Minimal, with potential for development

Site background

Bidston Moss landfill site was closed in 1995. The site operator (MWDA) has since worked in partnership with Groundwork Wirral to restore the site into a community open space, into which nature conservation issues have been incorporated. Restoration is principally in five phases; phases 1-4 have been completed, and phase 5 is due to be completed by 2001. Of particular interest to readers of this book is the use of paper mineral fibre as a soil substitute. Bidston Moss was also one of the first landfill sites to experiment with large-scale tree planting.

Habitat creation objectives

The principal objective was to provide an area of community open space, incorporating native woodland and meadow grassland. This will help to meet local planning targets for landscape, public open space and woodland creation, and should also provide benefits to biodiversity. The restored site will incorporate over 90,000 individual trees and 10 ha of meadow grassland. Additional objectives include:

- Education – through nature trails, tree planting and activities for children such as pond-dipping and "mini-beast safaris".
- Research – the restoration provides a good opportunity for specialist studies on landfill restoration, several of which have already been carried out.

Involvement of the local community has also been central to the restoration design process, particularly through the local action group Friends of Bidston Moss. Groundwork Wirral manages an Environmental Task Force on the site and currently has 11 young people learning practical countryside management skills such as tree planting and aftercare, grassland management and footpath maintenance.

Major constraints on restoration

Bidston Moss is situated on former marshland. On-site soil resources for restoration were very limited as it was a land-raising site. An immense volume of soil is required to restore a 37 ha site, implying major financial costs and logistical problems. Consequently, paper mineral fibre was used as a soil substitute.

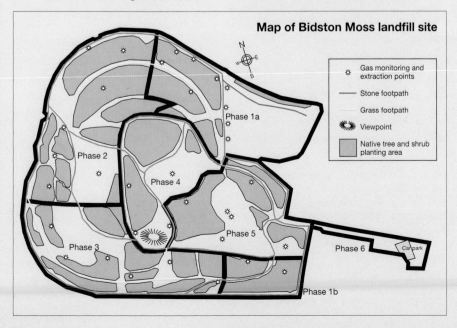

Bidston Moss landfill site

Photo: Duncan Watson

Techniques used

Provision of soil-forming material

Paper mineral fibre (a by-product of the paper pulp industry, supplied by the Bridgewater Paper Company Ltd) was used as a soil forming material in combination with other soil-forming materials brought in whilst the site was still operational. The paper mineral fibre increased the bulk of the soil and also supplied organic matter, therefore increasing soil quality. Substantial cost savings were made through the use of this material.

Step 1
Imported subsoil and paper mineral fibre were mixed together in a 1:1 ratio.

Step 2
After spreading, the subsoil and mineral fibre mixture was turned over several times in order to oxygenate the material and allow the mineral fibre to compost.

Step 3
The mixture was laid in its final position to a depth of 1-3 m.

Step 4
Clover and mustard seeds were sown, allowed to grow for 3-4 months and then

Map of Bidston Moss landfill site

Phase 1a

Phase 2

Phase 4

Phase 3

Phase 5

Phase 6

Car park

Phase 1b

Legend	
✸	Gas monitoring and extraction points
—	Stone footpath
	Grass footpath
✸	Viewpoint
▨	Native tree and shrub planting area

ploughed in to act as a green manure. These species also added nitrogen to the soil.

The result was a well-drained and fertile soil. Soil pH varied across the site depending on the nature of the imported subsoil, but in general was slightly alkaline with an average pH of 8.

Woodland creation

Two planting mixes were used for the top and the bottom of the slope. The planting mix for the top of the slope is shown below. Note that no more than 10% shrub species can be included in the mix for the site to be eligible for the Woodland Grant Scheme.

Several rides were incorporated into the woodland design. In addition to increasing habitat diversity, these provide access routes to landfill gas monitoring wells and will eventually form the basis for nature trails.

A seed mix of seven species, including bird's foot trefoil, red campion, pendulous sedge, foxglove and bluebell was planted amongst the trees as an attempt to create a woodland ground flora.

Grassland creation

The aim of grassland creation at Bidston Moss was to create a colourful meadow for landscape and educational benefits. The seed mix therefore included a variety of species. 80% of the mix consisted of grasses and 20% consisted of herb species including black knapweed, oxeye daisy, bird's foot trefoil, selfheal and meadow buttercup.

Aftercare and management

Management of young trees is very important during their first few years to ensure that their growth is not reduced as a result of competition from vigorous grasses and weeds. In Phase 1, herbicide was applied twice per year for the first two years, allowing the trees to grow tall enough for management to be no longer considered necessary. In Phase 2, biodegradable mulch mats were used to give the trees 18 months of protection; after this period, management was no longer considered necessary.

Meadow areas are mown once a year in September. Monitoring of woodland and grassland development has been carried out by the Cheshire and Wirral Wildlife Trusts.

Preliminary results

As a result of the high nutrient status of the soil, tree establishment has generally been very good. The trees have put on considerable annual growth, with most trees planted in Phase 1 now at least 3 m tall. Some species have fared better than others, with common and grey alder, willow, birch and oak especially prominent whilst others such as rowan, which is less tolerant of calcareous soil, are not doing as well. Tree growth on Phase 3 has been noticeably poorer than elsewhere, almost certainly as a result of this area's exposure to salt-laden winds

Photo: Duncan Watson

Woodland creation at Bidston Moss, four years after the trees were first planted as bare-rooted transplants.

blowing in off the Irish Sea. Netlon protective fencing has now been erected around these trees and it is hoped that establishment will benefit as a result.

Woodland ground flora species, with the exception of red campion, are tending to be out-competed by vigorous grass species as a result of the high nutrient status of the soil. In retrospect it may have been better to have waited until the tree canopy had developed and shaded out the grasses before introducing woodland ground flora species.

Similarly, high soil fertility in the meadow areas has prompted the dominance of grass species, and several of the planted herb species were not found in 1999. The high proportion of grasses planted, particularly aggressive species such as red fescue, is also likely to be a contributory factor in the comparative failure of the wildflower species.

Whilst in retrospect a few things could have been done slightly differently in order to maximise nature conservation benefits (e.g. it would have been preferable to use a woodland species mix consisting entirely of native species), the restoration of Bidston Moss provides an excellent illustration of the use of a soil substitute to compensate for the lack of on-site soil resources. The potential success of woodland creation at modern landfill sites is also demonstrated. The site also illustrates how the demand for public open space can be combined with nature conservation benefits, through both habitat creation and the provision of a valuable educational resource.

Planting mix for areas at the top of the slope

Trees (90% of mix)

Field maple *Acer campestre* 10%	Corsican pine* *Pinus nigra* 1%
Common alder *Alnus glutinosa* 15%	Oak *Quercus robur* 7%
Grey alder* *Alnus incana* 15%	Rowan *Sorbus aucuparia* 15%
Silver birch *Betula pendula* 15%	Willow *Salix cinerea* 5%
Scots pine *Pinus sylvestris* 2%	Willow *Salix viminalis* 5%

Shrubs (10% of mix)

Hazel *Corylus avellana*	Guelder rose *Viburnum opulus*
Hawthorn *Crataegus monogyna*	

* non-native species

Research into earthworm populations at Bidston Moss

An important part of the restoration process, particularly at sites where the use of soil-forming materials has created a poorly structured soil, is the establishment of a diverse soil organism community. Earthworms incorporate organic matter into the soil, promoting good structure, drainage and fertility.

Research at Bidston Moss (Pierce, 1998) funded by Bridgewater Paper Company Ltd. revealed an abundant earthworm population. Colonisation has clearly been enhanced by a number of earthworm introductions by the researchers. Inoculation of earthworms into poorly structured soil can therefore greatly speed up the development of soil structure and fertility.

Research was also carried out in response to concerns that paper mineral fibre might contain potentially toxic amounts of copper which could be passed on to species which predate earthworms. Results show that although copper is present in earthworms at the site, it appears that they can regulate their copper intake, and the copper is therefore not having a toxic effect.

The methods described here are presented purely as examples of landfill restoration and habitat creation techniques. They do not necessarily reflect the best practice standards contained within this book.

beneficial effects. These include increased water retention, aeration, crumb structure and nutrient supply. Organic matter can be supplied by the addition of organic wastes (see Table F.1.8). Materials such as manure should be composted and stored for at least 12 months before use to ensure that the manure is well rotted. Maximum rates of application are 30 tonnes / ha every three to five years. In practice, much lower amounts are likely to be required.

1.4   Soil testing

Soil testing (of pH, fertility, organic matter content etc.) is essential to the success of any habitat creation project. Soil resources for restoration, whether made up of topsoil, subsoil or soil-forming materials, from on site or imported from elsewhere, should all be tested at the earliest possible stage to ensure that the soil resource is suitable for the proposed habitat creation.

Where manipulation of soil fertility, pH etc. has taken place during restoration, regular soil testing (at least every 2 years) throughout the aftercare period is also highly recommended. Regular testing can be used to assess the success or otherwise of measures taken to alter soil condition, and therefore indicate when soil conditions have become suitable for habitat creation to proceed.

Soil sampling should take place across the entire site. A grid pattern of sample plots will ensure complete and regular coverage. This is especially important if the soil has originated from many different sources. The size of grid cells to use is site-specific and will largely depend upon the number of soil sources and on whether the soil has been mixed up or laid in distinct patches. As a rough guide, sampling at points 30 m apart will probably be accurate enough, although more detailed initial sampling may be required if the soil is very variable.

Soil samples should be analysed professionally rather than using DIY kits (these are often inaccurate). Nitrogen analysis in particular is notoriously difficult, even under laboratory conditions.

ADAS offer an analysis service for organic manures, giving the fertiliser value. They also analyse soils for pH, lime requirement, P, K and Mg content and a broad N content. Private laboratories will also conduct soil analysis. More information on soil sampling is given in English Nature & the Wildlife Trusts (1999) and the Flora Locale website (www.naturebureau.co.uk/pages/floraloc/floraloc.htm).

1.5   Soil storage

Storage enables the original soils present at a site (where available) to be used for restoration. As well as reducing costs, the use of on-site soil will in most cases improve the quality of habitat creation.

Soil storage also reduces final restoration costs since materials can be siphoned off as they are brought in with incoming waste during the active phase of the landfill. McKendry (1996) states that materials can be mixed together from various stockpiles and formed into new piles as a good method of mixing materials such as organic matter and soil forming materials.

Soil storage requires great care whatever the source material, but topsoil in particular requires very careful handling.

Stored soil should be cultivated after it has been spread to aerate the soil.

1.5.1   Topsoil

Storing topsoil in large heaps can destroy the soil structure and lead to the development of anaerobic conditions, with serious consequences for the success of any subsequent habitat creation. Although structure loss and anaerobic conditions are reversible, it is preferable to avoid this if at all possible; anaerobic conditions will kill soil organisms, and habitats will develop at a slower rate on initially structureless soil.

Restoration design should therefore be carefully planned to avoid unnecessary storage, although some storage is inevitable. Where topsoil storage is unavoidable, the following guidelines should be adhered to:

- Storage should ideally be for no longer than three months. If the storage period must be longer, the topsoil should be spread across a field to a depth of no more than 40 cm, and rotovated once a year to increase aeration. It is recognised that storing large volumes of soil in this way may not be practical due to the large amount of land required; if possible, it is preferable to plan restoration and habitat creation to avoid the need for long-term storage.
- Storage piles should be less than 2 m high.
- Storage piles should be created by loosetipping.
- Vehicles should not be driven over storage piles.
- Piles should ideally be covered with a light-coloured material such as tarpaulin. Apart from reducing water absorption, this can have an additional benefit by reducing the number of viable seeds within the

seedbank and hence reducing the potential weed problem. Covering material should not be dark in colour as this raises soil temperature and speeds up the degradation of humic matter, which can result in the development of toxic anaerobic conditions. The covering should be weighted down (e.g. with tyres) to prevent it being blown away by high winds.

1.5.2   Other materials

Subsoil and soil forming materials do not possess the well-developed structure of topsoil, and storage is therefore not as detrimental. However, the lack of structure can lead to toxic anaerobic conditions developing in storage piles. As with topsoil, anaerobic conditions can be reversed when the soil is spread, but it is preferable not to let them develop in the first place. Piles can also be prone to slippage if waterlogged. The following guidelines should therefore be followed for short-term storage:

- Storage piles should be less than 6 m high.
- Vehicles should not be driven over storage piles.
- Piles should ideally be covered with a light coloured material such as tarpaulin (see previous section).

If subsoil must be stored for longer periods, planning requirements may require that storage piles or bunds are seeded with grass. This has the effect of preventing weed growth and improving the aesthetic quality of the area during site operation.

1.6   Preparation of the site for habitat creation

1.6.1   Soil preparation
Creation of a tilth
A fine tilth should be created by harrowing (using a chain harrow, power harrow or cultivator) and rolling (using a Cambridge roller). This should be carried out at a suitable time; cultivation should not take place when the soil is wet, as this will destroy soil structure and cause compaction.

Soil stabilisation
Erosion of the soil overlying the cap should be avoided. Bare soil exposed to prolonged and heavy winter rain is especially vulnerable, although rain can erode unprotected soil at any time of year. It is therefore important to establish a cover of vegetation as soon as possible (Environment Agency, in prep.). If soil erosion is not likely to be a problem, areas

Photo: Melvyn Foxton

Ripping of soil prior to planting / seeding.

of exposed soil (especially on south-facing slopes) can be good for invertebrates and basking reptiles. However, prevention of soil erosion should take precedence on landfill sites.

Soil erosion can seriously compromise the effectiveness of capping systems, potentially leading to desiccation and damage. Vegetation also has a vital function in reducing the amount of water passing through the soil profile and reaching the top of the cap (Simmons, 1999). To stabilise the soil following placement, vegetation should therefore be sown at the earliest possible opportunity that is compatible with successful habitat creation.

- At sites where soil condition is suitable for habitat creation, the desired species should be sown or planted.
- At sites where soil fertility is very low, planting pioneer or nitrogen-fixing species should be considered.
- At sites where a nurse species is required to assist habitat establishment, the nurse species should be planted.

Table F.1.9 gives a selection of species that are suitable for soil stabilisation. Local strains of native species should ideally be used; if other species must be used, **they should not be allowed to persist in the community.** The best way of avoiding the persistence of undesirable alien species (or cultivated varieties of native species) is to avoid planting them in the first place.

Fast-growing grass species such as perennial rye grass (*Lolium perenne*), flattened meadow grass (*Poa compressa*) and creeping red fescue (*Festuca rubra* cultivar) have been recommended for slope stabilisation. However, the competitive nature of these species is generally not compatible with habitat creation, as they are likely to out-compete many of the more desirable plant species.

Terracing (spalling) can also be used to reduce the rate of water runoff and hence soil erosion. Terraces can be constructed from wood or lines of stones laid parallel to the contours (Environment Agency, in prep.). Alternatively, geotextiles can be used to cover and protect the soil from erosion. Geotextiles also promote vegetation growth by increasing the moisture retention capactiy of the soil. Geotextiles can be buried, or simply laid on the soil surface. Some are synthetic, such as densely woven mats or extruded grids. Other materials are biodegradable such as Geojute. Additionally, inert synthetics, gabions (wire cages filled with stone or concrete) or concrete blocks can be used. The selection of the most appropriate material will be site-specific and will largely depend upon the expected severity of the erosion problem.

1.6.2 Nurse species

Nurse species are planted to assist the establishment of the desired vegetation community. They are characteristically fast-growing, and pioneer nurse species are tolerant of poor soil conditions. Nurse species are not always required for habitat creation, and should not be used as a matter of course.

Nurse species may be necessary on very nutrient-poor sites where growth is very slow, or where slow-growing species

Table F.1.9. A selection of species suitable for soil stabilisation

	Species	Other information
Trees	Silver birch *Betula pendula*	Pioneer, tolerant of infertility. Native
	Downy birch *Betula pubescens*	Pioneer, tolerant of infertility. Native
Shrubs	Goat willow *Salix caprea*	Tolerant of wet soil. Native
	Grey willow *Salix cinerea*	Tolerant of wet soil. Native
	Ivy *Hedera helix*	Good ground cover. Native
Grasses	Common bent *Agrostis capillaris*	Wide soil tolerance. Native
	Creeping bent *Agrostis stolonifera*	Wide soil tolerance. Native
	Red fescue *Festuca rubra*	Wide soil tolerance. Native
	Smooth meadow-grass *Poa pratensis*	Wide soil tolerance, quick growing. Native
Herbs	Red clover *Trifolium pratense*	Wide soil tolerance. Native.
	Creeping buttercup *Ranunculus repens*	Wide soil tolerance. Native.
	Oxeye daisy *Leucantheum vulgare*	Wide soil tolerance. Native.
	Bird's-foot trefoil *Lotus corniculatus*	Wide soil tolerance, Salt tolerant. Native

such as heather are being sown (Gilbert & Anderson, 1998). They are generally not recommended on soils with a high nutrient content, particularly for grassland creation. A nurse is also not recommended if species are being allowed to colonise naturally.

If soil erosion is potentially a problem, other means of soil stabilisation such as geotextiles, large rocks or terraces may be used instead of, or in conjunction with, a nurse crop.

Planting nurse species may assist habitat development of the habitat in several ways:

- Improving soil fertility (in particular, nitrogen-fixing species can be used to boost nitrogen content). Nurse species also help to capture nutrients produced as a result of mineralisation before they are leached out of the soil (Chu & Bradshaw, 1996).
- Reducing soil water evaporation and maintaining a high moisture content. This assists seed germination and increases the survival of seedlings and saplings. A low-growing, sprawling drought-tolerant herb should be used, athough for woodland creation it is better to use a tree or shrub nurse species.
- Reducing soil erosion. A nurse will bind the soil and create stable soil aggregates through the accumulation of organic matter (humus) which increases the stability of soil aggregates and provides year-round protection from wind and rain (McKendry, 1996).
- Protecting slow-growing herbs from harsh conditions by moderating temperature fluctuations.
- Inhibiting the growth of annual weeds.

Nurse species are not intended to form part of the long-term vegetation community, and should therefore not persist once the habitat has been established. Typical nurse species are therefore generally short-lived and easily removed, for example by cutting before seed is set in the case of annual grasses, or by treating seedlings in the case of short-lived trees.

Some non-native species have been used as nurse crops in habitat creation projects. Using non-native species goes against the principles of habitat creation and local provenance outlined in Box E.3.3. **The use of native species is strongly recommended wherever**

possible. The use of non-native species can only be justified if there are over-riding economic and ecological reasons for not planting native nurse species, **and only if it can be guaranteed that the nurse species will not persist in the community.**

Selecting nurse species

The choice of species to use will depend on the purpose of the nurse crop.

- To increase fertility, use a nitrogen-fixing species (Table F.1.7).
- To stabilise soil, use a perennial sprawling herb (Table F.1.9).
- For general encouragement of seed germination, an annual grass or a cereal such as barley can be used. Cereals have abundant fibrous roots which are effective soil stabilisers, and tend to be annual species, which are easy to

eradicate. Highland bent (*Agrostis castellana*), a non-vigorous North American species, has been used for moorland creation on peat, and was found to be a suitable nurse species for this habitat (Gilbert & Anderson, 1998). The use of vigorous grasses such as perennial rye-grass (*Lolium perenne*) is generally not recommended, as they can be difficult to eradicate and can have negative impacts on sward diversity. However the biennial Italian rye-grass (*Lolium multiflorum*) is a frequently used and very effective nurse species.

Herbaceous species are best introduced as seeds. Nitrogen-fixing trees and shrubs are normally introduced as bare rooted transplants. If the nurse is sown as seed, sowing should be conducted between May and September. Shrub and tree species are best planted in autumn or winter.

Photo: Valerie Hack

The use of a nurse grass to stabilise a bare soil slope. In this instance, Italian rye-grass (*Lolium multiflorum*) has been used. The presence of the grass is sufficient to bind the upper layers of the soil with fibrous roots and prevent soil erosion. The sparse nature of the grass is beneficial as it permits the establishment of herb species within the gaps.

2 Grasslands

2.1 Background information

'Grassland' is a broad category of vegetation type loosely defined as being dominated by grass (graminoid) species (Rodwell, 1992). It encompasses a range of different grassland types that can be classified in various different ways. These types refer to the forms that the vegetation can take and the component species present; these are dictated by varying environmental conditions in different situations and previous management history. It is widely acknowledged that the same assemblage of species will almost always result given the same environmental conditions and management; this is the concept behind the NVC (see Box E.3.2). However, if one or more factor(s) are varied, the assemblage will be altered and another grassland type will result.

Grasslands are an attractive habitat with a wide range of associated wildlife. They can also be simple to create and maintain. Grasslands can develop on every soil type; it is therefore always possible to create grassland, regardless of the site conditions.

The ideal soil characteristics necessary to create a diverse grassland sward are good drainage and poor nutrient status. The creation of grassland is therefore a useful option where there is a limiting supply of nutrient-rich topsoil.

Semi-natural grasslands are divided into three groups based on soil pH: neutral, acid and calcareous. The conservation status of UK semi-natural grasslands is described in Box F.2.1.

2.2 Reasons for creating grassland

2.2.1 Primary objectives

When creating a grassland, one should have a clear idea of the reason why the grassland is to be created. In particular, a choice should be made whether the main objective of the grassland creation is to provide nature conservation benefit rather than to provide an agricultural crop (i.e. hay). Although these two objectives can be compatible, grasslands that are managed to maximise their nature conservation value cannot also be managed to maximise productivity (the usual objective of intensive agricultural management).

If nature conservation is the primary reason for creating a grassland on a restored landfill, the type of grassland to be created should be selected carefully, as grassland types have varying nature conservation value. A grassland consisting mainly of productive agricultural strains of

---

Box F.2.1. Conservation status of grasslands in the UK

Neutral grasslands

The UK Steering Group Report (Anon., 1995) states that unimproved neutral grassland has undergone a massive decline in the 20th century, almost entirely due to changes in agricultural practices. It is estimated that by 1984 the area of semi-natural grassland in England and Wales had declined by 97%, and losses have continued since then. Scotland has also suffered dramatic losses through agricultural modification of grassland. Recent estimates gauge the total extent of species-rich neutral grassland to be less than 15000 ha (Anon, 1995). As a result, old neutral grassland hay meadows are one of several grassland Priority Habitats in the UK Biodiversity Action Plan (UKBAP).A number of rare and scarce species can be associated with this habitat such as green-winged orchid (Orchis morio), wood bitter-vetch (Vicia orobus) and fritillary (Fritillaria meleagris). Additionally, lowland meadows are important for a number of birds and mammal species of conservation importance including skylark, lapwing, grey partridge and brown hare, as well as a large range of invertebrate species.

Acid grasslands

Acid grasslands have been lost at a similar rate and for similar reasons as neutral grasslands, with substantial losses resulting from agricultural intensification and, in some locations, forestry. The occurrence of lowland acid grassland is now thought to be restricted to less than 30 000 ha (Anon, 1995) and is concentrated in a handful of areas such as Breckland, the New Forest, Dorset, Suffolk and Shropshire. As a result lowland acid grassland is also a priority habitat type in the UKBAP.

Acid grassland can also support a significant number of rare plant species such as mossy stonecrop (Crassula tillaea), slender birds-foot trefoil (Lotus angustissimus) and clustered clover (Trifolium glomeratum). Many birds of conservation importance are also associated with acid grassland, including skylark, woodlark and stone curlew.

Calcareous grasslands

Calcareous grasslands have also suffered dramatic losses with current estimates of the remaining area being between 33000 and 41000 ha, mainly in Wiltshire, Dorset and the South Downs (Anon., 1995).

Upland and lowland calcareous grassland are both UK BAP Priority Habitats, and have major conservation value, supporting rare plants such as monkey orchid (Orchis simia) and pasqueflower (Pulsatilla vulgaris), and butterflies such as adonis blue, silver-spotted skipper and Duke of Burgundy fritillary.

---

grasses with a small amount of herbs will have little value to wildlife. In contrast, a grassland containing nectar-producing herbs with a wide diversity of species present will tend to have greater nature conservation value. One should also aim to create either neutral, acid or calcareous grasslands depending on the local soil type and the geographical location of the site. In addition, it is not acceptable to compile an ad hoc assortment of species for inclusion in a seed mix. Therefore, a species mix should always be based on naturally occurring grassland types as described by the NVC. It is strongly recommended that advice is sought from a suitably qualified ecologist on the most appropriate grassland type to be created and the species to be included.

It should be noted that any species mix based on an NVC type will not instantly

create an example of that NVC grassland. However, using the right species at the outset is a good starting point. A grassland consisting of appropriate native species is more likely to accrue nature conservation value than a grassland compiled of alien or inappropriate native species. Therefore, given appropriate management and a suitable length of time, it is possible that created grassland will acquire considerable nature conservation value. For this reason, grassland creation at landfill sites can potentially contribute to BAP Priority Habitat targets, and can also create potentially suitable habitat for a substantial range of species, thereby contributing to targets for a number of BAP Priority Species.

Even if a newly created grassland does not possess much inherent nature conservation value, the mere presence of the grassland may well enhance the conservation value of nearby existing grassland by acting as a protective buffer strip and thereby shielding the high quality grassland from adverse edge effects and other pressures. In addition, mobile species such as butterflies can benefit from the provision of new areas of grassland which act as 'stepping stones', enabling them to disperse to previously isolated grassland fragments.

Strategically positioning new grassland in relation to existing areas will facilitate the movement of species between sites, reducing the likelihood of local extinctions. The ideal scenario is to create new grassland adjacent to existing areas, but this will not always be possible. Placing new grassland as a linking habitat between two isolated fragments will assist in combating the effects of fragmentation. Additional features such as hedgerows or grassy boundary strips (see Section F.6) can serve as wildlife corridors between areas of conservation value (Kirby, 1995). This is of most benefit to mobile species such as mammals and birds, but may also benefit other species.

2.2.2 Secondary objectives

There are many secondary objectives for grassland creation on landfill sites. A selection is given below.

- Grassland is effective in preventing soil erosion since it is quick to establish and provide a protective cover on bare soil.
- Flowering herbs in a grassland sward can visually enhance the landscape and provide a valuable amenity resource for people living in urban areas. Other attractive species such as butterflies are common associates of many grassland types.
- Like other habitat types, grasslands can provide an educational resource for the study of various aspects of ecology concerned with that habitat or as an opportunity to study the success of grassland creation on landfill sites by undertaking long term monitoring.

2.3 Grassland creation on landfill sites – planning

As there is a relevant grassland type for all soil types, grassland creation is a versatile option for a landfill site, especially if the nature of the soil is variable or unpredictable. There are relatively few constraints imposed by the landfill site on grassland creation. Mowing grassland areas may be a

problem where above-ground gas and leachate control structures exist, but this can be easily overcome with a degree of planning.

Grassland creation can be a relatively low-cost exercise, especially if there is a source of seed close to or on the site. Where phased restoration is used, a newly-created species-rich grassland can be used as a seed source for subsequent grassland creation (see Cromwell Bottom case study number 2 and Penny Hill case study number 8). Grassland creation does not require large amounts of topsoil, which further reduces costs.

2.3.1 Basic principles
Restoration planning

Suitable materials for the creation of the chosen grassland type should be identified at an early stage. It is advised that the planning stage is used to determine exactly what type of grassland is desired; for example, a flower-rich spring-flowering grassland or a summer-flowering hay meadow. However, this decision will also in part be informed by both the nature and quantity of soils available and the type of nearby grassland habitats. If sufficient quantities of appropriate soil are available, the desired grassland is feasible. If soil resources are not sufficient, a soil forming material may be used with appropriate amelioration (Section F.1.2.4). If a suitable soil substitute is unavailable, the grassland type should be selected solely according to the nature of the soils / soil substitutes that are available (see *determining factors* below).

Grasslands require ongoing management, and the intensity of management necessary increases with soil fertility. If management resources are limited, it will be preferable to select a grassland type that requires only one or two cuts per year. Alternatively, using very infertile soils will reduce growth and hence reduce management requirements (see Section F.2.4.4). Most grasslands managed for nature conservation have low management demands.

When the grassland has established, it may be possible to harvest and sell seed (some seed houses will conduct contract harvesting) to generate an income. Alternatively, hay can be sold or the land rented out for grazing (if grazing is an appropriate management regime – this will depend on the grassland type and whether conditions at the site are suitable for livestock).

Constraining factors of a landfill site

Several constraints apply to grassland creation, but far fewer than for habitat types such as woodland, scrub and wetland. Consequently, there are a greater number of examples of grassland creation on landfills than any other type of habitat.

Minor constraints arise from the presence of pollution control infrastructure. Landfill gas wellheads are likely to be placed throughout the site at an average distance of 40-60 m apart on a site that has accepted substantial amounts of biodegradable waste (Environment Agency, in prep.). This does not prohibit grassland creation, but wellheads and underground pipework may affect the type of management that can be employed. Large agricultural mowing machinery may not be sufficiently manoeuverable to cut close to the wellheads; some strips of grassland may have to be left uncut. This is not ecologically detrimental since it increases habitat diversity. Altenatively, the grassland can be grazed.

Determining factors of a landfill site

The major determining factor for the successful creation of grassland is the matching of the chosen species with the nature of the soil, particularly pH. Species selection must therefore be made with the requirements of the species in mind. Selecting only those species that will tolerate the soil conditions at the site improves the chances of the species mix persisting.

Site design

Design considerations present few constraints. Access roads should be designed at the same time that the grassland is designed. If the grassland is to be grazed, access will be needed for moving stock and husbandry. Also, a wildflower grassland is a very attractive feature, and it may be appropriate to locate such grasslands where there is maximum opportunity for public appreciation. The layout of footpaths should be incorporated into the original site design, to avoid wasting seed on areas that will eventually become trampled.

2.3.2 Selecting a grassland type

The greater the species richness of the grassland the greater the conservation value. However, there should be high numbers of characteristic grassland species rather than species characteristic of other habitats (e.g. weeds and shrubs). Additionally, a grassland with a large proportion of herb species (such as 40%) is more favourable than one entirely consisting of grasses. All the plant species used to create the grassland should be native to the British flora.

The selection of the most appropriate grassland should be based on the following guidelines:

- The grassland type should have considerable potential nature conservation value; the grassland should therefore be modelled on a BAP Priority Habitat grassland type. Highly productive agricultural grasslands such as perennial rye-grass leys should not be created
- The selected grassland type should be appropriate given the available restoration materials. The most important characteristic is soil pH; a neutral grassland would only be appropriate if the available soil is of a neutral or very mildly acidic pH.
- If there are areas of existing semi-natural grassland close to the site with nature conservation value, there is a strong case for creating the same type of grassland as the existing areas. The main reason for this is that the existing grassland should be the most appropriate grassland type for that locality. Using the species composition of nearby grassland as a guide reduces the risk that inappropriate species will be introduced. However, if non-local soils or soil forming materials are used for restoration, a local grassland type may not be appropriate and ecological advice should be sought. Not all grassland types are common and widespread. Some types are scarce due to the rarity of the precise combination of environmental factors under which that grassland develops. The creation of rare grassland types in locations where they would not normally occur is not recommended.
- In contrast, some grassland types are rare because the traditional management that moulded the grassland is no longer practised. It is acceptable to create a once widespread habitat type that has become rare through changes in farming practices. It is advised that guidance on the rarity of various grasslands be sought before the final selection is made.
- Damp or inundated grasslands should not be created on the landfill cap (although it may be possible to create them in boundary areas).

- The grassland type should be appropriate to the site's:
  - geographical location,
  - altitude;
  - climate; and
  - soil type.
- Available management is also an important consideration. Grassland types have evolved under specific and constant management; should this change or cease altogether, the grassland type will change. For example, the choice of livestock species for grazing species can dramatically affect the species composition of the sward. Therefore, the likely nature of available management should be determined at an early stage, since this may affect the types of grassland which can be created.

The NVC can be used as a guide for selecting grassland types for creation, but it must be stressed that professional advice should be sought on this subject. NVC types suitable for creation on landfill are given in Table F.2.1 below.

Neutral, acid and calcareous grasslands are described in greater detail below, and examples of NVC communities with suggested seed mixes are given.

Neutral grasslands

The NVC describes 18 neutral grassland communities. The range of neutral grasslands encompasses the species-poor examples typical of agricultural grasslands that are widespread throughout Britain to the herb-rich traditional hay meadows that are now very restricted in their range. The spectrum also includes grasslands that are often

flooded and which have permanently damp soils.

Neutral grasslands are generally found as enclosed fields in lowland areas (i.e. below 300 m altitude), often on soils that do not dry out in summer, with soil pH between 5-6.5 and moderate to high nutrient status. The pH range of neutral grasslands is actually slightly acidic, but the term 'neutral' is used to differentiate these grasslands from grasslands on strongly acidic soils. The soils are often alluvial but can be either clay or loam-based, and are generally either a brown earth or meadow soil. Brown earths are well drained, whereas meadows occur on flat ground and have a water table that is never far from the surface.

Species-poor neutral grasslands with low conservation value tend to be dominated by perennial rye-grass (*Lolium perenne*), and are very productive and highly fertile. Neutral grasslands with high conservation value will be more species-rich, supporting a greater range of grass species, including meadow foxtail (*Alopecurus pratensis*), crested dog's-tail (*Cynosurus cristatus*) and sweet vernal-grass (*Anthoxanthum odoratum*). These are accompanied by a higher proportion of herbs compared to species-poor grasslands, including species such as meadow buttercup (*Ranunculus acris*), selfheal (*Prunella vulgaris*), oxeye daisy (*Leucanthemum vulgare*), dandelion (*Taraxacum officinale*) and daisy (*Bellis perennis*). These grasslands are typically either grazed or managed as hay meadows with aftermath grazing.

Species-rich neutral grasslands are typically managed as hay meadows; an example of a flower-rich hay meadow is given as a suitable NVC type for creation

Table F.2.1. Potentially suitable NVC grassland types that could be created on a restored landfill

Grassland type	NVC community
Neutral	MG4 (meadow foxtail – great burnet grassland)
Neutral	MG5 (black knapweed – crested dog's-tail grassland)
Neutral	MG8 (crested dog's-tail – kingcup grassland)[1]
Acid	U1 (sheep's fescue – common bent – sheep's sorrel grassland)
Calcareous	CG2 (sheep's fescue – meadow oat-grass grassland)[2]
Calcareous	CG10 (sheep's fescue – wild thyme grassland)[3]

1 Only suitable for creation off the cap, as this grassland type requires seasonally wet soils.
2 Southern Britain only.   *3 Northern Britain only.*

Box F.2.2. Example of neutral grassland NVC type.

NVC community MG5: *Cynosurus cristatus – Centaurea nigra* **grassland (crested dog's-tail – black knapweed)**

MG5 is a herb-rich grassland, with a greater proportion of flowers to grasses than some other grasslands.

Soil type
Soil type is the main determinant of grassland type. If the soil type is not of the correct nature for this grassland, the sward will not resemble MG5 regardless of the species that are introduced. The soil should be of a neutral pH, well drained and moderately fertile; ideally a brown earth, with topsoil and subsoil mixed in 50:50 proportions.

Management
MG5 grasslands are traditionally managed for hay, which promotes a high species richness. The sward is visually attractive which is a useful attribute for a grassland that is open to public access. They are normally grazed through winter until late April, when farmyard manure can be applied (although this is not essential). The sward is then left to grow until June when a hay cut is taken. Grazing is then resumed, unless a second hay cut is taken in September in which case grazing resumes after the second hay cut.

Benefit to wildlife
MG5 is a UKBAP Priority Habitat. The sward is rich in flowers, and a wide variety of insects therefore utilise this grassland. It is also of benefit to small mammals such as field mouse and therefore to birds of prey. After the hay is cut, grass and herb seeds fall onto the ground and are eaten by seed eating birds such as yellowhammer.

MG5a suggested seed mix
The following are a selection of species that can be included. Specialist botanical expertise should always be sought on the composition of the seedmix.

Red fescue *Festuca rubra*	10%	Ribwort plantain *Plantago lanceolata*	2%
Crested dog's-tail *Cynosurus cristatus*	30%	Black knapweed *Centaurea nigra*	5%
Yorkshire fog *Holcus lanatus*	6%	Red clover *Trifolium pratense*	2%
Cocksfoot *Dactylis glomerata*	5%	Daisy *Bellis perennis*	2%
Common bent *Agrostis capillaris*	20%	Meadow vetchling *Lathyrus pratensis*	2%
Sweet vernal-grass *Anthoxanthum odoratum*	5%	Oxeye daisy *Leucanthemum vulgare*	5%
Meadow fescue *Festuca pratensis*	2%	Field scabious *Knautia arvensis*	2%
Hard rush *Juncus inflexus*	2%	Yellow rattle *Rhinanthus minor*	1%
Bird's-foot trefoil *Lotus corniculatus*	5%		

Percentages refer to the percentage of the species in the sward (see Box E.3.2).

---

on a landfill site together with a seed mix (see Box F.2.2). Flower-rich hay meadows would be most suitable where the objectives of habitat creation are to produce a sward that is both attractive and of nature conservation value. These grasslands occur on less fertile soils and tend to be species rich, with many colourful perennial species. Additionally, these grasslands will withstand a degree of trampling outside of the flowering period, and could therefore be used as public recreation areas either before or after the hay is cut.

Acid grasslands
Acid grasslands are found on acidic, usually peaty or sandy soils, with pH between 3.5 and 6.5. The majority of acid grasslands occur in the north and west of Britain on soils that have been leached of nutrients over time as a result of high rainfall. Their natural distribution is generally restricted to areas where hard rocks such as granite or softer rocks such as greensand or sandstones occur or over sand and gravel deposits. Sandy soils are susceptible to leaching even if rainfall is relatively low, and thus sandy soils in the south are also commonly acidic. Acid grasslands are typically managed by grazing.

Acid grassland frequently occurs as a mosaic with some types of heath vegetation. Where very sandy and infertile soils are available, it may well be possible to recreate patches of heathland within acid grassland (see Section F.4).

Acid grassland is also found as a mosaic with bracken (*Pteridium aquilinum*) and gorse (*Ulex* spp.). Bracken is invasive, reduces soil quality and is poisonous to livestock, and is therefore not recommended for introduction. Gorse will grow on very poor soils and is a useful species to introduce, especially where soils are very infertile, as it is a nitrogen-fixer (see Section F.1.3.3). It can also provide habitat for rare birds such as Dartford warbler. However, large stands of gorse can constitute a fire hazard, and should therefore not be allowed to develop near to roads, footpaths and car parks.

Many acid grassland NVC types refer to communities that occur in the uplands of Britain (above 300 m altitude); it is unlikely that a landfill would be situated in such areas. However, there are some acid grassland types that occur in the lowlands. A widespread lowland acid grassland NVC community (and seed mix) is presented in Box F.2.3.

Calcareous grasslands
These grasslands occur on calcareous substrates such as chalk, limestone and calcareous superficials, with pH between 6.5-8.5. Calcareous grassland creation may be feasible if the available soil or soil forming material has an alkaline pH. The

---

Box F.2.3. Example of an acid grassland NVC type

NVC community U1: *Festuca ovina – Agrostis capillaris – Rumex acetosella* **grassland (sheep's fescue – common bent – sheep's sorrel)**

This grassland appears very tussocky, with a large proportion of bare earth, and becomes very dry in summer. The vegetation is often rather short with many semi-prostrate species. There is a wide range of grass species as well as herbs and mosses.

Soil type
U1 grassland occurs on base- and nutrient-poor droughty soils in warm lowland areas where rainfall is relatively low. It is the most common acid grassland in the south of Britain. The soil is usually a well-drained acid podzol with pH between 3.5 and 6.5.

Management
The sward benefits from light grazing by sheep or cattle (or mowing) throughout the year, although it can also be managed for hay. A certain amount of disturbance is beneficial; creating areas of bare ground provides basking sites for reptiles and habitat for invertebrates.

Benefit to wildlife
This grassland can support a variety of ground-nesting birds such as skylark and stone curlew, as well as a number of reptiles such as adder and slow-worm.

U1b suggested seed mix
The following are a selection of species that can be included. Specialist botanical expertise should always be sought on the composition of the seedmix.

Sheep's fescue *Festuca ovina*	33%	Common bent *Agrostis capillaris*	33%
Sheep's sorrel *Rumex acetosella*	33%		

Percentages refer to the percentage of the species in the sward (see Box E.3.2).

---

soils of calcareous grasslands are typically thin and well drained, and are often drought-prone during the summer. The sward comprises a number of species that would not survive in neutral or acid grasslands. Calcareous grasslands are typically managed by grazing.

There are 14 British calcareous grassland NVC types. These can divided into northern and southern types along an approximate line from Durham to the Mendips via Derbyshire and the edge of Wales. This divide is determined by annual levels of rainfall. Due to the geographic distribution of calcareous rocks, most (although by no means all) British calcareous grasslands are situated in the south of the country.

Examples of northern and southern calcareous grassland NVC types (with seed mixes) are given in Boxes F.2.4 and F.2.5 respectively.

2.3.3 Species selection
Once the grassland type has been selected, the next step is to compile a species list. An existing typical semi-natural grassland, on similar soils, close to the site will constitute an ideal model in terms of the species to use for creating new grassland (Gilbert & Anderson, 1998). The simplest method is to obtain a species list of the grassland and use the commonest species as the basis of the species list for planting.

In the absence of a local grassland to use as a guide, the NVC (Rodwell, 1991 *et seq.*) can be used to compile a species mix that is tailored to the site. The NVC gives floristic tables of constant species found in NVC types together with variations in abundance between types. The NVC can be consulted for lists of component species and their relative abundance, and the species list compiled from these (see Box E.3.2 for further information). Specialist advice should always be sought from a suitably qualified botanist who can advise on both the appropriateness of a grassland type, and on the selection of species that should be used.

The following guidelines specific to grassland creation are given to assist with species selection. These introductory guidelines are based on NCC guidelines for amenity-based grassland creation (Wells *et al.*, 1981). Indicative seed mixes for neutral, acid and calcareous grassland NVC types suitable for creation on landfill sites are given in Boxes F.2.2-2.5. However, these should only be used as a guide; they do not include those species that may be local to an area and give local grasslands their distinctive character. In addition, guidance on grassland creation

for butterflies is given in Box F.2.6.

Alternatively, an off-the-shelf seed mix can be purchased. However, it is strongly recommended that advice is taken as to the most appropriate composition of the mix. Whilst there are reputable seed merchants that sell well-researched seedmixes, there are some mixes for sale that are of lesser quality.

Seedmix design guidelines
Keep the seed mix simple – using more than 20 species will make the mix too expensive.

Species to use
Compile the species mix from the list of constant species (the characteristic species) of that grassland type in the same proportions as found naturally.
   Use species that are:
   ● native to the British Isles;
   ● not known to be invasive or very competitive; and
   ● common and widespread.

Species availability
A number of species are unavailable as seeds. A seed merchant should be consulted on the availability of a species. It is advised that if a characteristic species of the desired grassland type is unavailable as seed, it should be introduced in another

Box F.2.4. Example of southern calcareous grassland NVC type

NVC community CG2: *Festuca ovina – Avenula pratensis* grassland (sheep's fescue – meadow oat-grass)

This grassland is a short turf with a considerable variety of species, and is very attractive during the flowering season. It is widespread in southern regions and therefore an appropriate grassland for creation on southern landfill sites in calcaerous areas. Good quality CG2 grassland is becoming increasingly rare due to changes in management regimes and conversion to arable.

Soil type
CG2 grassland forms on thin, free-draining lowland calcareous soils in a warm dry temperate climate. Soil fertility is moderate, with pH between 7.0 and 8.5.

Management
The traditional management involves grazing. This can be provided by cattle or sheep.

Benefit to wildlife
This grassland is potential habitat for ground-nesting birds and many species of invertebrates including a number that are BAP Priority Species.

CG2 suggested seed mix
The following are a selection of species that can be included. Specialist botanical expertise should always be sought on the composition of the seedmix.

Sheep's fescue *Festuca ovina*	30%	Fairy flax *Linum catharticum*	1%
Crested hair-grass *Koeleria macrantha*	10%	Mouse-ear hawkweed *Hieracium pilosella*	2%
Common quaking-grass *Briza media*	5%	Small scabious *Scabiosa columbaria*	1%
Meadow oat-grass *Avenula pratensis*	10%	Wild thyme *Thymus praecox*	2%
Cocksfoot *Dactylis glomerata*	5%	Red clover *Trifolium pratense*	1%
Downy oat-grass *Avenula pubescens*	20%	Selfheal *Prunella vulgaris*	2%
Salad burnet *Sanguisorba minor*	1%	Devils-bit scabious *Succisa pratensis*	2%
Ribwort plantain *Plantago lanceolata*	1%	Black knapweed *Centaurea nigra*	2%
Bird's-foot trefoil *Lotus corniculatus*	1%	Oxeye daisy *Leucanthemum vulgare*	2%
Rough hawkbit *Leontodon hispidus*	1%	Yellow rattle *Rhinanthus minor*	1%

Percentages refer to the percentage of the species in the sward (see Box E.3.2).

Photo: David Hill

Abundant red clover amongst grass species within a hay meadow created at Cromwell Bottom landfill site (Case study no. 3).

form such as a plug or container plant. If this is not possible, the species should be omitted rather than substituted with another.

Soil pH
The pH of the soil is the most important factor governing the distribution of grassland types. The selected species should therefore be characteristic of grasslands with the same pH as the soil on the landfill site.

Proportions of grasses to herbs
It is recommended that advice is sought on the appropriate proportion of grasses to herbs. Grass species form the major component of grasslands, and often comprise 80% of the above-ground sward in a semi-natural grassland. This proportion should therefore be retained in the seed mix. In areas where the sward is likely to be subject to high levels of trampling or mowing, i.e. along a footpath, this proportion should be increased to 95%.

Box F.2.5. Example of northern calcareous grassland NVC type

NVC community CG10: *Festuca ovina – Thymus praecox* (sheep's fescue – wild thyme)
This is a species-rich grassland containing a variety of grasses and herbs. It is often closely grazed by rabbits or sheep, producing a short, springy turf. It requires moderately heavy rainfall (over 160 rain days per year) and thus occurs in upland situations with a cool and moist climate. The number of suitable landfill sites in upland situations is likely to be quite small.

Soil type
The soil is generally well drained, thin and calcareous, normally a brown earth with poor fertility and pH between 7.0 and 8.5.

Management
The traditional management involves light grazing throughout the year. This can be provided by cattle or sheep.

CG10 suggested seed mix
The following are a selection of species that can be included. Specialist botanical expertise should always be sought on the composition of the seedmix.

Sheep's fescue *Festuca ovina*	30%		Ribwort plantain *Plantago lanceolata*	2%
Common bent *Agrostis capillaris*	20%		Harebell *Campanula rotundifolia*	2%
Red fescue *Festuca rubra*	20%		Selfheal *Prunella vulgaris*	4%
Sweet vernal-grass *Anthoxanthum odoratum*	10%		Heath bedstraw *Galium saxatile*	2%
Wild thyme *Thymus praecox*	4%		Heath speedwell *Veronica officinalis*	1%
Common dog-violet *Viola riviniana*	1%		Yarrow *Achillea millefolium*	1%
Tormentil *Potentilla erecta*	2%		Yellow rattle *Rhinanthus minor*	1%

Percentages refer to the percentage of the species in the sward (see Box E.3.2).

The grass component is important for several reasons:

- Grass germinates quickly and establishes a fibrous root system which stabilises the soil;
- Some grasses are evergreen perennials and thus protect the soil from winter erosion; and
- Grass seed is cheaper than seed of herb species.

Relative abundances
- Every effort should be made to re-create the characteristic abundances of the species, as this is often what determines one type of grassland from another. However, it is important to note that grassland composition will change over time as the grassland matures.
- If seed or plants are used, advice should be sought on the weight of seed or plants per m^2 required to yield the correct proportions in the sward. For instance, some species produce large quantities of seed; only a small number of seeds may need to be sown at the outset for the species to become dominant. Conversely, some species reproduce so slowly that a high percentage of the seed mix may need to be of these species.
- Some species interact; for example, two aggressive grasses may counterbalance each other and help to prevent each other from

becoming dominant. Crested dog's-tail has been used to reduce the competitiveness of red fescue to ensure that the sward remains species-rich (Richard Brown, pers. comm.).

Longevity
Semi-natural grasslands generally consist of perennial species. Annual species require an appreciable amount of bare ground for the next generation of seeds to germinate. The amount of bare ground available each year can be unpredictable, and it is therefore inappropriate to base grassland creation purely on annual or biennial species.

Structure
Some herb species have a tall growth habit and are able to persist in an infrequently managed grassland. Species with a low or prostrate growth habit will not persist in a sward that is left uncut for most of the summer. Species selection therefore depends upon the aftercare management regime. If the grassland is to be managed for hay, taller species should be included. Grazed grassland should contain prostrate and small species.

2.4 Grassland creation – practical methods

It is recommended that ecologically-based creation methods are used if possible, such as strewing hay or using seed or topsoil originating from a local

species-rich grassland. This ensures that the species within the mix will be adapted to that area, characteristic of that locality and in the correct proportions. It also conserves local genetic diversity.

However, this may not be possible if there are no species-rich grasslands nearby, or if nearby grasslands are of an unsuitable type. Therefore, it may be necessary to compile one's own seed mix. If selected with sufficient care, an 'artificial' seed mix can result in a sward that closely resembles an NVC grassland type with nature conservation value. Whilst purpose-made grassland seed mixtures can be purchased, these tend to be very general in character, and often contain agricultural strains or alien species. It is best to use seed of native origin and if possible with local provenance (see Box E.3.2). Likewise, agricultural strains should be avoided. Many of these strains are suitable for amenity use and are cheaper than true wild seed. However, these are largely unsuitable for genuine habitat creation. If commercial seed must be used, the best option is to compile a mix by buying seed of various species separately.

If a no-management sward is required, it will not be possible to recreate a semi-natural grassland such as those described by the NVC; the characteristics of these grasslands are achieved and maintained largely as a result of management.

There are four stages in the creation of grassland, addressed in the following

Box F.2.6. Grassland creation for butterflies

Many typical grassland butterfly species have declined greatly in recent years in response to large-scale agricultural improvement, which eliminates the native plants upon which caterpillars of all species depend. Grassland creation on landfill sites therefore provides a good opportunity to benefit many of our declining butterfly species.

Factors to be considered in grassland creation for butterflies
The principal factor limiting the population of various butterfly species is the availability of its larval food plant. The caterpillars of many butterfly species rely on specific food plants, and it is therefore important that these species are included in planting mixes if butterflies are to be attracted to the site. The main food plants of a range of common grassland butterfly species are listed below.

Other factors that the design of grassland creation should take into consideration to maximise the value of grassland to butterflies include:

- Provision of plants whose flowers act as a good nectar source for adults. Examples include common knapweed (*Centaurea nigra*), greater knapweed (*Centaurea scabiosa*), thistles (*Cirsium* spp.) and teasel (*Dipsacus fullonum*).
- Variation in grassland structure. Species diversity will be maximised in a mosaic of different sward heights. This can be achieved by varying management between different areas.
- Provision of sheltering scrub. Whilst many species will flourish in open grassland, others require a degree of shelter, such as that provided by scattered scrub or hedgerows. Species diversity will therefore be higher if an element of scrub or hedgerow is incorporated into the restoration design.

Photo: David Hill

Marbled white butterfly on common knapweed.

Main food plants of widespread grassland butterflies

Butterfly species	Main food plant(s)
Small skipper	Yorkshire fog (*Holcus lanatus*)
Essex skipper	Cock's-foot (*Dactylis glomerata*) & creeping soft-grass (*Holcus mollis*)
Large skipper	Cock's-foot (*Dactylis glomerata*)
Green-veined white	Various crucifer species
Orange-tip	Cuckoo flower (*Cardamine pratense*) & garlic mustard (*Alliaria petiolata*)
Small copper	Common sorrel (*Rumex acetosa*) Sheep's sorrel (*Rumex acetosella*)
Common blue	Bird's-foot trefoil (*Lotus corniculatus*) – not cultivar
Marbled white	Various native grasses esp. red fescue (*Festuca rubra*)
Gatekeeper	Various native grasses e.g. bents (*Agrostis* spp.), fescues (*Festuca* spp.) & meadow grasses (*Poa* spp.)
Wall brown	Various native grasses e.g. cock's foot (*Dactylis glomerata*), yorkshire fog (*Holcus lanatus*)
Meadow brown	Various native grasses
Small heath	Various fine-leaved native grasses, e.g. fescues (*Festuca* spp.) & bents (*Agrostis* spp.)

sections:
- Site preparation (F.2.4.1)
- Species introduction (F.2.4.2)
- Aftercare (F.2.4.3)
- Long-term management (F.2.4.4)

2.4.1 Site preparation
The preparation of the site involves ensuring that the soil is in suitable condition. Ideal soil characteristics are given in Box F.2.7. Information on how to achieve these characteristics is given in Section F.1.

Use of a nurse species
Planting a nurse species may be necessary for grassland creation on infertile soils, but will usually not be required on soils with abundant nutrients unless there is a risk of soil erosion. The nurse species should be easily germinating and non-persistent, and should rapidly create cover and enhance the establishment of true grassland species. The nurse should be sown at the same time or before the grassland is created, depending upon whether there is a delay between site restoration and grassland creation. If there is a delay, establishing vegetation cover is important, and a nurse species can provide this (Wells, 1989). More details on nurse species are given in Section F.1.6.2.

Suitable grassland nurse species have specific characteristics: abundantly available seeds, rapid and high percentage germination rates, fast growth, and non-persistence in the sward. An annual or biennial species is therefore suitable. On neutral soils, the most commonly used is Italian rye-grass (*Lolium multiflorum*), but other annual or biennial species may also be appropriate. Agricultural species such as common oat, rape, mustard or barley can be used on neutral soils. Grasses are best to use as their fibrous roots hold the soil together. The physical presence of light cover whilst the seeds are germinating can also increase germination rates. The use of a straw mulch has been found to be effective (Gross, 1984), but this should be removed after the seedlings have produced their first true leaves.

Box F.2.7. Ideal soil characteristics for grassland creation

- **Correct pH:**
  - 3.5-5.0 for acid grasslands
  - 5.0-6.5 for neutral grasslands
  - 6.5-8.5 for calcareous grasslands

- **Adequate depth, at least 0.5 m deep**

- **Weed free**

- **Good structure, therefore:**
  - uncompacted, and
  - containing organic matter

- **Low fertility, therefore:**
  the ideal substrate is subsoil

- **Cultivated to a fine tilth**

Nurse management
Management of a nurse basically entails ensuring that it does not persist in the sward. Since they are short-lived species, they are easy to eradicate as many individuals will naturally die back, but some plants may persist. The nurse should therefore be mown once just before seed is formed to prevent the next generation from establishing. If the grassland sward is under 10 cm high when this cut is conducted, it should not be damaged. All cuttings should be removed.

Sowing rates
The weight of seed sown will depend on the species used. As an average figure, where grass seed is used as a winter cover in advance of habitat creation, the seed should be sown at about 46 kg/ha (Wells *et al.*, 1981). If a grass nurse is sown at the same time as the main habitat species, the rate can be reduced to around 10 kg/ha (Flora Locale, 1999). Annual species used to produce a colourful sward in the first year should be sown at 2 kg/ha. Further details can be found in Gilbert & Anderson (1998).

2.4.2 Species introduction
There are several methods that can be employed to introduce grassland species. Success rates will usually depend on whether the method is appropriate to a particular situation. The methods available include:

- Seed
- Strewn hay
- Plug plants (herbs only)
- Translocation of turves or individual species (seeds can be sown in gaps between turves)
- Addition of soil with a plentiful seed bank /fragment bank
- Natural colonisation

Seed
Sowing procedure
The sowing procedure is as follows:
- Prepare the site immediately prior to sowing. Clear the site of weeds such

as docks and thistles by spraying off the existing vegetation using a contact herbicide such as Glyphosate. Remove dead vegetation (this can be composted for use as a soil conditioner).

- Conduct the sowing in either autumn or spring. Autumn-sown seedlings stand a better chance of surviving drought the following summer, but risk being killed by winter frosts. The larger the seedlings, the better they can resist frost; spring-sown seedlings will tolerate winter frost better. If the seeds require pre-treatment such as vernalisation, an autumn sowing will be necessary, as frost will naturally supply the freezing treatment. Since most seed mixes are likely to contain some species requiring pre-treatment, best practice is always to sow in autumn.
- Create the seed bed by harrowing using a chain, disc or tine harrow to provide a fine tilth. This should be shallow (6-10 cm depth) to avoid excessive disturbance of the soil, and should only be conducted when the soil is moist (i.e. not wet or totally dry).
- Mix the seed with an equal volume of a carrier such as sand or barley meal to ensure that it is evenly distributed.
- Seed can be sown by hand, broadcast by tractor-mounted machinery such as a fertiliser spreader, direct drilled using a cereal seed drill or slot seeder, or hydroseeded. If broadcast, the seed container should be repeatedly agitated to prevent smaller seeds from settling to the bottom. Hydroseeding is a method of sowing whereby a liquid emulsion of seed, fertiliser and a binding agent is piped onto the receptor site. The binding agent allows the mixture to stick to the soil surface. Although expensive, hydroseeding has distinct advantages in a situation where the passage of a tractor is likely to

compact the soil (i.e. if it is clay-rich or wet).

- If the seed is drilled, the sowing rate should be 10 kg/ha at 0.5 cm depth with a drill spacing of 5 cm (English Nature & the Wildlife Trusts, 1999).
- If broadcast, suitable rates quoted vary from 12 kg/ha to 40 kg/ha, and can often be less than those specified by seed companies (Gilbert & Anderson, 1998; Highways Agency, 1993).
- After sowing, a light harrowing followed by rolling ensures good contact of the seed with the soil and boosts germination.

Seed sources
There are two ways of obtaining seed:
- Seed collected from semi-natural grasslands in the local area.

It is possible, although time-consuming, to collect seed from roadsides, grassland etc. provided that that grassland has established naturally and has not been reseeded. Collected seeds should be placed in a container such as a sack or paper bag. Plastic bags should be avoided as the high humidity retained around the seeds can encourage rot and reduce viability.

Areas of species-rich grassland near the site (if available) are probably the most suitable source of large amounts of seed, especially if the grassland is managed as a hay crop. The ideal time to obtain seed is when the majority of seeds are ripe, i.e. just after the hay is normally cut. Collecting seed by hand is time-consuming; the sward should be cut using an Allen scythe and the seed subsequently threshed out by hand into a collection container. Mechanical collection is possible; small combine harvesters can be used which automatically thresh out and collect the seed. Separating seed from hay reduces the bulk and eases problems of storage (green plant stems tend to retain moisture and increase the chances of the seed rotting, although this is not a problem if the hay is used immediately). Separating seeds from stems is a costly procedure, and it may therefore be more economical to use strewn hay as a seed source unless the seed has to be stored.

Wherever possible, it is recommended that seed should be obtained from local sources. If by using this method, some species might be omitted (e.g. due to germination difficulties), it could be possible to bulk up seed of that species from a commercial supplier.

It is illegal to collect seed from species listed on Schedule 8 of the Wildlife and Countryside Act. If a commercial seed merchant is used, one should ensure that the company is reputable.

- Seed bought in bulk from seed merchants

This method is usually expensive but is ideal if there is no nearby seed source. Commercial seed is often pre-treated, so good germination rates should be achievable.

Seeds of individual species can be purchased, or purpose-made seed mixes can be obtained (sold according to the type of grassland required and the characteristics of the receptor site). Buying seed of single species can be proportionally more expensive than purchasing a ready-made seed mix, but is usually preferable for habitat creation as it enables the species mix to be tailored to a specific site (Gilbert & Anderson, 1998). This is recommended as a best practice method.

A breakdown of a ready-made species mix specifiying seed numbers of component species (rather than weight) should be obtained from the supplier. The weight of seeds of different species varies considerably; obtaining details of seed numbers enables one to check the mix composition and ensure that there is a sufficient quantity of species with heavier seeds (Gilbert & Anderson, 1998).

Seed merchants often specify an excessive seeding rate to ensure 100% cover in year 1, which often constitutes a waste of seed. It is often possible to reduce the rate by as much as a third, especially on infertile soils, and still obtain a good cover of vegetation.

Seed obtained from seed merchants is mass-produced. The seed is therefore likely to be from a restricted number of sources with limited genetic diversity. Commercial seed will not generally provide local provenance strains. The mass introduction of similar genetic stock depletes the overall gene pool, with a resultant loss of within-species genetic variability. Other seed sources are therefore generally better for habitat creation.

An increasing amount of seed is now being obtained from direct harvesting an existing species-rich grassland, although only a limited number of seed merchants can supply seed harvested this way. The composition of a seed-mix obtained is this way may not closely reflect the composition of the grassland from which it is harvested, but the advantages of this method are that the origin of the seed is known and the genetic diversity of the seed is likely to be high. Furthermore, if the new grassland is within the local area of the harvested grassland, the seed will be of local provenance. Therefore, obtaining seeds harvested from local sites is always a best practice method and should be followed if practicable. See Gilbert & Anderson (1998) for more information.

Obtaining ripe seed and guaranteeing germination

If seed is collected and stored, several points are worth noting. For seed to germinate it must be ripe. Different species ripen at different times through the summer; a collection on one occasion only is unlikely to harvest ripe seeds of every species present. Additionally, it is unlikely that all plants of the same species will have ripe seeds at the same time (Wells *et al.*, 1981). This is a particularly important consideration when collecting hay to use as a seed source (see below). In general, the best seed collection months are August and September. Appendix 3 lists common British grassland species and the months in which their seeds ripen.

Even with ripe seed, the proportion of viable seeds (those capable of germinating) can be low (Grime *et al.*, 1988). The germination rate of fresh grass seeds is often high, but the rate of herb species tends to be much lower. Seeds often require pre-germination treatment such as scarification (scratching the hard seed coat to assist water penetration) or vernalisation (exposure to freezing temperatures for several weeks) to boost germination rates (Smith *et al.*, 1996;

Wells *et al.*, 1986; Wells *et al.*, 1981). Table F.2.2. lists some species which require seed treatment before sowing.

There are methods for treating seed en masse, such as agitating seed mixed with sharp sand. Most reputable seed companies will carry out pre-germination treatment if required.

If seed is home collected, it may be worth conducting viability trials prior to mass seeding. This would entail sowing small amounts of seed to investigate whether any species experience germination problems. Obviously, the seed from various species should be collected and retained separately so that it is possible to mark the areas with sown seed according to the species sown. If a species does not germinate, the remaining seed should be treated before sowing.

Strewn hay
Strewing methods
- Prepare the site immediately prior to strewing. Clear the site of weeds by spraying off the existing vegetation using a contact herbicide such as Glyphosate.
- Cut the hay from the donor site when the seed is ripe and collect it as bales or as loose hay. Do not allow the hay to dry out.
- Create the seed bed by harrowing using a chain, disc or tine harrow to provide a fine tilth. This should be shallow (6-10 cm depth) to avoid excessive disturbance of the soil, and should only be conducted when the soil is moist (i.e. not wet or totally dry).
- Strew the hay in a thin layer. As a general guide, hay cut from 1 ha of grassland can seed 2 ha of new grassland. The time taken between cutting and strewing should be minimised to prevent the hay from rotting.
- Shake the strewn hay on several successive days after application to ensure that the seeds are removed from their capsules, and to allow the hay to dry. This can be done manually using a pitchfork or

---

Table F.2.2. A selection of species requiring pre-germination seed treatment (preferably vernalisation)

Kidney vetch *Anthyllis vulneraria*	Sainfoin *Onobrychis viciifolia*
Clustered bellflower *Campanula glomerata*	Burnet saxifrage *Pimpinella saxifraga*
Wild carrot *Daucus carota*	Salad burnet *Poterium sanguisorba*
Meadow crane's-bill *Geranium pratense*	Cowslip *Primula veris*
Common rock-rose *Helianthemum chamaecistus*	Weld *Reseda luteola*
Horseshoe vetch *Hippocrepis comosa*	Great burnet *Sanguisorba officinalis*
Bird's-foot trefoil *Lotus corniculatus*	Bush vetch *Vicia cracca*
Black medick *Medicago lupulina*	Smooth tare *Vicia tetrasperma*

Case Study 3:

Cromwell Bottom landfill site – Tag Cut Loop, West Yorkshire
Creation of a range of habitats on an old landfill site

Site details

Site operator:	West Yorkshire Waste Management
Habitat created:	Species-rich grassland, woodland, ponds
Area of habitat created:	circa 8 ha
Existing nature conservation interest:	Site initially a former pulverised fly ash (PFA) lagoon that had developed into a range of habitats including wet woodland and calcareous grassland with several orchid species and the nationally scarce round-leaved wintergreen present.

Site background

Tag Cut Loop is one of a series of old PFA lagoons in the Calder valley for which planning permission was granted for landfill in 1983, despite considerable local opposition on the basis of the site's nature conservation importance. In response to this opposition it was agreed that site restoration would be designed to benefit nature conservation. Landfill operations at the site ceased in the early 1990s, and habitat creation works were completed in 1995.

Habitat creation objectives

The principal aim of restoration was to create a range of habitats in order to maximize biodiversity. These habitats included species-rich hay meadow, woodland and a number of ponds.

In addition, a small area of the site was not landfilled and has been largely left to colonise naturally since site closure. This area was also used as a receptor site for round-leaved wintergreen, translocated from elsewhere on the site.

Techniques used

Soil provision
Subsoil for restoration comprised spoil from local gravel-workings. A small quantity of the original topsoil, stored in sacks throughout site operation, was also used in restoration. The use of local soil should ensure that conditions are right for the establishment of species native to the local area. This is especially relevant to those parts of the site which have been left to colonise naturally, and in the long term should increase the conservation value of restoration.

Subsoil was loose-tipped onto the cap to an average depth of between 300 and 500 mm, to a greater depth on areas where tree planting was planned. The original topsoil was laid to a depth of 50 mm on areas where grassland creation was planned.

Woodland creation
Only species known to be already present in the valley were planted at the site. In particular, attention was focussed on planting pioneer species such as alder, birch and rowan, with the assumption that species characteristic of later seral stages such as oak would colonise naturally from nearby woodland. Additional features of the woodland creation were as follows:

- Particular emphasis was placed on ensuring that planting stock was of high quality; stock was carefully selected from well-established hedgerow nurseries.
- Trees were planted randomly in order to mimic natural woodland development.
- Planting on the top of the landform was avoided in order to minimise the risk of windthrow and reduce the likelihood of drought stress.
- A small number of old tree stumps, taken from incoming waste, were placed at random in the tree planting areas. These provided an additional microhabitat unlikely to occur naturally at the site for many years and also enabled a number of invertebrates to be introduced to the site.

Hay meadow creation
Seed harvested from a hay meadow created on another nearby landfill site was used as a seed source. This not only reduced restoration costs but also ensured that only species suited to the local environmental conditions were harvested for use at Cromwell Bottom. Additional features of the grassland creation were as follows:

- The presence of yellow rattle, which parasitises grasses, should help to prevent dominant grasses from out-competing less vigorous species and therefore help maintain a high species diversity.

- Sowing was carried out at relatively low rates, high enough to ensure a good covering of vegetation yet low enough to allow natural colonisation to take place in gaps in the sward.

Pond creation
Three ponds were created, one fed by surface runoff from the restored landform and two fed by an old canal adjacent to the site. All three were planted with small numbers of marginal species such as yellow iris, meadowsweet and marsh marigold, all grown from plants taken from local ponds. At the pond fed by surface water, species were only planted on the slope above the pond, in the hope that gravity would speed up colonisation of the rest of the pond.

A small number of rubble piles were constructed (using materials brought in with the waste) close to the ponds in order to provide refuges for amphibians and reptiles.

Aftercare and management

Initially the meadow areas were mown annually in September, thus mimicking traditional hay meadow management. However, following a re-structuring of the local authority, management carried out at the site has been minimal.

Preliminary results

Woodland
All trees are now at least four years old and survival rates are good. Average height at the in 1999 was approximately 1.5-2 m and there is no evidence of any windthrow as yet.

Species-rich grassland
Species diversity is good at present (see box over). However, in places the grassland is beginning to show signs of becoming more rank as a result of the lack of management and diversity will decline if left unmanaged for long.

Created pond at Cromwell Bottom immediately after creation

Created pond at Cromwell Bottom 4 years after creation

Ponds

Colonisation of the ponds by planted and self-sown marginal and emergent species has been good. A number of aquatic species are also present. However, one of the ponds in particular is starting to become overgrown by bulrushes and reeds, and its conservation value will therefore decline without management.

Area left to colonise naturally

This area is now dominated by birch scrub, which has flourished in response to the lack of management. Round-leaved wintergreen is still present but many of the orchids have disappeared as their habitats have been progressively shaded out.

A common theme of the preliminary results at this site is that the value of created habitats is beginning to decline in response to the lack of management. Cromwell Bottom therefore provides an excellent illustration of the importance of long-term management and the need to consider it as an integral part of habitat creation on landfill sites if the value of the created habitats is to be maintained.

Hay meadow species at Cromwell Bottom

Crested dog's-tail *Cynosaurus cristatus*
Sweet vernal-grass *Anthoxanthemum odoratum*
Yorkshire fog *Holcus lanatus*
Meadow foxtail *Alopecurus pratensis*
Red fescue *Festuca rubra*
Rough meadow-grass *Poa trivialis*
Wild oat *Avena fatua*
Red clover *Trifolium pratense*
Meadow buttercup *Ranunculus acris*
Bush vetch *Vicia sepium*
Ribwort plantain *Plantago lanceolata*
Oxeye daisy *Leucanthemum vulgare*
Yellow rattle *Rhinanthus minor*
Self-heal *Prunella vulgaris*
Eyebright *Euphrasia* spp.
Rough hawkbit *Leontodon hispidus*
Common mouse-ear *Cerastium fontaum* ssp. *holostoides*
Greater knapweed *Centaurea scabiosa*

The methods described here are presented purely as examples of landfill restoration and habitat creation techniques. They do not necessarily reflect the best practice standards contained within this book.

Case Study 4:

Heathfield Landfill, Devon
Heathland creation using litter from a nearby site

Site details

Site operator:	Viridor Waste Management Ltd
Habitat created:	Heathland
Area of habitat created:	1.8 ha
Existing nature conservation interest:	A small area of heathland has been retained within the site boundary

Site background

Landfilling of this former mineral extraction site commenced in 1979 and is on-going. Due to the rapid decline of heathland in Devon, planning conditions for the landfill ensured that heathland creation was incorporated into site restoration, alongside other after-uses including agriculture (grazing) and small-scale woodland creation. In association with the RSPB, the first phase of heathland creation was completed in 1996.

Habitat creation objectives

The principal objective was to create a substantial area of heathland using litter from a degraded area within the nearby Aylesbeare Common RSPB reserve. This method will ensure that local provenance species are used in the restoration and should also benefit the donor site through the clearance of invasive species such as bracken. As only the upper layer of litter was used this method also provides a comparatively low-cost restoration.

It is planned to link the new heathland with the remnant area of heathland within the site boundary, in order to maximise the value of both the created and existing heathland. A secondary objective involved increasing the value of the remnant heathland through clearance of invasive species such as birch and bracken.

Major constraints on successful habitat creation

- Soils suitable for heathland creation were not available on site; soil was imported from a local site approximately 1 mile away. The soil was a free-draining sandy loam with low nutrient status, and was of suitable texture for heathland creation, However, the pH (7) was a little too high – heathland mostly occurs on acid soils.

- The site lies close to a major estuary and accepts large volumes of domestic waste. A large number of gulls are therefore attracted to the site, leading to the potential problem of soil nutrient enrichment, particularly during the early stages of restoration when restored areas can prove very attractive to loafing gulls. Heathland is very much dependent on low soil nutrient status.

Techniques used

Soil treatment and laying
Step 1
A 150 mm layer of subsoil was laid over the cap.

Step 2
The imported soil was loose tipped on to the subsoil to a depth of 700 mm. To avoid compacting the soil, spreading was carried out during the winter at a time when the ground was frozen.

Step 3
A mixture of sulphur and bentonite (brimstone) was applied to the soil at a rate of 1 tonne/ha to lower the soil pH.

The benefits of treating the soil with brimstone to lower soil pH are illustrated by the results from a small trial area where untreated soil was laid to the same depth then covered with the same quantity of heathland litter as used on the treated areas. The untreated soil produced a grass-dominated sward with very little heather or gorse.

Heathland litter source
The chosen donor site was largely dominated by bracken, although invasion by bracken had taken place only recently and it was therefore anticipated that a substantial quantity of heather seeds would still be present within the seed bank. A 10 cm thick mulch of bracken / heathland litter harvested from 1.8 ha of heathland was found to yield up to 36,000 heather seeds per m². Bracken rhizomes were broken into pieces during harvesting, preventing the spread of bracken at the receptor site.

Application of heathland litter
Step 1
Bracken / heathland litter was laid to a depth of 10 cm over the treated soil shortly after it the soil was laid. The presence of grasses within the litter avoided the need for a nurse species, and no additional species were sown.

Step 2
The site was lightly rolled after the mulch was laid.

Aftercare and management

A large number of common gorse seedlings established from seeds present within the litter. Gorse can become dominant if not controlled, so a number of seedlings were removed, both by brushcutter and by hand in July of the first year. Similar management has also been carried out in each of the following years by RSPB volunteers and it is understood that the RSPB will continue to manage the site indefinitely. These labour-intensive methods were used in preference to a machine flail in order to protect the scarcer and less invasive western gorse, also present at the site.

A small number of ruderal weeds have been present within the heathland in each year since habitat creation was completed. Their presence indicates that the soil pH is probably still a little too high, and a second application of sulphur, in the form of pellets designed to leach into the soil, has been made in order to further reduce soil pH.

An active gas extraction system was put in place on the site at the time of soil placement, and there are a number of monitoring boreholes within the restored area. Damage to the heathland has been avoided by carrying out monitoring visits on foot instead of using a vehicle.

Photo: Duncan Watson

Heathland creation at Heathfield landfill site. This photograph was taken three years after the completion of habitat creation works.

Preliminary results

Despite a high proportion of common gorse and some ruderal species, significant amounts of characteristic heathland plants such as heather, western gorse, pill sedge and bristle bent have become established. One pair of stonechats were also present in 1999. With continued management and further ameliorative action to lower soil pH if necessary, the future for the heathland looks good.

For further details on this project, contact Pete Gotham, RSPB South West Regional Office, Keble House, Southernhay Gardens, Exeter, EX1 1NT.

The methods described here are presented purely as examples of landfill restoration and habitat creation techniques. They do not necessarily reflect the best practice standards contained within this book.

Case Study 4

mechanically with a hay-turning attachment on a tractor.

- Remove the hay from the site about a week after strewing, once the seeds have dropped, to prevent germinating seedlings from being shaded out.

If the amount of hay is limited, phase the seeding of the total area over several seasons. Protect unseeded areas from erosion by sowing a nurse species or a mix of commercial grass seed that does not contain herb species.

This method is applicable to a wide range of grassland types with perhaps the exception of wet meadows (see Section F.5).

It is vital that the donor and receptor site are very similar in terms of their physical attributes, particularly the soil type and drainage characteristics. The transportation of large amounts of hay may be expensive; this is only a realistic option if the donor and receptor sites are situated close together. The technique is ideal if there is already an area of grassland on the site that has been previously created and can now serve as a seed source. Transportation costs notwithstanding, hay strewing is a relatively cheap method for seeding a new grassland. Strewing is considerably cheaper than using commercial seed (which may cost £600-£1000/ha) and is considered best practice on economic and ecological grounds.

Probably the largest source of hay for this purpose will be from nature reserves that contain species-rich grassland. Nature reserve managers will be able to advise on whether hay from routine management is available for sale and use for grassland creation. The statutory conservation agencies can give information on suitable contacts.

There are several benefits to this method. Firstly, local provenance can be ensured. Secondly, the quality of the seed can be guaranteed if cutting and strewing are properly supervised. Thirdly, using strewn hay has been shown to reduce the number of weeds in the sward as the hay acts as a mulch, suppressing the germination of weed seeds.

Composition of the resultant sward

One problem that can arise from the use of hay is that species diversity and composition may not reflect the diversity and composition of the donor sward. Smith *et al.* (1996) found that seeds from herb species are more likely to drop out of their seed capsules and onto the ground in the period between cutting and spreading than grasses. Also, unripe grass seeds will ripen in storage, whereas herb species tend not to. Therefore, the resultant sward has a tendency to be dominated by grasses (Smith *et al.*, 1996).

In order to avoid this problem it may be necessary to employ a second method of seed harvesting specifically designed to collect herb species. Equipment that collects seed using a modified industrial vacuum or a brush harvester has been successfully used (English Nature & the Wildlife Trusts, 1999; Emorsgate Seeds, 1999). Alternatively, several cuts can be taken from the donor field in different areas and at different times so that herb seeds can be collected when they are ripe. Either method is an acceptable approach and should be considered to ensure that the resultant sward contains the correct proportion of herb species. For further details see Jones *et al.* (1995), Wells *et al.* (1986) and Smith *et al.* (1996).

In view of the difficulty of establishing some herb species with this method, it may be necessary to supplement the sward with plug or pot-grown herb plants (see below).

It should be appreciated that new grasslands are dynamic and their composition will change markedly over the first five to ten years. This change is most pronounced where seed has been used, as some species may not germinate for several seasons. Therefore, a sward may initially appear to lack the herb component, but the proportion of herbs may well increase given time and suitable management (Richard Brown, pers. comm.).

Plug plants

Plug plants are container-grown in 'cells' of about 20 cm³. Larger container-grown plants (e.g. 1 litre pots) are obtainable, although these tend to be prohibitively expensive for grassland creation.

Use of plug plants is a good method of propagating species which do not germinate well. However, plug plants are expensive; it is therefore not advised that the entire grassland is created from plugs or that plugs of grass species are used. It is not always a successful method, especially since plug plants can be very susceptible to drought immediately after planting. They usually require careful aftercare, including watering and weed control.

There are two best practice ways to use plug plants:

- Where local provenance seed is obtainable, the grassland can be created using either seed or strewn hay (see above), with certain poorly germinating species introduced as plug plants.
- Where local provenance seed is not available, create the grass component of the sward by seeding a sparse cover of a mixture of fine-leaved grasses (Table F.2.3). A small proportion of the site (for example 10%) can be planted with plugs of herb species. The plug plants will in time act as a seed source for colonisation of the remainder of the site, and will speed up the natural colonisation process. This method is relatively cheap but grassland can take a considerable length of time to develop.

Planting method

- Plugs should be planted into a patch of bare ground with no vegetation within 15 cm of the plant. Existing vegetation can either be removed using spot applications of herbicide or by hand (dead material should be removed). If the entire area is cleared (rather than just the patches into which the plugs are planted), the ground can be harrowed to create a fine tilth, which will boost the survival rate of the plugs.
- Plugs can be planted by hand using a spade, or with a dibber if the soil is not clay-rich.
- Planting density will vary according to

Table F.2.3. Grasses to plant with plug plants or wildflower seed

The grasses used must not be tussocky or too aggressive otherwise they will become dominant. The following species are appropriate in most soil conditions (adapted from Flora Locale, 1999).

Red fescue *Festuca rubra*
Crested dog's-tail *Cynosurus cristatus*
Small timothy *Phleum bertolonii*

Common bent *Agrostis capillaris*
Yellow oat-grass *Trisetum flavesens*
Sweet vernal-grass *Anthoxanthum odoratum*

the site and the budget. A rate of between 2 and 10 plugs per square metre has been recommended by the Highways Agency, giving between 30% and 50% cover (Highways Agency, 1993). Planting should take place in autumn or spring. Autumn planting allows the plants to become established before competition occurs from strong summer growth of weeds, but plants can be affected by heavy frosts in winter. Spring planting avoids frosts but plants can be more susceptible to drought. Spring planting should therefore be used in areas prone to frosts, and autumn planting in areas with dry summers.

- If the soil is very infertile, the plugs should be placed in pits filled with topsoil and a dose of slow-release fertiliser.
- The plugs should be plunged into water prior to planting and watered one week later. Subsequent regular watering of both spring and autumn planted plugs is advised.
- Selection of quality stock is important and only stock that has been 'hardened off' should be purchased. Plants that have been grown in heated greenhouses should be avoided, as they will be weak and fragile; outside-grown plants should be used.

Costs
Assuming a cost per plug of 22 pence and a planting rate of 3 per m², this method would cost £6600 per hectare. They can be planted at a rate of 125-350 plants per hour. Larger pot plants cost around 80 pence each, and planting rates are approximately half those for plug plants (Bisgrove & Dixie, 1994).

Translocation
Translocation is a general term for the transfer by human agency of any organism(s) from one place to another. Translocation in this case involves the physical movement of an entire grassland, including soil, with minimum disturbance caused to the soil and vegetation.

The translocation of a habitat by definition requires the destruction of the original donor site. This method is therefore only possible where an existing grassland is to be destroyed, either as part of the landfill development or as part of an alternative development nearby.

It is currently popular to justify the destruction of an existing grassland under the misconception that it will not be damaged if transferred to another site. On balance, however, most evidence shows that translocation usually results in a significant loss in overall diversity and thus nature conservation value, even if the procedure is conducted with care and the original management regime used on the grassland is reinstated on the receptor site (Winder & Robertson, 1993; Jerram, 1992; Jefferson *et al.*, 1999; Bryne, 1990). Note however that gauging the success of translocation is dependent upon detailed and thorough monitoring both of the original grassland and the 'new' grassland. Unfortunately, many previous attempts at translocation have not been monitored thoroughly and in particular, the original state of the grassland was not recorded. Therefore, any results that have been obtained are often difficult to interpret accurately. Translocation should therefore always be viewed as a last resort, as success in ecological terms (i.e. maintaining the original nature and species of the grassland) is less likely than failure.

Worthington & Helliwell (1987) reported that species richness often initally increases after translocation, but returns to pre-transference levels some five years after the operation. However, some of the original species were lost during the translocations described by this study; new species must therefore have colonised. If the original species were all characteristic of old grassland, it is likely that most (if not all) of the new species were undesirable invasive ruderal species.

In theory, translocation can be carried out on all types of grassland. It is difficult to translocate a grassland with scattered trees or shrubs intact, since the roots of woody species penetrate deeper than those of herbaceous species. Severing the roots of such species results in the above-ground growth becoming unstable, and the plants are liable to die.

Some studies have been conducted using translocated grassland turves placed intermittently as 'islands' on bare soil in the hope that the turves will act as seed sources. In practice this does not always work; weed growth is stimulated by soil disturbance, and they tend to dominate and shade out desirable species. Weed control is difficult, as many desirable species will also be affected by herbicides. Herbicide must therefore be applied carefully by hand. Pulling weeds manually is prohibitively time-consuming, and would have to be carried out for several years; many desirable species are slow colonisers, and areas of bare ground suitable for weeds would therefore persist for a long time. This method is therefore not recommended for use on landfill sites.

For translocation to be logistically possible, the donor and receptor site should be situated close together and linked by terrain that permits the passage of vehicles. The turves are very bulky, and transport costs are therefore likely to be high.

Of paramount importance is the consideration that the two sites should be as ecologically similar as possible (in terms of soil type, drainage, aspect, climate and management).

Translocation cannot be used on soils of a non-cohesive nature (e.g. sands and gravels) or soils consisting of industrial wastes.

Translocation of chalk grassland on Beddingham landfill site is described in Case Study 1.

Translocation methods
Translocation involves the transfer of three elements; vegetated turves and the A and B soil horizons. If the soil depth is not too great, the entire soil profile can be moved as a single turf.

Alternatively, the turf, A horizon and B horizon can be moved separately, which can be logistically difficult. Good planning and timing is essential to ensure that the minimum possible disturbance is caused and that soils are stored for the shortest possible time. Figure F.2.1 illustrates the steps involved in translocation.

- Prepare the donor grassland by mowing the vegetation to 5 cm tall and removing the cuttings.
- Using a disc harrow, cut the grassland into turves of a manageable size (ideally 1-2 m², although the exact size will depend upon the size of the bucket used to move the turves). Turf size should be as large as possible to minimise disturbance, but not so large that they tear in transit.
- The edge of the grassland that turf removal will advance from should be prepared by removing turf and soil to a depth of 0.5 m. This allows the equipment access to the side of the turves.
- Pick the turves up using an excavator with an articulated front bucket with cutting edges. The bucket is driven under the sward at the depth of the root zone, parallel to the ground surface. Place the cut turf on a trailer for transport to the receptor site.
- The A and B soil horizons should then be excavated separately. It is preferable to remove as much of both horizons as possible. On no

account should the horizons be mixed together or compacted; methods of soil handling should follow the guidelines given in Section F.1.6 and WMP26e (Environment Agency, in prep.) The horizons should be deposited at the receptor site in the same order (A horizon above B horizon).

- Re-lay the cut turves as soon as possible and do not leave them in direct sunlight for any length of time. If they must be stored, place them in the shade, covered with material such as tarpaulin or plastic sheeting.
- At the receptor site, lay the B horizon first, on top of the cap, followed by the A horizon. Vehicle movement across the laid soil must be minimised. The turves are then placed in position, taking care to place them in the same order in relation to the other turves, and at the same orientation as at the donor site. Do not leave gaps between turves exposing bare soil. To facilitate this, it is useful to draw up a diagram showing the location of the turves in relation to each other, and to individually mark the turves before they are transported to the receptor site.

It is vitally important that translocation is not conducted when the soil is wet. Therefore, although autumn is an ideal time to move plants, it is better to delay translocations until spring unless forecasts suggest that a prolonged dry spell is likely in autumn. If the following summer is dry, the turves should be regularly watered to assist establishment.

Storage of turves between removal and laying is not recommended, although it is possible for periods of less than 3 months in summer or five months in winter (Highways Agency, 1993). Stored turves should be placed on porous geotextile sheets away from direct sunlight and kept well watered.

Subsequent management
Careful management of any translocated vegetation is necessary. The seed bank and the grass component of the sward are likely to be stimulated as a result of soil disturbance, and increased growth of grasses and ruderal weeds will therefore occur. These should be controlled to maintain the characteristic composition of the grassland.

Spot treatment with contact herbicide can be applied by hand to perennial weeds. However, light management over the entire grassland will be most beneficial, limiting the growth of grasses

and controlling weeds. This should be in the form of light sheep grazing (not cattle) or mowing. Four cuts per year should be sufficient, but it is essential that the cuttings are removed.

Resume the original donor site management regime after the first post-translocation summer.

Translocation of individual species

Individual species can, in theory, be translocated if their existing habitat is being destroyed. The UK statutory conservation agencies should be consulted at the first possible opportunity as they will be able to give valuable advice. Also, a licence may be required to to uproot and move a species, particularly if it is rare. In all cases it is preferable to conserve rare species *in situ* if at all possible. Translocation is risky and there are no guarantees that the species will survive. It should not be considered as an easy or cheap option, but rather a last resort.

If permission has been obtained to translocate a species and a suitable receptor site has been selected, plans for the translocation should be made well in advance of operations. The receptor site should be as ecologically similar as possible to the donor site. A rare species is more likely to have very precise ecological requirements than a common species, and it is also more unlikely to tolerate deviations from these. The donor site should be studied carefully to ascertain the requirements of the species. A good example of this is the complex symbiotic relationship of some saprophytic orchids with fungi that infect their roots and enable the orchid to obtain nutrients from the soil. In the absence of the fungus, the plant is unable to survive. Thus if a saprophytic orchid is translocated to a site that does not support the appropriate fungus, the plant will not survive.

Although it may appear cheaper and easier to dig individual plants up and remove them, translocation will be more likely to succeed if a large turf containing the plant is removed. To maximise the chance of success, as large an amount of habitat as possible should be removed with the plant.

Method
- Remove a square metre of turf for each plant (with the plant at the centre).
- Minimise disturbance to the soil, especially around the roots of the plant. The depth of turf taken should be sufficient to avoid shearing deep

roots; in practice this should be at least 30 cm.
- Plant the turf in an excavated pit so that the final level of the soil is the same as in the original grassland.
- Water the cut turf after planting. Additional watering should be conducted in dry periods.
- Translocation is best conducted during the autumn, but take care to avoid frosty and wet conditions. Many species die back during winter and may therefore be difficult to find. The location of individual plants should therefore be carefully marked during spring or summer.

Post-translocation management should be carried out to control weeds and grasses stimulated by soil disturbance (see above).

Addition of soil with a plentiful seed bank or fragment bank

This method involves the removal of seed-rich topsoil from a donor site, and spreading the soil as the uppermost layer at the receptor site; the seed bank should contain species characteristic of the original grassland. This method is, like translocation, destructive, and should only be considered if the donor site is to be destroyed for other reasons.

One square metre of topsoil can be used to treat two square metres of a receptor site. It is therefore potentially possible to create an area of grassland twice the original size.

As for the other methods detailed in this section, the donor and receptor sites should be as ecologically similar as possible.

Method
- Prepare the vegetation at the donor site by allowing the grass to grow up ungrazed and then cutting for hay using a very low cut (about 5 cm high).
- Leave the hay for five days, and turn it every day (either mechanically or by hand). This allows the hay to dry and the seeds to ripen and drop onto the soil. Remove the hay after this five-day period.
- Remove the soil from the donor site and immediately transport it to the receptor site. It is important to keep the A horizon separate – strip this first, since most of the seeds will be concentrated in the top 5 cm of the soil. The B horizon can be used for bulking up, provided that the A horizon is used as the topmost layer. Use earth-moving equipment to move the soil, taking care to avoid compacting the soil. Soil handling procedures should follow official

Figure F.2.1. Sequence of operations for grassland translocation

Divide donor and receptor sites into equally-sized manageable sections (four sections have been used in this example).

Donor site

Receptor site

Establish depth of turf layer, A horizon and B horizon. Turf to be cut and removed in sections as described in the main text.

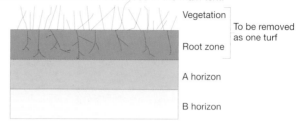

Vegetation

Root zone

To be removed as one turf

A horizon

B horizon

Remove turf (1) and A horizon (2) from 1st donor section. Store.

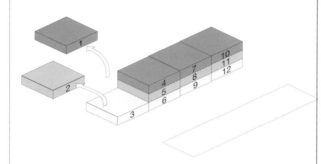

Place B horizon (3) on 1st receptor section. Store turf (4) from 2nd donor section.

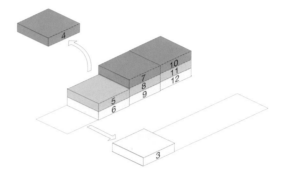

Place stored A horizon (2) on receptor site. Store A horizon (5) from 2nd donor section.

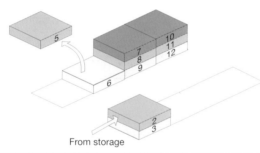

From storage

Move turf (7) from 3rd donor section to 1st receptor section. Move B horizon (6) from 2nd donor section to 2nd receptor section.

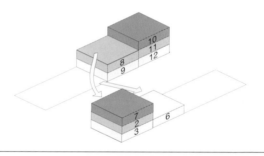

Move A horizon (8) from 3rd donor section to 2nd receptor section. Move B horizon (9) from 3rd donor section to 3rd receptor section.

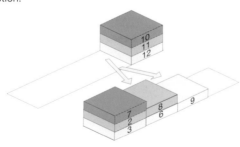

Move turf (10) from 4th donor section to 2nd receptor section. Move A horizon (11) from 4th donor section to 3rd receptor section.

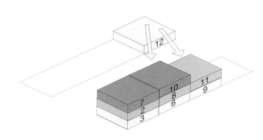

Place stored turf (1) on 3rd receptor site section. Move B horizon (12) from 4th donor section to 4th receptor section.

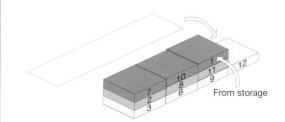

From storage

Place stored A horizon (5) and stored turf (4) on 4th receptor section.

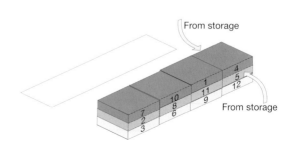

From storage

From storage

guidelines in WMP26e (Environment Agency, in prep.).

- Spread the soil evenly over the receptor site and roll it gently.

Sowing a nurse at the same time helps to control weeds, reduce soil erosion and creates conditions more suitable for the establishment of herbs.

The timing of this method is dictated by the time of seed production and must therefore be carried out during the summer.

Natural colonisation

This method entails leaving a site in a suitable condition to permit the germination and growth of seedlings, and allowing species to colonise via external seed rain. Seed rain is the natural influx of seed via various dispersal agents (mainly wind blow, but also agents such as birds and mammals). The closer a seed source to a site, the greater the probability of colonisation (MacArthur & Wilson, 1967). Species from the closest habitat to the site are the most likely colonisers of the new site, and the soil should therefore be prepared for this habitat. The species that successfully colonise are likely to be those that are well suited to the site.

The method is only suitable for small areas (less than 0.25 ha) at low risk of erosion that are located between or adjacent to areas of grassland so that there is an abundant local seed source.

To increase the success of this method, the following guidelines should be followed:

- A suitable source of seed must be present in very close proximity.
  Research on the seed rain falling on an arable field adjacent to a chalk grassland found that chalk grassland species formed a very small proportion of the total seed rain (Hutchings & Booth, 1996). Development of chalk grassland from natural colonisation would therefore be prohibitively slow, and it is likely that the site would become dominated by weedy ruderal species in the interim. Therefore, natural colonisation is not an appropriate method for the creation of chalk grasslands on landfill, even if a suitable seed source is situated close by. However, natural colonisation may well be feasible for other grassland types.

- A nurse species should be used.
  Natural colonisation is a slow process; bare patches are often visible for many years until the sward closes, and the risk of soil erosion is

high. It is therefore advised that a nurse is sown. The nurse cover should be uniform but sparse, with small areas of bare ground remaining between the nurse plants to act as germination sites for colonising species.

- The site should be managed by grazing or mowing.
  Studies have shown that colonisation by species characteristic of chalk grassland will be encouraged if the vegetation on the site is managed by grazing or mowing (Gibson et al., 1987). Management limits competition from aggressive ruderal species, and allows desirable species to become established.

The success of this method will depend on the similarity of conditions at the site to those under which the desired habitat develops. Particular attention should be paid to soil fertility, although drainage and pH are also important characteristics. In the research by Hutchings & Booth (1996) described above, it is possible that high nutrient levels in the ex-arable field discriminated against chalk grassland species which prefer low fertility. Methods of fertility reduction are detailed in Section F.1.3.3. See also Gilbert & Anderson (1998).

2.4.3 Aftercare

Regardless of the means of grassland creation, regular sward management in the first growing season is beneficial (Baines & Smart, 1991; Gilbert & Anderson, 1998). If grassland creation is conducted in autumn, it is unlikely that management will be required until early in the following summer.

There are three objectives of aftercare management:

- encouraging the establishment of desired species;
- weed control; and
- encouraging grass tillering (to increase ground cover).

Management by cutting or grazing prevents grasses from forming a dense mat and therefore encourages the establishment of herbs as well as permitting the establishment of species which are slow to germinate (Atkinson et al., 1995). Tussock-forming grasses can shade out other species; management prevents large tussocks from forming, and encourages grasses to produce above-ground shoots (tillers), forming a more even sward and reducing soil erosion.

Any species not characteristic of a

grassland can be viewed as a weed. Most weeds can be ignored as they will not significantly affect the nature of the grassland. However, some species are problematic, usually because they are prolific seed producers which if left uncontrolled will dominate the grassland to the detriment of other species. Control of such species is therefore imperative. The most noteworthy weed species are docks (Rumex spp.), thistles (Cirsium spp.), ragwort (Senicio jacobea) and willowherbs (Epilobium spp.). Cutting controls large broadleaved weeds by preventing them from flowering and setting seed. Perennial species will also be disadvantaged, which reduces the necessity of hand-pulling and the use of herbicides.

Cutting

The height of grassland vegetation should be kept below 10 cm for the first year after sowing. The sward should be cut to 5 cm in height. If the sward is spring- or summer-sown, the first cut should be conducted 6-8 weeks after sowing. If the sward is autumn-sown, cutting should be instigated in late May / early June when the sward is 10 cm tall. If a nurse has been used, the first cut should be taken before the nurse produces seeds. Translocated grassland should also be cut 6-8 weeks after the turves have been laid if translocation took place in spring.

For subsequent cuts, the sward should be rolled with a light roller and cut to a height of 5 cm with a tractor-mounted reciprocating blade or a rotary cutter. Never cut below 4 cm. If annual species have been sown to give colour in the first year, the cut should only be to 7 cm. One cut should be made early in the season before flowering (May), with another cut after flowering in August.

Cutting should be repeated whenever the sward reaches 10 cm tall and will probably be required four times in the first season. By the end of the first season it will usually be possible to start the long-term management regime, which will only require one or two cuts per year. If highly fertile soil has been used, the grass may grow so fast that four cuts will also be required in the second year. Alternatively, if the soil is very infertile, growth may be so weak that the first cut may not be required until the second season (Gilbert & Anderson, 1998).

Aftercare is a site-specific operation, and should be determined by the vigour of the growth of both desired and undesired species.

Cuttings should always be removed

from the site. The removal of cuttings reduces soil fertility and prevents non-aggressive species from being smothered; adequate management in the first and possibly second year will guarantee long-term savings in the amount of management required.

It should be noted that the sward is unlikely to be flower-rich in the first year due to the frequency of cutting, but the plants will become well-established during this period.

Grazing

Light sheep grazing is an alternative method of control. Cattle should not be used as the damage caused by their hooves would be detrimental to the establishment of grassland. Permanent grazing prevents herb species from flowering, but light grazing throughout the first year is beneficial as it controls weeds and promotes the establishment of desirable species. After the first year, the grassland can be grazed intermittently (particularly during winter), but not from May to October (see F.2.4.4).

Weed control

Cutting or grazing should be sufficient to prevent weeds from dominating the sward. If weeds are still a problem, spot applications of herbicide or hand-pulling may be required. The sward should be dense enough to suppress weed growth by the second year.

2.4.4 Long-term management

Grasslands require regular management to maintain the status quo. In ecological terms, grassland is a plagioclimax community; artificial intervention is necessary to maintain grassland in a similar state by arresting natural processes (particularly succession). If grassland is unmanaged, natural succession will occur, resulting initially in the domination of the grass sward by tussock-forming grasses. Tussocks shade out other species, leading to a decline in species richness and the domination of the sward by a limited number of aggressive grasses. Scrub and tree seedlings will also colonise, with the result that the grassland develops into scrub and ultimately woodland. Although there can be ecological benefits to allowing such natural processes to take place, the time and money invested in grassland creation is wasted.

The objective of long-term grassland management is to maintain the grassland in its desired condition. The main purpose of management is to:

- reduce the vigour of the grass component of the sward (preventing tussock formation and litter accumulation); and
- prevent nutrients from building up in the soil. If grassland is left unmanaged (or if cuttings are not removed), the decay of dead plant material releases nutrients back into the soil. This, coupled with external nutrient inputs from the atmosphere and from rainwater, leads to an increase in soil fertility over time which encourages the growth of aggressive species and reduces species-richness. Management should therefore aim to maintain soil fertility at a constant level (or even reduce it).

The management rationale and suggested regimes given in the following text are summaries of a larger subject. Further information can be gained from English Nature & the Wildlife Trusts (1999) and Sutherland & Hill (1995). Guidelines on monitoring created grasslands can be found in Mitchley *et al.* (2000).

Types of management

Fertiliser application

Since the objective of grassland creation is to produce and maintain a species-rich sward, the application of fertiliser is generally not recommended. This is because the addition of plant-available nutrients in the form of inorganic fertiliser or organic manure will serve to encourage the more competitive species in the sward to the detriment of other species. Most grasses are more responsive to fertiliser than herbs, and grasses are therefore encouraged at the expense of herbs, with the result that the species richness of the sward will decline. Fertiliser should only be applied if the plants exhibit signs of stress and disease. If this is the case, fertiliser can be applied sparingly in the form of organic farmyard manure or composted organic waste. Composted waste should be used with caution as the nutrient status may be unsuitable, and it may be saline and contain toxins. Composted waste should therefore be chemically analysed before use. Slow-release fertiliser is probably the ideal type to use.

Fertiliser should also be applied if the traditional management of the community being created includes fertiliser applications. For example, a grassland NVC community that is traditionally sheep-grazed would receive nutrient inputs in the form of sheep dung. A created grassland of this type should therefore also receive such inputs in order to maintain the species composition.

Cutting and grazing

Grasslands are traditionally managed by cutting to obtain a hay crop or grazing; the choice will depend upon whether the grassland is managed as a hay meadow or as permanent grazing pasture.

If a particular NVC community has been created, the management regime traditionally applied to this community should be instigated. Some NVC types are hay meadows, whereas others can be managed either as hay meadows or for permanent grazing. Both types have considerable nature conservation value. In terms of aesthetic landscape quality, a hay meadow is generally more appealing, and this would therefore be a useful management choice at sites where landscape aesthetics are an issue.

In general, neutral grasslands are managed for hay, whereas calcareous and acid grasslands are managed by permanent grazing. This is a broad generalisation, and it is worth replicating the management regime of other local grasslands. The local Wildlife Trust should be able to advise on an appropriate management regime for a specific site.

A regular management regime based on traditional hay meadow management will tend to favour tall and leafy species. These species persist by flowering and setting seed before the hay is cut and removed. Species characteristic of other habitats and management regimes will be disadvantaged.

Permanent grazing management will favour low-growing species. The result of grazing is a short sward which can be very species-rich. Typical chalk grassland is often very short, although this is due to the reduction in fertility caused by grazing rather than to high stocking densities – high stocking rates will reduce species-richness. Although dung from grazing animals adds nutrients to the system if deposited on site, many traditional forms of management involved taking livestock off-site at night, so that the majority of the dung was deposited elsewhere.

If a grassland is mown (either for hay cuts or as a substitute for grazing), It is essential that cuttings are removed.

Both management types (especially grazing) encourage grass tillering. This is beneficial as it creates an even sward and reduces the area of bare ground. To further encourage tillering, roll the sward in early summer.

Disturbance

An important component of the sward on

acid grasslands may be annual / biennial species or species with short-lived seeds. In this case it will almost certainly be necessary to build some form of regular disturbance into the management regime. Disturbance creates small areas of bare ground which act as germination sites for seeds that would be unable to germinate if they fell on a mat of vegetation (Grubb, 1977; Atkinson *et al.*, 1995; Grime, 1990). Areas of bare ground must be provided every year for annual species, as they must set seed each year in order to persist. For the continued persistence of perennial herbs, bare ground should be created on a rotation of at least three years. A secondary effect of grazing management is the creation of small areas of bare ground as a result of trampling by stock.

Management of flower-rich hay meadows
The cutting date affects sward composition, particularly the ratio of herbs to grasses. The effect of different cutting dates on sward composition was studied by Smith *et al.* (1996). In a long-established meadow, especially one that has been cut at the same date for many years, the most abundant species are likely to be those that produce the most ripe seed just before the cutting date. Desirable species can therefore be encouraged by cutting just after those species have set seed. In general, the results showed that the later the cutting date, the greater the number of grass seeds, whereas the number of herb seeds was greater from a mid-July cut than an early September cut. This is, however, only a general rule; there are several late-flowering (and hence late in producing ripe seed) herb species.

The optimum cutting date is therefore species- and site-specific (Marren, 1995). The diversity of the total grassland area (whether comprising one large area or several smaller areas) can be maximised by cutting on dates in different areas. This will encourage a wider variety of species, even if the whole site was orginally sown with a uniform species mix.

If the grassland forms one large area, it should be subdivided into management units with each unit being managed independently. The unit sizes chosen should be manageable and not so small as to inhibit the use of agricultural machinery. Separate areas of grassland can be treated as distinct management units. An important point to note is that the cutting date should remain consistent on each management unit, and should only be varied between units.

Photo: Melvyn Foxton

Hay making on a restored landfill site in West Yorkshire.

On infertile soils which do not permit vigorous growth, only one cut per year will generally be necessary. Two cuts per year will be necessary on fertile soils. Ideally, the grassland should also be grazed in the winter or mown (in warm weather) in the time between the hay cut (approximate dates: late June in the south, late July in the north) and mid-April to May (when management ceases to allow the hay to grow up) – Smith & Rushton (1994).

If ground-nesting birds are present, cutting should be delayed until after the chicks have left the nest. If the sward is managed for invertebrates, most species that have adapted to surviving in meadows can cope with hay cutting; there should be no drastic effects provided that the cut is no shorter than 5 cm (Ausden & Treweek, 1995).

A point worth noting is that hay cutting on moderately fertile sites can potentially yield 50 tonnes of fresh weight per hectare. It is therefore important to find a use for the hay, which can be a valuable commodity. One option may be to invite a contractor to cut and keep the hay.

On a more practical note, it is worth considering how the grassland will be cut. Tractor-mounted machinery is ideal, but steep slopes may well prevent tractor access. In these cases, a small hand-driven mower can be used such as those described by Bacon *et al.* (1997).

Permanent pasture
Grazing prevents grassland from succeeding into woodland. It also has other benefits: it diversifies the grassland structure (if the grazing pressure is not too high), creating a variety of microhabitats that benefit a variety of species. Structure can be provided by the presence of occasional tussocks, dead material and bare ground, and by a mixture of short and tall vegetation.

Cattle, sheep, ponies, horses or goats can be used as the grazing stock. Each species creates a different effect on the sward; the selection of species should therefore be made with care (Bacon, 1990; Gibson, 1997; Oates, 1993). Goats are browsers, and should therefore not be used in areas where they have access to planted trees. Rabbits can be effective grassland grazers; however, claims for damages can be made against site owners who fail to control rabbits on their property where the rabbits cause damage to adjacent crops etc. Rabbit grazing is therefore only viable on sites surrounded by land uses where this is not an issue.

The density of stock used is dependent on grassland type and soil fertility. Stocking rates are therefore site-specific, but general guidelines are given here. Sheep are ideal for newly created grassland as they create a short sward and the effect of trampling by sheep is not as severe as that from cattle. A low density of sheep (e.g. 2 sheep per hectare) can produce a varied sward structure important for nature conservation.

Note that the interaction between livestock and the public must be an important consideration at sites where public access is encouraged. In practice, grazing livestock is likely to be practical only on rural sites where recreation pressures are generally lower than on urban sites.

Other points that must be considered are:
- Stockproof boundaries in the form of hedgerows, fences or walls are required. The boundary of most conservation value is the hedgerow (see Section F.6.2 for details on hedgerow creation).
- Livestock should be given free access to drinking water and shelter.
- A stocksperson should be provided to attend to the welfare of the stock.
- Toxic plants should be absent from the sward. In particular, ragworts (*Senecio* spp.) must be controlled.

Management substitutes
There are certain methods or that can be employed to reduce the level of management required.

Germination niches can be created by physically breaking through the grass mat and creating areas of bare ground. Ideally, numerous small areas should be created rather than fewer large areas. The best tool to create germination niches is a chain harrow.

The growth of grasses can be suppressed by introducing yellow rattle (*Rhinanthus minor*). Yellow rattle is a characteristic herb of hay meadows and is semi-parasitic on the roots of grasses. This species can perform the useful function of reducing the vigour of grasses. Yellow rattle is an annual species, and its seeds must therefore be allowed to germinate every year to ensure the continued persistence of the plant in the sward. Cutting should be delayed

Photo: Valerie Hack

Yellow rattle *Rhinanthus minor*

until after yellow rattle has set seed, and germination niches should be provided. Including yellow rattle in a species mix can reduce the number of cuts required per year from two to one.

Yellow rattle can be introduced as part of the original grassland seed mix. Alternatively, it can be introduced after the grassland has been created. If the latter option is chosen, the following procedure should be followed (Flora Locale, 1999).
- Cut the grass to 5 cm tall.
- Sow yellow rattle seed in late summer or autumn at a rate of 1.2 kg/ha (do not work the seed into the soil surface).
- Keep the grass short from August to early March by cutting or grazing.

To retain yellow rattle within the sward, avoid cutting between March and the end of July/August to permit the plant to flower and set seed. This must be ensured each year, as yellow rattle does not produce seeds that lie dormant. If the sward is mown, it should be scarified annually to create germination niches.

Examples of long-term grassland management

1.   Summer-flowering hay meadows

These meadows flower through the summer, producing colourful swathes of perennial flowers intermixed with grasses.
- Cut once for hay (late June in the south and late July in the north) to a height of 5 cm.
- Southern meadows should be cut again one month later.
- Ideally, graze the aftermath growth by cattle or sheep from after the hay cut until late October / early November.
- If the sward is not very vigorous, no further grazing is required until after the next year's hay cut. If the sward is vigorous, graze until the end of April / end of May.

2.   Spring-flowering meadows

This type of meadow contains species that flower in early summer. Spring-flowering bulbs such as bluebells, daffodils and snowdrops can also be planted. On a landfill with public access, this type of grassland does not present an obstacle to recreational use. The cut can be delayed to allow the maximum number of people to enjoy the flowers in the early summer period. If a shorter sward is desired, the cut must be taken earlier.

- Cut once to 5 cm in early June.
- Either leave to grow up and then cut again in September, or:
- Following the first cut, mow on a three week interval or graze until September.

3.   Permanent pasture

This grassland type contains species tolerant of grazing, including low-growing and prostrate species. The abundance of these species will depend upon grazing intensity.

- Grazing regimes are site-specific and it is difficult to generalise on stocking rates and length of residence on the same area of pasture. If the stocking rate is low, the animals can in theory be left on the grass throughout the year. If the grassland is prone to waterlogging, especially if cattle are used, stock should be taken off in winter months to prevent the grassland becoming damaged through excessive trampling.
- Sheep are the recommended stock type, and the advised stocking rate for a medium level of grazing is given below:
  - Acid grassland: 25 LU/ha/yr
  - Neutral grassland: 50 LU/ha/yr
  - Calcareous grassland: 30 LU/ha/yr

LU = Livestock Unit. This is calculated depending on the weight of the sheep, therefore:

Light ewes are equivalent to 0.06 LU

Medium ewes are equivalent to 0.08 LU

Heavy ewes are equivalent to 0.11 LU

Source: Ausden & Treweek (1995).

at least 15 m;
- a minimum tree density of 1100 trees per ha is required;
- up to 20% of the area entered may be left unplanted;
- a maximum of 10% of the area may be planted with shrubs;
- there is a proportionally smaller payment per ha for woods greater than 10 ha in size; and
- rates are slightly different for natural regeneration and planting.

Larger grants are available for woodlands with public access or local community involvement. Advice on this and other schemes can be gained from the Farming and Wildlife Advisory Group (FWAG) and the Farming and Rural Conservation Agency (FRCA).

Community Forests
Community forests are regional initiatives with the objective of increasing the amount of woodland present within a designated locality. Current planning strategies encourage the expansion of community forests and may well favour planning applications that propose woodland creation. The woodlands are intended to comprise native broadleaved species of local provenance (as far as is practicably possible). Further details can be obtained from the Countryside Agency.

3.2 Reasons for creating woodlands

3.2.1 Primary objectives
The main objectives of woodland creation are:
- to expand the existing woodland resource in the locality;
- to help fulfil Biodiversity Action Plan targets; and
- to reverse fragmentation of existing woodlands by creating woodlands that link existing woods or form a 'stepping stone' between two woodlands.

3.2.2 Secondary objectives
There are many secondary objectives of woodland creation, a selection of which are given below:
- to produce timber and firewood, and therefore increase opportunities for traditional industries based upon wood products such as coppice poles and charcoal;
- to provide recreational opportunities;
- to provide shelter for livestock or provide habitat for game birds;
- to create an educational resource;
- to promote soil stabilisation;

- to enhance the attractiveness of the landscape;
- to compensate for industrial CO_2 emissions;
- to absorb dust and pollution (including noise); and
- as a (tax free) investment.

3.3 Woodland creation on landfill sites – planning

Until recently, landfill site restoration guidance advised against planting trees on landfills. This was primarily due to fears that tree roots could penetrate the cap, permitting water ingress and thereby increasing leachate production and allowing the uncontrolled migration of landfill gas. There were also fears that extraction of moisture from the cap could lead to the clay cracking and it was also thought that the trees could suffer die-back if their roots entered the fill as a result of exposure to landfill gas and the heat of biodegradation.

However, following recent research (e.g. Dobson & Moffat, 1993) this guidance has now been reconsidered. This research showed that 90% of tree roots are limited to the top 0.6 m of soil, and proved that a well-constructed clay cap (compacted to a minimum density of 1.8-1.9 g/cm³) should provide an effective barrier to roots due to the prevailing conditions of compaction and low oxygen concentration, both of which are hostile to root growth. Dobson & Moffat (1993) also state that there is little chance of tree roots penetrating a synthetic capping material such as HDPE.

3.3.1 Basic principles
Restoration planning
A number of factors must be considered at the outset of the restoration design process:
- The nature of the soil used in restoration will have a strong bearing on woodland creation and this should be fully considered. For example, if a very low fertility soil is used, nurse species may have to be planted to improve soil structure and fertility before other woodland species can be planted. Soil characteristics such as pH may also affect final species choice.
- Information on local woodland types / NVC communities should be sought.
- Long-term management must be fully considered. If woodland is planned which requires a high degree of ongoing management, resources for this management must be set aside. Failure to carry out

necessary management will reduce the success of woodland creation; it would be better to produce an alternative design at an early stage that requires a lower intensity of management if resources are limited.

An example of woodland creation using soil forming material is presented in Case Study 2. Other examples of woodland creation on landfill are presented in Case Studies 3 and 9.

Constraining factors of a landfill site
Landfill gas can cause considerable problems on old uncapped sites, creating anaerobic and occasionally toxic soil conditions. Furthermore, high temperatures resulting from biodegradation also causes unfavourable conditions by drying out the soil. These problems are significantly reduced on modern sites by the presence of an engineered cap and the active control of the gas within the landfill.

At modern sites the major constraint arises from the presence of pollution control infrastructure (above-ground wellheads and below-ground pipes). Trees and shrubs should not be planted over pipes or close to wellheads to which access must be kept clear for monitoring and maintenance. However, woodland may still be created; grassy areas within a woodland can be an important feature, and engineers should liaise with designers so that woodland rides and glades can be designed in conjunction with pollution control access points and access tracks (Figure F.3.1). A real-life example of woodland planting layout is given in Case Study 3.

At most sites accepting biodegradable waste, a considerable amount of settlement is expected in the first 2-5 years following restoration (settlement is generally much reduced after this period). At such sites, remedial works on pollution control infrastructure are likely to be required, which would almost certainly involve the digging up of the restored soil profile with potentially damaging consequences for newly-planted trees. As a general rule this constraint on woodland creation can be avoided by delaying tree planting until after the majority of settlement has taken place (i.e. after interim restoration). Note however that tree planting in areas unlikely to experience considerable settlement (e.g. steep slopes) may be possible at an earlier stage.

Another constraint is the necessity to lay at least 1.5 m depth of soil over a clay cap (1 m over a synthetic cap). This

Case Study 5:

Maw Green Landfill, Cheshire
Pond creation and translocation of great crested newts

Site details

Site operator:	Waste Recycling Group Plc
Habitat created:	Three ponds designed specifically as receptor sites for translocated great crested newts
Existing nature conservation interest:	Three ponds were present within the area of the proposed operational landfill. Two of these ponds supported populations of great crested newt

Site background

Ecological surveys during landfilling at the site in 1995 identified a population of great crested newts. Ephemeral ponds, often present in old quarry sites used for landfill, frequently provide a habitat for this species. Great crested newts and their habitat are protected under Schedule 5 of the Wildlife & Countryside Act 1981 and Regulation 39 of the Conservation (Natural Habitats etc.) Regulations 1994. In order to conserve the newts, suitable ponds were created on an area at the edge of the landfill site, and the newts were translocated into the new ponds during autumn 1996.

Habitat creation objectives

The principal objective of the pond creation was to provide compensatory newt habitat for the ponds to be lost during site operation. The location of the new ponds was governed by the requirement for water and an impermeable substrate, and they were therefore situated on clay at the base of the final landform where water levels could be maintained by surface water runoff. Additionally, the location chosen was within a short distance of the diverted Fowle Brook (see Case Study 6) to enable exchange of species to occur between the brook and the ponds.

Techniques used

Pond design
- Three new ponds were excavated in autumn 1994 to replace the ponds to be lost. The dimensions of the new ponds varied but were on average about 10 m x 8 m and thus of a similar size to the existing ones.
- The depth of the ponds varied, but in each pond around 50% was between 0.5 and 2 m in depth. This depth should be sufficient to prevent the ponds from completely freezing during cold weather and to ensure that the ponds did not rapidly become overgrown with emergent species such as common reed and

One of the three ponds created. Great crested newts were translocated into all three ponds. The photo was taken three years after excavation.

Photo: Duncan Watson

reedmace. The deeper water also provided a additional habitat for submerged aquatic plant species. Newts prefer depths of around 1 m (Gent & Gibson, 1998).
- Shelves were created to provide habitat for marginal plants and to create shallow water at the pond edges. Great crested newts require reasonably unvegetated pond margins to make courtship displays when breeding.
- The cover of submerged and emergent vegetation in great crested newt breeding ponds should ideally be around 25% (Gent & Gibson, 1998). To assist the establishment of vegetation, emergent plants were translocated from the existing ponds to the new ponds prior to newt translocation.

Additional habitat features
- Artificial hibernacula comprising piles of bricks were constructed in the surrounding grassland to provide

hibernation sites for newts. In addition, logs and hay piles were placed around the ponds to provide shelter.
- Small amounts of chopped straw were placed on the water surface in autumn to prevent algal blooms and to provide habitat for aquatic invertebrates.
- A willow was coppiced and transplanted and has established successfully.

Translocation of vegetation
Marginal and aquatic plant species were removed from the existing ponds in spring 1995. Marginal turves and aquatics were removed using a spade Turves were transported immediately to the new ponds and placed in position. Aquatics were replanted by pushing the roots into soft mud. Frogs and smooth newts were also translocated during this period. Some aquatic plants were also translocated using an excavator in winter 1995.

Photo: Duncan Watson

One of a number of artificial refuges created at the receptor site for use by translocated great crested newts.

Some mud and litter was transferred from the old ponds to introduce aquatic invertebrates and plant seeds.

Translocation of great crested newts
Prior to the translocation an amphibian-proof fence was erected around the three new ponds. This effectively prevented newts from coming to harm in nearby operational areas. In a similar way, additional ponds within the operational area (e.g. balancing ponds) were also fenced to prevent re-colonisation of the site and hence the need for further mitigation.

The ponds containing great crested newts were surrounded by newt-proof fencing, and pitfall traps were installed on the inside of the fence. Newts were captured leaving the pond in September and transferred to the new ponds.

As a final measure to ensure that no newts had been missed, the existing ponds were slowly pumped dry using a specially filtered pump to ensure that any newts remained behind. An ecologist was present on site throughout this operation to capture any newts found.

A translocation licence was obtained for this operation from English Nature. Note that the responsibility of assessing and issuing licences to obstruct and translocate great crested newts has recently been transferred to the Department of the Environment, Transport and Regions (DETR) in England and Wales. Over-riding public interest must now be demonstrated in order for a translocation to be approved, and it is very likely that translocation licences will be harder to obtain than was previously the case. General great crested newt

survey licences are still issued by EN / CCW. The situation in Scotland remains unchanged. See Baker (2000) or contact DETR for more details.

Management and aftercare

It is planned to mow the grassland surrounding the ponds annually in late summer to prevent the development of scrub and consequent shading of the ponds. Invasive emergent vegetation will also be managed if it starts to encroach upon open water in the ponds. The amphibian-proof fencing will be retained until all landfill operations have been completed.

Monitoring of the newt populations in the ponds was carried out in each of the first two years following the translocation.

Preliminary results

Surveys of the new ponds have revealed breeding smooth newts (by presence of larvae) in 1996. Great crested newt larvae were observed in August 1997 and the presence of juveniles was also noted in 1997.

Aquatic and marginal vegetation in the new ponds has also developed well following translocation.

One problem that has occurred has been a slight eutrophication of the ponds, almost certainly as a direct result of large quantities of gull guano within surface water runoff. In the early stages of restoration, gulls were attracted to the grassy bank above the ponds and even used to bathe in the ponds themselves. As a result one pond in particular now has a heavy covering of blanket weed, which is likely to act to the detriment of the newts. Fortunately, the restored grassland has developed and landfill operations have moved to another part of the site. The presence of gulls within the pond catchment is now much less frequent.

The methods described here are presented purely as examples of landfill restoration and habitat creation techniques. They do not necessarily reflect the best practice standards contained within this book.

Photo: Colin Carver / Windrush

Adult male great crested newt *(Triturus cristatus).*

Case Study 5

Case Study 6:

Maw Green Landfill, Cheshire
Stream diversion around landfill site

Site details

Site operator:	Waste Recycling Group Plc
Habitat created:	Wetland
Area of habitat created:	Stream of length 1300 m
Existing nature conservation interest:	Existing stream through site of local nature conservation importance. Stream feeds directly into Sandbach Flashes SSSI

Site background

Fowle Brook (a small stream) ran through the site for a distance of 600 m prior to landfilling. Rather than culvert the stream under the site, the site operator agreed to mitigate for the loss of habitat by diverting the stream around the site boundary. As a result, a 1300 m diversion was created in 1995. The site itself is still operational.

Habitat creation objectives

The primary objective of the stream diversion was to maintain, and if possible increase, the conservation value of the stream. The conservation value could be maintained by retaining substantial amounts of marginal and aquatic vegetation from the old course of the stream for translocation into the new section. It was also planned to improve the value of the stream in the long term, firstly by more than doubling the length and also by incorporating a variety of habitat features not present in the existing stream such as bends and shallow shelves.

Techniques used

Design and creation of the new channel
- The channel was excavated using a long-bladed bulldozer.
- The channel was constructed with gentle bends. Channel depth and width were varied along its length. As an additional feature, shallow shelves were created on the inside banks of bends onto which marginal and emergent species could be planted. These shelves were created after the water was allowed to flow through the channel.
- An embankment was created at the sides of the channel to prevent surface water runoff from the landfill flowing into the stream. The bank was seeded with a mix of grass and wildflower species.
- Once the entire length of the channel had been excavated, water

was allowed to flow through and translocation of emergent and marginal vegetation took place. To prevent excessive siltation affecting the adjacent SSSI (into which the stream flows), straw bales were placed at the downstream end of the diversion and secured using stakes to intercept and collect silt and plant fragments.

Translocation of vegetation from the existing stream course
Emergent and marginal plant species were removed from the existing stream in large turves using an excavator with a wide bucket attachment. Emergent vegetation tends to be fairly hardy and amongst the vegetation groups most likely to survive translocation, provided that it is not kept out of water for too long. Following removal, each clump of vegetation was transported immediately to the new channel for re-planting, and the length of time each plant was out of water kept to an absolute minimum. The translocation took place in early spring during the dormant period of plant activity to further minimise the risk of damaging the plants.

Straw bales were used to intercept silt and plant fragments downstream of the removal operations and hence prevent damage to the SSSI into which the stream flowed.

Planting in the new stream
The old stream course was considerably shorter than the diverted course. Therefore, although the maximum amount of vegetation possible was translocated from the original course, this needed to be supplemented with additional pot-grown plants purchased from a commercial supplier. Species purchased included water forget-me-not, marsh marigold and water mint, yellow flag and reed sweet-grass.

Care was taken to ensure that some silt and litter was transplanted with the

clumps of emergent and marginal vegetation in order to inoculate the site with invertebrates and plant seeds

To create an additional habitat, scattered shrubs were also planted on one side of the stream.

Aftercare and management

Immediate aftercare included:
- replacement of failed plants;
- removal of straw bales; and
- management of vegetation around the planted shrubs.

It is planned to dredge the stream once every 4-6 years between April and October. The effect on marginal species will be minimised by alternating the bank from which the work is conducted.

The Environment Agency and the site operator make regular checks of water quality. The site operator also carries out monthly monitoring of habitat condition, and ameliorative management (e.g. to combat bank erosion), is undertaken as necessary.

Preliminary results

The brook vegetation has established well, with good species diversity and few areas devoid of plants. Marginal, emergent and bank-side species are present, including yellow flag, water mint, common reed, reed sweet-grass, brooklime and greater pond sedge. Colonisation by invertebrates is also well underway, and the presence of several banded demoiselle dragonflies along the stream indicates that water quality is good. A heron has taken up residence along the stream, a further indicator that the habitat is developing well.

No evidence of problems due to erosion was evident in 1999, and water flow is good. However, there was a small problem with windblown litter from the adjacent operational area, which can be a consideration at any site where phased restoration takes place. It is understood

Photo: Duncan Watson

A section of the diverted stream. The photo was taken three years after the diverted section was excavated.

however that the site operator plans to increase the extent of litter fencing between the operational area and the stream in the near future.

The methods described here are presented purely as examples of landfill restoration and habitat creation techniques. They do not necessarily reflect the best practice standards contained within this book.

Case Study 6

Figure F.3.1. Woodland design and infrastructure

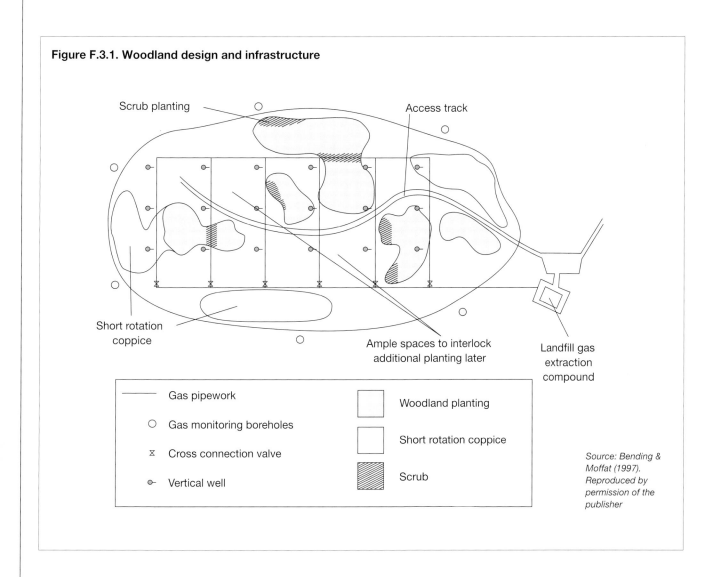

Scrub planting

Access track

Short rotation coppice

Ample spaces to interlock additional planting later

Landfill gas extraction compound

——	Gas pipework	☐	Woodland planting
○	Gas monitoring boreholes	☐	Short rotation coppice
⦻	Cross connection valve	▨	Scrub
⊙—	Vertical well		

Source: Bending & Moffat (1997). Reproduced by permission of the publisher

requires a large volume of soil. If on-site soil resources are insufficient, soil forming materials such as industrial waste products can be used (see F.1.2.4) providing that they meet the standards set out in Table F.1.2.

A final constraint regarding the location of woodland on a landfill site is that certain areas, particularly the top of the dome, may be subject to high wind speeds. Windthrow of the trees will have to be considered; methods to reduce the risk of windthrow are given in F.3.3.1.

Determining factors of a landfill site
In order to be create a local woodland type that will fit in with the surrounding landscape, soil conditions should be as similar to those in local woodlands as possible. Soil pH is the main determining factor of woodland type. Secondary factors are nutrient levels and soil hydrology.

Site design
Native woodlands occur in a wide range of situations from wet to dry soil regimes

and in a variety of locations from valleys to exposed hilltops. There is therefore no real constraint to the siting of a woodland on a restored landfill with the exception perhaps of site-specific landscape considerations.

Aesthetic considerations will play a part in the overall design, especially if the public is to be encouraged to use the restored site.

- An entire site covered in woodland can have an oppressive feel. For example, If a hillside is planted, leave the other side treeless to permit open views away from the site.
- Plant in irregular blocks and avoid unnatural geometric designs.
- Woodland edges and felling coupes should be irregular in size and outline, bearing in mind the edge effect.

A major consideration is the effect of the woodland on adjacent habitats. Woodland can have two main effects:
- Shading: open habitats such as

grassland or heathland will not perform as well if they are shaded by trees. Species that require warm or light conditions may be unable to survive.
- Seed dispersal: the seeds of some shrub and tree species are wind-dispersed and therefore constantly 'rain down' on adjacent habitats. If left unchecked, scrubby woodland comprised mainly of pioneer species such as birch, willow and alder will develop. The removal of woody seedlings is labour-intensive to perform by hand, so grassland areas enclosed by or at the edge of woodlands should be designed to allow mowing as a means of controlling tree and shrub invasion.

Overall size
New woodlands should be at least 2 ha, and preferably 5 ha in size; woods of less than 5 ha are dominated by the 'edge effect' (Peterken & Game, 1984). Woodland edges are very different in character from the core of a woodland

(Ferris-Kaan, 1991). A woodland should therefore have minimum dimensions of length and width of 220 m. Additionally, small woodlands may not be large enough to support a number of woodland bird species. It may not be possible to create a 5 ha woodland on many landfill sites, but the guideline that should be used is 'the bigger the better'. See Anderson (1994) for more details.

Woodland edge
Woodland edges are dominated by semi-shaded conditions with low humidity and are exposed to higher wind speeds than the woodland interior. Woodland edges can comprise areas of scattered trees, shrubs and grassland pockets. An ideal design is to plant a dense edge of scrub to reduce the amount of light entering the woodland from the side, and also to reduce wind and windblown seed penetration. Woodland edge species are mainly different from those found in the woodland core and are generally of two types: light-demanding species such as hawthorn *(Crategeus monogyna)*, aspen *(Populus tremula)*, bramble *(Rubus fruticosus)*, rosebay willowherb *(Chamanerion angustifolium)*, goldenrod *(Solidago virgaurea)*, field thistle *(Cirsium arvense)* and nettle *(Urtica dioica)*, and species tolerant of semi-shade (typically hedgerow species) such as primrose *(Primula vulgaris)*, red campion *(Silene dioica)*, wood speedwell *(Veronica montana)* and broad buckler fern *(Dryopteris dilitata)*. The perimeter of the woodland core should be surrounded by an edge strip between 10 m and 30 m wide (Peterken & Game, 1974; Cole, 1982), although the width should be increased to 100 m or more if spurs of scrub / scattered trees and grassland are incorporated.

Woodland edges also support different associated species. Scrub provides habitat for birds which distribute seeds through their droppings. Encouraging these birds speeds up the process of natural regeneration. Bird species attracted to woodland edges include species of conservation importance such as song thrush and bullfinch as well as a variety of warblers. Butterflies such as holly blue, gatekeeper and comma are also attracted to woodland edges, as are rarer species including small blue and some fritillaries. Associated mammals include bank vole, field mouse and wood mouse.

Detailed advice on the design of woodlands for birds is given in MAFF (1999).

Woodland inner core
The inner core is characterised by low light levels and higher humidity, and is protected from high winds. In semi-natural woodland the trees form a closed canopy which acts as a protective layer for the woodland environment below. The presence of an inner shady core separates woodland from parkland or a bank of scrub. This closure can be permanent, as in high forest, or intermittent, as in coppice woodland. To provide sufficient shade and provide territories for many bird species, the area of the inner core should be at least 2 ha. The inner core field layer is dominated by specialist shade-tolerant species such as bluebell *(Hyacinthoides non-scripta)*, greater woodrush *(Luzula sylvatica)*, yellow archangel *(Lamiastrum galeobdolon)*, wood sanicle *(Sanicula europaeus)* and butchers broom *(Ruscus aculeatus)*. Some of these species can survive in partial shade in the absence of other vegetation, but some shade is essential for the survival of many woodland herbs; for example, the leaves of dog's mercury *(Mercuralis perennis)* become scorched under direct sunlight (Peterken, 1981).

Both the woodland edge and the inner core should be created. Creating the woodland edge is relatively straightforward, but the essential part of woodland design is ensuring that there is a sufficient area of good quality woodland core. This can be achieved by designing a dense edge habitat with the primary objective of reducing light levels within the wood. If the edge habitat permits too much light penetration, opportunist edge species will be encouraged, and classic woodland herbs will be unable to survive.

To minimise the edge effect and provide habitat for specialist inner core species in the centre, the edge:core ratio should be as low as possible. The best shape is therefore a circle, but this will appear very unnatural, so in practice an uneven shape based upon a circle will be the best compromise (see Figure F.3.2.). One should not incorporate too many indentations and spurs around the edge of the wood as this extends the proportion of edge (unless it is compensated for by increasing the edge width). Size, shape and location of new woodlands can be assisted by landscape design principles but should be ecologically led.

Note that in practice, woodland creation on landfill must take account of access requirements to pollution control infrastructure (Figure F.3.1). Figure F.3.2 should therefore be used as a guide, but

should be adapted according to site-specific considerations. In the short term, it may not be possible to create a large inner core, although this will be possible in the long term after gas generation has ceased.

Woodland age structure
Mature woodlands should have a balanced age structure incorporating the full range from seedlings to mature trees and dead wood. Structural variation is created by disturbance, which occurs in natural woodlands as a result of windthrow, disease, fire or drought. Gaps in the canopy enable saplings to put on a burst of growth in an attempt to reach the canopy level. A wood of even-aged trees will take many years to develop a naturalistic structure and thus the age of the trees to be planted should be a major design consideration. Structural diversity can be promoted by the retention of existing mature trees, and dead wood should also be retained on site. Dead standing trees can be created by ring barking, but for safety reasons they should not be sited near footpaths or access routes.

In general, from an ecological perspective, the more naturalistic the created woodland, the better. Planting density and species composition of the trees and shrubs should be varied across the site, and planting in straight lines should be avoided. It is worth considering planting some areas with shrubs only, whilst other areas could comprise a dense thicket of scrub and a few trees that will be allowed to grow tall and broad. Additionally, some areas can be left unplanted to encourage natural regeneration.

Woodland microhabitats
The creation of microhabitats is perhaps of more importance for woodland than for any other habitat type, since natural woodlands contain many different microhabitat types. Microhabitats must be artificially created in newly-planted woods, and woodland design plays an important role. Woodland management will also affect the appearance and structure of the woodland, which again leads to the creation of other microhabitats. Examples of woodland microhabitats include:

Glades and rides
Glades and rides can be particularly relevant to woodland creation on landfill, due to the requirement to maintain access to pollution control infrastructure. They are essentially 'edge habitats' where

Figure F.3.2. Ideal woodland design to maximise biodiversity value

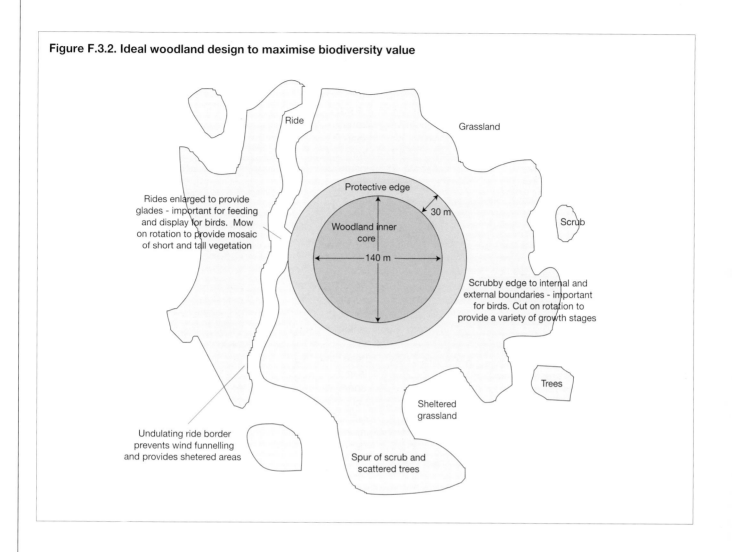

Ride

Grassland

Protective edge

30 m

Woodland inner core

140 m

Scrub

Rides enlarged to provide glades - important for feeding and display for birds. Mow on rotation to provide mosaic of short and tall vegetation

Scrubby edge to internal and external boundaries - important for birds. Cut on rotation to provide a variety of growth stages

Trees

Undulating ride border prevents wind funnelling and provides shetered areas

Sheltered grassland

Spur of scrub and scattered trees

semi-shade conditions prevail, and provide habitat for a range of species. The main difference between edge habitat created by rides and glades and the woodand edge itself is that conditions are sheltered within the wood, free from wind and cold temperatures. For the survival of woodland core species, it is important that core areas between rides and glades are not less than 2 ha. If site conditions do not permit this, a decision must be made on the required woodland type (either a shady woodland or a well-lit one), as it is impossible to incorporate both objectives in an area less than 2 ha.

Rides should be a minimum of 10 m wide (Watkins, 1990) or be wider than the height of the adjacent trees, whichever is greater, to allow good light penetration. Rides orientated east-west receive a greater amount of sun (an average of 10 hours per day) than north-south rides (an average of 6 hours per day).

Ride or glade edges should be scalloped to produce bays. These should ideally be mown to create grassland patches enclosed within scrub. Mowing

Photo: Duncan Watson

Woodland creation at a recently restored landfill site in north-west England. The ride forms a public footpath, provides access to pollution control structures and has value for species such as red campion.

will prevent scrub invasion and promote the survival of herb species such as foxglove, red campion, herb robert, wood speedwell and primrose. The sheltered conditions that result are also much valued by some butterfly species.

Grassland
Natural woodlands can contain appreciable amounts of grassland, which has the potential to be of considerable wildlife value. Grassland is found in access rides, glades and clearings and in areas with soils too thin to support trees. The same consideration of the woodland core applies to the design of grassland patches in that the areas of woodland outside should be at least 2 ha in size, with a minimum distance of 200 m between other grassland patches or the woodland edge. It is also good practice to ensure that grassland areas are no smaller than 30 m diameter. Grassland areas should be mown to prevent scrub invasion. The grassland shape should therefore be amenable to machinery and should be accessible by a ride.

Dead wood
Dead wood provides habitat for a range of invertebrates, mammals and fungi. Different species are encouraged depending on the type of dead wood present.
Forms of dead wood are:
- dead limbs on standing trees;
- decay columns and rot holes in standing trees;
- fallen dead wood; and
- stumps and coppice stools.

Dead wood such as failed trees or dead branches should not be removed. Dead wood can be provided from an early stage by introducing logs from a neighbouring wood or by using suitable material that enters the landfill as part of the waste. For maximum benefit to invertebrates, there should be a continuous supply of dead wood at all stages of decay. Tree species vary in the quality of dead wood they produce and thus their benefit to invertebrates. Rapidly decaying species such as birch are of less value than species that are more resistant to decay such as oak, beech, ash, hornbeam, elm and common lime. Note however that land managers have a duty of care toward visitors on public access land; dead and decaying trees should be felled on sites with public access if they are close to a footpath.

Photo: David Hill

Planting trees next to existing woodlands can increase the conservation value of woodland creation on landfill sites.

Other design issues
Linking other woodlands
The species diversity of isolated woodlands is likely to decline over time, as species cannot recolonise from nearby woodlands if local extinctions occur. Every new woodland fragment should therefore ideally either be situated close to existing woodlands or be independent of other areas for regeneration (i.e. large enough for local extinctions to be unlikely). The size of woodland necessary to ensure that species richness will be maintained is at least 5 hectares. Where woodland exists adjacent to the landfill site, planting should aim to link these areas or increase their size by planting at the edge, but preferably not adjacent to established scrub habitats on woodland edges which would become shaded (Kirby 1994); only plant adjacent to areas of true woodland. If a scrub edge must be planted up, create a new scrub edge to replace the one that will be lost. Alternatively, the new woodland can be placed between two isolated fragments to act as a 'stepping stone'. This will have little benefit to plant species, but may have a considerable effect on mammalian and invertebrate populations (Kirby, 1995). Woodlands should be larger than 3 ha to constitute attractive habitat for woodland birds. However, if several smaller woodlands are planted less than 1 km apart, birds can travel between woods and

the entire area is effectively treated as one woodland (MAFF, 1999).

Woodlands and wetlands
Woodlands should not be sited next to wetlands of conservation value. Swamps, bogs and fens will suffer from being in close proximity to woodland since the trees will take up moisture and hence dry out the wetland.
- Woodlands should not be planted as a ring around the perimeter of an existing wetland.
- Woodlands should also not be planted where they will intercept runoff water from the landfill that feeds a wetland.
The creation of ponds within woodlands provides an additional microhabitat. Such ponds will be very shaded and of a very different nature to unshaded ponds, supporting a limited range of specialised plants and invertebrates. Ponds should not be created above the cap.

Designing against windthrow
Shelterbelts can be used to provide shelter for newly planted trees in particularly exposed areas. However, the use of shelterbelts must be considered in the context of the landscape, particularly if non-native species are used, since they are very visible landscape elements and provide little conservation benefit. Fast-

growing native species such as willow and birch should be used if possible.

Alternative methods of avoiding windthrow are to ensure an adequate depth of rooting substrate (minimum 1.5 m depth), to coppice the woodland on a short rotation (7-10 years) or to restrict the composition of the woodland to small trees and shrubs. Oaks, field maple and aspen are particularly prone to windsnap and should not be planted in high windthrow hazard areas. Waterlogged soils also inhibit extensive root growth and hence enhance the likelihood of windthrow (Whitbread, 1992).

3.3.2 Selecting a woodland type

Of the twenty woodland types described by the NVC, only eight dry woodland types are suitable for creation on landfill sites. These can be divided into three very broad categories based primarily on soil type, altitude and geographical location. Soil type is one of the main determinants of the type of woodland that develops in a natural situation. Generally, acid soils support oak-dominated woodlands, whereas calcareous and neutral soils in southern Britain support beech or ash-dominated woodlands. This classification is very crude and ecological advice should be sought on what woodland types are appropriate in the project area.

Beech can be prone to windthrow and is rather difficult to establish. This leaves a choice of ash-dominated woodland on neutral soils or oak-dominated woodland on acid, more infertile soils. Although this appears to be a limited selection, there are a wide number of other tree and shrub species that are present both in the canopy and shrub layer of these woodlands. Rather than describe all available types of ash and oak woodland in detail, a widespread and commonly occurring woodland has been selected and given as an example in Box F.3.1. For further information on additional woodland NVC types see Rodwell (1991).

The species composition, structure and management of local woodlands, particularly ancient ones, provides another useful guide to the type of woodland that is appropriate (the local Wildlife Trust will be able to advise on this). This approach requires substantial planning and research in order to select the most relevant woodland type, but the returns are considerable in terms of nature conservation value. Additionally, the woodland will resemble a natural woodland in appearance and is therefore

---

Summary of woodland design guidelines

Woodland creation:
- Create all three layers of the woodland (canopy, shrub and field layers).
- Woodland size should be a minimum of 2 ha, and should ideally be larger than 5 ha.
- Try to ensure that an inner shady core is created.
- Only create rides and glades within the woodland if there is sufficient area of core habitat (although there may be a requirement for rides and glades in association with access requirements to pollution control infrastructure). Alternatively, design a well-lit woodland (essentially a parkland) with scattered trees and shrubs, or situate glades at the woodland edge.

If an open habitat of nature conservation value exists either on or adjacent to the landfill:
- Site the woodland some distance away (at least 30 m) from any other habitats of nature conservation value.
- Alternatively, plant the woodland with a wide grassland edge as a buffer zone.
- The buffer zone should be designed to facilitate management such as mowing to prevent the growth of tree and shrub seedlings and to maximise diversity of the grassland element.

Where grassland is also to be created, either within the woodland or at the edge:
- Ensure that these areas are accessible for management such as mowing or grazing.
- Scallop the edges to create sheltered conditions by planting shrub species.
- Rides should be a minimum width of 10 m.

---

likely to attract associated birds, mammals and invertebrates faster than a less well-designed wood.

3.3.3 Species selection
Canopy and shrub layer species

A wide range of species are acceptable for inclusion in a planting scheme to create woodland on landfill. However, there are several species that should not be planted on the landfill cap since they can grow roots in oxygen-depleted environments and thus may well be able to penetrate a clay cap. These species are lodgepole pine, white willow, crack willow and any poplar species except aspen (Bending & Moffat, 1997).

Ideally the relevant canopy and shrub layer species to include are native species listed as constant species in the constancy table of the chosen woodland NVC type. These constant species should be planted in the same proportions as in natural woodlands. However, it is strongly recommended that ecological advice is sought on the best species to include and the appropriate proportions.

Species should be appropriate to the environmental characteristics of the site. The major parameters that affect species selection are soil type (clay, silt, sand), soil pH, soil moisture content and woodland location. For example, dry woodland will be a feasible option for creation on the top

of the landfill cap, since rainfall will drain away from this area. Woodland situated around the base of the cap will receive run-off and thus a more water-tolerant woodland type should be created.

As a rule, therefore, the species selected should be:
- common;
- native;
- suited to the soil type and quality at the site;
- suited to the climate and geographical location of the site;
- be appropriate to the local area i.e. naturally occurring within the locality of the site; and
- be of British native origin and preferably of local provenance.

A considerable number of tree species possess limited distributions. To assist species selection, local seed zones have been defined by Herbert *et al.* (1999) (Figure F.3.3), and lists of native species appropriate for each seed zone are provided in Table F.3.1, together with an indication of suitable soil type for each species. However, it should be remembered that not all of these species will be suitable for immediate introduction on restored landfill sites. Table F.3.2 lists pioneer tree species most likely to tolerate conditions on a landfill.

If the rooting substrate is very hostile to

Table F.3.1. Native species appropriate to the numbered local seed zones in Figure F.3.3 (from Herbert et al., 1999)

Columns — Seed zone number: 101 102 103 104 105 106 107 108 109 201 202 203 204 301 302 303 304 305 401 402 403 404 405 40(6) — Soils: a b c d e f

Large and medium sized trees

Alder, black	Alnus glutinosa
Apple, crab	Malus sylvestris ssp. sylvestris
Ash	Fraxinus excelsior
Aspen	Populus tremula
Beech	Fagus sylvatica
Birch, downy	Betula pubescens
Birch, silver	Betula pendula
Cherry, bird	Prunus padus
Cherry, gean	Prunus avium
Elm, wych	Ulmus glabra
Hornbeam	Carpinus betulus
Lime, small-leaved	Tilia cordata
Lime, large-leaved	Tilia platyphyllos
Maple, field	Acer campestre
Oak, pedunculate	Quercus robur
Oak, sessile	Quercus petraea
Pine, Scots	Pinus sylvestris
Poplar, black	Populus nigra var. betulifolia
Poplar, grey	Populus canescens
Rowan	Sorbus aucuparia
Wild Service tree	Sorbus torminalis
Whitebeam	Sorbus aria sensu lato
Willow, crack	Salix fragilis
Willow, goat	Salix caprea
Willow, white	Salix alba
Yew	Taxus baccata

Small trees and shrubs

Blackthorn	Prunus spinosa
Box	Buxus sempervirens
Broom	Cytisus scoparius
Buckthorn, alder	Frangula alnus
Buckthorn, purging	Rhamnus catharticus
Butcher's broom	Ruscus aculeatus
Dogwood	Cornus sanguinea
Elder	Sambucus nigra
Gorse	Ulex europaeus
Guelder rose	Viburnum opulus
Hawthorn, common	Crataegus monogyna
Hazel	Corylus avellana
Holly	Ilex aquifolium
Juniper	Juniperus communis
Privet	Ligustrum vulgare
Rose, dog	Rosa canina
Rose, field	Rosa arvensis
Spindle	Euonymus europaeus
Spurge laurel	Daphne laureola
Wayfaring tree	Viburnum lantana
Willow, almond	Salix triandra
Willow, bay	Salix pentandra
Willow, eared	Salix aurita
Willow, grey	Salix cinerea
Willow, osier	Salix viminalis
Willow, purple	Salix purpurea

SOILS: a = wet sites b = light, dry soils c = heavy soils d = acid e = neutral / alkaline f = exposed sites

| Table F.3.2. Pioneer tree and shrub species that can be used as a nurse ||
Species	Comments
Aspen *Populus tremula*	Quick to establish
Blackthorn *Prunus spinosa*	
Bramble *Rubus fruticosus* agg.	
Common alder *Alnus glutinosa*	Nitrogen-fixing
Common gorse *Ulex europaeus*	Nitrogen fixing
Downy birch *Betula pubescens*	Quick to establish. Tolerates low fertility
Goat willow *Salix caprea*	
Grey willow *Salix cinerea*	
Hawthorn *Crategeus monogyna*	Tolerates browsing
Rowan *Sorbus aucuparia*	
Silver birch *Betula pendula*	Quick to establish. Tolerates low fertility
Wild cherry *Prunus avium*	Quick to establish. More fertile sites only

these characteristics is given in Section F.1. Further guidelines specific to woodland creation are given below.

Soil depth
The essential characteristics of a rooting substrate are that there is sufficient depth for the roots to grow unhindered before the cap is reached; the cap will not allow roots to penetrate. The risk of windthrow substantially increases if there is insufficient substrate to securely anchor the trees. At least 1 m depth of soil should be provided (1.5 m over a clay cap) (Dobson & Moffat, 1993; Environment Agency, in prep).

Drainage
Tree establishment is best where the restored landform promotes natural drainage and minimizes waterlogging. A slope gradient of about 1 in 10 is best for tree establishment (Simmons, 1999). Although trees can be established on slopes as steep as 1 in 3, slopes on landfills should not be greater than 1 in 4 to facilitate management and prevent excessive soil erosion.

In addition, a coarse drainage layer can be laid on top of the cap to allow rapid shedding of water and further prevent waterlogging. This may also have the effect of discouraging tree roots from reaching the cap.

Effect of soil type
The use of pure topsoil as rooting substrate for trees and shrubs is not recommended – the high fertility encourages the growth of grasses and other weeds which compete with the trees. The use of some topsoil can be beneficial if used locally where the trees are planted. For example, topsoil can be used to line the pits in which trees are planted, or a thin layer can be buried under the soil surface (or laid on top) to help initial establishment. Topsoil can also be mixed with low fertility subsoil or soil-forming materials to raise fertility to levels at which trees can establish.

Subsoil mixed with topsoil is probably ideal for woodland creation, although not essential; trees have been shown to perform well when planted into very infertile soil-forming materials such as crushed brick rubble, colliery shale, mineral overburden and river dredgings, provided that certain standards are met (Dobson & Moffat, 1993). Moderately infertile substrates such as subsoil may encourage a more diverse woodland by reducing the competitive ability of aggressive species. If very low fertility substrates are used (i.e. soil forming materials), they should be mixed with topsoil or soil conditioners to produce a suitable growing medium. Alternatively, nurse species can be used.

It is advised that very clay-rich soils are avoided, especially in drought-prone areas, as tree establishment can be difficult on these soils (Bending & Moffat, 1997; Dobson & Moffat, 1995b). Clay soils can be improved by the addition of sand, organic matter or coarse soil-forming materials.

Use of nurse species
Nurse species are likely to be required if:
- soil is poorly structured or likely to be

Table F.3.3. Common field layer species (from Gilbert & Anderson, 1998 and Francis, 1995)	
Woodland edge species	
Red campion *Silene dioica* S	Smooth brome *Bromus racemosus* S
Herb robert *Geranium robertianum* S	Wood false brome *Brachypodium sylvaticum* S
Pendulous sedge *Carex pendula* S	Foxglove *Digitalis purpurea* S
Bracken *Pteridium aquilinum* P	Hairy St John's wort *Hypericum hirsutum* S
Bramble *Rubus fruticosus* agg. S	Wood millet *Milium effusum* S
Wood avens *Geum urbanum* S	Hedge woundwort *Stachys sylvaticum* S
Hedge bedstraw *Galium mollugo* S	Greater stitchwort *Stellaria holostea* S
Hedge mustard *Alliaria petiolata* S	Upright hedge parsley *Torilis japonica* S
Arum lily *Arum maculatum* S	
Woodland core species	
Dogs mercury *Mercuralis perennis* P	Pignut *Conopodium majus* S
Bluebell *Hyacinthoides non-scripta* S	Sweet violet *Viola odorata* S
Yellow archangel *Lamiastrum galeobdolon* P	Wood anemone *Anemone nemorosa* P
Wavy hair-grass *Deschampsia flexuosa* S	Enchanters nightshade *Circaea lutetiana* P
Wild garlic *Allium ursinum* S	Wood sorrel *Oxalis acetosella* P
Sweet woodruff *Galium odoratum* S	Wood sage *Teucrium scorodonia* P
Bugle *Ajuga reptans* P	Common dog-violet *Viola riviniana* P
Primrose *Primula vulgaris* P	Ferns e.g. male fern *Dryopteris felix-mas* P

Note: S / P denotes whether the species should be introduced as seed (S) or a plug plant (P) – see Section F.3.4.2.

125

(*Fagus sylvatica*), hornbeam (*Carpinus betulus*), holly (*Ilex aquifolium*) and yew (*Taxus baccata*) should not be planted until moderate shade is present. These species are intolerant of droughty conditions and will perform better once the soil has had time to develop. Again, a Section 106 Agreement may be required to extend aftercare commitments.

Spacing

The closer the trees are planted, the quicker the canopy will close. Close planting will reduce the amount of aggressive grass growth and reduce overall short-term costs. However, if the trees are planted very close together, a greater amount of thinning will be required as part of long-term management. Additionally, close planting produces tall thin trees that are more liable to windthrow. Two factors to consider are the money available for long-term management and the introduction of field layer species. These species cannot be planted until canopy closure, and close planting enables this to be carried out at an earlier date.

Varying planting density across the site increases habitat diversity and the appearance of naturalness. Conifer plantations and commercial woodlands typically plant trees in long, straight rows which is far removed from the appearance of a natural woodland. To create a woodland with nature conservation value, the ideal method is to plant clumps of one to three species, and introduce variation by altering the clump size and between-clump distance. Clumps consisting of several species are usually not effective; fast-growing species tend to shade out the other species.

- Clumps of two to three species with similar growth rates are usually ideal.
- Clump size can be varied from just 3 individuals to clumps 40 m across.
- Between-clump distance can be varied between 8 m and 20 m.
- Trees should be planted 4 m apart on topsoil, and 10 m apart on poorer substrates.
- Shrubs can be planted 2 m apart between the trees.

(Rodwell & Patterson, 1994.)

Tree and shrub layers

Standards, bare rooted transplants and pot-grown trees

All species should be planted with care to increase the chance of successful establishment. British Standards have been formulated for quality of tree stock, planting methods and aftercare. These standards should be adhered to and

included in any specification for contractors. Excellent guidelines on planting methods are given in Brooks (1988).

If a grass nurse has been sown as part of interim restoration, it should be removed, either by spraying a 1 m^2 area around the trees with a non-selective contact herbicide or by cutting a 0.5 m^2 turf and replacing upside down around the newly planted tree.

Do not attempt to accelerate the creation of the appearance of woodland by using large standard trees. These are obtained as pot-grown specimens but are supplied with a much smaller root ball for the size of the above-ground growth than would be found naturally. Standards must be staked since they are very liable to windthrow, an important consideration on exposed landfill sites. They are prone to poor establishment and are very expensive.

Small pot-grown trees are available, but bare rooted transplants are generally preferable. Despite their smaller size, they have a greater proportion of roots to above-ground growth and therefore establish faster and do not require staking. They establish much faster in poorer substrates and are also cheaper than pot-grown plants. Transplants do, however, require careful handling prior to planting and during storage (see below).

Transplants are generally between 0.6 and 1.2 m tall when purchased. The quality of the stock is very important. The trees should possess a high proportion of roots to above-ground growth, be less than 1.5 m tall and possess a sturdy fibrous root system.

- Trees should be pit or slit planted (see Figure F.3.4). Tease apart the roots and place the tree in the hole with the roots spread out. Ensure that the soil used for backfilling is crumbly so that all the roots make contact with soil. Standards require a large pit filled with a mixture of soil and high quality compost. An application of inorganic fertiliser will stimulate root growth.
- Keep the trees in a plastic bag until they are placed in the hole – any time exposed to the open air can dry out and kill the roots. If the roots appear dry when removed from the bag, immerse them in warm water for three minutes.
- Firm the soil surface gently after planting – take care to avoid compaction of the soil. The surface of the soil should gently slope away from the plant to avoid water accumulating around the stem.
- Water the soil with at least one bucket of water per plant. Pour the water on gently to avoid washing away loose soil.
- Tubes to protect the trees from grazing should also be installed if

Table F.3.4. Comparison of planting material costs of direct sowing with cost of planting transplants (from Willoughby *et al.*, 1996)

Species	Seed					Transplants			
	Number ha^{-1}	Germination kg^{-1}	£ kg^{-1}	£ ha^{-1} kg^{-1}	£ ha^{-1} inc sowing	Number ha^{-1}	£ plant^{-1}	£ ha^{-1}	£ ha^{-1} inc planting
Oak	100000	200	3.50	1750	1790	2500	0.30	750	1000
Scots pine	100000	112000	185.00	165	180	2500	0.12	300	550
Ash	100000	8000	8.00	100	115	2500	0.25	625	875
Beech	100000	2400	12.00	500	515	2500	0.25	625	875
Birch	100000	150000	80.00	53	53	2500	0.15	375	625
Wild cherry	100000	3000	21.00	700	700	2500	0.20	500	750

Notes: Transplant prices are average prices for 1+0 or 1+1 stock as appropriate for each species.
If seed can be collected from local woodlands, the cost of seed may be reduced.
Cost of seeding is assumed to be £20/ha for oak (drilled) and £15/ha for all others.
Cost of planting is assumed to be £250/ha.

required (see below); these also provide some support for the young plants.

Bare rooted transplants can be stored for up to three weeks by heaping them together in a dry, dark and chilled (but frost free) area. The entire heap should be covered with plastic or tarpaulin to prevent evaporation.

For longer-term storage in winter, the whips should be 'heeled in'. This entails planting the trees in bunches in crumbly soil with the entire root mass covered in a relatively frost-free area. The trees should be at an angle of 45 degrees to the ground to minimise 'wind rock'. They can be stored in this way for up to three months in winter, but only for two weeks in the growing season. The trees must be regularly checked to ensure that they do not dry out.

Seeds
During the period between planting and establishment, new trees are vulnerable and require a degree of maintenance. Establishment is the stage at which the trees no longer require protection, and their growth rate increases considerably once this stage is reached. Trees grown from seeds reach this stage quicker than planted trees, and it is therefore worth considering using seeds, seedlings or both as a planting method to reduce the amount of aftercare required.

Many tree seeds are large and easily handled and therefore easy to introduce. Another advantage is that local provenance can be guaranteed if they are collected from nearby woods. Seeds with a hard coat such as acorns and hazel nuts can be introduced by dropping them on the ground and pressing them in with a heel. Seeds encased in a fleshy coat such as blackberries, rosehips, hawthorn berries and holly berries require pretreatment before germination, such as passing through the gut of a bird. These species are therefore best introduced naturally by birds or as seedlings or transplants (Baines & Smart, 1991).

However, the length of time before the area has the general appearance of woodland will be considerably longer using seeds than using transplants, and the time taken for the development of conditions suitable for the introduction of field layer species will also be much greater. The aftercare period should therefore be extended until the canopy has started to develop through a Section 106 Agreement (see Section D.3). This may have implications for planning conditions and affect the choice of after-use.

Due to EC Directives on forestry reproductive material (66/404/EEC and 71/161/EEC), seeds of the following species are restricted from sale unless from a registered source: Scots pine (*Pinus sylvestris*), black poplar (*Populus nigra*), aspen (*Populus tremula*), pedunculate oak (*Quercus robur*), sessile oak (*Quercus petraea*) and beech (*Fagus sylvatica*). This Directive is soon to be amended to include the following species: alder (*Alnus glutinosa*), silver birch (*Betula pendula*), downy birch (*Betula pubescens*), wild cherry (*Prunus avium*) and small-leaved lime (*Tilia cordata*). This can make seed of local provenance hard to obtain. However, small amounts of seed can be collected or sold from unregistered sources (sufficient to produce less than 1000 plants) if the new woodland is to be used for conservation rather than commercial purposes. Guidance from the Forestry Authority should be sought on this issue (Flora Locale, 1999).

A tested method to encourage establishment of tree from seeds is to sow a grass nurse crop at the same time. Italian rye-grass (*Lolium multiflorum*) has been used to good effect, and cereals such as wheat can also be used (see Section F.1.6.2 for more information).

Seeds should ideally be broadcast in mid-late April during a cold moist spell. Sowing rates should be 100 000 viable seeds per hectare – this produces a density of 10 000 trees per ha after 10 years, accounting for tree failure (Willoughby *et al.*, 1996). Note that this figure excludes the number of nurse seeds sown.

Seeds can be stored in hessian bags in a dry dark place. The seeds should be dry at all times and if possible stored off the floor. If suitable conditions are not

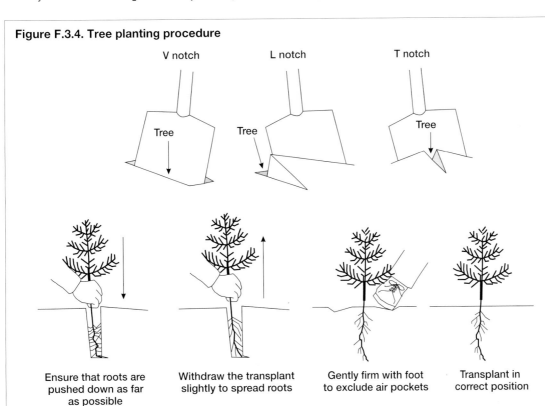

Figure F.3.4. Tree planting procedure

V notch   L notch   T notch

Tree   Tree   Tree

Ensure that roots are pushed down as far as possible

Withdraw the transplant slightly to spread roots

Gently firm with foot to exclude air pockets

Transplant in correct position

Source: Dobson & Moffat (1993). Crown copyright is reproduced with the permission of the Controller of Her Majesty's Stationery Office.

Mechanical control

Mechanical control of vegetation by cutting is usually carried out with a strimmer, as the distance between trees will be too narrow or uneven to use a ride-on mower. Cuttings should always be removed – leaving them will hinder the establishment of field layer species. Care should be taken not to catch the trees with the strimmer blades. The best time to carry out mechanical control is early to mid-July.

Herbicides

Following initial weed control with herbicide prior to tree and shrub planting, a second generation of weeds will grow up from the seed bank. Once these have germinated and grown several true leaves they can be sprayed with a non-selective herbicide. However, these herbicides are also capable of killing the trees; extreme care must be taken during application. Weed control must therefore be carried out by hand using a knapsack sprayer and a shield to ensure that the application does not touch the trees. Grass-specific herbicides are available but these are very expensive and generally little used. The best time to apply herbicide is late May, and the effects should last for the entire season without the need for a second application.

Alternatively, a residual pre-emergent herbicide can be used, which stays active in the soil and acts on seeds as they germinate. The length of residence in the soil will depend on the soil type – the herbicide will remain in sandy soils for two months at best, up to four months at best in clay or humus-rich soils. Correct timing is therefore essential for maximum effect; residual herbicides should be applied in February or March, in time for the weed seeds to germinate in the spring. Note that this method can only be used if the trees and shrubs are introduced as saplings.

Weed control – second season onwards

If mechanical methods are used to control weeds, cutting should be carried out annually until the trees have grown above the surrounding vegetation and appear to be establishing well. Further management will be unnecessary once the woodland canopy develops and begins to cast appreciable shade.

If herbicides are used, a second application of non-selective contact herbicide (with or without residual pre-emergent herbicide) will usually be sufficient. If topsoil has been used, treatment in the third year will probably also be necessary.

Watering

Plants will benefit greatly from watering during the first six months after planting. Regular watering is essential for large plants such as standard trees. The logistics of watering large areas will probably make this a difficult task. To offset the need for watering, thick mulches such as coarse bark which reduce soil water evaporation should be used.

Fencing

It is worth considering fencing newly planted areas, especially if public access to the site is to be encouraged. Areas planted with ground flora may need to be fenced to prevent trampling. Stands of planted trees may require fencing as protection from grazing animals such as rabbits, deer, cattle and sheep.

Wind fencing may be required on exposed areas. Windrock (loosening of newly planted trees by strong wind) is a common factor in tree failure. Wind fencing can be placed around blocks of trees, along the length of a hedgerow or at strategic positions such as in the line of the prevailing wind. Wind fencing is cheaper than individually staking trees; stake ties require monitoring to prevent the ties restricting tree growth, and are labour-intensive to install.

Replacement of failed individuals

Individuals of any of the three layers should be replaced if they die within five years of planting. The specification of the planting contract should make it clear that the responsibility to replace dead plants lies with the planting contractor, as this encourages good planting practice in the first instance.

Thinning

Thinning is standard forestry practice, and involves the regular removal of a proportion of the tree layer as the individual trees grow in height and girth. This provides more space for the remaining trees to grow whilst retaining straight stems, and encourages better quality timber. Thinned trees and dead wood should not be removed in woodland managed for conservation.

Timber quality is not an important consideration in conservation woodlands, so thinning is not required for this purpose. However, if the trees are planted very close together, they will soon start to crowd each other, producing a dense thicket of even-aged saplings with little or no light penetrating to the woodland floor. There are two methods which can be used to promote a more diverse age structure:

- Non-intervention: allowing the woodland to develop as a dense thicket will induce self-thinning (the death of less vigorous specimens), leaving more space for remaining trees. Self-thinning takes longer, but produces a more natural woodland.
- Active thinning: felling and removing a proportion of the trees by hand. This requires more resources, but produces a diverse age structure in a shorter time. Active thinning should begin when the trees begin to crowd each other; on productive sites, this may be necessary within five years after planting, whereas on less productive sites it may not be required for several years.

Dead wood should be retained within the woodland, either left where it is cut or piled into heaps. This provides habitat for fungi, lichens, mosses and invertebrates.

Control of invasive perennials

Invasive alien species such as rhododendron (*Rhododendron ponticum*) and japanese knotweed (*Fallopia japonica*) should be removed at the earliest opportunity if they colonise the woodland. These species are hard to eradicate once established and have detrimental effects on woodland diversity.

3.4.4 Long term management

Long-term management should be considered at the outset of restoration design – intended management can be integral to habitat creation design.

Guidance given here on long-term management is brief and serves to illustrate basic principles. For further details on woodland management see Sutherland & Hill (1995), Buckley (1992), Andrews & Rebane (1994) and Brooks (1988). The Forestry Commission have produced a series of leaflets on the management of semi-natural woodlands (Forestry Commission, 1999).

Traditional management practices such as coppicing evolved from the necessity to obtain products from woodland. However, these practices had incidental beneficial effects on wildlife, and traditional management is therefore often continued in woodlands that are managed for conservation. For example, coppicing has recently been resumed in several ancient woodlands to encourage populations of rare butterflies such as high brown and pearl-bordered fritillaries.

Newly created woodlands obviously have no management history or pre-existing wildlife value. It is therefore probably most appropriate to introduce a

Case Study 7:

Nantmel Landfill, Powys

Wetland creation as part of a new leachate treatment system

Site details
Site operator: Powys County Council
Habitat created: Wetland
Area of habitat created: Stream of length 1300 m
Existing nature conservation interest: Minimal on the site itself. Otter and white-clawed crayfish present in river catchment downstream of the site.

Site background

Nantmel landfill is a relatively small site that was closed several years ago. As a result of the high annual rainfall in this part of Wales, leachate production is still very high, with up to 600 tonnes produced per day in the worst weather (the third largest volume at any site in Wales). The site was not designed as a containment landfill and lies at the top of a slope. Leachate breakout has occurred in a number of places, causing considerable contamination of both the site and the land below. Of even greater concern from a nature conservation perspective were the impacts on the local river catchment into which much of the leachate flowed, which was known to support otters and the rare white-clawed crayfish. Both these species are UK BAP priority species and are known to be highly sensitive to pollution.

Remedial works were carried out on the site in 1996, involving re-engineering of the cap and the design and construction of a new leachate treatment system. More than 5 ha of various wetland habitats were also created.

Habitat creation objectives

The principal objective was low-cost, effective treatment of the large volumes of leachate produced at the site. Leachate removal and treatment off-site was not an option as the nearest suitable treatment works is over 50 miles away.

As a final component of the leachate treatment system a 4.5 ha wetland area was created on land directly below the site. Whilst this was primarily designed to be part of the leachate treatment system, the potential benefits to biodiversity were fully considered from the outset.

Remedial works also involved the clean-up of three polluted streams, and their diversion into a holding pond designed to intercept leachate in the case of breakout. All these features were also specifically designed to benefit nature conservation.

The remainder of the site was restored to rush-pasture, the traditional land-use in the local area.

Remedial works and habitat creation techniques

Leachate treatment system

A brief summary of the leachate treatment system is given below. Contact the Waste Management Department, Powys County Council for further information.

Discharges of various constituents of the leachate into the local catchment are monitored daily and at present do not exceed 0.1 mg/l ammonia and 9 mg/l nitrate. Water quality in the stream below the site has therefore improved considerably, and white-clawed crayfish

---

Summary of Nantmel leachate treatment system

Stage 1
Leachate from the site is collected in a holding tank and aerated through repeated circulation to encourage oxidation of iron and other heavy metals. The leachate is also pumped through plastic filters, which further aerates it and promotes further oxidation of leachate components. The system can cope with large volumes of leachate, but a number of storm tanks have also been constructed to enable the system to cope in the event of prolonged periods of heavy rain.

Stage 2
The leachate is pumped through two vertical flow reed beds. This removes much of the remaining iron and also considerably reduces ammonia levels (down to around 20 mg/l).

Stage 3
The final stage of treatment, prior to discharge into the river catchment, involves the pumping of leachate into a 4.5 ha wetland area. This comprises several bunded enclosures through which the leachate slowly percolates into collection drains for discharge into a stream. Leachate typically remains in the wetland for about 2 days prior to discharge. The wetland has a pronounced effect on ammonia and nitrate levels. Bacterial action, plant root uptake and the physical adsorption of nitrogen into the soil by cation exchange all contribute to reducing contaminant levels within the leachate.

Photo: Duncan Watson

Wetland created as part of leachate treatment system at Nantmel.

and otter have returned. The treatment system has also received a special commendation from the Environment Agency.

Creation of a species-rich wetland

The wetland area that forms the final stage of the leachate treatment was originally a rush-dominated pasture with low species diversity. Its transformation to a species-rich fen has taken place purely as a result of the introduction of treated leachate, which in addition to regularly inundating the area, has greatly increased its nutrient status. Plant species have colonised naturally, and the site now has considerable nature conservation value. Species diversity has been further increased by the creation of additional microhabitats as a result of the varying topography provided by the bunded enclosures. Species present in the wetland in 1999 are listed below.

stripped and re-profiled to remove pollutants, and left to re-vegetate naturally. The principal objective of re-profiling the streams (and the pond creation below) was to prevent leachate pollution downstream of the site. However, vegetation has colonised rapidly, and the streams are now of conservation value in themselves. Species present along the streams in 1999 included marsh birds-foot trefoil, fen bedstraw, bog stitchwort, soft rush, meadowsweet, bladder sedge and sharp flowered rush.

Pond creation

A pond approximately 1 ha in size was constructed at the foot of the site, into which the three streams were diverted. The pond has an engineering function; it is designed to hold water and hence prevent its release into the catchment in

the case of leachate breakout. Another primary objective of the pond was to create habitat of conservation value.

The pond was created simply by stripping contaminated soil, profiling the bed and leaving it to fill naturally, fed by the streams. It was designed to incorporate shallow shelves, an area of deeper water and an island. A small number of emergent and aquatic plants were translocated from another pond nearby, but otherwise it has been left to colonise naturally. To provide potential habitat for otters, a number of large boulders were placed at the waters edge as potential sprainting sites. It is also understood that the local Wildlife Trust have been approached with regard to the creation of an artificial otter holt.

Preliminary results from the pond are very encouraging. Vegetation development has been good and large numbers of brown trout are now present. Even better news is that otters have been seen regularly with several spraints recorded on the specially designed rocks.

The methods described here are presented purely as examples of landfill restoration and habitat creation techniques. They do not necessarily reflect the best practice standards contained within this book.

Wetland plants present at Nantmel in 1999

Floating sweet-grass	Tufted hair-grass
Flag iris	Marsh cinquefoil
Great willowherb	Wild angelica
Soft rush	Marsh valerian
Creeping buttercup	Purple moor-grass
Meadowsweet	Lady fern
Reed canary-grass	Great burnet
Lesser spearwort	Greater bird's-foot trefoil
Marsh bedstraw	Betony
Bog stitchwort	Common hemp-nettle
Kingcup	Creeping bent
Pill sedge	Smooth meadow-grass
Marsh woundwort	Rough meadow-grass

At present, the vegetation is regulated by the regular inputs of treated leachate, and the site therefore effectively manages itself. With high volumes of leachate expected to be produced for at least the next 50 years, management requirements are therefore considered to be minimal for the foreseeable future.

Stream diversion

Prior to remedial works, three streams running through and adjacent to the site had become heavily contaminated with leachate. As a result, the substrate was coated with heavy metal deposits with high levels of algae, resulting in low vegetation diversity.

Part of the course of each stream was diverted. Re-engineering of the site also took place to divert leachate away from the streams. Leachate breakout into the streams was further prevented by the construction of intercepting ditches between the streams and the landfill.

The new stream courses were soil-

Photo: Duncan Watson

Created pond at Nantmel. The rocks in the bottom right of the photograph were designed specifically to be used as a sprainting site for otters.

Case Study 7

Case Study 8:

Penny Hill Landfill, Worcestershire

Creation of calcareous grassland using seed-rich hay supplemented by commercial grass seed

Site details
Site operator: Shanks Ltd
Habitat created: Calcareous grassland
Area of habitat created: 4 ha
Existing nature conservation interest: The site lies between two SSSI limestone grasslands.

Site background
Penny Hill Landfill is a relatively small site (4 ha) located within an old limestone quarry. The site lies between two SSSI calcareous grasslands and therefore planning conditions required the creation of calcareous grassland as part of restoration. Landfilling operations ceased in 1996 and creation of limestone grassland was carried out in two phases before completion in late 1998.

Habitat creation objectives
The objective of restoration was to create calcareous grassland of a similar species composition to the neighbouring SSSIs.

Given the potential for the site to increase the conservation value of the adjacent grasslands, species of local provenance were used in the restoration. Seed-rich hay from the adjacent SSSIs was the principal source of material.

A further objective was to use the site as an educational resource, with public access encouraged once the grassland develops and landfill gas production declines. Given the rural setting of the site, it is unlikely that large numbers of people would use the site, and public access is therefore not likely to cause excessive damage to the grassland.

Major constraints on successful habitat creation
The landform of the site was steeply sloping; soil erosion was a potential problem, particularly during the early stages of restoration.

Provision of the soil
Species-rich calcareous grassland requires a soil that is both infertile and calcareous. At Penny Hill the "soil" used for restoration comprised 700 mm of red marl (infertile subsoil), covered by 300 mm of limestone fines (both infertile and calcareous). The red marl originated from a local source whilst the limestone fines came from the site itself. Use of these materials provides an excellent illustration of how low-cost, locally available soil-forming materials may be successfully used in habitat creation schemes on landfill.

Seed sources
1. Seed-rich hay
Hay was harvested from the adjacent SSSI grassland. Unfortunately, the amount of seed derived from the hay was fairly small, and it was necessary to supplement it with commercial seed. Commercial seeds were restricted to grass species only, so that all the herbs were of local origin. Although the hay originally only contributed a small proportion to the sward, it is anticipated that with appropriate management, this proportion will increase over time.

2. Commercial grass seed
A mixture of nine perennial non-aggressive grasses were sown (see over).

In addition, Italian rye-grass, a biennial species, was sown as a nurse to prevent soil erosion, provide an instant "green cover" and promote good conditions for herb establishment.

Techniques used
Restoration took place in two phases, one completed in 1997, the other in 1998. Techniques used were similar for each phase.

Step 1
In August the site was levelled, harrowed and rolled to produce a seedbed. Large stones, which would reduce seed germination, were removed.

Step 2
Triple super phosphate fertiliser was applied at a rate of 150 kg/ha. Fertiliser was required since the limestone fines were extremely infertile.

Photo: Duncan Watson

Calcareous grassland at Penny Hill landfill site, created using strewn seed-rich hay. The photo was taken just one year after sowing. Although the cover is not yet 100%, the grassland has the potential to become a diverse community with considerable conservation value.

Seed mix used at Pennyhill landfill site

Species		%
Common bent	*Agrostis capillaris*	20
Sweet vernal-grass	*Anthoxanthum odoratum*	0.5
Quaking-grass	*Briza media*	2
Upright brome	*Bromus erectus*	1.5
Sheep's fescue	*Festuca ovina*	20
Red fescue	*Festuca rubra*	20
Crested hair-grass	*Koeleria macrantha*	4
Small timothy	*Phleum pratense* ssp. *bertolonii*	10
Yellow oat-grass	*Trisetum flavescens*	2
Nurse		
Italian rye-grass (Westerwolds variety)	*Lolium multiflorum* "Westerwolds"	20

Step 3

The site was seeded with the commercial mix of grass species (see above) at a rate of 30 kg/ha. The site was rolled after sowing to ensure that seeds made good contact with the soil.

Step 4

The nearby SSSI grassland was harvested by cutting and collecting seed-rich grass and herb flower heads. A relatively small quantity of hay was harvested, and there was not enough to cover the entire phase area. The hay was therefore spread in a series of "islands" across the site from which it was hoped the grassland species would spread over

time. Approximately 4-5 m³ of loose hay was strewn, covering an area of around 50 m².

In subsequent years, seed has been shake from the hay immediately after harvesting and then spread across the site. This has proved much more effective than spreading the hay itself, being much less time-consuming and covering a much greater area.

Harvesting of the donor site has been carried out at a number of different times of year to ensure that the full range of species were introduced to the site.

Aftercare and management

The nurse species was strimmed twice in the first year (in June and August) to prevent it from re-seeding. It was cut again in June of the second year using a scythe mower. The removal of the nurse has been largely successful, according to a survey carried out in June 2000, although small amounts are still present throughout the site.

More seed will be harvested from the adjacent SSSI in each of the next few years and used to treat some of the barer areas within the created grassland.

The long-term management regime has yet to be finalised, but will take the form of either mowing or grazing.

Preliminary results

A survey in June 2000 suggests that the creation of herb-rich grassland using hay from the SSSI has been reasonably successful; species which are naturally slow to colonise new ground are present on seeded areas. A substantial number were characteristic of the donor grassland, including eyebright, hay rattle, cowslip, salad burnet, greater knapweed, bird's-foot trefoil, red clover, black medick, soft brome, red fescue, sweet vernal grass, white clover and rough meadow grass. There was also evidence that some species had dispersed to areas that had not been spread with hay, although vegetation cover was greater and more diverse in areas treated with hay. Further hay treatments are likely to speed up the development of the grassland.

The developing herb-rich grassland, although containing many of the species from the SSSI, is closer to the neutral grassland NVC community MG5 than it is to the donor site chalk grassland community CG3 - few of the most strongly calcicolous associates of CG3 are at present becoming established. This indicates that more work is required to fully establish herb-rich chalk grassland, but the initial success of the grassland creation is an encouraging start.

Prior to Phase 2 of the restoration, several upright spurge (*Euphorbia serrulata*) plants were found growing on an area of the red marl subsoil, with over 50 plants present in 1999. Upright spurge is known from only a handful of sites and is included in the vascular plant Red Data Book. This area was consequently left out of Phase 2 of the restoration and is being allowed to develop naturally. Upright spurge characteristically occurs on limestone and is known from the area around the site, although the exact origin of the plants is uncertain (it could have come in with the imported marl). Whatever its origin, it provides an excellent illustration of the benefits of regular ecological monitoring, even in areas appearing at first glance to be devoid of any nature conservation interest.

The methods described here are presented purely as examples of landfill restoration and habitat creation techniques. They do not necessarily reflect the best practice standards contained within this book.

Photo: Valerie Hack

Upright spurge at Penny Hill landfill site.

management regime similar to that employed in local woods, especially if the new woodland is intended to extend an existing woodland.

Long-term woodland management is not essential for all woodland types; the need for management is decided by the desired form of the woodland. However, even in non-intervention woodlands, some management may be required in the interests of public safety. Dead and dangerous trees/branches should be removed near paths or car parks.

Management should aim to maximise habitat diversity and it is advised that traditional management regimes are used to produce one of the three woodland types listed below, as these generally yield substantial wildlife benefits.

Long-term monitoring (once every five years) will show how a management regime is affecting the overall wildlife value of the woodland and will also reveal if any sensitive or rare species have colonised the woodland. If this has occurred, there may be good reason to modify management to favour these species. Guidelines on monitoring created woodlands can be found in Mitchley *et al*. (2000).

The timing of management operations should be sympathetic to wildlife. Thinning and felling should be conducted outside of the bird breeding season (mid March to mid September). Likewise, mowing of rides etc. should not be conducted in spring or summer if ground nesting birds are present. Coppicing should only be carried out when the trees are leafless (i.e. late autumn – winter.

Management should aim to create one of the following types of semi-natural woodland:

Non-intervention high forest
These woodlands are permitted to develop with little management and are closest to natural woodland. The tree layer comprises standard trees of a variety of species that are typically close together. The shrub layer is also present with a wide diversity of species, but the field layer may be relatively sparse. Dead wood is left where it falls, and as a consequence these woodlands have good invertebrate populations. High forest may be grazed either by domestic stock or by deer, but this is not essential.

Pasture woodlands
These woodlands tend to comprise a mosaic of open glades amongst patches of both open and dense woodland. Parkland is an extreme form of wood pasture. Tree species are typically long-lived and permitted to grow to great size, although they are often pollarded for timber. Canopy species are usually sessile / pedunculate oak, lime, beech or ash. Pasture woodlands are permanently grazed (usually by sheep, deer or cattle), which restricts the natural regeneration of trees and results in the absence of scrub layer and woody field layer species, but there is often an abundance of epiphytic lichens. This type of woodland is likely to be inappropriate for urban sites. More information on the management of this woodland type can be found in Chatters & Sanderson (1994).

Coppice woodlands
Areas of coppice woodlands are regularly cut (to ground level), and the stumps allowed to regenerate. Several shoots sprout from each stump, and over time, the stumps develop into large coppice stools. The frequency of coppicing can vary from 5 to 30 years. Species that are typically coppiced are hazel, sweet chestnut, hornbeam, gean and alder. Occasional standard trees such as sessile / pedunculate oak and ash are left uncut. Coppiced areas can be lightly grazed some 5 years after cutting, which can promote natural regeneration and the development of a diverse moss flora. The regular disturbance caused by coppicing discourages dead wood specialists and mature woodland species. To maximise habitat diversity, areas of long rotation should be mixed with areas of short rotation. This management is ideal if the local community or other volunteers can be involved as a source of willing hands to carry out the coppicing.

Other management issues
Windthrow
Unless widespread, this natural event should not be viewed as disastrous and in fact can be beneficial to the woodland as a whole. Gaps in the canopy provide variations in light levels and affects the tree, shrub and field layers. Fallen trees also provide additional dead wood habitat. It may be wise to adopt a coppicing management regime on sites with a high risk of windthrow. More information is given in Dobson & Moffat (1993).

Alien invasive species
Undesirable or invasive alien species such as rhododendron and sycamore should be controlled if they colonise the woodland.

Dead wood
As much dead wood should be retained as possible; dead standing trees (snags), stumps and fallen trees and branches are all valuable. Ideally, dead wood should be left *in situ*. Alternatively, it can be collected into piles situated in a shady location.

4 Heathlands

4.1 Background information

Seventy-five percent of British heathland has been destroyed since 1800. Furthermore, the 57000 ha remaining in the UK represents at least 20% of the European resource (Farrell, 1989) and heathland is therefore a Priority Habitat within the UK Biodiversity Action Plan. BAP targets for heathland conservation require the creation of 6000 hectares by 2005. There is therefore an excellent opportunity for heathland creation on landfill sites in appropriate areas to contribute directly to biodiversity targets. Heathland creation may also contribute to BAP targets for several Priority Species associated with the habitat, including a number of reptiles, invertebrates and birds.

Heathland is typically dominated by dwarf shrub vegetation, notably heather (*Calluna vulgaris*) and various *Erica* species, whilst trees are characteristically absent. Heaths can occur on soils ranging from acid to neutral but the soil must be infertile. There is a very fine distinction between soils of acid grassland and heathland, demonstrated by the common occurrence of these habitat types in a mosaic. In general, heathland soils are more infertile than acid grassland soils.

It is important to note the distinction between **dry** heathland and **wet** heathland. Dry heathlands are generally southern in distribution and typically form on dry, droughty mineral soils in lowland (<250m altitude) areas with low rainfall. Wet heathland is generally northern in distribution, forming on wet soils and in upland areas with high rainfall. It should be noted that this is a simplistic classification, since dry heaths do form in upland areas and wet heaths occur in the southern lowlands. Other types of heath such as montane, lichen-rich heath and maritime heath also exist but are unlikely to be relevant at most landfill sites.

Due to fears over potential damage to the integrity of the landfill cap, permanently waterlogged areas should not be created on sites which have accepted biodegradable wastes. The creation of wet heathland is therefore not likely to be possible at the majority of landfill sites. Lowland dry heathland (less than 250 m altitude) is greatly restricted in its distribution by the occurrence of suitable soil and climatic conditions. Heathland creation will not therefore be appropriate at landfill sites across large areas of the country.

4.2 Reasons for creating heathlands

Heathland creation on landfill can directly contribute to BAP targets for this Priority Habitat simply by creating additional examples of heathland. Creating potentially suitable habitat for a range of associated species may also contribute to targets for a number of BAP Priority Species.

Heathland creation also helps to reverse the effects of habitat fragmentation. Habitat fragmentation is a major threat to species, as fluctuating populations are more liable to extinction if there is an absence of a nearby source of colonising individuals. The creation of new heathland that enlarges or connects existing heaths is therefore of great value.

As with all habitats, careful attention must be paid to soil type and depth as well as to the species used in the creation of heathland on restored landfill sites. A newly created heathland will not have the same nature conservation value as a long-established example of the same habitat, and is not likely to support rare or uncommon species in the short term. However, this does not constitute a reason for not creating heathland; as the habitat matures over time, the nature conservation value of the heathland is likely to increase.

Even if a newly created heathland does not possess much inherent nature conservation value, it can act as a buffer habitat to existing heathland, and act as a 'stepping stone', facilitating the movement of mobile species between previously isolated heathland fragments.

4.3 Heathland creation on landfill sites – planning

Provided suitable restoration materials are available and the site is in an area where heathland creation is appropriate, the landfill environment presents no more constraints on heathland creation than any other type of site. In certain areas heathland creation is therefore likely to be one of the most effective after-uses for landfill sites. See the case study in Section E.3.2.6 for an illustration of the potential value of heathland creation on landfill in parts of Dorset.

4.3.1 Basic principles
Restoration planning

Good planning at the outset of the site design process is essential for successful heathland creation. At this stage, issues such as the availability of restoration materials and seed sources should be fully considered. Their availability will play a major part in determining whether heathland creation is appropriate.

Heathlands require long-term management, and provision for this should also be made at this stage. Careful thought should be given to work specifications for contractors including the appropriate British Standards. Advice on site design should be sought from the local Wildlife Trust and the statutory UK conservation agencies.

Constraining factors of a landfill site

On sites that have accepted biodegradable waste, attention must be paid to the layout of the various habitats with respect to pollution control infrastructure. Heathland is likely to be less constrained by pollution engineering than other habitats; leaving bare areas for access to well heads etc. may even be beneficial, for example by providing basking sites for reptiles. Care should be taken where heathland is to be created within a mosaic containing associated habitats such as woodland – design should ensure that trees in particular do not restrict access to infrastructure.

Dry heathland requires well-drained soils. The presence of a low-permeability layer below the soil (the cap) therefore has implications for heathland creation, and measures that promote free drainage may have to be considered.

Determining factors of a landfill site

The major determining factor for the successful creation of heathland on landfill is the availability of suitable soils. The nature of heathland soil is extremely important to the success of the project: the soil must be freely drained, acidic and very infertile. Heathland creation should not be attempted if these conditions cannot be guaranteed.

Site design

The following factors should be considered during heathland design:

- A variety of microhabitats should be incorporated into the design. Small sheltered areas of bare ground such as sand banks, particularly south-facing areas, can be of considerable value to invertebrates and reptiles.
- Dry heaths often form a mosaic with acid grasslands; the creation of a mosaic of these habitats may be appropriate at certain sites.
- The presence of scrub or trees on heathlands is usually considered undesirable as in the absence of management, trees are likely to

become dominant over time. However, heathland trees can support important invertebrate and bird populations, and the incorporation of small woodland areas can therefore provide a valuable addition to the biodiversity of the site. In this case, ongoing management will be required to prevent scrub invading the open heathland.

- Existing heathland within or adjacent to the site should be incorporated into site design to maximise linkage and the creation of larger heathland blocks. Existing heathland, or newly-created heathland on earlier phases, may be utilised as a seed source for habitat creation provided that operations and restoration are carefully planned.

4.3.2 Selecting a heathland type

The NVC (Box E.3.2) can be used as a guide for selecting the heathland type appropriate for creation on landfill. However, it is strongly recommended that ecological advice is sought on the most appropriate heathland type to create at a specific site as well as the most appropriate species to introduce.

Dry heathland is dominated by heather.

Common associates are bell heather (*Erica cinerea*) and grasses characteristic of acid soils such as sheep's fescue (*Festuca ovina*) and wavy hair-grass (*Deschampsia flexuosa*), along with various lichen and moss species. Gorse and silver birch are also commonly associated with heathland, but should not be permitted to cover large areas.

NVC community H1 has been selected as appropriate for creation on landfill sites (Box F.4.1). This is a relatively low diversity community, and given that the introduction of associated moss and lichen species is not feasible, only requires the introduction of two plant species.

In principle, species selection will be guided by the constancy table of the NVC community type required. However, in most cases heathland creation will involve using seed or other material collected locally and therefore the species used will in any case closely reflect the NVC type found on the donor site.

4.4 Heathland creation on landfill sites – practical methods

It is recommended that ecologically-based creation methods are used if

possible, such as using seed or cuttings collected from local heathlands.

There are four stages in the creation heathland, addressed in the following sections:

- Site preparation (F.4.4.1)
- Species introduction (F.4.4.2)
- Aftercare (F.4.4.3)
- Long-term management (F.4.4.4)

4.4.1 Site preparation
Soil type and quality

Under natural conditions, lowland heathland forms on acidic, well drained, infertile soils. The levels of all three main plant nutrients (nitrogen, phosphorous and potassium) must be low. If this is not the case, the substrate must be treated to reduce acidity and nutrient levels for heathland creation to be successful (see below).

The natural parent substrates of heathland soils include sands, gravels, shales and sandstones. Heathland creation is therefore most likely to be viable where soils from these substrates or similar soil-forming materials are available for restoration. Several soil forming materials have also been shown to support heathland, including china clay waste, sand and gravel overburden and colliery spoil; it may therefore be possible to incorporate these into restoration in certain areas. Subsoil or any other infertile soil forming material should be used in preference to topsoil. If topsoil has to be used, fertility reduction will be essential.

Materials such as sand and gravel overburden and china clay waste are likely to contain little organic matter, and will therefore be poorly structured. They may therefore be prone to compaction, erosion and drought. To alleviate this, the material should be graded, ripped and / or ploughed.

As for other habitat types, the best soil for restoration will generally be that already present on site. However, sufficient soil resources will not be available at many sites. If soil or soil-forming materials must be imported (and even if on-site resources are used), action to reduce soil fertility and pH may be required before vegetation can be established (see below). In some cases, nutrients and lime may need to be added to achieve the germination of heather seeds, but it is generally more likely that these factors will need to be reduced.

The nutrient and pH status of the soil is critical to the successful establishment of heathland; soil testing should be conducted before any heathland species are introduced. Numerous tests should be made across the entire site, especially if there are areas of soil originating from

---

Box F.4.1. Example of a heathland NVC community

NVC community H1: *Calluna vulgaris – Festuca ovina* (**heather – sheep's fescue**)
This heathland is of simple species composition but has a complex physical structure provided by the various growth phases of the heather.
H1 heath is confined to base-poor and infertile sandy soils in the lowlands of Britain especially in the east. The majority of this heathland occurs in the Brecklands of East Anglia. This habitat was once widespread but is now rare due to reclamation for agriculture and forestry and the cessation of the traditional management practices of burning and grazing.

Soil type
The soil type is the main factor determining whether creation of this heathland is possible. The soil must be acidic (pH between 4 and 5), free draining and infertile.

Management
Unlike grassland, H1 does not require annual grazing or mowing to prevent species being lost from the community. Light grazing by sheep or cattle is beneficial as it promotes structural diversity and prevents scrub invasion. Control of invasive tree or shrub species such as pine, birch and bracken is necessary, and should be carried out by cutting, burning or grazing.

Benefit to wildlife
This heathland type is favoured by many species that require areas of warm bare ground. Such species include solitary wasps, ants, reptiles and a variety of ground nesting birds.

H1a constant species
Heather *Calluna vulgaris* (7-10)   Sheep's Fescue *Festuca ovina* (1-6)
(Bracketed figures refer to characteristic abundance given on the Domin scale (Box E.3.2))

different sources. Nutrient levels suitable for heathland creation are given in Section F.1.3.3, and soil pH should be between 3.5 and 5.5. Further details can be found in Environmental Advisory Unit (1988).

Amelioration of the soil to reduce fertility and pH is best conducted after the soil has been laid. Any additives will require thorough mixing with the original soil, and this is easiest to achieve if the soil as a whole is cultivated after the additives have been applied. This subject is covered in more detail in Section F.1.

Methods of reducing soil fertility

- *Dilution*: Subsoil or a suitable low-fertility alternative can be added to topsoil to dilute nutrient levels. The additive should be spread evenly across the site and thoroughly worked in by cultivation.

- *Nutrient stripping*: A cereal crop can be grown on the site to take up soil nutrients. Five years of cropping on agricultural land by adding nitrogen to increase the uptake of other nutrients has succeeded in depleting phosphorus levels to close to that of heathland, but pH and calcium remain high (Gilbert & Anderson, 1998; Evans, 1992; Welch & Wright, 1996).

Methods of reducing pH

- *Bracken mulch*: Spreading a 10 cm layer of bracken mulch over a site has been found to reduce pH from 6.7 to 4.7 over a 29-month period (Welch & Wright, 1996).

- *Sulphur*: The addition of elemental sulphur at a rate of 3 tonnes/ha on Breckland soils has been shown to reduce pH from 5.7 to 2.9 in only 2 months (Chambers & Cross, 1996). Care must be taken not to contaminate ground water or nearby waterbodies with sulphur.

- *Peat*: Adding buried peat to arable soil reduces soil pH to around 2.5 (Davey *et al*., 1992). However, the oxidation of the peat generates unwanted sulphuric acid, and one must therefore be careful not to use too much peat. The careful mixing of peat with arable soils can also be effective at reducing calcium levels. The use of peat cannot generally be advocated on environmental grounds (peat bogs are themselves a Priority Habitat) and is also unlikely to be financially and logistically viable. The only circumstances in which peat may become available for heathland creation would be a situation where a nearby peatland site is being destroyed for other reasons.

Increasing nutrients and pH

Small quantities of fertiliser may need to be added to induce growth in heather seedlings if very poorly structured soils or soil-forming materials are used for creation. Advice should be sought before any fertilisers are added, since nutrient levels can be hard to deplete once increased. To enable heather to germinate on very peaty soils, lime may have to be sparingly added to raise the pH of the soil. This has a secondary effect of promoting microbial activity, which releases nutrients.

If china clay waste, sand and gravel overburden or colliery spoil are used as restoration materials, some fertilisers may need to be added just before seeding to encourage the growth of the nurse crop (see below) as well as to promote germination of heather seeds. In all cases, soil sampling should be conducted before any additions. This will highlight which major nutrients are deficient and more importantly, the amount that is needed. In general, application should be at a low rate of about 25-100 kg / ha using a balanced NPK fertiliser. Fertilisers should not usually be added in the second season after initial creation Gilbert & Anderson (1998).

Nurse species

The establishment of heathland on a landfill site will often benefit greatly from the use of a nurse species regardless of which method of species introduction is used, especially if the site is on a slope. On flatter areas, a nurse is not so essential, and there is a danger that the nurse will restrict the establishment of the heath species (Gilbert & Anderson, 1998). Nurse crops prevent soil erosion whilst heather seed is germinating, provides shelter and high humidity for the heather seedlings, and reduces frost damage.

The most suitable nurse species is a matter of debate. Sheep's fescue (*Festuca ovina*), wavy hair-grass (*Deschampsia flexuosa*) and common bent (*Agrostis capillaris*) are most suited for ground stabilisation, but large amounts of native wild seeds of these species are hard to obtain. Collecting seed of these species from local grassland or heathland may be possible, but it is unlikely that enough seed will be collected in this way to treat large areas. Wavy hair-grass should not be used in lowland areas as it can be invasive.

Species used with effect in the past are highland bent (*Agrostis castellana*) (Anderson *et al*., 1997) and crested dog's tail (*Cynosurus cristatus*) (Parker, 1995). Highland bent in particular is a good nurse species, forming a thin but widespread sward for 4 years before gradually thinning out and disappearing (Gilbert & Anderson, 1998). However, highland bent is an alien species, and on sites adjacent to areas of conservation value it may not therefore be appropriate to use this species. Crested dog's-tail is not a characteristic member of the heathland community, and it may therefore also not be appropriate to use this species if there is a danger of it spreading onto nearby heathlands.

Heather and sheep's fescue growing on a landfill site.

Photo: Duncan Watson

Alternatively, wild oat (*Avena fatua*) and barley (*Hordeum vulgare*) have been used to good effect (Parker, 1985).

Sowing rates for the nurse crop will vary depending on the species used, but will be approximately 15-25 kg / ha. The nurse can be drilled as for sowing grassland or broadcast by hand.

The sowing rate given should provide a thin cover with plenty of bare ground between the plants. If nutrient levels are low, the nurse is unlikely to become rank or thick. However, if this does occur, it should be managed by cutting once or twice per year to 10 cm tall (Gilbert & Anderson, 1998). Cuttings should always be removed.

Leaching of soil nutrients by rainfall will assist the heather in dominating the nurse species over time. This requires freely draining (and preferably sandy) soil. However, drainage on landfill sites is largely dependent upon the soil material used and the gradient of the landform above the cap. Incorporating a layer of coarse gravel above the cap should promote free drainage. Gravel should be anchored in place using terracing formed by gabions which prevent the subsurface movement of the gravel in the drainage flow.

Alternatives to a nurse species
A geotextile or woody material such as heather litter can be used instead of a nurse. Suitable types of geotextile are honeycomb forms or the biodegradable Geojute. These materials protect the new sward in the same way as a living nurse species, and can also be very effective at preventing soil erosion.

Weed control
Non-heathland species such as bracken, bramble and other weedy species are undesirable and should be controlled before the introduction of heather. Bracken is particularly undesirable as it is invasive and hard to control once well-established.

Soil should be treated before seeding takes place if bracken rhizomes are present. Treatment consists of rotovating the soil, exposing the rhizomes to the air and rendering them vulnerable to dessication and frost. This should be followed by an application of the fern-specific herbicide Asulam.

If agricultural or other non-heathland soil has been used for site restoration, there may be a considerable number of weeds present in the seed bank. Failure to control these will inhibit the growth of heathland species (especially heather) and may cause the scheme to fail (Gilbert & Anderson, 1998). Spot applications with

Photo: Duncan Watson.

Heathland created using seeds collected from an existing heath. This photo was taken three years after the completion of site restoration.

non-specific herbicide is probably the best method of weed control.

4.4.2 Species introduction
The following methods can be used to introduce heathland species:
- Heathland topsoil
- Heather litter
- Seed harvested from heathland
- Commercially available seed
- Planting
- Translocation of heathland turves

Heathland topsoil
The application of heathland topsoil is the best way to create a replicate NVC community, but this approach is limited by the availability of a suitable donor site. Suitable heathland topsoil may be available from forestry firebreaks or as part of the management of nearby heathland. Soil may also be available from existing heathland which is being destroyed as part of site development.

The costs of this method are very site-specific, and a general cost estimate is therefore difficult to make. The major cost incurred will be the transport of the topsoil from donor to receptor site, so care should be taken to ensure that the donor site is as close to the receptor site as possible. Note also that collection and spreading costs are also expensive.

Heathland topsoil can supply seeds, rhizome fragments, stem bases and tillers of heather and other heathland species. The location of the seed bank in the donor soil can vary; it may be located in the

organic (O) or the mineral (A) horizons, but in general the majority of seeds will be contained in the first 40 mm of soil. Seed bank tests can be used to locate and quantify the seed bank – see Gilbert & Anderson (1998) and Bullock (1996) for more details.

Section F.1 gives more detail on soil handling and storage, but a summary of methods is given below.

Removal of topsoil from donor site
Any existing vegetation should be cut to ground level by flailing or forage harvesting (which also permits the harvesting of seed). The soil should be rotovated to the depth of the seedbank or to 50 mm, whichever is greater, before being stripped. Soil should not be removed from existing heathland during the bird breeding season (March to July) if ground-nesting birds are present or during periods of greatest sensitivity to reptiles (April-May and September are the most sensitive months, but reptiles will be active from April-September inclusive). For best results, remove soil in October/November.

Soil storage
Soil storage is detrimental to soil quality. Soil should therefore be stripped immediately prior to use in restoration. If storage is unavoidable, soil should be stored in piles less than 1.5 m high and covered with plastic or tarpaulin. On no account should these piles be subjected to vehicular traffic.

Spreading

The bulk of the soil for restoration (subsoil, soil-forming materials etc.) should be laid prior to the application of heathland topsoil, following the general guidelines given in Section F.1.

The stripped heathland topsoil should then be loose-tipped on top and spread evenly using a back-acter. Topsoil can be mixed 50:50 with suitable subsoil, enabling an area up to twice the size of the donor site to be treated. Alternatively, topsoil can be mixed with mineral wastes such as china clay waste, enabling an area up to five times the area of the donor site to be treated.

For best germination results, spreading should be carried out in spring or autumn. Spreading should not be conducted when the soil is wet.

Heather litter

Litter consisting of fallen leaves and seeds accumulates under heather plants on heathlands. Spreading this litter over the receptor site can be used to introduce heathland species and is generally regarded as the best practice method.

The principal advantage of this method is that no damage is caused to the donor site. The main disadvantage is that although it is possible to collect appreciable quantities of dwarf shrub species, it is unlikely that the full species complement will be collected, and undesirable species may also be picked up. Missing species should therefore be supplemented with purchased seed, whilst provision should be made to remove undesirable species before they become established.

Before time and money is spent storing and / or spreading litter, the viability of the seeds should be tested by conducting germination tests. Ideally, viable seed density should be approximately 300-500 seeds per m^2 of litter, which allows it to be spread at 100-150 g / m^2.

In 1988 this method cost approximately £2000-£2500 per ha (if litter is spread by hand) and £1200-£1500 (if litter is spread mechanically) (Environmental Advisory Unit, 1988).

Method of collection

Litter can be collected by hand or, when larger quantities are required, with a vacuum. Using a vacuum causes disturbance, and collection should therefore not take place during the bird breeding season (March-July) or during periods of greatest sensitivity to reptiles (April-May and September are the most

sensitive months, but reptiles will be active from April-September inclusive). Heather litter should preferably be collected from medium aged stands (10-15 years) on upland sites and old stands (15-25 years) on southern sites. Approximately 30-40 kg can be collected per day by hand, and 80-100 kg using a vacuum (Environmental Advisory Unit, 1988).

Heather litter can be stored for several years if kept in paper or hessian bags in dry conditions. Woody material can be sieved out prior to storage to reduce bulk.

Spreading

Litter can be spread by hand or mechanically (by hydroseeding or fertiliser spreader). Once the seeds have germinated and started to establish, large pieces of litter should be removed as they will inhibit further germination. Litter is a very concentrated source of seeds; only 100-200 g / m^2 is required. Litter is light and vulnerable to wind blow, and may therefore need to be used in conjunction with a nurse crop.

Spreading can be conducted either in spring or autumn (autumn is preferable).

Seed harvested from heathland

Heather shoots containing ripe seed can be harvested from an existing heathland with a forage harvester or a combine harvester (for large quantities). Seeds can also be collected using a vacuum or a brush collector (Gilbert & Anderson, 1998), which causes less damage to the donor site. If a harvester is used, only the

top 350 mm of the heather should be harvested to ensure that a high proportion of seed to woody material is collected.

Harvesting should be conducted between September and November. Heather seed ripens later than that of other species; two collections should therefore be made to harvest the full range of heathland species.

In 1988 costs per hectare for two people conducting mechanised harvesting at a rate of 2 ha per day varied between £150 / ha (EAU, 1988) to £320 / ha (North York Moors National Park Committee, 1991).

If cut material is to be stored for long periods, it should be dried and baled to prevent it from composting. For short-term storage, the material can be heaped into small mounds (maximum height 1.5m); the small loss of viable seeds which will occur will not be of great consequence. The mounds should be covered in tarpaulin or plastic.

Spreading

Spreading should take place in either early spring or autumn. Woody material should be spread with the seed to act as a protection against winds. The seeds may take up to three years to germinate. Recommended seeding rates in the published literature vary from 1000–10000 kg / ha, but as a general rule, seeds should be spread over an area between twice and three times the size of the donor site (Gilbert & Anderson, 1998; Parker, 1995). After application, the site should be rolled with a ring roller to press the seed gently into the soil.

Photo: Duncan Watson

Heathland regeneration after the removal of litter and soil for use in heathland creation at a site in Dorset. This photo was taken 3 years after the removal of soil and litter from the site.

If the amount of seed is limiting, it should be spread evenly across the site and bulked up with seeds of a grass nurse species.

Spreading can be conducted in spring or autumn (autumn is preferable).

Commercially available seed

The major disadvantage of this method for heathland creation is that the seed is unlikely to have been grown locally; the three previous methods are therefore recommended in preference to the use of commercial seed wherever possible.

If heathland topsoil, heather seed or heather litter are unavailable locally, heathland creation is in any case likely to be inappropriate. However, in areas where the remaining heathland resource is very small, local heathland seed sources may be unavailable, yet heathland may still be a valid habitat to create; in this case, commercially grown seed will be required. Due to the relative youth of the market for heathland species, many species are difficult to obtain although species such as gorses (*Ulex* spp.), heaths (*Erica* spp.) and various heathland grasses are actually relatively easy to grow from seed. One solution to this problem is therefore to commission a seed company to harvest the seed of each species and use it to bulk up numbers in a nursery. Other species that germinate poorly e.g. bilberry (*Vacinnium myrtillus*) are relatively easy to introduce as plugs (Gilbert & Anderson, 1998).

This method can be expensive, costing approximately £2000 / kg according to Parker (1995). However, prices seem to have fallen recently, with one quote as low as £40 / kg obtained from a seed company.

Seed should be sown with a nurse crop or substitute such as woody material to weight the seed down and provide sheltered conditions for germination.

Seeds can be sown in autumn or spring. Heather seeds require moisture to germinate and establish, and summer drought can affect spring-sown seed. Autumn is therefore probably the best time to sow lowland sites. However, heather seedlings are also vulnerable to frost, and smaller seedlings are more likely to die than larger ones; spring-sown seedlings are therefore better able to resist winter frosts. Spring sowing will be more effective than autumn sowing if the seedlings are watered or if there is adequate spring and summer rainfall.

Direct planting of heathland species

This method is very slow and expensive, and plants of local provenance are unlikely to be obtainable. It should therefore only

be attempted when all the preceding methods are not available. If direct planting appears to be the only option, further consideration may need to be given as to whether heathland is the most appropriate after-use.

Nursery plants are expensive; costs have been quoted at between £5000 and £12,000 per ha (Environmental Advisory Unit, 1988). To keep costs to a minimum, small clumps covering about 10% of the total area should be planted. These will eventually spread and colonise the surrounding area. To prevent soil erosion, the remaining bare soil should be planted with a nurse crop at the same time as the nursery plants. The site should be fenced for at least five years after planting to protect the young heather plants from grazing.

Lowland sites should be planted in autumn or early spring, and upland sites should be planted in spring or late summer.

Translocation of heathland turves

This process of heathland translocation is very similar to the translocation of grassland; (see Section F.2.4.2 for procedure). This method necessarily involves the destruction of the donor site and should therefore only be used where a nearby heathland is being destroyed for other reasons. Turf translocation can also be useful for the transference of heathland invertebrates.

For translocation to have any chance of succeeding, it is essential that the donor and receptor sites are ecologically similar. Due to the susceptibility of translocated vegetation to drought, regular watering is essential between July and September. Turves should be as large as possible (the recommended size is 1 m x 2 m) and should be tightly packed into prepared pits on the receptor site. Translocation should be carried out in autumn or spring. An account of heathland translocation is given in Pywell *et al.* (1995) and Pywell (in press).

Estimating the cost of translocation is extremely difficult, as factors affecting costs will vary from site to site. The major cost will be the transport of the turves between sites, and is therefore dependent on the location of the receptor site in relation to the donor site. However, the method will undoubtedly be very expensive and therefore only practical for small areas.

4.4.3 Aftercare

The objectives of aftercare are:
- Weed control
- Protection of plants from trampling and grazing

Weed control

Non-heathland weed species need to be controlled whilst the heather plants are growing. Once the heather canopy closes, heathland is less susceptible to weed invasion, but before this occurs, weeds should be spot-treated with a non-selective herbicide. Herbicide should be carefully applied with a knapsack sprayer to avoid the risk of damaging the heathland plants. Weed control is likely to be necessary on sites where nutrient levels are higher than on typical heathland.

Protection from trampling and grazing

Germinating heather is vulnerable to trampling and high levels of grazing, particularly from rabbits. Rabbit grazing produces different growth forms of heather. Isolated plants are grazed into a domed 'topiary' form, and in such circumstances will not merge into a continuous area of heath. Newly established heathland should therefore be rabbit fenced until the heather plants form a canopy. Fencing should be left in place for at least five years after planting.

4.4.4 Long term management

The majority of heathland originated as a result of human activity, with the exception of some montane and maritime types, and was maintained by the traditional management practices of cutting, burning and grazing. In the absence of management, heathland will be invaded by scrub and tree species, and will eventually develop into woodland.

The long-term management of heathland must therefore be considered at the outset of restoration design; without some form of long-term management, heathland creation will ultimately be unsuccessful.

Advice on management given here represents only a brief summary of a large body of literature. For further details of heathland management techniques see Gimingham (1992) and Sutherland & Hill (1995). Guidelines on monitoring created habitats can be found in Mitchley *et al.* (2000). The methods are described with reference to grassland and woodland habitats, but can be adapted for monitoring heathland.

Control of invasive plants

The first objective of management is to prevent the invasion of woody shrubs such as common gorse (*Ulex europaeus*) and rhododendron (*Rhododendron ponticum*), trees such as silver birch (*Betula pendula*), downy birch (*Betula pubescens*) and Scots pine (*Pinus sylvestris*), and bracken (*Pteridium aquilinum*). All of these species will eventually shade out heather if they become established, resulting in the loss of heathland species and the replacement of heathland by woodland.

Tree and shrub control

Measures used specifically to control invading seedlings are:

- The use of woody heather cuttings spread over the site as a mulch to reduce the availability of germination sites for other species;
- hand pulling of seedlings; and
- cutting of saplings.

Invading plants that grow to saplings or larger require felling, either with hand saws or with a scrubcutter or chainsaw. Conifer species will not regrow, but deciduous species will coppice and send up new shoots after being cut. Cut stumps should therefore be treated with a systemic herbicide to prevent regrowth. Guidance should be sought on the best type of herbicide to use and any restrictions controlling their use (a licence may be required to use herbicides).

Bracken control

Bracken is an invasive fern, forming a dense canopy that shades out lower-growing species. Dead bracken fronds form a thick litter layer which inhibits the germination of other species. In addition, decaying fronds release chemicals into the soil which are toxic to other plants.

Bracken can be easily introduced by accident if topsoil from a heathland containing bracken is used for creating new habitat; the best method of control is therefore prevention (see Section F.4.4.1). The plant will also spread by vegetative growth from adjacent areas. Bracken is very difficult to eradicate if it becomes well-established, and in this case, best practice is to instigate a programme of

control rather than to attempt elimination. Newly-colonising bracken should be controlled as soon as the plant is discovered, regardless of the area covered by the plant, since elimination may be possible in the early stages of colonisation. Control will also prevent the spread of the plant into new areas.

The most effective method of controlling bracken is a combination of herbicide (such as the fern-specific Asulam) and cutting. The two treatments should be carried out twice a year in June and August for four consecutive years. This should reduce the vigour of the plant sufficiently so that subsequent treatment can be limited to a cut every three years or a cut and herbicide application every six years.

The ground must be cleared of dead vegetation following cutting or herbicide treatment; bracken litter will inhibit the growth of heather seedlings.

Traditional heathland management

Heathlands are traditionally managed by burning, cutting or grazing. Management controls the invasion of scrub and grasses and maintains the heather in a bushy and vigorous condition. Management should ideally aim to create areas with differing age structures; this creates a larger number of microhabitats and is thus likely to be of maximum benefit to biodiversity. There are four recognisable growth phases of heather: pioneer (3-10 years), building (7-13 years), mature (12-30 years) and degenerate (>30 years); areas of all four growth phases should be present.

Note however that heather cannot support heavy grazing or intensive management; heavy grazing in particular will result in the replacement of heathland with grassland, as has happened on many upland sites. Management should

not commence until the new heathland is at least five years old.

Cutting

Relatively even ground is required for tractor-mounted cutting machinery to work efficiently. Cutting can also be carried out by hand using scrubcutters. The heather should be cut to 150 mm height for the first 2-4 years and then at 200 mm height in subsequent years (Environmental Advisory Unit, 1988). Cuttings should always be removed. The cut should be made in late summer, and consideration given to using the cuttings for other heathland creation projects or on another part of the landfill. Different areas should be cut in different years to create a varied age structure.

Burning

Burning cannot be recommended as a management tool on landfill due to obvious safety concerns regarding the presence of landfill gas and pollution control infrastructure.

Grazing

Grazing is the most cost-effective method for controlling scrub invasion and maintaining a diverse range of microhabitats, and also controls invasive grass species. Grazing can also increase biodiversity by providing habitat for dung-dependent invertebrates. The grazing animals most commonly used are ponies, sheep and cattle. The choice of grazing animal will affect the results obtained; each species exhibits a different food preference, grazing style and trampling effect.

Grazing levels should be low (< 1 ewe/ha), and to maintain a diverse age structure a rotational grazing regime should be adopted.

5 Wetlands

5.1 Background information

Wetland creation presents an ideal opportunity for integrating drainage requirements and nature conservation at restored landfill sites. The objectives of wetland functionality and conservation are not mutually exclusive and wetland habitats can therefore serve both these roles.

Wetland creation over capped areas is not recommended on sites which have accepted biodegradable waste (Environment Agency, in prep.) because the presence of permanently waterlogged soil or standing water above the fill is considered likely to increase the risk of leachate generation. Leachate generation may be increased both through increased infiltration of water into the fill and as a result of potential damage to the cap caused by differential settlement under wetland areas.

Wetland creation above pollution control infrastructure also cannot be recommended as it conflicts with the requirement for long-term maintenance of access to monitoring points. Furthermore, the typical domed profile characteristic of most restored landfill sites is in any case largely inappropriate for wetland creation. However, there are frequently parts of a site which have not been landfilled where wetlands can be created (Barker, 1994).

Wetlands naturally form in low-lying areas or in depressions over impermeable or waterlogged soils. There is therefore plenty of scope for creating wetlands at the edge of the filled area, particularly on sites where the final landform is raised above the existing ground level (land raising sites). Note however that at most landfill sites the area which can be devoted specifically to wetland habitats will be small. Consequently, the greatest value of most created wetlands at landfill sites will be their contribution to overall site biodiversity. Provided the wetland type is selected carefully, there is plenty of opportunity to link the habitats created on top of the filled area with those around the edge to increase the overall nature conservation value of the site. Schemes that create a wide variety of habitats also tend to be viewed favourably by planners (Barker, 1994).

Balancing ponds are often created on landfill sites to collect runoff and act as silt traps and monitoring points before water is discharged off-site (Barker, 1994). Modern restoration practices create shallower gradients on landfills than have been used in the past, which permits a greater volume of water to be absorbed by the soil. However, water still drains relatively rapidly off the cap. This water is normally lost from the site through drainage channels, but there is no reason why it should not be collected and used for ecological benefit within the site boundary. An additional benefit is that flash flows and inputs of suspended silt into the main drainage system are reduced.

Management of wetlands and waterbodies is site-specific and depends on the intended habitat type and the species that establish. However, management is usually low key and does not require a large amount of resources.

5.1.1 Ponds and other waterbodies

Most open waterbodies are of value to wildlife regardless of their depth, size or seasonal permanence. Furthermore, the conservation importance of such waterbodies is becoming greater, particularly in agricultural landscapes where many farm ponds have been drained and infilled during the last century to facilitate agricultural improvement.

Ponds are important to a variety of wildlife:

* All six British amphibian species breed in ponds.
* Ponds support a range of invertebrates, notably dragonflies and damselflies.
* Ponds and lakes can also support a range of birds and mammals.

Ponds are rarely found in isolation but usually occur in association with other wetland habitats; the entire system can be viewed as a zonation or gradient from open deep water through wet margins, swamp and marsh to drier ground.

5.1.2 Bogs, fens and marshes

Bogs are wetland habitats that form on peat and possess a very low nutrient status. The water is generally acidic and the habitat created is very hostile to all but a restricted range of highly adapted species. The major input of water to bogs is from rainfall.

Fens also develop on peat but the source of water for their development is surface runoff, springs or watercourses. Fens can be base-poor or base-rich resulting in the formation of either poor fens or rich fens.

Marshes are permanently waterlogged, often base-rich and quite fertile, with pH generally in the range 6.5-7.5. Marsh vegetation is typically very lush with tall plants and often a high species richness. Marshes naturally occur on low riverbanks, flood plains and lake shores.

Reedswamp can be viewed as a type of marsh and forms at the boundary between marsh and open water.

Fens and bogs both require peat as the rooting substrate and building block of the habitat. Peat takes many thousands of years to accumulate; the global resource of peat is dwindling and is now so small that the large-scale use of peat for restoration purposes is neither morally nor economically justifiable. The creation of bog and fen habitats is therefore not recommended.

There is, however, potential to create marsh habitats around the edge of the filled area on a landfill site.

5.1.3 Wet woodlands (carr)

Wet woodland (also termed carr woodland) naturally occurs as a stage in the successional sequence from open water to dry woodland. The habitat typically comprises scattered willows or alder beneath which is a short layer of ferns, sedges, grasses and a rich assemblage of mosses.

Creation of wet woodland could be a viable option at many landfill sites, particularly in association with other woodland creation, provided that a suitable source of water is available.

5.1.4 Wet grassland

There are two types of wet grassland: inundation grassland and flood meadows. Inundation grassland usually forms within a drier grassland around a seasonal pond within which the water level fluctuates. The grass species are tolerant of frequent flooding but only by shallow water. Flood meadows usually occur in flat-bottomed, low-lying river valleys. Although low-lying fields adjacent to rivers often flood naturally, ditches were dug across many traditionally-managed flood meadows to increase the period of water retention. The purpose of this was to keep the meadows flooded for several months over winter, preventing the ground from freezing and thus encouraging the early growth of grass in the spring. These swards were typically very productive and were grazed for much of the summer.

The creation of flood meadows is unlikely to be appropriate at landfill sites. However, the creation of small areas of inundation grassland may be possible in association with open waterbodies situated off the landfill cap itself. These can have particular value for breeding waders (Ward, 1994).

5.2 Reasons for creating wetlands

5.2.1 Primary objectives

Waterbodies created on landfill sites will probably be small, and are therefore unlikely to directly contribute towards national BAP targets for creation of new areas of this habitat. Wet woodlands have been identified as a Priority Habitat, although the size of woodland possible at the edge of a landfill site will probably provide only a small contribution to national BAP targets for creation of this habitat.

Nevertheless, wetlands on landfill sites are able to provide a significant contribution to biodiversity and may be able to contribute directly to local BAP targets. The greater the species richness and structural diversity that can be created, the greater the diversity of associated wildlife. It is therefore likely that the creation of any wetland type will benefit a wide range of species, possibly including BAP Priority Species such as great crested newt, water vole and reed bunting.

5.2.2 Secondary objectives

- Waterbodies provide a useful drainage function by collecting and controlling surface water runoff.
- Waterbodies can attract wildlife by the provision of drinking water, nesting sites and feeding opportunities. This can benefit adjacent habitats.
- Wetlands and waterbodies provide an excellent educational resource, not least to demonstrate the success of habitat creation on landfill sites.

5.3 Wetland creation on landfill sites – planning

5.3.1 Basic principles

Restoration planning

The wetland type (or types) to be created should be determined at the early stages of restoration and design; engineers and designers should be consulted to ensure that the drainage characteristics of the restored site will be appropriate for the desired wetland type.

Availability of creation materials such as soil, seeds and plants should also be considered during the planning and design stage.

Wetlands should be located in areas exposed to the least risk of water pollution, and every effort should be made to prevent any polluted water from entering new wetlands. However, one of the main reasons for creating ponds on older landfill sites was to intercept potential leachate breakout. Pollution will not necessarily destroy the nature conservation value of a wetland, and there are measures that can be taken to reduce the adverse effects of leachate (see Section F.5.4.1). This should therefore not be used as a reason not to create wetlands on landfill sites.

Wetlands require a degree of management although this is often not as intensive as for other habitats. The financial requirements of management should be considered at the planning stage.

However, the most important factor to consider is the provision of a sufficient amount of water to create and maintain wetlands. This applies particularly to ponds, but a guaranteed water source is essential for all wetland types.

There are three main sources of water that potentially can be used in wetland creation (Williams *et al.*, 1997). These are:

- Runoff water from the landfill cap
- Groundwater
- Inflow streams / rivers / flushes

Runoff water

Runoff water comprises water that runs off the landfill surface and water that percolates through the soil. Runoff is likely to be the most suitable water source for wetland creation at a landfill site; wetland creation methods given in Section F.5.4 assume that runoff water will be used. The quality of surface runoff will depend on the catchment quality; the route taken by the water should be considered, and water flowing through areas of bare ground or high fertiliser application should not be used. Note that buffer zones should be created to intercept and clean surface water before it enters the wetland (see Section F.5.4.1). Buffer zones should be vegetated; semi-natural habitats can can therefore be used, provided that they will not be adversely affected by the quality of the surface runoff that will flow through them.

The surface area of any restored landfill should be large enough to provide sufficient water to sustain at least a small wetland area. However, the actual size of the wetland created is inherently dependent on the amount of water available to feed it. Site engineers should be able to calculate the quantity of water likely to be available; this should play an integral part in restoration and site design. Landform design is also crucial to wetland creation – to maximise the water supply to a wetland, the restored landform should be designed to direct water towards one place. For wetland creation to be successful, it is therefore essential that consultation between site engineers and habitat creation planners takes place at an early stage in the restoration process.

Runoff from access roads should be avoided. Locally collected surface runoff from hard surfaced areas within the site such as roads, car parks and buildings can be used to if water is in short supply, since the volume of such water will be relatively small and pollutants can be dealt with. Water from car parks may contain oil; an oil trap should be placed in the inflow to prevent oil from entering the wetland. Suspended sediment should be removed by passing the water through a silt trap before it enters the wetland. A silt trap is a pit placed just before the runoff enters the pond. The water enters the pit

A small pond created specifically for educational activities such as pond dipping at Bidston Moss Landfill Site, Merseyside.

Photo: Duncan Watson.

and floods over into the inlet pipe for the wetland once the pit is full. Slowing the rate of water flow in this manner causes suspended silt to be deposited in the pit. Silt traps help to control nutrient inputs and prevent the pond from silting up, but will require periodic maintenance to remove accumulated silt. The size of the silt trap will depend on the volume of inflowing water.

Groundwater
Wetland can be created by excavating a hole below the water table and letting it fill with water. However, using groundwater is probably not applicable on landfill sites, although there may be an opportunity for wetland creation in this manner if the landfill is situated in an old sand or gravel pit which has not been completely used for waste disposal.

Using ground water has the advantage in that the water is usually unpolluted. However, if a wetland is to be created on an old landfill site with a poorly engineered lining system, leachate may seep into the groundwater. In this case, water testing should be conducted as part of the planning stage. It is preferable to treat polluted water before it enters a wetland, although there are examples of using wetlands as part of leachate treatment (see Case Study 7).

Inflow streams / rivers / flushes
Where available, watercourses and flushes can be used as a water source for wetland creation. Water quality is hard to control, however, since the inflow water will originate from outside the landfill area and will be affected by catchment land-use. Problems are likely to arise where the catchment includes intensive agriculture or urban areas. For example, in agricultural areas, the quality of the inflowing water may be unsuitable due to high levels of plant nutrients such as nitrogen and phosphates, heavy metals or large amounts of suspended sediment. Polluted inflow streams should not be used for wetland creation unless they can be cleaned through other constructed wetlands.

Determining factors of a landfill site
The quantity of water available will determine the depth of waterbodies which can be created. Water depth determines the distribution of wetland plant species within waterbodies and other wetland habitats.

Another important factor is the pH of the water. Dissolved mineral salts in runoff water will gradually increase water pH, whereas a wetland fed only by rainwater will be more acidic. Species

vary in the pH range they can tolerate; some plants have narrow tolerance levels whilst others can tolerate a much wider pH range. The water pH therefore determines which species can survive on the site (acid-tolerant species will not persist in alkaline water and *vice versa*). The ideal pH of water is 6.5 to 7.5 (Barker, 1994), since this will permit the greatest latitude when selecting appropriate species. In practice this is also the typical pH of the water in man-made waterbodies and wetlands.

Constraining factors of a landfill site
As previously mentioned, wetlands should not be created on top of the filled area. A second constraint of the landfill environment is that waterlogged, unstable wetland soil inhibits vehiclular access. Wetlands must therefore be placed so that they do not interfere with access to pollution control infrastructure and other site maintenance activities. A further constraint is the potential effect of flooding on nearby areas; wetlands should not be placed adjacent to areas that would suffer damage if they are flooded.

Wetland design
In a landfill context, wetlands should always be situated at the edge of the filled area. The boundaries of most landfill sites are likely to extend beyond the edge of the filled area,

which should provide suitable space for a wetland. The creation of features such as ponds is worthwhile even in small areas.

The existence of wetland adjacent to the site is a good reason to create another. In general, conservation benefits will be maximised by developing a wetland complex with other existing wetland habitats such as streams, floodplains, wet woodlands, flushes and ponds, and by linking some of these areas together so that the various elements can interact. An existing wetland site is likely to act as a good colonisation source for wetland species and can also provide a good source of translocation material. The nearby wetland does not need to be of the same type, as most wetland species are generalists and can colonise more than one wetland type.

Wetland complexes are usually of more value to overall biodiversity than a single wetland habitat as they provide a wider range of microhabitats and hence support a larger number of species. A wetland complex could include some or all of the wetland types suitable for creation on landfill sites. Wetland design should be incorporated into the restoration of the rest of the site where possible (e.g. wet woodland creation at the edge of the cap in conjunction with dry woodland creation on the cap itself). A potential wetland

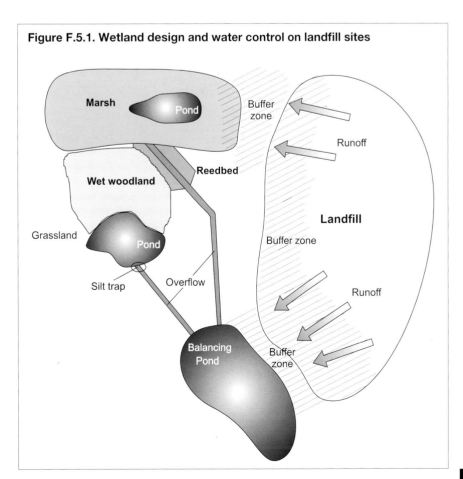

Figure F.5.1. Wetland design and water control on landfill sites

design is shown in Figure F.5.1

However, if only a very small area is available for wetland creation, it is preferable in this case to create one wetland habitat of a reasonable size rather than attempting to create tiny examples of a wide range of habitats.

Pond creation
If possible, ponds should be linked to existing wetland areas such as marshes or wet woodlands. This is likely to be of greater benefit to wildlife than an isolated pond.

If several ponds can be created, the size, depth and annual water level fluctuations of the ponds should be varied (i.e. some ponds should be allowed to dry out occasionally and others remain inundated).

Suitable pond management during the early stages of colonisation will increase species richness in a shorter time. Ponds also require a degree of long-term management.

Landfill sites may contain balancing ponds created as part of on-site water management. Balancing ponds are used for retaining large volumes of storm water runoff whilst releasing a smaller, more manageable flow into the drainage system. This prevents erosion and flooding elsewhere on the site, and stops large quantities of water from entering the drainage system at once. Balancing ponds are different from typical ponds, since their water levels constantly change, filling after a storm and slowly draining away, and they are unattractive to some wetland species for several reasons. Firstly, if the pond is empty for most of the time, many aquatic species cannot survive. Secondly, water entering balancing ponds may be turbulent and silt-laden, which can uproot or otherwise damage plants, promote algal blooms and cloud the water.

However, adaptations to the design of balancing ponds can improve their conservation value.

- Retaining water in the pond during dry periods and reducing the height that the water level drops by increasing the surface area of the pond will enable aquatic plants to survive and hence permit the survival of a wide range of other species. It is unwise to retain water levels at full capacity as this reduces the ability of the pond to cope with additional flood water. However, keeping the pond half-full creates a permanent waterbody and retains the ability to control flood water.
- Water turbulence can be reduced by

allowing incoming water to seep in rather than being channelled through culverts. For any water control system, it is important to reduce the speed of water flow as much as possible without halting drainage altogether.

- Rather than feeding the water into an external drainage system, the water from balancing ponds can be used to feed a wetland complex, although provision for extremely high flood volumes can be built into the system by creating a storm culvert to an offsite drainage system or a soakaway. Alternatively, the balancing pond can be used to feed a second pond using a narrow pipe linked to a sluice or located near the top of the pond which will only feed the second pond when the balancing pond is full.
- The balancing pond can also be used as part of a water treatment system by feeding into a reedbed and a sediment trap or other type of nutrient stripping unit.

Marsh creation
The easiest method of creating a marsh is to situate the habitat at the edge of a waterbody. This will supply the constant high water levels that are necessary to maintain the marsh in good condition and hinder the development of woodland since the soil will be too wet for most trees to grow. However, even away from waterbodies, marsh creation should be possible as long as there is a constant source of water to keep the soil waterlogged. Siting the marsh where it will intercept runoff water and compacting the soil to impede drainage should suffice. The nature of most restored landfill sites provides an ideal source of water as runoff is directed quickly off the cap.

Marshes require a degree of management to promote high species richness, but management need not be intensive.

Marsh habitats are sensitive to pollution, and adequate buffer strips should be created (Section F.5.4.1) if the water source is likely to be polluted. Potential sources of pollution on landfill sites are bare soil (soil particles and dissolved nutrients can both act as pollutants), litter and uncapped waste. Leachate is not a significant potential problem on modern sites.

A variety of substrates can be used to create a marsh and nutrient levels are not critical. Marsh creation is not as prone to failure as other habitat types as marsh plants are usually easy to transport and establish.

Wet woodland creation
Wet woodland is likely to form naturally over time as water-tolerant tree species such as willow and alder colonise open wetland habitats. Creating the wet woodland tree layer is also very simple. Creating the field layer is more difficult, and there is little published information regarding field layer creation. However, it is likely that this layer will also develop naturally over time, and tree layer creation will have conservation benefits to wildlife even if the field layer is not authentic.

Wet grassland creation
The principles that should be followed for wet grassland creation are identical to those for dry grassland creation (Section F.2), with the exception that there must be an adequate supply of water to keep the soil moist and that the species introduced will be slightly different. The water table in wet grassland is usually about 0.5 m below the soil surface, although this should rise in the winter to flood naturally occurring wet grasslands. Wet grassland can therefore be created as a fringe to a marsh or a waterbody where the soil level rises greater than 0.5 m above the height of the water.

Wetland design for species
If rare or interesting wetland species are known to exist nearby, this is an excellent reason to create new wetlands specifically designed for these species. For example, designing ponds for amphibians is not complicated (see Box F.5.1 for details on pond creation for great crested newts). The provision of emergent and submerged aquatic plants will create good habitat for dragonflies and damselflies. Areas of bare mud are used by wading birds as well as a considerable range of scarce plant species.

Other design considerations
Provision for visitor access
Wetlands, particularly ponds, can be attractive landscape features and their use by the public should be encouraged, as long as the conservation interest is not compromised. However, marsh vegetation is very vulnerable to trampling. To prevent trampling damage, boardwalks (raised walkways, usually made from wood) can be constructed across wetland areas. Boardwalks also serve the secondary purpose of leading visitors away from sensitive areas where access is not desirable.

If wetlands are large enough (>2 ha) they may provide habitat for various species of wader and wildfowl, (Gilbert & Anderson, 1998). Many of these are highly susceptible to disturbance and public access to such areas should therefore be strictly controlled.

Bird hides can be installed (with the access tracks screened) to allow people to watch birds without causing disturbance.

Aesthetic design considerations
The following points should be considered when designing a wetland (Williams *et al.*, 1997):

- Locate wetlands in low-lying situations (preferably on level ground) so that the setting appears natural.
- Allow good views across the water.
- Design most of a waterbody edge to be natural and well vegetated, but allow good close-up access at one restricted point such as a boardwalk.
- Vegetation should be low or absent at access points to wetlands.
- Shallow ponds in winter will often have dense and tall vegetation in summer and the appearance will therefore change and may obscure views.
- Trampling of waterbody edges can create areas of bare mud which can be beneficial, but this should be confined to localised areas. Barriers can be formed from scrub, banks and ditches to restrict access to waterbodies.
- Consider the safety aspects of wetlands. Do not create steep-sided deep waterbodies; create shallow shelves at places where the edge is accessible.

Photo: David Hill

Wetlands provide habitat for species such as this migrant hawker dragonfly.

5.3.2 Selecting a wetland type

For most habitat types the ideal method of habitat creation is to attempt to create a replicate example of an existing habitat type that forms naturally such as those described by the National Vegetation Classification (NVC) (Rodwell, 1991 *et seq*.). However, the situation is more complex for wetlands. A wetland complex is unlikely to support only one NVC community; it will contain a range of habitats and plant communities. There are a series of zones within a waterbody which are primarily dictated by water depth, with different communities occurring at different depths. Habitats such as wet grassland and wet woodland can also be subdivided into various communities resulting from complex interactions between large numbers of

---

Box F.5.1. Pond creation for great crested newts

The great crested newt (*Triturus cristatus*) is specially protected under Schedule 5 of the Wildlife & Countryside Act 1981 and Annex II of the EU Habitats & Species Directive. It is also a BAP Priority Species. One of its principal habitats is ephemeral ponds which are frequently found in the disused quarries in which many landfills are situated. This has resulted in several examples of habitat creation for great crested newts at landfill sites (for example see Case Study 5), usually in association with translocation of the species from an area being developed. Changes to the procedure for licensing translocation of great crested newts have recently occurred, and translocations are likely to be harder to justify unless over-riding public interest can be demonstrated (Baker, 2000). However, the creation of great crested newt habitat need not be restricted to sites at which translocation is carried out, and pond creation for this species should therefore be considered as part of site restoration, particularly in areas where great crested newts are known to be present. The principal habitat requirements for great crested newt are given below:

- Great crested newts require well-vegetated ponds with sufficiently clear areas around the edges to allow males to display during the breeding season. They prefer a moderate growth of aquatic vegetation (especially water starwort) – the cover of submerged and aquatic vegetation should be around 25% (Gent & Gibson, 1998).
- A small amount of shading of the pond from adjacent scrub or trees is probably beneficial, but ponds become progressively less suitable as breeding habitat for great crested newts as shading increases above 5%, and certainly as it exceeds 20% (Cooke *et al.*, 1994).
- Ponds should ideally be at least 100 m^2 (i.e. 10 m x 10 m) in size, although great crested newts do use smaller ponds. A two hectare pond might support 2000 adult newts. Ponds that contain fish generally do not support great crested newts due to predation of newt larvae.
- Great crested newts do not tolerate regular drying out of ponds (although drying out every few years, which kills fish and controls aquatic vegetation, is tolerated). Ponds at least 1 m deep are therefore required, but pond design should include shallow margins to allow easy access to and from the water.
- The nature of terrestrial habitats surrounding the pond is very important. A mosaic of scrub, woodland and rough grassland habitats is thought to be best for great crested newts, although note that trees and scrub should not shade the pond. Arable or intensively managed grassland habitats adjacent to the pond will generally not support newts.
- Corridors such as hedges and ditches are used for dispersal and should therefore be incorporated into the habitat design. For further information on habitat design and management for great crested newts and other amphibians see Gent & Gibson (1998).

environmental factors. There is often no predictable outcome for a given set of factors. Whilst guidance on the nature of the various communities can be obtained from the NVC, it is very difficult to attempt to faithfully recreate one particular NVC community.

The NVC can assist wetland creation by showing which species of plants grow in association with each other and thus illustrate which species should be included in a mix in order to create a characteristic community. Furthermore, this can be used as a guide for the correct water depth needed for different species. For example, if yellow flag establishes naturally within a pond, one can infer that plants commonly associated with this species such as meadowsweet, ragged robin and marsh thistle would also survive if introduced to the site.

Most man-made waterbodies are eutrophic (nutrient-rich), so plant species characteristic of eutrophic water should therefore be selected. The NVC can identify which species are characteristic of eutrophic conditions and thus suitable for inclusion. Local wetlands are another useful guide, and can be used as a guide for the species to include as well as giving an indication of the location of the species in relation to water depth.

5.3.3 Species selection
Standard guidelines that should be followed when selecting species are outlined below.
- Species should be native to Britain. Some naturalised alien species are notoriously detrimental to wetlands. These species can be exceedingly damaging to all forms of aquatic life and are expensive to control. A list of species to avoid is given in Table F.5.1.
- Species should be common and widespread.
- Species should be perennial and long-lived with an effective means of vegetative spread.
- Highly competitive native species should be avoided.
- When selecting species for a waterbody, submerged aquatic species should be included since these oxygenate the water. Other species should include floating aquatics, marginals and emergents.

An informed judgement should be made regarding the selection of species based upon the water pH, substrate type, soil water content (if a terrestrial habitat), and water depth (if an aquatic habitat). Part of wetland construction is trial and error: the

wetland is sculpted and planted and then left undisturbed. Plants that are adapted to the conditions will survive and fill gaps left by those species that do not survive.

There are basically three types of wetland plants, categorised according to their location in relation to water depth. The full range of species types should be introduced. Table F.5.2 lists some wetland plants with a brief description of their habitat requirements and wildlife value.

- **Aquatic species**

These are divided into three different categories:

Submerged aquatics grow in water of a depth generally greater than 10 cm, and are rooted. These species perform the useful role of oxygenating the water. Examples of submerged aquatic species are spiked water-milfoil (*Myriophyllum spicatum*) and rigid hornwort (*Ceratophyllum demersum*).
Floating-leaved aquatics are also rooted to the bottom and require a water depth of at least 10 cm. Examples are broad-leaved pondweed (*Potomogeton natans)* and white water-lily (*Nymphaea alba*).
Free-floating aquatics are not rooted to the bottom. Examples are ivy-leaved duckweed (*Lemna trisulca*) and frogbit (*Hydrocharis morsus-ranae*).

- **Emergent species**

These species grow out from water and their stems and leaves emerge above the surface. Some emergent species such as reedmace (*Typha latifolia*) and common reed (*Phragmites australis*) can be invasive in shallow waters. These species can be controlled by cutting or increasing the water depth.

- **Marginal species**

Marginal plants have their roots in wet mud rather than water, although they are tolerant of water levels up to about 6 cm depth. They will also withstand winter flooding provided that it is not for prolonged periods. Marginal species are

those such as yellow flag (*Iris pseudoacorus*), purple loosestrife (*Lythrum salicaria*) and ragged robin (*Lychnis flos-cuculi*).

5.4 Wetland creation on landfill sites – practical methods
It is recommended that ecologically-based methods are used to create wetlands if possible. The use of topsoil, dredgings, water, mud and vegetation from local wetlands is the most appropriate method for achieving ecologically sound habitat creation (although care must be taken not to introduce exotic species). If such methods are used, local provenance is ensured, the proportions of the species are likely to be appropriate and there is a high probability that other species essential for the creation of a functional ecosystem such as bacteria, algae and invertebrates will also be introduced. However, these materials are often in short supply and purchased seed or pot grown plants which are unlikely to have local provenance may have to be used if local material is unavailable.

There are four stages in the creation of wetland, addressed in the following sections.
- Site preparation (F.5.4.1)
- Species introduction (F.5.4.2)
- Aftercare (F.5.4.3)
- Long-term management (F.5.4.4)

5.4.1 Site preparation
Pond creation
Ponds of all sizes can have benefits to wildlife, from small areas of waterlogged ground to shallow seasonally wet pools to large deep ponds. Ideally, the size of newly created waterbodies should be varied from 1 m^2 upwards.

An example of a pond and wetland margin design is shown in Figure F.5.2. Ponds are best excavated mechanically. Whilst compaction of the soil beneath a waterbody is beneficial to prevent post-creation subsidence and water loss,

Table F.5.1. Wetland species that should never be planted (Adapted from Flora Locale, 1999). These species should be removed immediately if accidentally introduced	
Any *Hydrocotyle* species except the native *Hydrocotyle vulgaris*	
Any *Crassula* species, particularly New Zealand pygmyweed *Crassula helmsii*	
Water fern *Azolla filiculoides*	Canadian pondweed *Elodea canadensis*
Water hyacinth *Eichornia crassipes*	Nutalls' pondweed *Elodea nutallii*
Balsam (any species) *Impatiens* spp.	

compaction of soil surrounding a waterbody should be avoided. As a result of such compaction, runoff is likely to enter the pond at speed, carrying sediment and possibly causing soil erosion. This can lead to nutrient enrichment of the water with consequential algal growth and a loss of more sensitive species.

Excavated soil can be used in other restoration projects around the site or used in situ to create islands, screening bunds (especially if birds are to be encouraged) or to dam another area in order to retain water.

Pond lining and soil
Once the pond has been dug, it should be lined to increase water retention. Three main materials are recommended for lining ponds; concrete, butyl and clay. At many landfill sites it is likely that there will be an abundance of clay, and being a natural material, it is advised that clay is used as the liner wherever possible. However, it is best not to use clay on wetlands that are likely to have highly fluctuating water levels unless a depth of greater than 60 cm can be applied. For more details on this and other types of lining see Merritt (1994).

A clay lining should be at least 30 cm thick and can be placed on any substrate. This thickness should prevent sharp materials, bricks etc. from cutting through the clay, and should also prevent toxic materials from leaching through. It is vital that the clay is compacted to produce a watertight barrier. The clay should be spread evenly across the bottom and sides of the excavated waterbody, ideally with a hydraulic excavator which does not need to track over the material and is able

to exert considerable pressure. A roller can be used on larger sites to further compact the clay. To ensure maximum compaction, the clay should be slightly moist when applied. Ensuring that the clay liner is compacted is essential for successful pond creation.

Soil should be placed on top of the pond liner as a rooting substrate for aquatic and marginal plants. A soil capping of 300 mm will provide sufficient rooting depth for most species (Merritt, 1994). The soil used for this purpose should not be rich in nutrients, as the nutrients will dissolve into the water. This can cause algal blooms which reduce the amount of light filtering through the water column and hence reduce the survival of aquatic plants.

Although topsoil may potentially provide the best growing medium for aquatic plants, it is also more likely to generate algal blooms. If topsoil must be used, it is best to place aquatic and marginal plants in baskets or hessian bags containing topsoil. If topsoil is used for seeding (see Section F.5.4.2), it is preferable to introduce it slowly in small amounts.

The best substrate to use for pond creation is subsoil (Williams *et al.*, 1997). This can be spread across the bottom of the pond in varying depths. Once the pond has filled with water, whole plants can be introduced by throwing them into the water attached to a weight, allowing them to sink and take root. Around the pond edges, plants can be pushed into the mud by hand or introduced as turves placed into shallow excavations. Placing a subsoil layer across the base of the pond allows plants to grow without restriction; a more naturalistic effect is created compared to that obtained with plants

Yellow flag *Iris pseudacorus*, a common marginal species.

placed in pots or bags of soil.

Barker (1994) advocates the addition of a 300 mm deep layer of gravel, sand or any other coarse material at the base of the pond. This acts as a suitable rooting substrate for plants, and silt will gradually accumulate providing a source of nutrients. A layer of gravel placed on top of a soil layer will also help to hold the soil in place.

The following points should be considered when designing waterbodies (Williams *et al.*, 1997):

- Pond edges should be vegetated as soon as possible, if necessary by

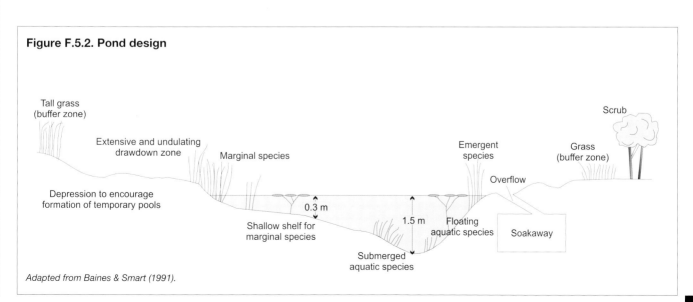

Figure F.5.2. Pond design

Tall grass (buffer zone)

Scrub

Extensive and undulating drawdown zone

Marginal species

Emergent species

Grass (buffer zone)

Depression to encourage formation of temporary pools

Overflow

0.3 m

Shallow shelf for marginal species

1.5 m

Floating aquatic species

Soakaway

Submerged aquatic species

Adapted from Baines & Smart (1991).

Table F.5.2. Wetland plants, their requirements and attributes (from Andrews & Rebane, 1994)

Species	Type of plant	Requirements and wildlife value
Broad-leaved pondweed	Submerged	Rivers and drains. Good seed production.
Curled pondweed	Submerged	Seeds eaten by wildfowl.
Fennel pondweed	Submerged	Tolerates brackish, polluted and turbid water to some degree. Seeds and tubers eaten by wildfowl.
Horned pondweed	Submerged	Seeds eaten by wildfowl.
Rigid hornwort	Submerged	Unrooted. Tolerant of nutrient-rich waters. Good invertebrate habitat but can smother other aquatic plants.
Spiked water-milfoil	Submerged	Favours lime-rich waters. Excellent invertebrate habitat.
Water crowfoots	Submerged	According to species, fast-flowing rivers to ponds and ditches. Some have floating leaves. Seeds used by waterfowl.
Water starwort	Floating – submerged	Good invertebrate habitat.
Duckweeds	Floating – unrooted	Free-floating. Plants eaten by wildfowl.
Frogbit	Floating – unrooted	Free-floating. Unpolluted ditches. Local. Overwintering buds eaten by wildfowl.
Watercress	Floating – unrooted	Favours calcareous water.
Amphibious bistort	Floating – rooted	Also on damp ground. Good invertebrate habitat. Good seed production taken by wildfowl. Good duckling foraging habitat.
White water-lily	Floating – rooted	Rivers and lakes. Good for water scorpions, some snails and dragonflies. Good duckling foraging habitat.
Yellow water-lily	Floating – rooted	Rivers and lakes. Good for water scorpions, some snails and dragonflies. Good duckling foraging habitat.
Arrowhead	Emergent	Rivers and drains. Brood foraging habitat.
Bogbean	Emergent	Acid waters and peat
Bulrush	Emergent	Swamps and open water to 1.5 m depth. Winter cover for wildfowl but very invasive.
Common club-rush	Emergent	Pools and rivers. Seeds eaten by wildfowl.
Conmon spike-rush	Emergent	Damp ground. Very good seed producer. Used by duckling broods, Benefits from some cattle grazing.
Erect bur-reed	Emergent	Ditches and margins of rivers. Good invertebrate habitat and seeds eaten by wildfowl.
Mare's-tail	Emergent	To 1 m depth. Good invertebrate habitat. Seeds eaten by wildfowl. Cover for duckling broods.
Reed	Emergent	To 1.5 m water depth. Ungrazed areas with high water levels. Readily grazed by cattle. Prime habitat of reed warbler. Winter cover for wildfowl.
Reed sweet-grass	Emergent	Areas subject to frequent flooding. Highly invasive and limited value. Favoured grazing by cattle.
Water plantain	Emergent	Shallows, margins of ponds and ditches
Brooklime	Marginal	Damp ground and shallows.
Flowering rush	Marginal	Damp ground and shallows.
Fool's watercress	Marginal	Favours calcareous water.
Great willowherb	Marginal	Damp ground when ungrazed.
Marsh marigold	Marginal	Damp ground.
Marsh woundwort	Marginal	Damp ground.
Meadowsweet	Marginal	Damp ground.
Purple loosestrife	Marginal	Damp ground and water margins. Good butterfly plant.
Reed canary-grass	Marginal	Mostly ungrazed/partly grazed wet fields.
Rushes	Marginal	Damp ground. Seeds eaten by wildfowl.
Sedges, e.g. greater pond sedge	Marginal	Damp ground and water's edge. Very good seed producers. Nesting cover for wildfowl.
Water figwort	Marginal	Damp ground. Good nectar and seed producer.
Water forget-me-not	Marginal	Damp ground.
Water mint	Marginal	Damp ground and shallows. Good nectar plant.
Yellow flag	Marginal	Damp ground.

planting a low-density grass cover as a nurse (Section F.1.6.2). Ideally, dredgings containing plant fragments and entire plants should be used for this purpose as this will create vegetative cover very quickly. The edge slope should not be shallow to reduce the risk of runoff carrying sediment into the pond.

- For a pond to remain permanently wet, the water should be at least 1 m deep, but there is little reason to create a waterbody greater than 2 m deep. Most plant species will not grow in very deep water and there is little additional benefit for other groups.

- Deep waterbodies should only be created if the water can be kept unpolluted; shallow water is largely vegetated by tall emergent species that are better able to withstand polluted water. Deep water plants such as submerged aquatics are more sensitive to pollution, especially if the water becomes turbid.

- Water depth in a waterbody should be varied. This can be achieved by cutting shallow shelves on some edges and leaving a deep central area. Varying water depth and permanence creates different habitats, maximising the biodiversity potential. Most wildfowl species, for example, feed mainly in water that is less than 50 cm deep.

- Creating a wide drawdown zone (the edge of the waterbody where the water level fluctuates between winter and summer) will maximise the value of the pond to wildlife. The slope of this zone should be as shallow as possible and need not be an even gradient; small depressions in this area will fill with temporary pools. Temporary pools are an increasingly uncommon habitat type; many rare plants and a considerable number of invertebrates are found in this type of environment. Marginal and semi-terrestrial species may also colonise this type of habitat.

- Undulating margins should be created, forming bays of sheltered water. These provide conditions suitable for aquatic and emergent plants, and plant litter can accumulate which provides habitat for invertebrates. On large waterbodies, wave action is often considerable and may even prevent vegetation from establishing. In these cases, sheltered bays are often the only place where abundant vegetation is present.

- Excavated soil from wetland creation can be used to create one or several islands. Islands form an undisturbed habitat which is especially useful if the pond edge is grazed and trampled. If the main objective of wetland creation is to provide nesting habitat for birds, the provision of islands is very important. The size of waterbody is an important consideration. Isolated waterbodies less than 0.5 ha in size generally attract few waterbird species apart from moorhen and mallard, and islands in such waterbodies will therefore be of relatively little value to birds (Merritt, 1994). Indeed, creating an island in a small pond may constrain the design to the detriment of more appropriate species. The further an island is from the shore the more attractive it is to birds. A four-metre wide channel will deter foxes but will not prevent stoats, mink, weasels and rats from reaching an island. Low, flat islands are usually the most attractive to birds. For further details on island design see Merritt (1994). The height of the island above water level will dictate the habitat type of the island. High islands will become grassy and eventually dominated by scrub, whereas if the slopes are gentle and the islands are often submerged, mud banks will be created. To reduce the need for management, islands should be grassy with occasional winter flooding to prevent scrub invasion. However, access to islands should be possible in case management is necessary.

Marsh creation

If the watertable is not close to the surface, an impermeable liner will be necessary for marsh creation. The same considerations apply as for pond lining (see above). Compacted clay is the preferred material to use as a liner. Once the clay is laid and compacted, a substrate layer should be placed on top.

If the marsh is linked to a pond, there should be no break in the liner from the pond to the marsh, but the depth of the liner can be lessened and the marsh created as a large shelf at the edge of the pond. The water from the pond then soaks into the soil of the shelf creating and perpetuating marsh conditions. If the marsh is separate, there must be some provision for runoff to enter the system even if only a small volume. It is important to ensure that the water table is kept permanently close to or at the soil surface.

The ideal soil to use is river or pond dredgings arising from routine watercourse management (the Environment Agency should be able advise on the location of nearby dredging operations). If this is unavailable, subsoil should be used, with small amounts of composted organic matter mixed well with the subsoil. Soil forming materials such as gravel, pebbles, sand or brick rubble can be used, but it is preferable to incorporate some organic matter or top/subsoil into such materials. See Merritt (1994) for further details. At least 300 mm of soil should be laid, particularly where periodic drying occurs; a clay liner can crack under such conditions if not adequately protected (Gilbert & Anderson, 1998).

Wet woodland creation

To create conditions suitable for wet woodland, clay-rich soils that are prone to waterlogging should be laid, and runoff directed from the cap onto the creation site. Alternatively, an impermeable layer of clay or other suitable lining that does not permit water drainage can be created (see above), with a considerable depth of soil (such as 1.5 m) laid on top. This depth of soil is necessary to prevent tree roots from reaching and penetrating the liner, and wet woodland creation will not be appropriate unless the lining can be laid as part of initial site restoration.

Semi-natural wet woodlands are usually dominated by grey willow (*Salix cinerea*), although several other species of willow are also commonly associated with the various types of wet woodland. Alders are unsuitable for permanently waterlogged soils but are suitable where water drains through slopes into streams or other waterbodies. In contrast to dry woodland creation, the field layer should be left to develop naturally after willow is planted as the canopy layer. Although some species of shade-tolerant herbaceous wetland plants are available commercially, the field layer mainly comprises mosses and herbaceous species that are difficult to purchase. Soil or mud from an existing wetland will provide a source of propagules, but the seeds and spores of plants should be introduced by mobile species such as birds over time.

Wetland microhabitats

- *Dead wood:* dead wood provides habitat for specialist invertebrates, fungi, lichens and mosses, and can be introduced in the form of logs, large branches or entire dead trees.
- *Bare shingle:* Gravel beaches favour several rare species of aquatic beetle. They can be created by

Photo: David Hill.

Pond created at Cromwell Bottom landfill site (see Case Study no. 3)

placing a butyl or plastic liner on the ground covered with a layer of sand or gravel. The gradient of the beach should be as gentle as possible.

- *Scrub:* A dense area of scrub provides nesting habitat for birds and good terrestrial habitat for amphibians. Scrub can be situated close a waterbody, but should not surround more than half of the waterbody edge as species such as great crested newts cannot tolerate heavily shaded water.

- *Habitat piles:* Piles of cut vegetation may be used by breeding grass snakes.

- *Reedbeds:* Beds of common reed can be of value to breeding birds and a variety of invertebrates especially when they cover a large area. Reedbeds are a BAP Priority Habitat, although targets focus on the creation of reedbeds over 20 ha in size. The creation of reedbeds of this size is unlikely to be possible at landfill sites.

Wetland buffer zones

Wetlands, especially ponds, require good water quality, and hence an absence of pollutants. Pollutants can include nitrates, soluble phosphorus, biocides, metals, and sediment-bound toxins washed in with soil particles. High nitrogen levels favour nuisance species such as water fern (*Azolla filiculoides*), duckweed (*Lemna* spp.) and algae. An additional problem is high Biological Oxygen Demand (BOD) resulting from the decay of organic matter. Fast-growing algae such as blue-green algae produce large amounts of biodegradable matter that produces toxic

chemicals and deoxygenates the water. Therefore, an excess of organic matter within the water should be avoided.

Buffer zones protect wetlands from pollutants entering from the surrounding area and can be very effective at controlling water quality. For wetlands fed by runoff, buffer zones should comprise tall grasses or herbaceous vegetation. Such buffer zones reduce areas of bare soil and slow down the rate of water flow. Woodlands are an unsuitable buffer zone habitat; they absorb water and hence reduce the volume entering the wetland. A buffer zone should not contain tile drains or runnels as these increase water flow rate. Buffer zones intercept waterborne and sediment-borne pollutants, and should be wider on the side of the slope from which most water and sediments will be derived.

Buffer zones can also protect wetlands against the effects of herbicide and fertiliser spray drift. In these cases, they should be a minimum of 20 m wide. Ponds with muddy edges and large populations of annual plants need extra protection from spray drift.

Buffer zones in waterbodies
Extensive stands of emergent, submerged or floating plants can assist pollution control by intercepting airborne pollutants, absorbing excess nutrients and slowing down the spread of contaminants through the pond (Haycock & Worral, 1996). Reedmace and common reed are both very tolerant of pollution and are able to drastically reduce nutrient levels in water. Incoming water in the form of streams or drains should be

passed through sediment traps and / or reedbed filters to remove sediment and pollutants.

Reedbeds
Reedbeds can be purely functional, created with the sole purpose of treating leachate or other polluted water, or they can be created as part of a wetland complex for their nature conservation value and for general improvement of water quality.

Reedbeds can have considerable benefits for wildlife (LeFeuvre; 1998, Mills *et al.*, 1998). Even small reedbeds can form a habitat for breeding birds such as sedge warbler, reed warblers and reed bunting, whilst larger reedbeds may provide habitat for BAP priority species such as bittern. The improvement of water quality by reedbeds will have general benefits for a wide range of aquatic plants and invertebrates, which in turn provides benefits for other species such as wildfowl. Box F.5.2 summarises the principles of reedbed creation and management.

Pollution control measures for waterbodies prior to species introduction

Excessive levels of nutrients in a waterbody (and the resultant algal blooms) can be treated in several ways:

- The most effective method of reducing nutrients is to plant a large bed of common reed or reedmace, as these species are very effective at absorbing nutrients. If reedbeds are used to ameliorate an existing excess of nutrients in a waterbody, the entire reedbed should be cut each year to remove the nutrients from the system. Harvested reed should ideally be composted in heaps which can also serve as reptile habitat. Both of these natural methods can be slow to act, but will be successful in the long term.

- A very effective method of controlling algae is to place bales of barley straw in the water for a one month period. Toxins released by the breakdown of fungi growing on the barley kill the algae. However, this only treats the symptom, not the cause.

- If the water source for a new pond is polluted and cannot be rectified, pond design should be altered to one that can better cope with pollution. It is better to create shallow ponds with large drawdown zones and swampy margins as opposed to deep water, since submerged aquatic species cannot tolerate much pollution.

5.4.2 Species introduction

Wetlands can develop a good range of species very quickly (within 3-4 years), especially if there are other wetlands close by. The major reason for introductions is to speed up the development of a mature community. This applies particularly to waterbodies.

Methods of introducing wetland plant species include:
- Dredged spoil
- Hand planting
- Seeds
- Translocation of soil or vegetation from existing marsh
- Mud/water/leaf litter from existing waterbodies

Dredged spoil

Dredged spoil is the recommended method of obtaining material for transplantation and is the most effective way of obtaining plant propagules for large-scale planting. This is therefore regarded as the best practice method. It is cheap (often free) and obtainable in large amounts. Also, if spoil can be obtained from a local source, local provenance of the plants is assured. Dredgings from both running and still waters are generally suitable, as the majority of wetland plant species are very adaptable. Dredgings can contain seeds, roots and shoots, all capable of producing new plants. An additional benefit of using dredgings is that aquatic invertebrates are also likely to be introduced.

Routine watercourse management is undertaken by Internal Drainage Boards (IDBs) in a number of regions to keep the centre of waterways free of vegetation and to maintain adequate water depth. The Environment Agency should be able to advise on the location of current dredging works. Dredging may also be conducted by farmers or conservation bodies, and these may be able to supply material if requested.

However, dredgings are bulky and cost a considerable amount to transport. Another disadvantage is that there is no control over the type of species that will be introduced, a point to be wary of if there are alien species present at the donor site. The donor site should be inspected prior to the acceptance of any spoil to check the nature of the vegetation and thus the likely nature of the seed composition. Silt (see below) should be dried for a period of no more than two days to reduce weight and volume and to enable non-watertight containers to be used, both of which will reduce transport costs. Clumps of plants should not be allowed to dry out.

Dredgings from the bottom of a waterbody will be different from those taken from the sides. Bottom dredgings are generally structureless, sloppy silt, usually rich in seeds from a wide range of aquatic plants, and probably also containing seeds or fragments of emergent and marginal species. The easiest method to introduce this type of dredging is to use an excavator with an articulated bucket at the edge of the pond. The material should be scooped up and placed in the water at the receptor site as gently as possible.

Side dredgings tend to comprise clumps (usually the size of the excavator bucket) of marginal and emergent plants with soil still attached to the roots. These clumps should be left intact without disturbing the soil around the roots as this will assist the establishment of the plants. Clumps should be picked up by an excavator and placed gently in position where the eventual water depth will be shallow (no deeper than 50 cm) or along the waterbody edge. Ideally, a shallow excavation should be made in the soil to receive the clump. It is important not to place the clump upside down, but apart from this, planting does not require great precision.

Box F.5.2. Reedbed creation and management

Common reed can tolerate a variety of water depths and conditions where the water is above or below the soil surface. The optimum water depth for reedbed wildlife is 5-30 cm above the surface in summer and 30-100 cm in winter (Hawke & José, 1996). The soil used for the substrate should be pure clay or clay-rich. The base of the reedbed should be gently shelving to allow shallow flooding. If possible, the reedbed should be adjacent to an area of open water in order to maximise the benefit of the reedbed for wildlife. There should be a large reed-water interface with 20% open water. For full details see Hawke & José (1996).

Creation

Reedbeds can be created using cuttings or rhizomes for large areas, and pot / plug-grown plants for small areas, at a density of 4 plants per m². The use of seed is not advised as it requires complex pre-germination treatment.

Planting rhizomes is an effective method of reedbed creation; a length of rhizome 15 cm long is sufficient to produce a plant, as long as a dead stem is attached to act as an oxygen supply tube. Spring is the best time to plant rhizomes. They can be hand-planted by transplanting a 30 cm diameter clump, which should be placed into a pre-dug hole without disturbing the soil around the rhizomes. Alternatively, an excavator can be used to collect rhizomes and substrate together to a depth of 30 cm from a donor site. These are then transported to the receptor site and spread by hand or with a digger. This method can be carried out in wet or dry conditions, but not during frosty weather. Rhizomes should not be submerged completely after planting.

Aftercare

Once the rhizomes have been planted, a settling-in period of two weeks should be allowed, followed by flooding to a depth of 20-100 cm for two weeks to reduce weed growth. Thereafter, weed control is conducted by flooding, creating water depths of 30 cm on a periodic basis, each flood lasting for two weeks. Hand-pulling may also be necessary until the reed canopy is complete.

Management

Reedbed management involves cutting and harvesting the reeds and manipulating water levels. Reed should be cut on a four-year rotation. An entire reedbed should not be cut at any one time; it should be divided into smaller areas cut in different years.

Ideally, one should be able to manipulate water levels. Periodic flooding is necessary for weed control, but the water level should be dropped to below the soil surface when cutting is carried out. It is important that water levels are gradually reduced over a one-month period to allow mobile species to move out of the reedbed to deeper water. Water control is normally achieved using sluices and outfalls. Reed cutting will have to be conducted by hand if the ground is not allowed to dry out before cutting, as machinery will sink. Generally, small areas of reed can quite easily be cut by hand, but large areas will necessitate the hire of a mechanised reed mower.

Hand planting

Planting by hand is more precise than the above method and is therefore a better method for introducing more sensitive and easily damaged species. Plants that have been purchased as plugs should also be hand planted. The advantage of planting individuals by hand is that the exact location of a plant can be chosen to match its ecological requirements. Plug plants are also relatively cheap and easy to establish. It may also be possible to obtain plant fragment from nearby waterbodies (with the owner's permission).

Marginal plants with soft roots can be pushed into bare soft mud (taking care not to damage the roots). Deep water plants should be weighed down with a stone so that the roots reach the mud at the bottom of the waterbody.

Pit planting may be necessary if:

- the plant is rhizomatous (i.e. grows by extension of an underground horizontal stem);
- the mud is hard; or
- the plant is to be introduced into a bank above the water level.

The pit should be large enough to accommodate all the roots without the roots being crushed together. Soil should be firmed around the roots, taking care to avoid compaction.

It is not always necessary to introduce entire plants. Shoot cuttings can be used (5-10 cm long), especially if they contain a short length of rhizome. One large rhizomatous plant can be used to create many small plants by cutting the rhizome into pieces (each piece should contain at least two rhizome buds). Introducing plants in this way should only be carried out outside the growing season.

Willows can easily be propagated with 20 cm lengths of stem. Remove any leafy branches and push the cuttings into the ground, leaving 6 cm exposed. These root easily and will soon sprout from the stem buds. These willow 'pegs' can be used to establish banks of scrub at the side of a waterbody or can be used to stabilise the bank whilst the waterbody is still immature. Alternatively they can be used to establish willow carr.

One should be wary of purchasing plants from a garden centre, since the plugs may contain seeds of aggressive alien species such as New Zealand pigmyweed.

Pot grown plants should be given space to spread sideways; the ideal spacing is about 1 m.

Timing

Aquatic plants should be planted in May-August. Marginal and emergent species should be planted in winter or spring, but not in frosty conditions.

Planting marginal and emergent species should be delayed until the waterbody has filled with water, which may take several months if the pond is entirely fed by runoff. Submerged aquatic plants can be introduced whilst the pond is filling; these plants will oxygenate the water and keep it fresh. It is anticipated that the aftercare period will be used for most of the planting works and also to impose any remedial works on water quality such as controlling algal blooms.

If a created wetland is flooded with water before planting, access can be problematic. It is therefore advised that planting is conducted before flooding. If possible, water should be collected in a holding pond in order to supply an appreciable amount of water immediately after planting. If this is not possible and access is required to wet areas, tracked machines can be used that will not cause severe damage.

Protection against wave action

Waves can damage emergent and marginal plants and may be a problem on waterbodies greater than 25 m². A line of stakes or willow pegs can be pushed into the mud between the plants and open water to protect new planting. Alternatively, a line of submerged barley bales can be placed along the waterbody edge, which also has the advantage of controlling algal blooms and providing habitat for aquatic invertebrates.

Storage of plants before planting

Wetland plants are very susceptible to desiccation, and will probably die even if exposed for only a short time. The removal of plants from their original habitat or from pots should be delayed for as long as possible. Plants can be stored temporarily (up to three hours) by covering them completely with plastic sheeting and placing them under a lightproof cover (which should not be black). Alternatively, they should be wrapped in damp newspaper and placed in the shade to reduce evaporation.

For longer storage (up to four days) the plants should be placed with their roots in shallow water to keep them moist, with the stems and leaves kept out of the water and covered with plastic. Again it is important to keep the plants in the shade. The majority of the leaves and stem can also be pruned off to further reduce evaporation of water from the plant.

Seeds

Locally collected seeds can be used, or seeds can be purchased from a commercial seed house. Seed should be hand broadcast or distributed using a fertiliser spreader (see Section F.2.4.2) in spring or autumn. Commercial seed should be applied at the rate advised by the seed house.

Translocation of soil or vegetation from an existing marsh

Soil and vegetation from an existing marsh is an ideal material for creating a new marsh. Even small amounts of soil from another wetland habitat are worth obtaining, since such soil is likely to contain a large amount of seeds and root fragments. However, sources of wetland soil are scarce, and should only be taken from a marsh which is being destroyed for other reasons. In exceptional circumstances, it may be possible to remove randomly located small turves from an existing marsh, provided that permission has been given by the landowner. The statutory UK conservation bodies should also be consulted if this operation is being considered.

Environmental conditions on the receptor site should be similar to the donor site. The most important factors that will determine the success of this method are soil and water pH, but the amount of inflowing water and the depth of the water table should also be similar.

Large-scale removal

The procedure involved is very similar to that for grassland translocation (see Section F.2.4.2), although the chances of success are higher. Marsh soil is wet and therefore has a fragile structure. Compacting the base of a marsh to retain high water levels is acceptable, but soil used as a rooting substrate must not be compacted.

The soil should be removed separately from the vegetation. The vegetation should be removed in turves of manageable size such as 1 m x 1 m using an excavator, and stored temporarily whilst the soil is stripped and moved to the receptor site. If there is a limited amount of turf available, creating complete cover may not be necessary; it is possible to use turves as colonisation nuclei. The turves should be concentrated in the centre of the site.

Small-scale removal

If soil is in short supply, it can be spread as a thin upper layer to permit the roots, seeds and rhizomes within to germinate and sprout. Small amounts of turves can

Case Study 9:

Stadt Moers Park, Merseyside
Integration of habitat creation into an urban country park

Site details

Site operator:	Knowsley Metropolitan Borough
Habitat created:	Woodland, grassland
Existing nature conservation interest:	Tushingham Pond, within the site boundary but retained during landfill operations, is of local nature conservation importance

Site background

Landfilling at what is now Stadt Moers Park was completed in 1981, but as with many old landfill sites, restoration at the time was limited. The standard of capping is very variable (the cap varies in thickness from over 1 m to as little as 2 cm in places where the cap has been disturbed or has settled). With the land remaining largely derelict, Knowsley Council took over the site in 1983 and over the next few years the site was gradually restored to its present state. Restoration has yet to be completed in a small area in the north east of the site. Further development of the site is currently being considered, a process involving consultation with the local community.

Restoration objectives and site layout

Restoration objectives for this large (90 ha) urban site included the creation of formal parkland, woodland (in association with the Mersey Community Forest), garden allotments and a picnic site, in addition to habitat creation for nature conservation. The objectives originally included the provision of a number of sports pitches, but differential settlement has meant that this after-use has had to be reviewed.

Successful restoration to such a wide range of after-use interests required that the site be divided into separate zones to ensure that the interests of one after-use were not compromised by those of another. The site is divided into four quadrants by the M57 motorway and the main Liverpool – Manchester railway line. Each quadrant is a substantial size, enabling different after-uses to be created in separate quadrants.

The south-east quadrant was set aside for a less formal after-use designed to benefit nature conservation, incorporating woodland and grassland creation and the integration of Tushingham Pond (retained intact during the operational life of the

site). Environmental education is a major objective for this part of the site, involving the creation of nature trails, production of interpretative material and the encouraging of school visits. The two quadrants to the west of the motorway are devoted to parkland and garden allotments, and to the north of the railway there is a picnic area and visitor centre.

Constraints upon successful habitat creation

Vandalism is a common problem at urban sites and Stadt Moers is no exception. Particular problems experienced have included damage to young trees and damage from the use of scrambling motorbikes. In response to the latter, special motorbike-proof gates have been constructed at the entrance to all quadrants and motorbike use of the site is now much less prevalent.

An additional problem, also common at old, partially restored landfill sites, is a lack of resources for carrying out essential management work. As a result,

areas of grassland at Stadt Moers have been left to natural succession.

Habitat creation in the south-east quadrant – techniques used

Soil provision
The south-east quadrant was capped, albeit to a variable standard, prior to the completion of landfilling operations and covered with a thin layer of a heavy clay loam soil. No remedial engineering works have since taken place. In 1988 a layer of local subsoil (originating as spoil from nearby road and house building projects) was loose-tipped onto the site and covered with a 50 mm layer of topsoil and an organic starter agent.

Woodland
Large areas of the south-east quadrant were planted with trees in 1995-96. Native species were preferred, including common alder, willow, silver birch, pedunculate oak and Scots pine. The woodland areas were designed to form a mosaic of habitats with areas of grassland already present.

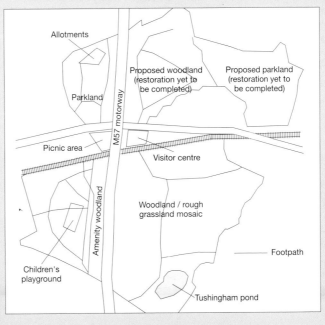

**Stadt Moers Park
– site layout**

Grassland

Much of the grassland present in the south-east quadrant is thought to have developed naturally. Differential settlement has led to damp areas forming and as a result a number of different communities have become established.

A small area of species-rich grassland (<1ha) was created several years ago using commercial seed, mainly as an experiment, and is managed by annual mowing in September. Species planted included cowslip, southern marsh orchid, black knapweed and oxeye daisy, all of which are still present. Additional species such as yellow rattle have colonised naturally. The presence of yellow rattle, which parasitises grass species, has helped to maintain the herb-rich nature of the sward.

Wetland

The main wetland area at the site is Tushingham Pond. The pond formed in a derelict quarry and was not landfilled during the operational phase of the site. The pond has been integrated into the restoration by allowing natural colonisation to take place on an area of quarry spoil in a strip 20-30 m wide on its northern side.

Results

Woodland

Many trees planted as recently as 1995 are now up to 6 m tall, indicating very rapid growth. Good numbers of birds such as willow warbler and whitethroat were present in 1999. The most successful trees, as would be expected, have been pioneer species such as willow, alder and birch. Other species such as oak and Scots pine have fared less well so far. It is uncertain what will happen to the trees when their roots meet the clay cap or come into direct contact with the waste below.

Photo: Duncan Watson

Damper areas have formed at the site as a result of settlement. These have been colonised by plants such as reed canary-grass and now support threatened bird species such as reed bunting.

Grassland

Much of the grassland is dominated by tall, aggressive species, principally due to the lack of management. The majority of the grassland is therefore relatively species-poor and of limited conservation value.

A number of ecologically interesting areas have developed however, particularly where differential settlement of the waste has caused wet areas to form on top of the cap. Such areas have been colonised by plants such as reed canary-grass and bird species such as reed bunting and snipe, both of which are of considerable conservation importance.

The formation of such wetland areas on the cap of modern sites is unlikely due to higher standards of engineering, and in any case would be unacceptable due to the increased risk of emission of landfill gas or leachate. However, on old sites such as Stadt Moers where the reduced rate of landfill gas and leachate production does not necessarily justify the costs of remedial engineering works, such areas can provide habitats of relatively high conservation value.

Wetland

Tushingham Pond already holds Site of Biological Interest (SBI) status and is shortly to become a Local Nature Reserve. The pond itself supports a diverse plant community and a range of invertebrates including a number of dragonflies and damselflies. Bird species present include kingfisher and little grebe. An interesting willow-dominated community has developed naturally on the retained quarry spoil adjacent to the pond. A number of orchids have been recorded here including southern marsh, northern marsh and bee orchids. The pond and surrounding area provide an excellent illustration of how areas retained during site operation can increase the value of habitat creation carried out as part of site restoration.

Zonation of different after-uses

Stadt Moers Park provides a good example of the integration of nature conservation interests into a primarily amenity-based after-use at an old, urban landfill site. The nature conservation value of restoration has been increased by the zoning of separate after-uses into well-defined areas within the site. Bird species such as snipe are unlikely to utilise habitat immediately adjacent to amenity areas such as football pitches; however, the careful zonation of after-uses allows amenity and conservation interests to co-exist on the same site.

The methods described here are presented purely as examples of landfill restoration and habitat creation techniques. They do not necessarily reflect the best practice standards contained within this book.

Photo: Duncan Watson

This existing pond was retained throughout site operation as a result of its conservation and amenity value. It is now an integral part of the restored site.

Case Study 9

be spread throughout the marsh as above.

Mud / water / leaf litter from other waterbodies

Mud, water or leaf litter from an existing water body is a valuable source of characteristic pond life such as invertebrates, microorganisms and seeds. In the absence of the availability of dredgings or other sources of wetland plants, small amounts of water or mud will assist in the development of the natural array of species found in wetland communities.

5.4.3 Aftercare

Some form of aftercare will be required for at least five years after wetland construction. The objectives of aftercare management are:

- to replace failed individuals;
- to control water nutrient levels;
- to control water levels in reedbeds for weed control; and
- to protect plants from grazing and trampling.

Ponds are likely to require the most immediate aftercare in the form of nutrient control and replanting in gaps left by failed individuals. Generally, little aftercare is required for other wetlands. Some manipulation of the water levels may be required; the most effective weed control is flooding which kills terrestrial weeds. If flooding is not possible, handpulling of weeds is effective, and herbicides approved for use adjacent to water can also be used (advice should be sought from the Environment Agency on suitable herbicide).

Wetlands and marginal and emergent vegetation may require fencing to give protection from trampling and grazing. It is advisable to prevent stock access to a pond or a wetland for the first year to allow the plants time to establish.

Waterbodies require a period of settling in immediately after construction. Water quality is likely to deteriorate, primarily due to nutrients dissolving into the water from soil. This usually induces a profuse growth of algae which can smother aquatic plants and produce anaerobic conditions. If the use of topsoil within the pond has been minimised and only relatively small amounts of sediment enter the pond, problems with algae should not be too serious or long-lived. There are several measures that can be used to reduce potential problems:

- Install a silt trap to collect and remove sediment from incoming water.
- Introduce submerged aquatic plants

to the pond as soon as possible.

- Plant a bed of common reed or reedmace in the area where the majority of the incoming water enters the pond. This will remove sediment and nutrients from the water and slow down the water flow rate.
- Install several barley bales near or at the edge of the pond (any further into the pond will make their removal very difficult). These can be left for three months and then removed, replacing them if algae are still a problem. To be effective, the bales must be partially rotted and placed in water in February/March before the algal blooms appear.
- Minimise disturbance to the soil at the bottom of the pond.

Profuse algal growth can be removed with nets. Care should be taken not to remove plants, invertebrates and amphibians with the algae. The water should become clear within three months, and other plant species can be introduced when the water quality starts to improve. Introducing plants will disturb the water and add more soil, so it is likely that water quality will temporarily deteriorate. Barley bales should be added if water quality does not improve.

Pond vegetation should generally not require management in the first two years after planting. Subsequently, some vigorous species such as reedmace and common reed may need to be controlled to prevent them from encroaching into the middle of the pond. Wetlands will require some degree of management after the first year, although this should not be intensive (see below).

5.4.4 Long-term management
Wetland management

The nature of a wetland will change naturally as it develops. As old plants die, a layer of semi-decomposed litter builds up below the growing parts of the plants. Over time the plants will become raised above the water level and conditions will become drier, a process called terrestrialisation. A continual supply of water is required to combat this process, although one may have to accept that the wetland may not remain as wet as when first created.

The basic objectives of management are as follows:

- The maintenance of species diversity. This can be achieved by using grazing or mowing as management, which maintain diversity by preventing the

dominance of vigorous species. The removal of cuttings after mowing removes nutrients from the wetland system, which again discourages the dominance of vigorous species. Grazing also removes dead litter which would otherwise contribute to nutrient accumulation.

- The creation of complex structural mosaics. A complex vegetation structure contains a wide diversity of microhabitats, and is best achieved by low-intensity management. The absence of any management allows a small number of vigorous species to dominate, resulting in low structural diversity. High-intensity management creates very short vegetation, also with low structural diversity. Low intensity management creates a mosaic of short areas, taller stands, poached areas with bare mud and puddles of water and trampled areas.
- The prevention of terrestrialisation. Maintaining an adequate water supply by channelling as much runoff as possible through the wetland should ensure that litter does not build up to the point where the wetland dries out.

Regular ecological monitoring enables interesting habitats and species to be identified, and management can be tailored to suit these. Monitoring also enables potential problems such as the build-up of algae or the dominance of vigorous species to be identified at an early stage, enabling remedial management to take place before the conservation value of the wetland is reduced. Guidelines on monitoring created habitats can be found in Mitchley *et al.* (2000). The methods are described with reference to grassland and woodland habitats, but can be adapted for monitoring some wetland habitats.

Grazing

Grazing is a good management option, preferably with cattle (sheep are prone to diseases associated with hoof rot). Grazing reduces sward height, controls aggressive grasses and rushes, and creates bare ground germination niches (Fojt, 1994). Cattle will also create muddy poached waterbody margins, which can be of benefit to a wide range of plants and invertebrates.

Although it is impractical to obtain cattle just for the purposes of grazing a small amount of marsh, if other areas of the landfill are grazed with cattle, it is a relatively simple matter to let them graze the wetland as well.

Grazing should take place in late summer and autumn but care should be taken not to overstock; this will cause far more damage than under-management. Optimum stocking rates are very site-specific; it is difficult to give general guidelines. Advice should be sought before deciding on the appropriate stocking rate.

Mowing

Mowing is an alternative option for sites that cannot be grazed. However, because the bearing capacity of wet soil is poor, mowing very wet areas is best carried out when the ground is frozen. On drier areas, provided that wide tyres are used, a tractor-mounted mower can be used. Wide tyres will prevent the machinery from sinking and avoid excessive soil compaction. Alternatively, a hand-held strimmer can be used. It is important that cuttings are removed from the site. Mowing is only necessary once a year.

Pond management

A good background to pond management is given in Biggs *et al*. (1994). The basic objective of pond management is to retain areas of open water. Aggressive emergent species such as reedmace and common reed are liable to encroach towards the centre of a pond and reduce water depth, and these species may therefore need to be periodically cut back or pulled out, but the removal of large stands of vegetation in one go should be avoided. Removal by hand should be conducted in winter, and the cuttings removed.

Vigorous aquatic species may also dominate and choke a pond; these should be removed gently by hand, taking care not to remove any invertebrates or amphibians. Plants should only be removed if there are no areas left free of aquatic plants. To prevent a pond from being choked by one species, periodically remove a proportion of the stand.

Periodic drying out of shallow ponds is not necessarily detrimental to the health of the pond as shallow ponds will tend to support species that can tolerate the

occasional lack of water.

Ponds which are filling with silt can be dredged, but this can reduce the conservation value; a better option may be to create a new pond and allow the original pond to silt up.

Very shaded ponds will not support as many species as non-shaded ponds, but they do provide habitat for some uncommon invertebrate species. Invertebrate surveys should be carried out before cutting back overhanging vegetation. If the diversity of the shaded aquatic vegetation is poor, shade-tolerant species such as yellow flag can be planted. Decaying leaf litter will deoxygenate the water and should be removed if it builds up.

Areas of bare mud need to be actively managed if they are to be retained. Regular flooding may not prevent colonisation of perennial plants in the long term. However, germination of plants will be inhibited on areas of bare mud that are flooded in spring. Another effective method of maintaining open mud is to encourage trampling and grazing by cattle.

6 The agricultural landscape

6.1 Background information

Despite the benefits of habitat creation as an after-use for landfill sites, many sites (particularly those with old planning permissions) are likely to be restored to agriculture. Restoration to agriculture is the most likely choice of after-use in the following situations:

- On previously agricultural land of grades 1-3 (to ensure that the most productive land remains in production).
- Where the surrounding landscape is predominantly agricultural.
- Where restoration to agriculture has been agreed with the landowner or where a financial return from the land is required.

Many typical farmland species have declined drastically in recent years. For example, populations of previously common farmland birds such as skylark, linnet and tree sparrow have declined by over 50% in the last 25 years. Whilst these declines are mainly due to changes in agricultural practices, the introduction

of an ecologically-sensitive component into the restoration of landfill sites to agriculture can provide considerable benefits to the conservation of some of our most threatened species.

The creation of ecologically sensitive landscape features in restoration need not necessarily affect agricultural production. Agricultural restoration on landfill is already constrained by factors such as the existence of pollution control infrastructure; landscape features can be incorporated around these constraints. For example, landfill gas wellheads may be located within a conservation headland or alongside a hedgerow.

Details of restoration for an agricultural after-use such as methods of laying soil, methods of seeding agricultural swards etc. are beyond the scope of this book. Instead, guidance is given on the creation of specific landscape features to benefit nature conservation within an agricultural after-use. The guidance demonstrates that objectives for agriculture can be met in conjunction with benefits to nature conservation and therefore provides an

opportunity for the Waste Planning Authority to secure additional benefits from agricultural restoration.

The following features are described in this section. They are illustrated in Figure F.6.1.

- Hedgerows (F.6.2)
- Grassy field margins (F.6.3)
- Conservation headlands (F.6.4)
- Beetle banks (F.6.5)

Farms traditionally also contained small areas of woodland and ponds. In addition, traditionally managed agricultural grasslands are more species-rich than the intensively managed grasslands typically found today. For the restoration of landfill sites to agriculture to benefit nature conservation, consideration should therefore also be given to the creation of species-rich grasslands, small woodlands and ponds. The methods involved for the creation of these habitats are detailed in Sections F.2, F.3 and F.5.

A considerable number of grants are available that might be applicable to the creation of various habitats such as herb-

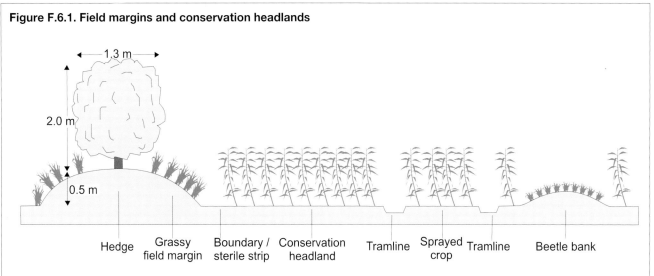

Figure F.6.1. Field margins and conservation headlands

Hedge | Grassy field margin | Boundary / sterile strip | Conservation headland | Tramline | Sprayed crop | Tramline | Beetle bank

Adapted from: Boatman (1990). Game Conservancy Council, Fordingbridge. Reproduced with kind permission of the publisher.

- *Hedge:* Trim hedges every other year, keep to a maximum height of 2 m.
- *Grassy field margin:* Used by overwintering insects and as a nest site by game birds. At least 1 m wide, and preferably on a bank. Perennial grasses and other non-weedy herbaceous species. Avoid spray and fertiliser drift. Top vegetation every 2-3 years to avoid scrub encroachment and prevent grass seeding into sterile strip.
- *Boundary/sterile strip:* Purely to prevent invasion of crop by aggressive weeds. At least 1 m wide. Maintain by rotovation in February/March.
- *Conservation headlands:* Usually 6 m wide. Area of crop treated with selective pestcides to control grass weeds, cleaver and diseases whilst allowing most broadleaved weeds and beneficial insects to survive.
- *Sprayed crop:* Treat as normal, but avoid drift into headland and use only safer aphicides.
- *Beetle Bank:* 0.4 m high and 1.5 m wide. Avoid herbicide drift.

rich grasslands, or landscape features such as hedgerows. The application and extent of these grants is beyond the scope of this publication. Further information can be gained from the Farming and Wildlife Advisory Group (FWAG) or the Farming and Rural Conservation Agency (FRCA).

6.2 Hedgerows

Hedgerows are a relatively simple feature to create and can bring considerable nature conservation benefit. There are no major constraints to hedgerow creation on a landfill site since a variety of soils can be used. Hedgerows can also provide a useful screening function by hiding structures such as wellheads and boreholes. Hedgerow design should also be fully integrated with pollution engineering design from the outset. In this way, pollution control infrastructure can be located along the course of hedgerows. This maximises the area of the site which can be used for agriculture or habitat creation. Access to monitoring infrastructures must also be provided; an access track bounded by hedgerows on

each side is a good way of allowing access whilst providing wildlife habitat. To further maximise the nature conservation value of the area, the access track itself can be grassland or a conservation headland.

Hedgerows were traditionally used to create a stockproof barrier and to demarcate boundaries. The structure of the hedgerow was tailored to the type of stock in question; sheep-proof hedgerows were bushy at the base, whereas cattle-proof hedgerows were taller and wider.

Hedgerows are a valuable habitat in their own right, with considerable value to nature conservation. In recognition of this, species-rich hedgerows are an UK BAP Priority Habitat. Not only do they provide a habitat for a selection of tree and shrub species, they also provide shelter, food and nesting sites for many birds of conservation importance such as tree sparrow, linnet, bullfinch, song thrush and corn bunting. Hedgerows also provide habitat for small mammals and many invertebrates. The creation of hedgerows, especially if they are planted with a

diverse number of species and managed in a way to benefit wildlife, will have considerable conservation value and can contribute to targets for local BAPs.

Hedgerows have a valuable function as wildlife corridors, allowing the dispersal of mobile animals and invertebrates such as mice, voles, birds and butterflies by providing suitable cover (Andrews, 1993). They can therefore help to combat the effects of habitat fragmentation by allowing the transfer of individuals between discrete areas of habitat.

Hedgerows are often combined with other features such as a bank, ditch or standard trees. Standards (full size trees at intervals along a hedgerow) are important elements of the hedge habitat. They are used by a wide range of invertebrates and birds such as tawny owl and great spotted woodpecker, especially if there is abundant dead wood on the tree. A water-filled ditch is not an appropriate feature to create above the cap on a landfill (see Section F.5), but ditches can be created at the edge of the site away from the filled area. Ditches can support several shade-tolerant wetland plants such as yellow flag, as well as a wide range of invertebrates. These additional features bring associated wildlife value and enhance the hedgerow as an entire unit.

6.2.1 Hedgerow design

Careful design allows a range of objectives to be met, combining the nature conservation benefits of hedgerows with landscape enhancement. Hedgerows can be located to create the appearance of a traditional agricultural landscape by demarcating field boundaries and lining tracks.

Hedgerows should be used as linking habitats. They can link two existing woodlands on either side of the site, or link existing woodlands to newly created ones on the site itself. This is likely to speed up colonisation of new woodland by mobile species such as small mammals. Hedgerows can also be used to link areas of rough grassland or scrub.

Landscape enhancement can be achieved by using a dense hedgerow as screening for pollution control infrastructure or access roads.

There are two components of traditional hedgerow design, the hedge plants themselves and a physical element such as a stone bank, an earth bank, a dry stone stone wall, and / or a ditch. Increasingly, hedges are planted in association with a stockproof fence.

A stone bank is usually built from alternate layers of stone and turf, although

Photo: David Hill

Hawthorn is the main species planted to create hedgerows. The berries provide food for birds during autumn and winter.

the turf tends to grow over the entire structure. Stone banks probably originated in areas where stones were too scarce (or of unsuitable quality) for the construction of dry stone walls. Earth banks consist of a mound of earth, often the result of excavating a parallel ditch, and may be faced with stone. Dredgings from the ditch were usually placed on top of the bank.

The combination of traditional hedgerow elements varies across the country; local forms of hedgerow evolved through different styles of management. It is important to create a hedge of local style to retain landscape character. Some hedges are planted as a single line, others as two parallel but staggered lines; this detail should also be reproduced faithfully. Also, hedgelaying styles vary in different areas. Local stone should be used for walls or banks associated with hedgerows.

Hedges themselves often comprised three parts; trimmed hedgerow shrubs and trees, intermittent standard trees, and woodland ground flora (a hedgerow could almost be said to be a linear woodland).

6.2.2 Species selection

Hedgerow species composition varies according to geographical locality, but the main hedgerow species is always hawthorn (*Crategeus monogyna*). Northern England and Scottish hedges are usually dominated by hawthorn with occasional blackthorn (*Prunus spinosa*) and few other accompanying species, whereas southern hedges are characteristically rich with species such as dog rose (*Rosa canina* agg.), guelder rose (*Viburnum opulus*) and field maple (*Acer campestre*). The best guide to

appropriate hedgerow species is to include those that are present in local hedgerows, especially those that are ancient and species-rich.

Standard trees are usually good timber species. Ash and oak were commonly used in dry northern areas, with a wider diversity in the south including beech, lime and horse chestnut as well as ash and oak. However, horse chestnut is an alien species and limes, although native, are relatively scarce, so planting these species is not recommended.

Table F.6.1 lists common hedgerow shrub and standard species, with an indication of the geographical are and soils for which they are appropriate. Field layer species suitable for planting in hedgerows are the woodland edge species listed in Table F.3.3.

Table F.6.1. Common hedgerow shrub and standard species

	Species	South Britain	North Britain	Acid soil	Neutral soil	Calcareous soil
Shrubs	Hawthorn *Crategeus monogyna*	✓	✓	✓	✓	✓
	Blackthorn *Prunus spinosa*	✓	✓	✓	✓	
	Hornbeam *Carpinus betulus*	✓			✓	✓
	Field maple *Acer campestre*	✓			✓	✓
	Crab apple *Malus sylvestris*	✓	✓	✓	✓	
	Hazel *Coryllus avellana*	✓	✓	✓	✓	✓
	Dog rose *Rosa canina*	✓	✓	✓	✓	✓
	Holly *Ilex aquifolium*	✓	✓	✓	✓	
	Privet *Ligustrum vulgare*	✓			✓	✓
	Guelder rose *Viburnum opulus*	✓			✓	✓
	Wayfaring tree *Viburnum lantana*	✓			✓	✓
	Dogwood *Cornus sanguinea*	✓			✓	✓
	Buckthorn *Rhamnus catharticus*	✓				✓
	Spindle *Euonymus europaeus*	✓			✓	✓
Standards	Pedunculate oak *Quercus robur*	✓	✓	✓	✓	
	Sessile oak *Quercus petraea*	✓	✓	✓	✓	
	Ash *Fraxinus excelsior*	✓	✓		✓	✓
	Beech *Fagus sylvatica*	✓		✓	✓	

Photo: David Hill

Species such as spindle add diversity to hedgerows.

6.2.3 Site preparation

The principles of site preparation (soil type, soil handling etc.) are basically the same as for woodland creation (Section F.3.4.1). The only major difference from woodlands is that hedgerow soil is not shaded to the same degree as woodland soil, so the natural suppression of weeds is not as effective. Hedgerow aftercare and management costs will be reduced if nutrient-poor soil is used. If the soil is nutrient-rich, weed control becomes difficult once the field layer species are introduced. Although topsoil will be used in adjacent areas for agricultural restoration, it should be possible to spread nutrient-poor soil along the line of the hedgerow.

It is important that any vegetation present along the line of the hedgerow is removed before the hedge is planted. The quickest method is to spray using a contact systemic herbicide.

6.2.4 Planting methods

Planting methods for tree, shrub and field layer species are given in Section F.3.4.2.

Hedges are usually planted as two staggered rows. Occasionally, usually to save costs, only a single row is planted, although the resultant hedgerow is less wide and dense and consequentially of less benefit to wildlife. For double rows, the rows should be 23 cm apart, and the plants in each row should also be spaced 23 cm apart. For single row hedges, the plants should be spaced 20 cm apart.

The best type and size of plants for hedgerows are bare rooted transplants (i.e. 2 years old, 450-600 mm high). These are cheap, quick to plant and establish well. They should be planted into a strip 600 mm wide and 300 mm deep that has been tilled or dug over to produce a fine tilth.

Hedgerow standards can also be planted as bare-rooted transplants at the same time as the main hedge species. When the hedge is trimmed or laid (see Section F.6.2.6), the standards should obviously be left uncut. Plants intended for standards should be visibly marked in some way so that they are not inadvertently cut.

6.2.5 Aftercare

Aftercare management for hedgerows is essentially the same as for woodlands (Section F.3.4.3), and involves:
- Weed control
- Protecting the plants from grazing and wind

In addition, pruning the top growth of the hedge species in the first year is beneficial. The plants should be cut back to 40 cm high. This encourages additional root growth and the growth of side shoots, and results in a bushy, dense hedgerow with a wide base. Pruning is not necessary if the hedgerow is to be managed by laying (see Section F.6.2.6).

Weed control

Mulches are very effective at controlling weeds; mulch sheeting specifically for hedgerows is sold in 20 m rolls. However, if field layer species are introduced, mulch sheeting must be removed before these species can be planted. It is best to wait at least five years until the hedge has become established and some shade is cast before planting the field layer.

Weed control can be problematic after field layer species have been planted. One method of control is to spray a grass-specific herbicide. Weeds can also be controlled by strimming in late autumn after the field layer herbs have set seed. If weeds are controlled by strimming, cuttings must be removed.

Protection from grazing and wind

Newly planted hedges require protection from grazing. Tree tubes protect trees from rabbits and hares, but fencing will be required if livestock are present. In this case, rabbit fencing can be used, which removes the need for tree tubes. To protect hedges from deer grazing, ensure that there is at least a 0.75 m gap between the fence and the hedge.

Wind rock of newly planted trees can cause many failures on exposed sites. Tree tubes are effective, but a wind-proofing fence parallel to the hedge provides the best protection. Purpose-made fencing materials are sold in rolls.

6.2.6 Hedgerow management

The ideal hedge should be 1.5-2.0 m high and 2.5 m wide at the base, tapering to 1.5 m at the top, with few gaps and scrubby vegetation at the base. A good physical structure can be maintained by management.

Traditional hedgerow management is hedgelaying. This is a skilled task, involving:
- removing thin and straggly growth;
- trimming the remainder of the hedge to about 2 m high;
- cutting most of the way through the stem of the hedge plants just above ground level, leaving a thin hinge;
- laying the stems on top of each other at an angle of 45 degrees or lower; and
- holding the stems in place with vertical wooden stakes and thin poles woven horizontally between the stakes.

Hedgelaying should be carried out about 10 years after planting, and repeated every 12 to 15 years. This is an effective method of maintaining a stockproof barrier, producing a dense hedge that also provides habitat for nesting birds. Full details of hedgelaying methods are given in Brooks (1988).

Currently, the most common method of hedgerow management is cutting every 2-3 years with a tractor-driven flail. The disadvantage of this method is that it tends to produce a 'leggy' hedge with a sparse bottom half. Although the form of the hedge created by flailing is less beneficial for nesting birds than a laid hedge, it can still provide habitat for birds if carried out sensitively.

Hedgelaying and flailing should be carried out in winter, before early April in the south and early May in the north.

Hedgerow standards were traditionally managed by pollarding. Pollarding involves the regular removal of large limbs at a height above the browsing level of stock (c 2.5 m). No more than half the limbs should be removed at any one time. Pollarding is by no means essential; standard trees can simply be left unmanaged.

6.3   Grassy field margins

The field margin is the strip between an arable crop and the field boundary. Under intensive management, fields are sprayed with herbicide to control annual weeds and ploughed right up to the boundary, leaving only a thin strip. This practice reduces the conservation interest of the field margin and potentially of the adjacent hedgerows (if present). The creation of grassy field margins can therefore provide conservation benefits as well as providing a buffer zone preventing the spread of invasive weeds from the hedge into the crop. On a landfill site, grassy field margins created for wildlife benefit can also act as access tracks or sites for above-ground pollution control infrastructure.

Creating a permanent herb-rich grassy field margin provides habitat for beneficial invertebrates such as rove beetles, ground beetles and spiders that feed on crop pests. Field margins are also important for some species of conservation importance such as grey partridge and brown hare. Grey partridges breed in field margins and their chicks depend on invertebrates for food.

Permanent grassy field margins do not benefit arable weeds that require regularly ploughed land. These species benefit from the creation of conservation headlands (see Section F.6.4).

Methods for creating grasslands (Section F.2) can be used for creating grassy field margins. The following points should be considered:
- Both topsoil and subsoil are suitable

substrates for field margins. Topsoil may contain a sufficient seed bank, therefore avoiding the need for seeding.
- If seed is required, a general grassland mix for the appropriate soil pH will be suitable.
- If the strip is not to be used for access, wildflowers intolerant of trampling such as black knapweed (*Centaurea nigra*) and meadow cranesbill (*Geranium pratense*) can be added to the seed mix.
- For low-use tracks, sprawling flowers can be added such as scentless mayweed (*Tripleurospermum inodoratum*) and scarlet pimpernel (*Anagallis arvensis*).
- Alternatively, rough grassland can be created, comprising coarse tussocky grasses. Appropriate grass species include cock's-foot (*Dactylis glomerata*), tall fescue (*Festuca arundinacea*), false oat-grass (*Arrhenatherum elatius*) and tufted hair-grass (*Deschampsia cespitosa*), although the exact selection of species will depend on the soil type.
- On margins used as tracks, a thinly-sown seed mix of non-aggressive species will leave small areas of bare ground, enabling attractive annual or biennial species such as corn poppy (*Papaver rhoeas*) and foxglove (*Digitalis purpurea*) to be included in the seed mix.

Field margins should be managed by light grazing or cutting at least once a year. Cutting should be carried out in late summer to avoid disturbing ground-nesting birds, and cuttings should always be removed. Herbicides and pesticides should not be applied to the field margin.

On arable fields, it is best to leave a 1 m bare strip between the edge of the crop and the grass strip to prevent invasion of the field margin species into the crop. This bare strip should be ploughed annually at the same time as the rest of the field. It can also be sprayed with herbicide in March if necessary, but this should generally not be required. If herbicide is applied, a shield should be used to ensure that the spray does not drift into the field margin.

6.4   Conservation headlands

A conservation headland is a strip usually 6 m wide that is not treated with herbicide or fertiliser between the crop edge and the first tramline on an arable field. Although technically a field margin, the management of conservation headlands

differs from grassy field margins in that headlands are regularly ploughed. They should therefore not be created above pollution control infrastructure, but they can be used as access tracks.

Conservation headlands were originally developed to improve the breeding success of grey partridge. Partridge chicks are primarily insectivorous in their first two weeks of life and depend upon insects found on broadleaved weeds. The ideal location of a headland is adjacent to a hedge or area of scrub that provides cover for birds close to their feeding areas.

Conservation headlands also provide habitat for arable weeds. Many arable weeds are now rare; cereal field margins are now a UK BAP Priority Habitat. It is not appropriate to sow rare arable weeds, but species such as corn poppy can be sown, creating an attractive show of colour. Butterflies are encouraged by the presence of larval food plants and nectar-producing flowers. For example, garlic mustard (*Alliaria petiolata*), the larval food plant of the orange tip butterfly, is often found in field edges. Seeds produced by headland vegetation provide food for seed-eating birds such as linnet, tree sparrow and goldfinch. Headlands may also be used as nesting areas by farmland bird species such as skylark.

Conservation headlands are ploughed and seeded with the same crop as the rest of the field. The headland is then treated with a selective herbicide that favours broadleaved herbs at the expense of grasses. It is important not to turn the furrows into the grassland strip at the edge of the field as this creates bare ground which is ideal habitat for several notifiable arable weeds such as black grass (*Alopecurus myosuroides*) that can be very invasive and difficult to eradicate.

6.5   Beetle banks

A beetle bank is an earth ridge usually created by two ploughlines extending from one end of an arable field to the other. They can also be created by tipping a raised mound of additional soil in a long strip. Beetle banks are permanent structures and are therefore an ideal location for pollution control monitoring structures.

The bank is sown with tussock-forming grasses, providing habitat for many invertebrates as well as small mammals. The primary reason for creating beetle banks is to boost populations of many types of insects including species such as rove and ground beetles that predate crop pests. This reduces the severity of crop pest attacks and the subsequent need for pesticides.

Beetle banks should be 0.4 m high and 1.5 m wide. Sufficient space should be left at the end of the beetle banks next to the field boundary to permit the passage of a tractor (e.g. 25 m). The banks are sown with a 50:50 mixture of cocksfoot (*Dactylis glomerata*) and yorkshire fog (*Holcus lanatus*) at a rate of 8 g per m^2 by drilling or hand broadcasting. Sowing should take place in either autumn or spring. If sown in spring, a broad-spectrum non-residual herbicide should be used first to kill any invading weeds. A herbicide shield should be used when spraying the crop to avoid spraying onto the beetle banks and killing the grass.

The seed heads of the grasses on the beetle bank should be mechanically cut and removed to prevent them from seeding into the field. Further information can be obtained from Andrews & Rebane (1994).

Even the width of a tramline can make a significant contribution to the conservation of arable weeds such as common poppy.

Photo: David Hill

APPENDIX 1

Assessment of the effectiveness of a range of bird control techniques in trials at three operational landfill sites in the West Midlands

1 Introduction

Few objective studies have been reported which compare the effectiveness of various techniques used to control large concentrations of birds at operational landfill sites in the UK. For this reason, Ecoscope Applied Ecologists supervised some simple trials of a range of bird control techniques and monitored the effects on bird numbers and behaviour at three sites in the Midlands region over the winter of 1998/99. The results have been used to assist in the formulation of best practice guidelines described in Section C.2.

2 Scope & objectives of study

The study aimed to observe the general effect on bird numbers and behaviour following the introduction of specific examples of a range of bird control techniques, with a view to assessing the potential effectiveness of different types of method at a range of sites.

Examples of the following methods were tested at two sites. Bird numbers and behaviour were monitored at both these sites plus a third 'control' site where the effects of natural factors could be identified. Methods tested were:
1. Noise stimuli
2. Birdscarer kites
3. Recorded distress calls
4. Birds of prey

It was not possible to test the complete range of variations of each technique during the course of this study, but although it is acknowledged that differences in the effectiveness of such variations can be substantial, the principles behind each method are very similar. It was therefore considered that effects on bird numbers, and particularly bird behaviour, would be generally comparable, enabling a broad assessment of the effectiveness of each method to be made at a range of sites.

3 Methodology

Each method was operated for a two-week period at each trial site with the exception of falconry which, due to resource constraints, was operated at one site for a one-week period only. In general, specialist bird controllers were not employed to carry out the trials; with the exception of falconry, it was the responsibility of site staff to operate the control methods.

Trial sites and the control site selected for participation in the study met the following criteria:
- they received a substantial amount of domestic / household waste;
- no bird control was being operated prior to the trials;
- their operational licence did not require continuous bird control (allowing scope to stop and start different methods as required); and
- they were located close enough to one another that similar external factors (e.g. climate, distance from coast) acted upon bird numbers, but were far enough apart so that numbers at one site would not be affected by the imposition of bird control at another.

Trial sites and the control site chosen were as follows:
1. Wilnecote Landfill Site, Staffordshire (control site)
2. Ufton Landfill Site, Warwickshire
3. Waresley Landfill Site, Worcestershire

All three sites are operated by Biffa Waste Services Ltd.

3.1 Bird monitoring

Bird monitoring visits were made to each site twice weekly from November 30th 1998 until April 1st 1999. At all sites, gulls and corvids frequently used the surrounding area for loafing (gulls) and daytime feeding (corvids). All birds present on site and within the immediately adjacent area were counted on each visit. Due to access and time constraints, the area surveyed at each site was defined as all fields and quarry areas that could be viewed from the site. Investigations revealed that very few gulls were ever present beyond this area at any of the study sites although this was not the case with corvids (see results).

Species monitored were restricted to gulls and corvids (rook, carrion crow and jackdaw) for the following reasons:
- Large birds create a much greater air strike risk and have a much higher impact on visual amenity than small passerines.
- Gulls are the only species group with the potential to spread pathogens.
- Gulls and corvids have a much greater potential for impacting upon sensitive habitats than smaller birds.
- There were logistical difficulties in counting small birds accurately in the short time available.

Counts effectively represented a 'snapshot' of bird numbers using the site at any one time, as flocks of both gulls and corvids were prone to constant movements, both to and from sites and within sites. Accurate counts were made when possible, although block counts (typically in tens) were made when numbers were high. In addition to the counts, the location and behaviour of birds were recorded on each visit, and weather data were also recorded.

All monitoring visits took place during the time at which gull numbers were highest, this being at least one hour after the first domestic waste delivery of the day and at least one hour before dusk.

3.2 Bird control

Each trial, with the exception of falconry, was carried out for two weeks. A minimum of two weeks without bird control before and after each trial was monitored, to enable the comparison of bird numbers and behaviour before, during and after the operation of control methods. Staff carrying out bird control were unaware of when bird monitoring visits would take place.

3.2.1 Noise stimulus methods

Rope bangers were operated at both trial sites for two weeks in December. At Ufton, due to staff errors, operation continued for several days beyond the two-week period. At each site two ropes were used per day, one in the morning, one in the afternoon. Rope bangers were chosen for the trial as they require low operating effort – each rope lasts approximately five hours once lit. Other methods such as blanks cartridges and rockets require more staff time, which was not available at either of the trial sites.

3.2.2 Birdscarer Kites

Two weeks in January were set aside for trials using a Helikite at both trial sites. However, wet and windy weather throughout this period meant that the kite could only be put up on certain days (see results). There was therefore little opportunity to collect any meaningful data on bird numbers during periods of kite use.

3.2.3 Recorded distress calls

A handheld Scarecrow Patrol bio-acoustic system (supplied by Airfield UK Ltd.) was operated for two-week periods at each trial site in February and March. The equipment contains a digital chip holding the distress calls of eight species including herring gull, black-headed gull, common gull and rook. At each site the system was generally operated from within the compactor or other vehicles on the operational face.

Operating instructions for this system are quite specific and observations made during bird monitoring indicated that the system was not always used in the manner recommended by the manufacturer, particularly at Ufton. This is perhaps understandable, especially during the first few days of operation, as staff seemed to become quickly disillusioned when immediate effects were not apparent. Results may therefore show the method to be less effective than it would have been if it been used more intensively.

It should also be noted that the chip used did not contain lesser black-backed gull calls (although such chips are available), despite this being the commonest large gull species at all the sites. The supplier advised that herring gull calls work just as well on lesser black-backs, so results are not thought to have been greatly affected.

3.2.4 Falconry

A one-week trial using birds of prey was carried out at Ufton in February. As mentioned previously, further trials were not possible due to budget constraints. Birds and operator were supplied by NBC (Environmental Services) Ltd. Three birds were used each day (one saker/peregrine hybrid and two lanner/peregrine hybrids) in the standard manner used by the contractor at other sites.

Table 1: Percentage species composition of gulls at each site over the course of the monitoring visits

Species	% species composition at each site		
	Wilnecote	Ufton	Waresley
Black-headed gull	66	64	28
Common gull	<1	1	<1
Lesser black-backed gull	24	23	68
Herring gull	9	11	3
Great black-backed gull	<1	<1	<1

4 Results

4.1 Gulls

Figures 1-3 show total numbers of gulls (all species) recorded at Wilnecote, Ufton and Waresley Landfill Sites respectively on each monitoring visit. Table 1 shows the proportion of the total number made up by each individual species, over the course of the whole study.

4.1.1 General observations and their implications for interpretation of results

At all sites wide fluctuations in numbers occurred between visits that cannot be related to the presence of bird control. Certain fluctuations are constant between sites; for example, low numbers were recorded at all sites on December 30th and January 19th. On both these days, winds were blowing at Force 6 or above. Strong winds, leading to blowing litter, are known to deter gulls from visiting landfill sites. Numbers also varied depending on the time of visit or day of the week. Other fluctuations are more site-specific; for example, relatively low numbers at Ufton throughout January may have been due to the nearby presence of several flooded fields, which provided alternative feeding and bathing grounds. The occurrence of such fluctuations over the short time period of this study has major implications for the assessment of the effect of each bird control trial on gull numbers.

Species composition, whilst similar at Wilnecote and Ufton, is markedly different at Waresley where the most numerous gull species is lesser black-backed rather than black-headed. This may have implications for the apparent success of different control methods as certain species are likely to be more susceptible than others to scaring by the use of different methods.

Figure 1 indicates a gradual reduction in gull numbers from late February onwards at the control site. This is a result of wintering gulls, the vast majority of which were adults, departing for breeding areas. At Ufton and Waresley, which are

further south and west than Wilnecote, this decline in numbers began earlier, and consequently there are implications for trials taking place late in the monitoring period when declines in numbers may be due to primarily natural factors rather than to control techniques.

The following sections describe the effects of bird control on bird numbers and behaviour observed during the monitoring visits. Changes in the mean gull numbers before, during and after each trial are shown in Tables 2-4. It should be noted that while the use of mean numbers illustrates the scale of any reduction in gull numbers it can obscure changes in gull numbers that took place during the period of each trial. For this reason Figures 2-3 should also be read in conjunction with these results.

4.1.2 Noise Stimuli Trials

Table 2 shows that at both trial sites the mean number of gulls (all species) present during the period when rope bangers were operating was significantly lower than during the period before and after the trial, when no bird control was operating. However, even during the period of operation the mean number of gulls present at both sites was still substantial.

Figures 2 & 3 show that at Ufton, during the first week of the trial, total gull numbers remained close to the 2000 mark, before falling to around the 1000 mark during the second and third weeks. Numbers then rose again to around the 2000 mark following the cessation of the control operation. However, at Waresley a different pattern was evident with numbers reduced to around 250 on the first day of the trial, gradually increasing during the first week to a peak of over 2000 early in the second week.

Observations on the location and behaviour of gulls during the trial indicated the following:

Ufton – During the first week, gulls were never observed feeding on exposed waste

Table 2. Mean gull numbers before, during and after operation of noise stimulus methods

	Mean number of gulls:			Significance of reduction during period of bird control
	preceding two weeks	noise stimuli in use	following two weeks*	
Ufton	3638	1369	1929	t test: p < 0.05
Waresley	2353	1132	1891	t test: p < 0.05

* N.B. figure relates to the mean over the following week at Ufton due to staff error in continuing use beyond finish date

but were generally found loafing on the far side of the site from the bangers. They also seemed more wary than usual, being easily startled by the visiting ornithologist with many leaving the site. Early in the second week, gulls were noted around the operational area again. Later in the week gulls were again restricted to the far side of the site and became increasingly wary. Reasons for this apparent habituation before a return to more wary behaviour are not clear.

Waresley – No birds were recorded around the operational area throughout the first week. Birds were seen only in the air or loafing in fields some 500 m from the site. However, by the start of the second week, large numbers of gulls had returned to the operational area and although put to flight by a banger going off, most resettled within two minutes. By the end of the second week, habituation to the bangers was such that gulls began to resettle within 30 seconds of being startled by a banger going off.

4.1.3 Birdscarer Kites

Trials using a Helikite were very much inhibited by poor weather during the trial period. At the two trial sites use of the Helikite was restricted as follows:

Ufton
Week 1 – up all day on day one, not used subsequently despite attempts to raise it as wind too strong.
Week 2 – not used all week due at first to strong winds followed by dense fog.

Unfortunately, bird monitoring visits were all carried out on days when it was not possible to use the Helikite. A direct assessment of its effectiveness could not therefore be made at this site.

Waresley
Week 1 – up for two full days and three half days during the week. Periods of non-use were due to strong winds and/or heavy rain.
Week 2 – up for half a day on day 1, thereafter not used, due first to strong winds and then to dense fog.
One bird monitoring visit was carried out whilst the Helikite was in use.

Clearly, quantitative data on the effect of the Helikite on bird numbers could not be obtained, due to the constraints upon its use. Note however that such weather conditions are fairly typical of a British winter and that the inability to use the kite in poor weather is a useful observation in itself.

Observations on gull behaviour at Waresley made during the one pertinent monitoring visit and supplemented by observations by site staff suggested that the presence of the Helikite initially deterred gulls from feeding, and consequently very few were seen around the site. However, on the first full day of operation a number of gulls returned to the site and were feeding on exposed waste within four hours of the Helikite being put up. Numbers subsequently increased and although the immediate area around the kite was avoided, habituation clearly took place within a very short time.

4.1.4 Recorded distress calls

Table 3 shows that at both sites the mean number of gulls was substantially lower during the period of operation, although at neither site was the reduction statistically significant.

Problems exist for both sites when interpreting data on gull numbers. The manufacturers concede that the method can take a few days to clear gulls from a site; such a pattern is evident in Figures 2 and 3, which show initially high numbers steadily falling over the period of use. However, at both sites numbers remained low or even continued to fall following cessation of operation, most likely as a result of birds departing for breeding areas. Therefore, the extent of the effect of recorded distress calls on gull numbers is not clear. Observations of gull behaviour in response to the playing of distress calls are therefore likely to be more useful in assessing the effectiveness of this method. These are summarised for each site below:

Ufton
During the first few days, gull numbers and behaviour appeared to be unaffected. The site manager commented that using distress calls on the operational area did shift the gulls, but only to loafing areas on the far side of the site or onto adjacent fields. These birds subsequently returned to the operational area within two hours. During the second week, numbers were much reduced (although see above), but gulls present continued to behave in a similar manner. Use of distress calls did

Table 3. Mean gull numbers before, during and after operation of distress calls

	Mean number of gulls:			Significance of reduction during period of bird control
	preceding two weeks	distress calls in use	following two weeks	
Ufton	2451	1333	51	t-test not significant at p < 0.05
Waresley	412	136	83	t-test not significant at p < 0.05

Table 4. Mean gull numbers before, during and after operation of falconry

	Mean number of gulls:			Significance of reduction during period of bird control
	preceding two weeks	falconry in use	following two weeks	
Ufton	2723	318	2553	t-test: p < 0.01

not at any time result in the gulls leaving the area en masse.

The value of these observations is constrained by the probable failure of site staff to use the equipment exactly as outlined in the manufacturer's instructions. Note however that such failure is likely to represent the situation at a large number of landfill sites where recorded distress calls equipment is used. It is therefore an important observation in itself, highlighting the need for staff to be properly trained and correct operation of equipment to be closely monitored.

Waresley
Gulls were cleared from the site by the first use of the equipment. Their departure was slow, spending a few minutes circling over the site before dispersing some distance (out of sight). This reaction is similar to that described in the literature (e.g. CAA, 1998). For the first few days, gulls continued to return to the site every 2-3 hours before being dispersed in a similar manner. Very few gulls were seen in the vicinity of the site for the next few days although by the end of the second week small numbers of gulls were observed loafing adjacent to the site, indicating a possible habituation effect. It should be noted that gull numbers immediately prior to the trial were considerably lower than those earlier in the winter.

4.1.5 Falconry
Table 4 shows that the mean number of gulls present at or around the site was significantly lower during the period when birds of prey were used to control bird numbers than during the period before operation (t-test; p < 0.01). It is also noteworthy that numbers quickly returned to previous levels upon cessation of the trial. Figure 2 shows further that gull numbers reduced substantially during the period of the trial. Monitoring visits were carried out on days 2 and 4 of the five-day trial, with a peak count of gulls of 550 on day 2 of falcons being used, falling to 85 on day 4.

Observations on gull behaviour made during the monitoring visits are as follows:

On the second day of falconry operation flocks of gulls repeatedly flew over the site, attempting to land on usual loafing areas on several occasions and once attempting to feed on exposed waste. On each occasion gulls were quickly dispersed by the use of a falcon.

By the fourth day gulls were rarely seen in the air over the site and never attempted to land either on or near to the site throughout a two hour visit.

This behaviour and the figures above are supported by the contractor's report for the trial period, which noted large numbers of gulls (c 3000) present at the start of the week. Numbers and activity were reduced steadily throughout the week until by the last day no gulls were present on site with very few prospecting over the site. Despite quite strong winds (Force 4-5) on the first two days, the weather had little effect on bird control operation throughout the trial.

4.2   Corvids
Figures 4-6 show total numbers of corvids (all species) recorded at the three sites on each monitoring visit. Table 5 (below) shows the proportion of the total numbers made up by each species, over the course of the whole study.

4.2.1 General observations and their implications for interpretation of results
The pattern of use of landfills by corvids has important implications for bird control. Unlike gulls, corvids can obtain food from covered waste and are therefore not dependent on exposed

waste present only during site operation. They therefore often feed on sites outside operational hours when there is less disturbance. Furthermore, when they do use sites during the day they may use areas some distance from the operational cell where major gull concentrations are based. Nevertheless, the landfill is still an obvious attractant, with large numbers of corvids consistently present in the area surrounding each site. Implications for the results are twofold:

1. During operational hours corvids were frequently recorded in surrounding fields and parts of the site away from the operational cell. Hence, most bird control methods, which were predominantly used close to the operational area during operational hours only, had little effect on corvid numbers during the day and no effect on corvids using the site outside operational hours.

2. The high mobility of corvids and the variation in food sources surrounding each site led to large fluctuations in numbers recorded. Birds that were within the study area on one visit could easily be feeding outside the study area on the next. Such fluctuations over the short time period of this study effectively mask any changes in corvid numbers that may have occurred as a result of bird control methods in use.

Trends in corvid numbers at the control site appear to indicate numbers rising steadily to a peak in mid-January, and then declining until the end of the monitoring period, as birds departed for breeding areas. This trend has obvious implications on assessment of changes in numbers resulting from bird control, particularly during the latter stages of the period,

Table 5. Percentage species composition of corvids at each site over the course of the monitoring visits

Species	% species composition at each site		
	Wilnecote	Ufton	Waresley
Jackdaw	18	47	56
Rook	41	21	32
Carrion crow	41	32	12

Table 6. Mean corvid numbers before, during and after noise stimulus use

	Mean number of corvids:			Significance of reduction in corvid numbers during period of bird control
	preceding two weeks	noise stimuli in use	following two weeks*	
Ufton	130	350	53	N/a
Waresley	184	400	343	N/a

* N.B. figure relates to the mean over the following week at Ufton due to staff error in continuing use beyond finish date

although the trend was less apparent at the two trial sites. It is not clear from the results how differences in species composition between sites might affect bird control, although they do highlight the site-specific nature of bird populations at landfills.

The following paragraphs describe the effects of bird control on bird numbers and behaviour observed during the monitoring visits. Changes in mean corvid numbers before, during and after each trial are shown in Tables 6-8. The limitations of using mean numbers described for gulls also apply for corvids.

4.2.2 Noise stimulus methods
Table 6 shows that at both sites numbers of corvids (all species) were actually higher during the period of noise stimulus use. The increase is not thought to be a direct result of bird control, but may reflect the large variations in corvid numbers inherent in this study method, as shown by Figures 4-6.

It is clear from the above that corvid numbers in the immediate area of the two landfills were not reduced in any way by the use of noise stimuli. Observations on bird behaviour during the trials indicated very little change from that observed during the weeks preceding and following the trial, with birds predominantly feeding in surrounding fields and small flocks occasionally feeding on site even when rope bangers were in use.

4.2.3 Birdscarer kites
The limitations of this trial are similar to those described for gulls. Observations

during the one pertinent monitoring visit at Waresley showed crow numbers in surrounding fields to be unaffected by the presence of the Helikite, although no assessment of the kite's ability to keep corvids from feeding on site could be made.

4.2.4 Recorded distress calls
Table 7 shows that although crow numbers on and around both sites were lower during the period whilst recorded distress calls were in use, the reductions were not significant. Indeed, numbers fell further during the period following cessation of bird control, suggesting a natural decline in numbers due to departure for breeding areas.

Corvids were almost certainly unaffected by the use of recorded distress calls, despite the use of a rook distress call chip. The normal behaviour of corvids at the two sites involved most birds feeding in surrounding fields during the day. This behaviour meant that the operator of the distress calls equipment rarely came into contact with corvids from his position in the operational area. Corvids feeding on site outside operational hours were presumably also unaffected as the equipment was not in use.

4.2.5 Birds of prey
Table 8 shows that the mean number of corvids was actually higher during the period of birds of prey use than in the previous week. However, this increase is not thought to be directly related to the presence of birds of prey.

Observations on crow behaviour are important. On the first visit, corvids appeared to show no fear of the falcons, clearly unfamiliar with avian predators capable of catching them. This resulted in several birds being caught and killed over the first three days. However, on the second visit corvids appeared much more wary of the birds of prey and none were seen on or immediately adjacent to the site. These observations support the contractor's report, which reported that no corvids were seen on the last day of the trial. It must also be stressed that the contractor is confident that crow numbers in the surrounding area could be further reduced during a longer trial, although corvids would still not be prevented from using the site outside operational hours.

5 Discussion
The implications of the results for the use of each method at a range of sites are discussed below:

5.1 Noise stimuli
The results show that gull numbers can be significantly reduced by the operation of noise stimuli, at least in the short term. However, habituation can occur within a week, as illustrated at Waresley. For more intensive methods such as rockets or cartridges, used only when required, there is less scope for habituation although it is likely to take place over the long term.

The tendency of birds to remain wary as a result of noise stimuli use renders them more easily dispersed by other

Table 7. Mean corvid numbers before, during and after operation of distress calls

	Mean number of corvids:			Significance of reduction in corvid numbers during period of bird control
	preceding two weeks	distress calls in use	following two weeks	
Ufton	166	120	106	t-test not significant at p < 0.05
Waresley	304	139	135	t-test not significant at p < 0.05

Table 8. Mean corvid numbers before, during and after use of falconry				
	Mean number of corvids:			Significance of reduction in corvid numbers during period of bird control
	preceding two weeks	falconry in use	following two weeks	
Ufton	166	210	256	n/a

methods, as illustrated at Ufton when gulls dispersed simply as a result of the ornithologist's presence. Noise stimuli used in combination with other methods may therefore be very effective.

The above notwithstanding, rope bangers, even prior to habituation were unable to clear the large numbers of gulls present at both trial sites from the area surrounding each site. It is therefore likely that for all types of noise stimuli, although the operational landfill itself may be kept clear, the area around the site will not. This has important implications for many sites.

The use of noise stimuli would appear to have little effect on corvids, which often tend to feed in surrounding areas during the day, moving onto sites outside operational hours. Moreover, where corvids do feed on site during the day, habituation to noise stimuli is likely, as with gulls.

5.2   Birdscarer kites
Use of a Helikite is clearly very dependent upon the weather. On this basis alone, a Helikite cannot be expected to provide a consistent method of bird control. Use of a more traditional kite, may be possible on days when weather conditions preclude the use of a Helikite, and such a combination of the two may attain fuller coverage.

From the limited observations made during the course of this study it is clear that gulls can become habituated to kites very quickly. No firm conclusions about the effect of kites on corvids can be taken from the results, although clearly the day-time use of surrounding fields is unaffected, as is use of sites outside of operational hours if kites are taken down at the end of the day. Whilst the exact length of time for birds to become habituated to kites will vary between sites, they are clearly only useful as a short term bird control measure. As such they may be most useful when operated in conjunction with other bird control methods, or to keep birds away for short periods whilst the use of other methods is not possible.

5.3   Recorded distress calls
The fact that at both sites, trials took place during the time when gulls (and corvids)

were beginning to depart for breeding sites makes any direct link between use of distress calls and a reduction in gull numbers impossible to prove. For this reason few definite conclusions can be drawn from this study.

From behavioural observations it would appear that the method can be very successful at sites with relatively small numbers of gulls, such as Waresley. At sites with much higher gull numbers it is likely to be less effective, although had the method been used in accordance with the manufacturer's instructions at Ufton, better results may have been obtained. It should be considered however that use at the intensity required to have a positive effect will be difficult at many sites where bird control is the responsibility of staff for whom other tasks assume a higher priority.

The use of distress calls from a point in the operational area (such as a compactor) minimises their effectiveness against corvids, which do not require exposed waste on which to feed. No conclusion can be drawn from our results as to whether an area can be cleared of corvids using distress calls, although even if it were possible it would require the use of specialist vehicles and staff, thus greatly increasing costs and manpower. Corvids would also still be able to feed on site outside operational hours.

5.4   Falconry
The intensive use of falconry was without doubt the most effective method used during the study. By the end of the five-day trial the site was clear of gulls, with the only birds seen being restricted to small flocks flying over at irregular intervals. Habituation to this method is unlikely to occur as it provides a direct threat to the birds. Once a site is clear it should therefore be possible to virtually eliminate gulls from a site through continued operation. It is clear from subsequent monitoring visits that gulls' return to the site was almost immediate following the removal of the falcons. Therefore bird control using birds of prey must be continuous to consistently keep a site clear of gulls.

The effect of the method on corvids was less clear cut during the very short trial

period. However, it is likely that corvids can be kept away from sites and their immediate surroundings by the use of birds of prey, once they become aware of the threat posed by unfamiliar predator species. However, it is possible that corvids will continue to use sites during periods when bird control is not operating.

One concern over the effectiveness of falconry as a bird control method is their perceived inability to fly during wet and windy weather. Fortunately, during this trial the weather posed no constraint on successful operation, with no prolonged periods of rain and winds no greater than Force 4-5 throughout the week. The contractors acknowledge that severe weather does prevent the falcons from flying and therefore successful bird control using birds of prey will require supporting methods, such as noise stimuli or distress calls to be used at times when flying falcons is not possible. Note also that numbers of gulls on landfill sites are known to be reduced during severe weather, particularly during strong winds, and therefore impacts from not being able to operate birds of prey are likely to be reduced.

6 Summary and conclusions
At all three sites in this study:
- Gulls were the major species group of concern as they can be present in very large numbers (counts greater than 3000 were recorded at all sites).
- Corvids were present in relatively high numbers at times (up to 700 at all sites) but require different methods of control due to differences in ecology and behaviour.
- Large variations in bird numbers, species composition and behaviour are apparent even between the geographically similar sites studied here. Such site-specific differences may have important implications for the effectiveness of different types of bird control over a range of sites.

The results of this study are not intended to provide definitive guidelines on the effectiveness of every method used to control numbers of birds at landfill sites in the UK. The following difficulties in achieving such an objective were encountered, principally due to a shortage of time and resources:

- Variations of each method could not be tested, e.g. different types of noise stimuli.
- Combinations of different methods were not tested.
- Control method trials were too short for habituation effects to be fully tested.
- The operation of control methods was not a priority for site staff: some methods may not have been used to their full potential.
- In many cases too little monitoring data were collected to rule out effects of natural factors upon bird numbers.

However, the study results do provide a good indication of the effectiveness of different bird control methods in reducing numbers of problem species at a range of landfill sites. Conclusions relating to a range of methods are as follows:

- **Noise stimuli** – these methods can significantly reduce numbers of gulls at landfill sites. However, they do not appear to be able to clear birds completely from the surrounding area and also suffer from habituation effects.
- **Kites** – these can keep sites clear for a short time, but habituation occurs very quickly. Certain types of kite can only be used in certain weather conditions.
- **Recorded distress calls** – These appear to be able to clear birds from a site, when used properly, at least where concentrations of gulls are relatively small. The potential problems of habituation are not clear however. Their effectiveness when used on large, highly persistent flocks is also unclear and further research is required before more definite conclusions can be made.
- **Falconry** – The use of certain falcon species can be very successful in significantly reducing bird numbers not only on site but in the surrounding area, probably to the point of virtual elimination. There are no habituation problems although action needs to be continuous to keep birds away.

There are disadvantages to each method. This suggests that a combination of methods is required in order to achieve consistent results.

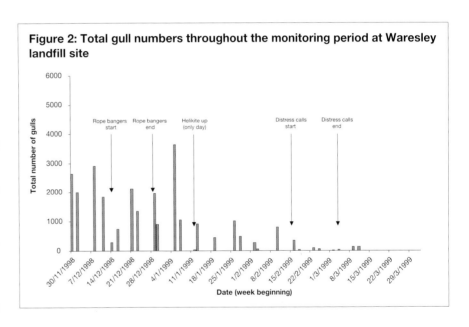

Figure 1: Total gull numbers throughout the monitoring period at Wilnecote landfill site (control site)

Figure 2: Total gull numbers throughout the monitoring period at Waresley landfill site

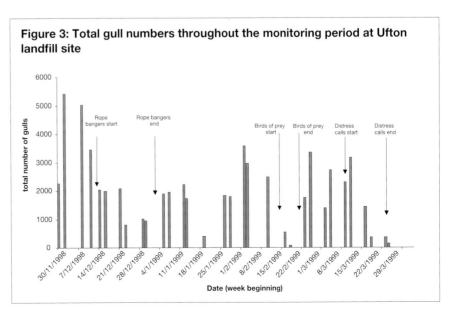

Figure 3: Total gull numbers throughout the monitoring period at Ufton landfill site

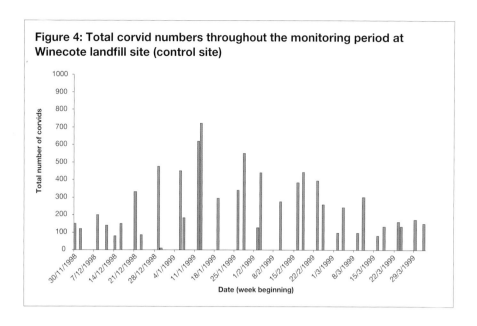

Figure 4: Total corvid numbers throughout the monitoring period at Winecote landfill site (control site)

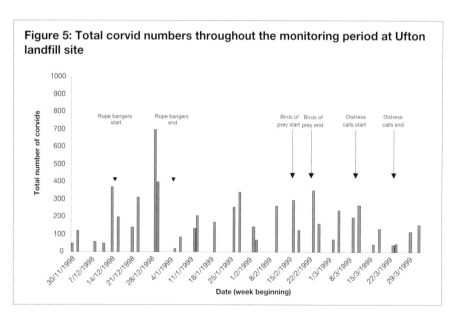

Figure 5: Total corvid numbers throughout the monitoring period at Ufton landfill site

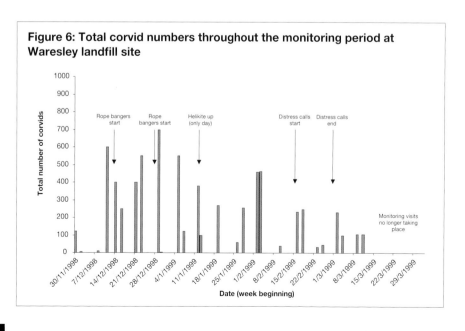

Figure 6: Total corvid numbers throughout the monitoring period at Waresley landfill site

APPENDIX 2

Useful Contacts

British Standards Institute
Customer Services, 389 Chiswick High Road, London W4 4AL.
Tel: 0208 996 9001
www.bsi.org.uk
Produces British, European and international standards.

British Trust for Conservation Volunteers
36 St Mary's Street, Wallingford, Oxfordshire OX10 0EU.
Tel: 01491 839766
www.btcv.org
The largest organisation in the United Kingdom promoting practical conservation work by volunteers. BTCV also produces handbooks on practical management techniques.

Countryside Agency
Dacre House, 19 Dacre Street, London SW1H 0DH.
Tel: 020 7340 2900
www.countryside.gov.uk
Statutory body working to conserve and enhance the countryside. Statutory consultee on all waste plannng applications.

Countryside Council for Wales (CCW)
Plas Penrhos, Fford Penrhos, Bangor, Gwynedd LL57 2LQ.
Tel: 01248 385500
www.ccw.gov.uk
Statutory body responsible for Wales' biodiversity and natural features. Statutory consultee on all waste planning applications. Regional offices also exist.

Department of the Environment, Transport and the Regions (DETR)
Eland House, Bressenden Place, London SW1E 5DU.
Tel: 020 7890 3333
www.detr.gov.uk
Issue licences for great crested newt and other Annex II species translocations. Details of countryside legislation available on web page.

English Nature (EN)
Northminster House, Peterborough PE1 1UA.
Tel: 01733 455000
www.english-nature.org.uk
Statutory body responsible for England's biodiversity and natural features. Statutory consultee on all waste planning applications. Regional offices also exist.

Environment Agency (EA)
Rivers House, Waterside Drive, Aztec West, Almondsbury, Bristol BS12 4UD.
Tel: 01454 624400
www.environment-agency.gov.uk
Has a range of functions relating to regulation, management and monitoring of the environment in England and Wales. The EA is consulted on waste planning applications and is responsible for issuing licences to deposit controlled waste.

Environmental Services Association
154 Buckingham Palace Road, London, SW1W 9TR.
Tel: 020 7824 8882
www.esauk.org
Trade association representing companies providing waste management and environmental services.

Farming and Rural Conservation Agency (FRCA)
Nobel House, 17 Smith Square, London SW1P 3JR.
Tel: 0171 238 5342
www.maff.gov.uk/aboutmaf/agency/frca/frca.htm
MAFF agency. Assists government in design, development and implementation of policies on the integration of farming and conservation, environmental protection and rural economy.

Farming and Wildlife Advisory Group (FWAG)
National Agricultural Centre, Stoneleigh, Kenilworth, Warwickshire CV8 2RX.
Tel: 01203 696699
www.fwag.org.uk
Organisation providing conservation advice to farmers.

Flora Locale
www.naturebureau.co.uk/pages/floraloc/floraloc.htm
Email: floralink@naturebureau.co.uk
A non-profit organisation created to promote best practice in the sourcing and use of native plants for all types of large-scale projects, from the restoration of damaged nature reserves to the creation of natural woodlands and new wild plant communities on industrial waste tips and intensively farmed land.

Forestry Commission
231 Corstophine Road, Edinburgh EH12 7AT.
Tel: 0131 334 0303
www.forestry.gov.uk
Provides details of Woodland Grant Scheme and Certificates of Authenticity to producers of forestry seeds, plants and cuttings. Produces publications giving advice on tree establishment, selection and planting.

Institute of Wastes Management
9 Saxon Court, St Peter's Gardens, Northampton, NN1 1SX.
Tel: 01604 620426
www.iwm.co.uk
Professional body representing predominantly UK-based waste management professionals.

Joint Nature Conservation Committee (JNCC)
Monkstone House, City Road, Peterborough PE1 1JY.
Tel: 01733 562626
www.jncc.gov.uk
UKBAP Action Plans and lists of protected species under various pieces of legislation can be downloaded from the website.

Royal Society for the Protection of Birds (RSPB)
The Lodge, Sandy, Bedfordshire SG19 2DL.
Tel: 01767 680551
www.rspb.org.uk
Europe's largest wildlife conservation charity. They publish a variety of books and reports on habitat management for birds and other species. Regional offices also exist.

Scottish Environment Protection Agency (SEPA)
Erskine Court, Castle Business Park, Stirling FK9 4TR.
Tel: 01786 446885
www.sepa.org.uk
Has a range of functions relating to regulation, management and monitoring of the environment in Scotland. SEPA is consulted on waste planning applications and is responsible for issuing licences to deposit controlled waste.

Scottish Natural Heritage (SNH)
12 Hope Terrace, Edinburgh EH9 2AS.
Tel: 0131 446 2277
www.snh.org.uk
Statutory body responsible for Scotland's biodiversity and natural features. Statutory consultee on all waste planning applications. Regional offices also exist.

Soil Survey and Land Research Centre
Cranfield University, Silsoe Campus, Silsoe, Bedfordshire MK45 4DT.
Tel: 01525 863000
www.cranfield.ac.uk/sslrc/
Publishes a number of soil maps and other publications. Also offers a range of other soil-related surveys, including site survey and laboratory analysis.

The Wildlife Trusts
The Kiln, Waterside, Mather Road, Newark, Notts NG24 1WT.
Tel: 01636 677711
www.wildlifetrust.org.uk
The Trusts exist to promote the protection of wildlife across the UK. Numerous county offices exist – contact the head office for details.

APPENDIX 3

Months in which ripe seed is available from wild populations of 112 grassland species in central England

May

Taraxacum officinale

June

Taraxacum officinale

July

Anthriscus sylvestris
Arrhenatherum elatius
Briza media
Bromus erectus
B. racemosus
Carex flacca
C. hirta
Cynosurus cristatus
Dactylis glomerata
Deschampsia cespitosa
D. flexuosa
Euphrasia nemorosa
Festuca arundinacea
Fritillaria meleagris
Helianthemum nummularium
Hieracium pilosella
Holcus lanatus
Hordeum secalinum
Hypochaeris radicata
Leontodon hispidus
Leucanthemum vulgare
Luzula campestris
Lychnis flos-cuculi
Medicago lupulina
Plantago lanceolata
Polygala calcarea
Ranunculus bulbosus
Rhinanthus minor
Rumex acetosa
Sanguisorba officinalis
Senecio integrifolius
Taraxacum officinale
Tragopogon pratensis
Trisetum flavescens
Viola hirta

August

Agrostis stolonifera
Alopecuris pratensis
Anthyllis vulneria
Avenula pratensis
Briza media
Bromus erectus
Carex flacca
C. hirta
C. spicata
Centaurea nigra
C. scabiosa
Centaurium erythraea
Cerastium fontanium
Cirsium acaule
Conopodium majus
Crepis capillaris
Dactylis glomerata
Danthonia decumbens
Filipendula vulgaris
Gentianella amarella
Geranium dissectum
G. pratense
Helianthemum nummularium
Heracleum sphondylium
Hordeum secalinium
Holcus lanatus
Knautia arvensis
Koeleria macrantha
Lathyrus pratensis
Leontodon hispidus
Leucanthemum vulgare
Lotus corniculatus
Luzula campestris
Lychnis flos-cuculi
Medicago lupulina
M. sativa
Melilotus altissima
Onobrychis viciifolia
Ononis spinosa
Phalaris arundinacea
Picris hieracioides
Plantago lanceolata
P. media
Primula veris
Prunella vulgaris
Ranunculus bulbosus
Rhinanthus minor
Rumex acetosa
Sanguisorba minor
S. officinalis
Scabiosa columbaria
Silene alba
Stellaria graminea
Succisa pratensis
Thymus praecox
T. pulegioides
Tragopogon pratensis
Trifolium campestre
T. pratense
Trisetum flavescens
Veronica chamaedrys
V. officinalis
Vicia angustifolia
V. cracca
Viola hirta

September

Agrimonia eupatoria
Angelica sylvestris
Anthoxanthum odoratum
Asperula cynanchica
Astragalus danicus
Blackstonia perfoliata
Campanula glomerata
C. rotundifolia
Carlina vulgaris
Centaurea scabiosa
Cirsium acaule
Clinopodium vulgare
Crepis capillaris
Danthonia decumbens
Daucus carota
Elymus repens
Festuca rubra
Filipendula vulgaris
Galium verum
Gentianella amarella
Heracleum sphondylium
Hippocrepis comosa
Leontodon autumnalis
L. hispidus
Linum catharticum
Lotus corniculatus
L. uliginosus
Molinia caerulea
Onobrychis viciifolia
Ononis spinosa
Pastinaca sativa
Phleum pratense
Picris hieracioides
Pimpinella saxifraga
Plantago lanceolata
P. media
Primula veris
Prunella vulgaris
Ranunculus acris
Reseda lutea
R. luteola
Sanguisorba minor
S. officinalis
Scabiosa columbaria

Serratula tinctoria
Silaum silaus
Stachys officinalis
Stellaria graminea
Succisa pratensis
Thymus pulegioides
Tragopogon pratensis
Trifolium pratense
Vicia hirsuta

October

Achillea millefolium
A. ptarmica
Carlina vulgaris
Daucus carota
Galium verum
Gentianella amarella
Leontodon autumnalis
Lotus uliginosus
Pimpinella saxifraga
Potentilla erecta
Ranunculus acris
Sanguisorba officinalis
Scabiosa columbaria
Silaum silaus
Succisa pratensis

November

Galium verum
Pimpinella saxifraga

GLOSSARY

Acronyms

ADAS	Agricultural Development and Advisory Service	**FWAG**	Farming and Wildlife Advisory Group
BAP	Biodiversity Action Plan	**HDPE**	High Density Polyethylene
BOD	Biological Oxygen Demand	**HTA**	Horticultural Trading association
BD	Bulk Density	**JNCC**	Joint Nature Conservation Committee
BS	British Standard	**MAFF**	Ministry of Agriculture, Fisheries and Food
CAA	Civil Aviation Authority	**MoD**	Ministry of Defence
COD	Chemical Oxygen Demand	**NCC**	Nature Conservancy Council
CCW	Countryside Council for Wales	**NVC**	National Vegetation Classification
DETR	Department of the Environment, Transport and Regions (formed from DoE and DoT)	**PPG**	Planning Policy Guidance Note
DLG	Derelict Land Grant	**SAC**	Special Area of Conservation
DoE	Department of the Environment	**SEPA**	Scottish Environment Protection Agency
DoT	Department of Transport	**SNCI**	Site of Nature Conservation Interest
EA	Environment Agency	**SNH**	Scottish Natural Heritage
EcIA	Ecological Impact Assessment	**SPA**	Special Protection Area
EIA	Environmental Impact Assessment	**SSSI**	Site of Special Scientific Interest
EN	English Nature	**WDP**	Waste Development Plan
EU	European Union	**WLP**	Waste Local Plan
FRCA	Farming and Rural Conservation Agency	**WPA**	Waste Planning Authority

Definitions

Aftercare	Work carried out following soil placement to establish and maintain the after-use. Aftercare includes soil treatment, cultivation, planting and other management within the initial five-year aftercare period.
After-use	The long-term use established on a landfill site following restoration, e.g. nature conservation, amenity, agriculture, etc.
Alien species	A species alien to the British flora. Also termed non-native species. A species that is introduced to a location outside of its natural range can also be termed alien.
Ancient	Term applied to habitats such as woodlands. The definition varies between habitats but will imply the habitat is long-established (i.e. at least several hundred years old).
Anticoagulant	A substance which prevents coagulation (clotting of the blood), commonly used in rat poisons.
Bare rooted stock	Tree and shrub stock supplied with bare roots (i.e. not planted in a pot).
Biodegradable waste	Waste containing organic compounds able to be broken down by the process of biodegradation
Biodegradation	The decomposition of matter by bacteria or other living organisms.
Biodiversity	The variability among living organisms from all sources including terrestrial, marine and other aquatic ecosystems and the ecological complexes of which they are part; this includes diversity within species, between species and of ecosystems.
Bird-strike	The potentially fatal collision between birds and aircraft.
Cambridge roller	A type of agricultural roller used for several purposes. It is useful when creating a fine tilth on a seedbed.
Canopy closure	(Of woodland): a canopy is considered to be closed when the edges of the adjacent trees meet, thus no longer permitting direct sunlight to penetrate through the canopy to the woodland floor.
Cell	Specific compartment within a landfill site within which waste is deposited.
Climax species	The species which will dominate / persist in a community once a habitat is fully established.
Coir	A type of biodegradable geotextile used for soil stabilisation purposes.
Compaction	1. The compression of waste within a landfill.
	2. The compression of soil leading to conditions unsuitable for vegetation establishment.
Conifer	Any evergreen tree of a group usually bearing cones, including pines, yews and firs.
Container-grown plant	A plant that has been grown (and subsequently sold) in a pot. Compared to bare-rooted stock, container plants are more expensive. However, container plants tend to be sturdier and better able to withstand drought. Storage is also easier as bare rooted stock require careful handling (cf bare rooted stock)
Controlled waste	Combined term referring to domestic, commercial and industrial wastes. A licence is needed to dispose of controlled waste at a landfill site.
Corvid	General term used to refer to birds of the crow family (Corvidae), e.g. carrion crow, rook, jackdaw.
Cultivar	A cultivated variety of a wild plant species, i.e. a strain that has been modified from the true wild form.
Deciduous	(Of a tree): shedding its leaves annually.
Ecological Impact Assessment	The process of identifying, estimating and evaluating the ecological consequences of proposed or current actions.
Ecosystem	A relatively self-contained community of interacting organisms, e.g. grassland, woodland, soil.
Ecotype	Naturally occurring variant of a species which is adapted to a particular suite of environmental conditions.
Edge effect	An ecological effect occurring at the boundary between two different habitats. Conditions at the edge will be different from those in either habitat, and these conditions will extend some way into each habitat. This may affect species dependent upon conditions occurring in one or other habitat (e.g. woodland ground flora species requiring deep shade will not survive near woodland boundaries where light levels are higher).
Environmental Impact Assessment	The process of identifying, estimating and evaluating the environmental consequences of proposed or current actions.
Establishment period	The time between sowing / planting and the time at which the plant is self-supporting (i.e. no longer requiring care such as watering).
Eutrophication	Nutrient enrichment of a habitat by natural or artificial means.
Flight-line	Typical route followed by flocks of birds between feeding sites and breeding / roost sites.
Geomembrane	An impermeable synthetic material, used to line and cap some landfill sites.
Geotextile	Synthetic or natural permeable material used for erosion control, soil reinforcement and drainage.
Grass	Any plant of the family Gramineae.
Grassland	A habitat dominated by grass species (or a mixture of herbs and grass), with an absence of woody species.
Groundwater	Water filling pore spaces within rock / soil.
Guano	Seabird excrement.
Habitat creation	The creation of habitats of nature conservation interest on a site where they do not currently exist (regardless of whether or not they previously existed on the site). Cf habitat restoration.

Habitat restoration	The improvement of existing habitats (cf habitat creation). Also referred to as habitat enhancement.
Habituation	The process of becoming accustomed to a particular stimulus, leading to that stimulus having a diminished effect, e.g. birds learning to ignore regular bangs.
Heathland	A habitat dominated by dwarf shrub species.
Herb	A non-woody seed-bearing plant (excluding grasses, sedges, rushes and ferns).
Hibernacula	Places used by an animal for hibernation during the winter months.
Hydroseeding	A method of seeding used especially for inaccessible locations. The seed is mixed with a slow release fertiliser in a water suspension. The resultant semi-liquid is then sprayed onto the receptor surface under pressure.
Inert waste	Waste that will not undergo chemical or biological reaction (biodegradation) within a landfill.
Interim restoration	Establishment of temporary vegetation cover after replacement of part of the full subsoil depth.
Landfill cap	A low-permeability layer placed directly above the waste as part of restoration, to prevent the uncontrolled migration of landfill gas and reduce the generation of leachate.
Landfill gas	Gaseous product of the biodegradation of waste, consisting mainly of methane and carbon dioxide.
Landform	The final profile of the restored landfill site.
Land-raising site	A waste disposal site which results in the final landform of the filled area lying above the height of the surrounding land. The majority of landfill sites are land-raising sites.
Leachate	Liquid output from the biodegradation of landfill waste.
Legume	A plant capable of assimilating nitrogen from forms unavailable to non-leguminous plants. Legumes fix nitrogen with the aid of symbiotic bacteria in their roots.
Long-term management	Work carried out after the five year aftercare period to maintain / enhance the after-use. Also termed post-closure management.
Loosetipping	A method of depositing soil onto the desired location that avoids detrimental compaction of the soil. The soil is deposited from a tipping trailer and then evened out.
Management	The control of vegetation for a specific purpose in order to control certain species or achieve a certain structure.
Mulch	Mulches are placed on the soil to prevent the growth of weeds and conserve moisture. They can be made from bark chippings, stone, plastic sheeting or other light-proof material.
National Vegetation Classification	A system of classifying all natural and semi-natural vegetation communities specific to Britain (Rodwell, 1991 *et seq.*).
Native origin	A plant of native origin is a plant whose genetic makeup has been inherited from plants which grow in the wild. It is the progeny or direct descendant of wild individuals that have naturally regenerated at the site of collection (i.e. the place of native origin) and which (based on all the available evidence) has been unaffected by recent introductions or plantings of the same or related species. Unlike cultivated varieties, plants of native origin have not been subject to levels of human interference or selection processes induced by *ex situ* cultivation that have resulted in distinctive changes to its wild traits (Flora Locale, 1999).
Nature conservation value	A term applied to habitats or species. High nature conservation value is assigned either to a species or value habitat if it scores highly using standard nature conservation criteria as devised by statutory nature conservation organisations such as English Nature.
Nurse species	A species planted as part of restoration / habitat creation to assist the establishment of the habitat by providing shelter from harsh conditions (e.g. high winds) to the desired habitat species also planted. Nurse species can also act as soil stabilisers and fertilisers. Their presence is usually only short term, and they are removed during or at the end of the establishment period.
Overtipping	The practice of landfilling wastes to a height above the final landform contours to compensate for settlement reducing the final landform height.
Parent material	The original rock from which a soil is formed by weathering
Pioneer species	A plant species capable of colonising new habitats, creating conditions suitable for the establishment of other species. For example, birch is a pioneer tree species; oak generally does not naturally colonise woodland until a tree canopy is already established.
Plant community	Particular assemblage of plant species indicative of the prevailing environmental conditions.
Plug plant	A plant grown in cells smaller than a container-grown plant.
Poaching	The trampling of soil by livestock, creating small areas of bare ground and an uneven soil surface. Poaching can also be caused by the traffic of machinery.
Podzol	A type of acidic soil. Iron and aluminium oxides are leached from the A horizon and deposited in the B horizon. Eventually, the deposited iron can from an impermeable iron pan, leading to waterlogged conditions developing in the A horizon and above.
Post-closure management	Work carried out after the five-year aftercare period to maintain / enhance the after-use. Also termed long-term management.
Precipitation	The deposition of a solid substance from a solution (in chemical reactions).
Priority	A term applied to habitats and species, listed in the UK Biodiversity Action Plan as being of priority nature conservation importance.

Provenance	(Of plants): The origin of the propagative material (e.g. a habitat or a plant nursery).
Pulverised Fly Ash	By-product of burning fuel in power stations, sometimes used as a soil-forming material.
Putrescible waste	Organic waste that is easily biodegradable, i.e. waste that rots / decomposes within a short period of time.
Ramsar site	International site designation under the Ramsar Convention on Wetlands of International Importance.
Restoration	The process that returns a landfill site to a condition suitable for its after-use. Restoration includes design, soil placement and aftercare.
Ruderal species	As defined by Grime (1979). A species that is adapted to growing in disturbed habitats.
SAC	Special Area of Conservation. European site designation under Council Directive 92/43/EEC (1992) on the conservation of natural habitats and of wild flora and fauna.
Seed bank	The reservoir of dormant seed within the soil.
Semi-natural	(Of habitats): Affected by human management (e.g. grazing, burning, coppicing).
Settlement	The sinking of the landfill surface as a result of the compaction of the waste under its own weight and the reduction in waste volume as a result of biodegradation.
Shrub	A woody species that usually does not attain a mature height as great as a tree.
SNCI	Site of Nature Conservation Interest. Non-statutory designation on a county level. Also referred to as County Wildlife Sites.
Soil	The upper layer of earth in which plants grow, consisting of weathered rock and (usually) organic matter.
Soil horizon	Layers within undisturbed soil formed by soil processes of weathering, humus accumulation and plant/animal activity.
Soil forming material	A material such as brick rubble or china clay waste which can be used as a soil substitute. Given sufficient time and weathering, these materials can form soils suitable for the establishment of most habitats.
SPA	Special Protection Area. European site designation under Council Directive 79/409/EEC (1979) on the conservation of wild birds.
SSSI	Site of Special Scientific Interest. Statutory site designation under the 1981 Wildlife and Countryside Act.
Stabilisation	The biodegradation of organic waste to stable products.
Stress tolerator	Defined by Grime (1979). A plant adapted to stressed conditions such as drought-prone / nutrient-poor soils or extreme climatic conditions.
Subsoil	Layer of soil immediately below topsoil, with lower nutrient levels and organic matter content, and lighter colour than topsoil. Usually below the depth of cultivation.
Succession	A natural ecological process whereby one habitat is replaced by another over time (if unchecked, succession will generally lead to dry woodland). Management of semi-natural habitats (e.g. grazing, cutting) usually has the affect of arresting succession and maintaining early successional habitats.
Sward	An expanse of ground layer grass / herb / dwarf shrub vegetation.
Tilth	Top layer of loose soil created by cultivation (e.g. harrowing) prior to seeding with a fine particle texture and an absence of clods.
Topsoil	Top layer of soil characterised by higher fertility and organic matter content (and hence darker colour) than the subsoil beneath (usually cultivated).
Translocation	The transfer of a species (or habitat) from one location to another, with the intention that they become permanently established in their new location.
Transplant	A tree / shrub sapling purchased for woodland planting, generally between 0.6-1.2 m tall when bought.
Vernalisation	(Of seeds): Exposure to prolonged freezing or cold temperatures. This treatment is required for the seeds of some plant species to break dormancy and thus permit germination.
Volatilisation	Evaporation.
Wetland	A wide category containing various examples of habitat that are wet and heavily influenced by moisture content.
Windthrow	The toppling of trees by wind.
Woodland	A habitat dominated by tree or other woody species.

References

ADAS (1985). Pests on refuse tips. MAFF Leaflet 605. Ministry of Agriculture, Fisheries and Food, Alnwick.

Akeroyd, J. (1994). *Seeds of destruction? Non-native wildflower seed and British floral diversity*. Plantlife, London.

Anderson, P. (1994). *Roads and nature conservation: guidance on impacts, mitigation and enhancement*. English Nature, Peterborough.

Anderson, P. (1995). Ecological restoration and creation: a review. *Biological Journal of the Linnean Society*, **56** (Suppl.), 187-211.

Anderson, P., Tallis, J.H. & Yalden, D.A. (1997). *Moorland management project, Phase III*. English Nature/Peak Park Joint Planning Board, Bakewell.

Andrews, J. & Rebane, M. (1994). *Farming and Wildlife: A practical management handbook*. Royal Society for the Protection of Birds, Sandy.

Andrews, J. (1993). The reality and management of wildlife corridors. *British Wildlife*, **5**, 1-7.

Anon. (1994). *The UK Biodiversity Action Plan*. HMSO, London.

Anon. (1995). *Biodiversity: The UK Steering Group Report*. HMSO, London.

Anon. (1998). *UK Biodiversity Group Tranche 2 Action Plans. Volume II – terrestrial and freshwater habitats*. English Nature, Peterborough.

Aspinwall & Co. (1998). *The Sitefile Digest*. Aspinwall & Company Ltd, London.

Association of Local Government Ecologists (ALGE) and the South West Biodiversity Initiative (1998). *A biodiversity guide for the planning and development sectors. A South West regional perspective*. Unpublished report, October 1998.

Atkinson, M., Trueman, I., Millet, P., Jones, G. & Besenyei, L. (1995). The use of hay strewing to create species rich grasslands. II. Monitoring the vegetation and seedbank. *Land Contamination and Reclamation*, **3**, 108-110.

Ausden, M. & Treweek, J. (1995). Grasslands. In *Managing Habitats for Conservation* (eds W.J. Sutherland & D.A. Hill). Cambridge University Press, Cambridge. 197-229.

Bacon, J., Harris, S. & Southwood, R. (1997). Making hay in a small way. *Enact*, **5**, 8-11.

Bacon, J.C. (1990). The use of livestock in calcareous grassland management. In *Calcareous grasslands – ecology and management* (eds S.H. Hillier, D.W.H. Walton & T.C.E. Wells). Bluntisham Books, Bluntisham. 51-56.

Baines, J.C. (1989). Choices in habitat re-creation. In *Biological Habitat Reconstruction* (ed G.P. Buckley). Belhaven Press, London.

Baines, C. & Smart, J. (1991). *A guide to habitat creation* (2nd edn). London Ecology Unit, London.

Baker, A. (2000). Protected species legislation re-defined! *Ecology and Environmental Management In Practice*, **28**, 1-4. Institute of Ecology and Environmental Management, Winchester.

Barker, C. (1995). The creation of wetland habitats on landfill sites. *Waste Planning*, **16**, 9-13.

Barnes, A. (1997). *A Biodiversity Action Plan for Purbeck*. Royal Society for the Protection of Birds, Sandy.

Baxter, A. (1999). Evaluation of bird control on landfill sites; recent progress. *North West Environmental Trust News*, **6**, 13-15.

Bending, N.A.D. & Moffat, A.J. (1997). *Tree establishment on landfill sites: Research and updated guidance*. Forestry Commission, Edinburgh.

Biggs, J., Corfield, A., Walker, D., Whitfield, M. & Williams, P. (1994). New approaches to the management of ponds. *British Wildlife*, **5**, 273-287.

Bisgrove, R. & Dixie, G. (1994). Wild Flowers: plugging the gap. *Enact*, **2**, 18-20.

Bloomfield, H.E., Handley, J.F. & Bradshaw, A.D. (1982). Nutrient deficiencies and the aftercare of reclaimed derelict land. *Journal of Applied Ecology*, **19**, 151-158.

Boatman, N. (1990). Field Boundary Vegetation. *The Game Conservancy Review of 1989*. No. 21. Game Conservancy Council, Fordingbridge. 58-61.

Bradshaw, A.D. & Chadwick, M.J. (1980). *The restoration of land*. Blackwell Scientific Publications, Oxford.

Bradshaw, A.D. (1983). The reconstruction of ecosystems. Presidential address to the British Ecological Society December 1982. Journal of Applied Ecology, **20**, 1-17.

Brooks, A. (1984). *Woodlands: a practical conservation handbook*. British Trust for Conservation Volunteers, Wallingford.

Brooks, A. (1988). *Hedging: a practical conservation handbook*. British Trust for Conservation Volunteers, Wallingford.

Bryne, S. (1990). *Habitat transplantation in England. A review of the extent and nature of the practice and the techniques employed*. England Field Unit Report No. 104. Nature Conservancy Council, Peterborough.

Buckley, G.P. & Knight, D.G. (1989). The feasibility of woodland reconstruction. In *Biological Habitat Reconstruction* (ed G.P. Buckley). Belhaven Press, London. 171-188.

Buckley, G.P. (ed). (1992). *Ecology and management of coppice woodlands*. Chapman and Hall, London.

Bullock, J.M. (1996). Plants. In *Population Census Techniques* (ed W. J. Sutherland). Cambridge University Press, Cambridge. 111-138.

Bullock, J.M. (1998). Community translocation in Britain: Setting objectives and measuring consequences. *Biological Conservation*, **84**, 199-214.

CAA (1998). *Aerodrome bird control*. Civil Aviation Authority, London.

Chambers, B.J. & Cross, R.B. (1996). Recreating lowland heath on ex-arable land in the Breckland Environmentally Sensitive Area: Vegetation in forestry, amenity and conservation areas. *Aspects of Applied Biology*, **44**, 393-400.

Chatters, C. & Sanderson, N. (1994). Grazing lowland pasture woods. *British Wildlife*, **6**, 78-88.

Chu, L.M, & Bradshaw, A.D. (1996). The value of pulverised refuse fines (PRF) as a substitute for topsoil in land reclamation. II: Lysimeter studies. *Journal of Applied Ecology*, **33**, 858-865.

Cole, L. (1982). Does size matter? In *An ecological approach to Urban Landscape Design* (eds A. Ruff & R. Tregay). Occasional Paper No 8. Department of Town and Country Planning, University of Manchester. 70-82.

Cooke, S.D, Cooke, A.S. & Sparks, T.H. (1994). Fluctuations in night counts of crested newts at eight breeding sites in Huntingdonshire 1986-1993. In *Conservation and management of great crested newts: proceedings of a symposium held on 11 January 1994 at Kew Gardens, Richmond, Surrey* (eds A. Gent & R. Bray). English Nature Science No. 20. English Nature, Peterborough.

CSL (1998). *Evaluation of a large fixed netting system as a means of excluding birds from a domestic waste landfill*. Unpublished report, Central Science Laboratory, York.

Davey, A., Dunsford, S. & Free, A. (1992). Feasibility studies for heathland creation on arable land in the Suffolk Sandlings. In *Proceedings of the Seminar on Heathland Habitat Creation* (eds A. Free & M.T. Kitson). Suffolk Wildlife Trust, Ipswich.

DETR (1999a). *The new Environmental Impact Assessment (EIA) Regulations*. DETR Circular 2/99.

DETR (1999b). *Limiting Landfill. A consultation paper on limiting landfill to meet the EC Landfill Directive's targets for the landfill of biodegradable municipal waste.* DETR, London.

Dobson, M.C & Moffat, A.J. (1995a). A re-evaluation of objections to tree planting on containment landfills. *Waste Management and Research*, **13**, 579-600.

Dobson, M.C. & Moffat, A.J. (1995b). *Site capability assessment for woodland creation on landfills*. Research Information Note 263. Forestry Commission Research Division, Wrecclesham.

Dobson, M.C. & Moffat, A.J. (1993). *The potential for woodland establishment on landfill sites*. HMSO, London.

DoE (1986). *Landfilling Wastes. A technical memorandum for the disposal of wastes on landfill sites*. Waste Management Paper 26. HMSO, London.

DoE (1994a). *Landfill completion*. Waste Management Paper 26a. HMSO, London.

DoE (1994b). *Planning and nature conservation*. Planning Policy Guidance Note PPG 9. HMSO, London.

DoE (1995). *Landfill design, construction and operational practice*. Waste Management Paper 26b. HMSO, London.

Duffey, E., Morris, M.G., Sheail, J., Ward, L.K., Wells, D.A. & Wells, T.C.E. (1974). *Grassland Ecology and Wildlife Management*. Chapman and Hall, London.

Ecoscope Applied Ecologists (1998). *Enhancement of the environmental benefits of farm woodlands.* Final report to MAFF. Ecoscope, Muker.

Ecoscope Applied Ecologists. (1999). *Report on ecological issues associated with development of Cabot Park, Avonmouth*, 1999. Unpublished report. Ecoscope, Muker.

Emorsgate Seeds (1999). *British wild flower and wild grass seeds*. Catalogue. Limes Farm, Tilney All Saints, Kings Lynn, Norfolk. PE34 4RT.

English Nature and the Wildlife Trusts (1999). *The lowland grassland management handbook* (2nd edn). English Nature, Peterborough.

Environment Agency (1999). *Library of license conditions and working plan specifications*. Unpublished consultation draft.

Environment Agency (in prep.). *Landfill restoration and post closure management*. Waste Management Paper 26e.

Environmental Advisory Unit (1988). *Heathland restoration: a handbook of techniques*. British Gas Southern plc., Southampton.

EU (1979). *On the conservation of wild birds*. Council Directive 79/409/EEC. EU, Brussels.

EU (1992). *On the conservation of natural habitats and wild fauna and flora*. Council Directive 92/43/EEC. EU, Brussels.

EU (1999). *On the landfill of waste*. Council Directive 1999/31/EC. EU, Brussels.

Evans, C. (1992). Heathland recreation on arable land at Minsmere. In *Proceedings of the seminar on heathland habitat creation* (eds A. Free and M.T. Kitson). Suffolk Wildlife Trust, Ipswich.

Farrell, L. (1989). The different types and importance of British Heaths. *Botanical Journal of the Linnean Society*, **101**, 291-299.

Ferris-Kaan, R. (ed.) (1991). *Edge management in woodlands*. Forestry Commission Occasional Paper 28. Forestry Commission, Edinburgh.

Flora Locale (1999). Web pages at: www.naturebureau.co.uk/pages/floraloc/floraloc.htm

Fojt, W. (1994). The conservation of British fens. *British Wildlife*, **5**, 355-366.

Forestry Commission (1999). The management of semi-natural woodlands: Forestry Practice Guides 1-8. Forestry Commission, Edinburgh.

Francis, J.L. (1995). The enhancement of young plantations and new woodlands. *Land Contamination and Reclamation*, **3**, 93-95.

Francis, J.L., Morton, H.J. & Boorman, L.A. (1992). The establishment of ground flora species in recently planted woodland. *Aspects of Applied Biology*, **29**, 171-178.

Gent, A.H. & Gibson, S.D. (eds). (1998). Herpetofauna workers' manual. JNCC, Peterborough.

Gibbons, D., Avery, M., Baillie, S., Gregory, R., Kirby, J., Porter, R., Tucker, G. & Williams, G. (1996). Bird Species of Conservation Concern in the United Kingdom, Channel Islands and Isle of Man: revising the Red Data List. In *RSPB Conservation Review* No. 10 (ed. C.J. Cadbury). RSPB, Sandy. 7-18.

Gibson, C.W.D., Watt, T.A. & Brown, V.K. (1987). The use of sheep grazing to recreate species-rich grassland from abandoned arable land. *Biological Conservation*, **42**, 165-183.

Gibson, C.W.D. (1997). *The effects of horse and cattle grazing on English species-rich grasslands*. English Nature Research Projects No. 210. English Nature, Peterborough.

Gilbert, O. & Anderson, P. (1998). *Habitat creation and repair*. Oxford University Press, Oxford.

Gimingham, C.H. (1992). *The lowland heathland management handbook*. English Nature Science No. 8. English Nature, Peterborough.

Gough, M.W. & Marrs, R.H. (1990). A comparison of soil fertility between semi-natural and agricultural plant communities: implications for the creation of species-rich grassland on abandoned agricultural land. *Biological conservation*, **5**, 83-86.

Grime, J.P., Hodgson, J.G. & Hunt, R. (1988). *Comparative plant ecology* (3rd edn). Blackwell Scientific Publications, Oxford.

Grime, J.P. (1990). Mechanisms promoting floristic diversity in calcareous grasslands. In *Calcareous grasslands – ecology and management* (eds. S.H. Hillier, D.W.H. Walton and T.C.E. Wells). Bluntisham Books, Bluntisham. 51-56.

Gross, K.L. (1984). Effects of seed size and growth form on seedling establishment of six monocarpic perennial plants. *Journal of Ecology*, **72**, 369-387.

Grubb, P.J. (1977). The maintenance of species-richness in plant communities: the importance of the regeneration niche. *Biological Reviews*, **52**, 107-145.

Halley, R.J. (ed). (1982). *The agricultural handbook* (17th edn). Butterworths, London.

Hammond, D. (1999). Watch the birdie. *Waste Manager*, **28**, 16-19.

Hawke, C. & José, P. (1996). *Reedbed management for commercial and wildlife interests*. Royal Society for the Protection of Birds, Sandy.

Haycock, N. & Worral, P. (1996). Constructed wetlands (use of wetlands as biological treatment systems). *Enact*, **4**, 17-20.

Herbert, R., Samuel, S. & Patterson, G. (1999). *Using local stock for planting native trees and shrubs*. Forestry Commission Practice Note No. 8. Forestry Commission, Edinburgh.

Highways Agency (1993). The wildflower handbook. In *Design manual for roads and bridges*. Volume 10, Environmental Design Section 4, Horticulture Part 1 HA 67/93. Department of Transport, Scottish Office Industry Department, The Welsh Office and Department of the Environment for N. Ireland.

Hodgson, J.M. (1997). *Soil survey field handbook*. Soil Survey and Land Research Centre, Cranfield University, Silsoe.

Horton, N., Brough, T. & Rochard, J.B.A. (1983). The importance of refuse tips to gulls wintering in an inland area of south-east England. *Journal of Applied Ecology*, **20**, 751-765.

Hutchings, M.J. & Booth, K.D. (1996). Studies on the feasibility of re-creating chalk grassland vegetation on an ex-arable field. I. The potential roles of the seed bank and the seed rain. Journal of Applied Ecology, 33, 1171-1181.

ICRCL (1987). *Guidance on the assessment and redevelopment of contaminated land*. ICRCL Guidance Note 59/83. Department of the Environment, London.

Ingelmo, F., Canet, R., Ibanez, M.A., Pomares, F. & Garcia, J. (1998). Use of MSW compost, dried sewage sludge and other wastes as partial substitutes for peat and soil. *Bioresource Technology*, **63**, 123-129.

Jefferson, R.G. Gibson, C.W.D, Leach, S.J, Pultney, C.M. Wolton, R. & Robertson, H.J. (1999). *Grassland habitat translocation. The case of Brocks Farm*, Devon. English Nature Research Report No. 304. English Nature, Peterborough.

Jerram, R. (1992). *Five years of monitoring grassland transplantation at Potatopot, West Cumbria*. English Nature Research Report No. 36. English Nature, Peterborough.

JNCC (1996). *Birds of Conservation Importance*. Press release. Joint Nature Conservation Committee, Peterborough, 31st May 1996.

Jones, G. (1990). Learning from experience. Landscape Design, **193**, 40-44.

Jones, G.H., Trueman, I.C. & Millett, P. (1995). The use of hay strewing to create species rich grasslands. I. General principles and hay strewing versus seed mixes. *Land Contamination and Reclamation*, **3**, 104-107.

Kent, M. & Coker, P. (1992). *Vegetation description and analysis – a practical approach*. Belhaven Press, London.

Kirby, K.J. (1981). Woodland evaluation and assessment for nature conservation. CST Note 25. Nature Conservancy Council, Peterborough.

Kirby, K. (1995). *Rebuilding the English countryside. Habitat fragmentation and wildlife corridors as issues in practical conservation*. English Nature Science No. 10. English Nature, Peterborough.

Lefeuvre, J. (1998). Reedbeds as living assets. *Enact special supplement*, 3-4.

Leslie, D. (1984). *Gull scaring – three years of success*. Lancashire County Council, Preston.

Lewis, R.R. (1990). Wetlands restoration/creation/enhancement terminology: suggestions for standardization. In *Wetland Creation and Restoration: the status of the science* (eds. J.A. Kusler & M.E. Kentula). Island Press, Washington. 417-422.

MacArthur, M.H. & Wilson, E.O. (1967). *The theory of island biogeography*. Princeton University Press, Princeton.

MAFF (1999). *Farm woodlands for birds: advice on their design and management*. Ministry of Agriculture, Fisheries and Food, London.

Marren, P. (1995). Harvests of beauty: the conservation of hay meadows. *British Wildlife*, **6**, 235-243.

Marrs, R.H. & Gough, M.W. (1989). Soil fertility – a potential problem for habitat restoration. In *Biological Habitat Restoration* (ed. G.P. Buckley). Belhaven Press, London.

Marrs, R.H. (1985). Techniques for reducing soil fertility for nature conservation purposes: a review in relation to research at Ropers Heath, Suffolk, England. *Biological Conservation*, **34**, 307-332.

McKendry, P.J. (1996) Landfill restoration: soils, specifications and standards. *Waste Management and the Environment*, **6**, 36-41.

Merritt, A. (1994). *Wetlands, industry & wildlife. A manual of principles and practices*. Wildfowl and Wetlands Trust, Slimbridge.

Mersey Forest and Red Rose Forest Partnership. (1999). *Creating community woodlands on closed landfill sites*. The Mersey Forest, Warrington.

Mills, S., Taylor, D. & Wetton, J. (1998). Reedbeds in Somerset and Normandy – their creation and use. *Enact special supplement*, 7-9.

Mitchley, J., Burch, F., Buckley, P. & Watt, T.A. (2000). *Habitat restoration monitoring handbook*. English Nature Research Report No. 378. English Nature, Peterborough.

Mitchley, J., Burch, F. & Lawson, C. (1998). *Habitat restoration: project development of monitoring guidelines*. English Nature Research Project No. 284. English Nature, Peterborough.

Moffatt, A.J. & Bending, N.A.D. (1992). Physical site evaluation for community woodland establishment. Research Information Note 216. Forestry Commission Research Division, Wrecclesham.

Morris, P. & Therivel, R. (1995). *Methods of Environmental Impact Assessment*. UCL Press, London.

Natural Environment Consultants (1995a). *Masons landfill site, Great Blakenham, Suffolk. Bird control study 1994-1995*. Unpublished report prepared for Haul Waste Disposal Ltd.

Natural Environment Consultants (1995b). *Salt Ayre landfill site, Lancaster. Gull control study, June-September 1995*. Unpublished report prepared for Haul Waste Disposal Ltd.

NCC (1989). *Guidelines for the selection of biological SSSI's*. Nature Conservancy Council, Peterborough.

NCC (1990a). Handbook for Phase I habitat survey – a technique for environmental audit. England Field Unit, Nature Conservancy Council, Peterborough.

NCC (1990b). *Review of NCC policy on species translocations in Great Britain*. (NCC BD P9021). Nature Conservancy Council, Peterborough.

Newbold, C. (1989). Semi-natural habitats or habitat re-creation: conflict or partnership? In *Biological Habitat Reconstruction* (ed. G.P. Buckley). Belhaven Press, London.

North York Moors National Park Committee (1991). *North York Moors Moorland Management Programme* 1985-90. NYMNPC, Helmsley, York.

Oates, M. (1993). The management of southern limestone grasslands. *British Wildlife*, **5**, 73-82.

Ortiz, N.E. & Smith, G.R. (1994). Landfill sites, botulism and gulls. *Epidemiological Infection*, **112**, 385-391.

Parker, D.M. (1995). *Habitat creation – a critical guide*. English Nature Science Series No. 21. English Nature, Peterborough.

Peterken, G. & Game, M. (1984). Historical factors affecting the number and distribution of vascular plant species in the woods of central Lincolnshire. *Journal of Ecology*, **72**, 155-182.

Peterken, G. (1981). *Woodland conservation and management*. Chapman and Hall, London.

Petts, J. & Eduljee, G. (1994). *Environmental Impact Assessment for waste treatment and disposal facilities*. John Wiley & Sons, Chichester.

Petts, J.I. (ed). (1999). *Handbook of Environmental Impact Assessment*. Blackwell Science, Oxford.

Pierce, T. (1998). *Earthworm inoculation at Bidston Moss and related investigations*. Unpublished report.

Pywell, R.F., Webb, N.R. & Putwain, P.D. (1995). A comparison of techniques for restoring heathland on abandoned farmland. *Journal of Applied Ecology*, **32**, 400-411.

Pywell, R.F. (in press). *Heathland translocation and restoration*.

Rackham, O. (1994). *The illustrated history of the countryside*. Phoenix Illustrated Orion Publishing Group, London.

Reijnen, R., Foppen, R., Ter Braak, C. & Thissen, J. (1995). The effects of car traffic on breeding bird populations in woodland. III. Reduction of density in relation to the proximity of main roads. *Journal of Applied Ecology*, **32**, 187-203.

Rodwell, J. & Patterson, G. (1994). *Creating new native woodlands*. Forestry Commission Bulletin 112. HMSO, London.

Rodwell, J.S. (ed). (1991 et seq.). *British Plant Communities*. Volume 1. Woodlands and scrub (1991). Volume 2. Heaths and mires (1991). Volume 3. Grasslands and montane communities (1992). Volume 4. Aquatic communities, swamps and tall-herb fens (1995). Volume 5. Maritime and weed communities and vegetation of open habitats (2000). Cambridge University Press. Cambridge.

Rowell, T.A. (1988). *The peatland management handbook*. Nature Conservancy Council, Peterborough.

RSPB/EN/ITE. *The wet grassland guide: managing floodplain and coastal wet grasslands for wildlife*. Royal Society for the Protection of Birds, Sandy.

RSPB/NRA/RSNC (1994). *The new rivers and wildlife handbook*. Royal Society for the Protection of Birds, Sandy.

Shimwell, D.W. (1971). *The description and classification of vegetation*. Sidgwick & Jackson, London.

Simmons, E. & Baines, D. (1998). *Landfill gas and leachate control applied to arable after use*. MAFF, London.

Simmons, E. (1992a). The importance of restoration in waste disposal by landfill. *Wastes Management*, December 1992, 12 -13.

Simmons, E. (1992b). Landfill site restoration for wildlife. *Waste planning*, **3**, 3-7.

Simmons, E. (1999). Restoration of landfill sites for ecological diversity. *Waste Management and Research*, **17**, 511-519.

Simpson, N. & Jefferson, R. (1996). *Use of farmyard manure on semi-natural meadow grassland*. English Nature Research Report No. 150. English Nature, Peterborough.

Smith, R.S, Pullan, S. & Shiel, R.S. (1996). Seed shed in the making of hay from mesotrophic grassland in a field in Northern England: effects of hay cut date, grazing and fertiliser in a spilt-split-plot experiment. *Journal of Applied Ecology*, **33**, 833-841.

Smith, R.S. & Rushton, S.P. (1994). The effects of grazing management on the vegetation of mesotrophic (meadow) grassland in Northern England. *Journal of Applied Ecology*, **31**, 13-24.

Sol, D., Arcos, J.M. & Senar, J.C. (1995). The influence of refuse tips on the winter distribution of Yellow-legged Gulls. *Bird Study*, **42**, 216-221.

Soutar, R.G. & Peterken, G.F. (1989). Regional lists of native trees and shrubs for use in afforestation schemes. *Aboricultural Journal*, **13**, 33-43.

Sutherland, W.J. & Hill, D.A. (eds). (1995). *Managing habitats for conservation*. Cambridge University Press, Cambridge.

Treweek, J. (1999). *Ecological Impact Assessment*. Blackwell Science, Oxford.

Vanclay, F. & Bronstein, D.A. (eds). (1995). *Environmental and Social Impact Assessment*. John Wiley & Sons, Chichester.

Ward, D. (1994). Management of lowland wet grassland for breeding waders. *British Wildlife*, **6**, 89-98.

Warren, R. & Fuller, M. (1990). *Coppice woodlands, their management for wildlife*. Nature Conservancy Council, Peterborough.

Watkins, C. (1990). Woodland management and conservation. Nature Conservancy Council, Peterborough.

Welch, G. & Wright, M. (1996). Arable to heath: a progress report. *Enact*, **4**, 10-11. English Nature, Peterborough.

Wells, T.C.E., Bell, S.A. & Frost, A. (1981). *Creating attractive grassland using native plant species*. Nature Conservancy Council, Shrewsbury.

Wells, T.C.E., Frost, A. & Bell, S. (1986). *Wildflower grasslands from crop grown seed and hay bales*. Focus on Nature Conservation No. 15. NCC, Peterborough.

Wells, T.C.E. (1989). *The establishment and management of wildflower meadows*. Focus on Nature Conservation No. 21. Nature Conservancy Council, Peterborough.

Whitbread, A. (ed). (1992). *Research and survey on the ecological effects of the 1987 storm*. Research and Survey in Nature Conservation. Nature Conservancy Council, Peterborough.

Williams, P., Biggs, J., Corfield, A., Fox, G., Walker, D. & Whitfield, M. (1997). Designing new ponds for wildlife. *British Wildlife*, **8**, 137-150.

Willoughby, I., Kerr, G., Jinks, R. & Gosling, P. (1996). *Establishing new woodlands by direct sowing*. Research Information Note 285. Forestry Commission Research Division, Wrecclesham.

Willoughby, I. & Moffat, A. (1996). *Cultivation of lowland sites for new woodland establishment*. Research Information Note 288. Forestry Commission Research Division, Wrecclesham.

Winder, F.L.R. & Robertson, H.J. (1993). *Progress reports on monitoring of grassland transplant sites*, Brampton Meadow, Cambs 1987-1991. English Nature Research Report No. 37. English Nature, Peterborough.

Wood, C. (1995). *Environmental Impact Assessment – a comparative review*. Longman, Harlow.

Worthington, T.R. & Helliwell, D.R. (1987). Transference of semi-natural grassland and marshland onto newly created landfill. *Biological Conservation*, **41**, 301-311.

INDEX